THE COLOR OF LOVE

BOOK FORTY
LOUANN ATKINS TEMPLE WOMEN & CULTURE SERIES
BOOKS ABOUT WOMEN AND FAMILIES, AND THEIR CHANGING ROLE
IN SOCIETY

THE COLOR OF LOVE

Racial Features, Stigma, and Socialization

in Black Brazilian Families

ELIZABETH HORDGE-FREEMAN

UNIVERSITY OF TEXAS PRESS *Austin*

The Louann Atkins Temple Women & Culture Series is supported by Allison, Doug, Taylor, and Andy Bacon; Margaret, Lawrence, Will, John, and Annie Temple; Larry Temple; the Temple-Inland Foundation; and the National Endowment for the Humanities.

Portions of the introduction and chapters 1, 3, and 6 were previously published in Elizabeth Hordge-Freeman, "What's Love Got to Do With It? Racial Stigma and Differential Treatment in Afro-Brazilian Families," Special Edition: Rethinking Race, Identity, and Nationalist Ideologies in Latin America, *Journal of Ethnic & Racial Studies*, Vol. 36, no. 10, 1507–1523. Reprinted by permission of the publisher (Taylor & Francis Ltd., http://www.tandfonline.com).

Requests for permission to reproduce material from this work should be sent to:
  Permissions
  University of Texas Press
  P.O. Box 7819
  Austin, TX 78713-7819
  http://utpress.utexas.edu/index.php/rp-form

⊗ The paper used in this book meets the minimum requirements of ANSI/NISO Z39.48-1992 (R1997) (Permanence of Paper).

LIBRARY OF CONGRESS CATALOGING-IN-PUBLICATION DATA

Hordge-Freeman, Elizabeth, 1979–, author.
  The color of love : racial features, stigma, and socialization in black Brazilian families / Elizabeth Hordge-Freeman. — First edition.
      pages   cm — (Louann Atkins Temple women & culture series; book forty)
  Includes bibliographical references and index.
  ISBN 978-1-4773-0238-5 (cloth : alk. paper) — ISBN 978-1-4773-0788-5 (pbk. : alk. paper) — ISBN 978-1-4773-0789-2 (library e-book) — ISBN 978-1-4773-0790-8 (non-library e-book)
    1. Blacks—Brazil—Salvador—Social conditions.   2. Families, Black—Brazil.   3. Blacks—Socialization—Brazil.   4. Blacks—Race identity—Brazil.   5. Racism—Brazil.   6. Brazil—Race relations.   I. Title.   II. Series: Louann Atkins Temple women & culture series ; bk. 40.
  F2659.N4H65 2015
  305.800981—dc23
                                                    2015006358

doi:10.7560/302385

FOR MY SON, NATHANIEL.
FOR ESSENCE, SONIA, LAURYN, AND GABRIELLE.
AND FOR BLACK GIRLS OF THE AFRICAN DIASPORA.

CONTENTS

ACKNOWLEDGMENTS

ONE OF THE MOST GRATIFYING PARTS of this project is recognizing the institutions, departments, and individuals that made this research possible. First and foremost, I thank the Brazilians and their families who are the backbone of this research and who kindly opened their homes and their hearts to me. Generous to a fault with their time, families met me one day and often invited me to return to their homes for several hours of interviews the very next day. Many even accepted my request to return weeks, months, and years later. They shared with me private experiences and moments, and patiently answered what they perceived as my odd questions. I have a debt of gratitude to these families that I will never be able to fully repay. I hope that I have represented them in all their complexities, and take full responsibility for any shortcomings.

The institutional support of Duke University, the University of North Carolina–Chapel Hill (UNC), the State University of Feira de Santana, the Federal University of Bahia, *Brazil Cultural*, and the University of South Florida (USF) were fundamental to this project, which began as my dissertation in the Department of Sociology at Duke University. I thank my dedicated "Dissertation Dream Team" committee members Eduardo Bonilla-Silva (co-chair), Linda George (co-chair), Lynn Smith-Lovin, Linda Burton, and Sherman James for supporting me, coaching me, and encouraging me throughout the process. Words cannot express my gratitude for the training and tough love that each of you gave and continue to give me. I thank John French for providing some of the most prolific feedback on my earliest work. Kia Lilly Caldwell and Gladys Mitchell-Walthour provided invaluable professional and personal support. Kia's expertise and coffee breaks to discuss my research at all stages of its development were tremendously helpful. Gladys's contacts paved the way for me as I pursued my research in Salvador, Bahia, and she was an endless fountain of resources. France Winddance Twine's book *Racism in a Racial Democracy* is why I am a sociologist. I appreciate her investment in my research and detailed feedback during various stages of this project.

This research would not be possible without financial support from a number of sources, including the American Sociological Association/National Institute of Mental Health Minority Pre-Doctoral Fellowship and the Ford Foundation Dissertation Fellowship. Throughout my time as a graduate student, the Duke University Graduate School of Arts and Sciences funded me generously with summer fellowships and conference grants, which planted the seed of my dissertation and helped me make my first contacts with families and researchers in Salvador. The UNC/Duke Consortium of Latin American and Caribbean Studies (CLACS) and Afro-Latin Working Group afforded an intellectually stimulating space to develop my ideas and connect with other scholars. CLACS awarded me fellowships, travel grants, and conference funding to present my findings and develop my Portuguese. In addition, I am also proud to have been one of the founding members of Duke Sociology's Race Workshop, which served as a continual source of intellectual and personal engagement. I presented my work at the workshops numerous times, and critical comments helped me to better conceptualize the project.

This project would also not have been possible without the collaboration of a cadre of brilliant Brazilian researchers and scholars. Of great initial help were the contacts of my committee member Sherman James, including Antonio Alberto Lopes, Gildete Lopes, and Maria Ines Barbosa. They form part of a group of accomplished scholars and activists that also includes Michel and Ecyla Chagas, who generously hosted me during my trips to Brazil, patiently answered personal questions about race, introduced me to Afro-Brazilian culture, and welcomed me with the warm hospitality for which Brazilians are known. I cannot thank Javier Escudero, Patricia Burgos, and *Brazil Cultural* enough for their incredible professional support and unparalleled personal encouragement. My connection with Javier and Patricia began with them helping me find housing in Salvador, and it quickly blossomed into a professional relationship lasting over five years. In partnership with *Brazil Cultural*, we launched USF's Brazil study abroad program, which helped me to conduct follow-up interviews for two summers in Salvador.

There are a number of other Brazilians without whom this project would not have come into fruition. Deserving very special recognition is Edna Araújo at State University of Feira de Santana, who moved heaven and earth to help secure my visa and implement my research agenda in Brazil. Going far beyond what I could have imagined, she incorporated me as a visiting research collaborator at the university, hosted me in her home, and helped me to become integrated into a forward-thinking interdisciplinary research community. Similarly, for their friendship and assistance I would also like to thank Luzia Maria, Lúcio Mágano Oliveira, Roberto Lacerda, Nelia Almeida, the Oliveira Family, the Miranda Family, Eduardo Esteban, Maria Lúcia da Silva (AMMA Psique e Negritude), Silvio Humberto, and Sales Augusto dos Santos. Each of them introduced me to the cultural and racial complexities of Salvador while offering critical insights into my research. Research mentor Nancy de Souza e Silva spent too many hours to count *tirando minhas dúvidas* about the idiosyncrasies of Afro-Brazilian family life. A truly remarkable researcher and oral historian, she offered insights that filled in the gaps and greatly expanded my understanding of Brazilian society.

After completing my PhD from Duke in May 2012, I joined the USF faculty as an assistant professor in sociology, with a joint appointment in the Institute for the Study of Latin America and the Caribbean. Despite their busy schedules, Donileen Loseke and my chair, Elizabeth Aranda, read chapters and provided feedback. I also thank my colleague and faculty mentor Bernd Reiter, who read chapters and provided critical feedback, encouraged me to publish other pieces in my downtime, and convinced me to pursue worthwhile diasporic projects. At USF I am indebted to three talented graduate students, Kaitlyn Robison, Amber Gregory, and Sophia Daniels, who had the supernatural ability to interpret my research requests and deliver what I needed. Sophia worked with me for over a year and was truly an invaluable research assistant.

During my first semester at USF, Cynthia Spence invited me to serve as the distinguished faculty facilitator to organize the ten-day UNCF/Mellon International Faculty Seminar in Salvador. I thank Cynthia for giving me, a new assistant professor, the honor of leading a group of seasoned faculty members to Salvador to study "Afro-Aesthetics in Brazil . . . and Beyond." In partnership with Javier Escudero from *Brazil Cultural*, we organized an amazing group of panelists, presentations, and visits, some of which have been incorporated into the research for this book. In this seminar I was challenged to reconsider my intellectual positions and push my analysis even further by feminist powerhouse Beverly Guy-Sheftall.

While I was completing this book a number of people cheered me on, offered coffee breaks, made me laugh, sent friendly e-mails, or suffered through my endless rants about my research. For all the ways they assisted me, I thank Becki Bach, Dianne Penderhughes, Carol Stack, Jaira Harrington, Maxine Leeds Craig, Regina Baker, Candis Watts, Victor Ray, Trenita Brookshire Childers, Theresa May, Mary Freeney, Ted Williams, and Brenda Tindal. Nmeregiri Nwogu, a longtime supporter and tremendous ally, must be acknowledged for reading all of my drafts, taking my midnight phone calls, answering random e-mails, and being a kindred spirit. I would also like to thank the University of Texas Press and especially Meg Wallace for her diligent editing and valuable suggestions.

Research can be isolating, but I had the luxury of having two of the most devoted friends and colleagues in the history of friendships. We created a graduate school support group and named ourselves T.O.T. to formalize our feminist posse. To say that my dear friends Sarah Mayorga-Gallo and Rose Buckelew devoted time and emotional and instrumental support is simply not enough, as their friendship knew no bounds. Sarah's home and cooking were my sanctuary when I was hungry, pregnant, and suffering through dissertation mania. She has always nurtured me with incredible love and kindness, reading my work and pushing me to be a better scholar and, most important, a better person. In Rose, I met my match in someone who was willing to ask the hard and uncomfortable questions, but wise enough to know when to relax and take a break. Even though time and circumstances inevitably change relationships, I will be forever indebted to them for sharing this journey with me.

Considering how important family bonds and family history have been to me, it is no coincidence that I became a sociologist who studies families. For instilling in me spiritual grounding, integrity, and a love of learning, I thank my parents, Larry and Patricia Hordge, and my grandparents, Johnie Lewis, Louise Lewis, and Maggie Hordge. I am convinced that I would be a different person if I did not have my siblings Theresa, Larry Jr. (L.B.), Jenifer, Christina, and Jeanette, who keep me grounded, make me laugh, and inspire me to excellence by example and by threat of merciless teasing. I also appreciate my mother-in-law, Mrs. Collins, who helped take care of my son, Nathaniel, when I was working and traveling for conferences and interviews. Likewise, the bright smiles and brilliance of my wonderful nieces, Essence, Sonia, Lauryn, and Gabby, remind me why this project is necessary.

And last but not least, I want to thank God, who has blessed me in innumerable ways and placed McArthur and Nathaniel in my life. McArthur, a brilliant artist and encouraging husband, championed my research even when it meant that I would be in Brazil for over a year. Against his better judgment, he weathered a long and extremely tumultuous international flight to visit me in Salvador and even learned a few words of Portuguese to impress (and entertain) me. When I returned from the field, McArthur befriended the group of Brazilian friends who returned with me, encouraged me to create and follow a writing schedule, celebrated my writing progress, and assured me that I could do anything ("Pode, Pode!"). After the birth of our son, Nathaniel, in 2011, I returned to the field twice for over two months of follow-up interviews, and McArthur remained in the United States with Nathaniel. An amazing team, McArthur, my sister Jenifer, and my mom, have been the backbone of my family support system, coordinating and synchronizing their schedules so Nathaniel would be cared for with love. When the path to my manuscript promised land was paved with uncertainty and sleepless nights, McArthur stood beside me as the beacon that guided me to the end. The culmination of this project is an achievement that we all share—a challenging labor of love surpassed only by the birth of our son. I am confident that even bigger achievements are in store, now that I have both McArthur and Nathaniel lighting my path.

THE COLOR OF LOVE

THE FACE OF A SLAVE

Aw, yes! In a family, people are happy to have children. They have the dark one first, . . . but when the white one comes everything changes! The white one is treated really well and the dark one is forgotten. The black one is punished because it is said to have the "face of a slave."

ANA, A DARK-SKINNED BLACK WOMAN, a college student at the Federal University of Bahia in Salvador, Brazil, leaned in toward me and whispered the above statement as we chatted in a small classroom about my proposed research. Provocative and persuasive, her comments echoed my sense that racial hierarchies infiltrate Afro-Brazilian families in ways that might affect how people feel about and treat their children. In this powerful and compelling assertion, she challenged the notion of the Brazilian "racial democracy," the idea that in Brazil social relations reflect racial egalitarianism. She did so by highlighting how racial features—or, rather, the internalization of hierarchies that privilege whiteness—could be the basis on which love and affection is granted or denied in families.

I had always been intrigued by the ambiguity of the "tender and tense ties" of family and the possibility that the sacred institution could leave family members without sanctuary.[1] Ana's comments validated my interest in shifting the gaze on the politics of love and race in families from romantic or conjugal partnerships toward other close family relationships. Whereas the family has been conceptualized as an "intimate site of implementation" of dominant social hierarchies, rarely are nonsexual relationships considered important elements of these intimate sites.[2] To me it seemed plausible, even inevitable, that the racial politics and phenotypic hierarchies that affect romantic relationships could influence love in parental, sibling, and extended family relationships as well. By revealing the emotional dimensions of race and emphasizing differential treatment,

Ana's comment was an inkling that I might be able to trace how language, emotion, and interactions in families contribute to racialization, the process by which racial meaning is attached to people's bodies.

Our brief conversation took place in Salvador, Bahia, Brazil, a city that for several decades has been praised for its strong African presence and recognized with prestigious monikers such as Black Rome.[3] Bahia is located in the Northeast Region of Brazil, considered the most racially diverse region in the country. Instead of idealizing the racial mixture in Bahia, Ana's comments substantiate researchers' admonitions that "interracial unions and multiracial children are no panacea for enduring problems of stratification."[4] Understanding how one's placement into racial categories is influenced by racial appearance (phenotype) and affects life chances takes on particular importance in light of the 2010 Brazilian Census, which reveals that whites are no longer the numerical majority in Brazil. According to that census, the Instituto Brasileiro de Geografia e Estatística estimates the population is 48 percent white, 43 percent brown/mixed-race, 8 percent black, 1 percent yellow, and 0.5 percent indigenous.[5] Those who might view these statistics as a turn in the racial tide have to reconcile these demographic shifts with sobering statistics that place blacks and browns at the bottom end of every major social indicator in Brazil, including literacy, completion of high school, employment, income, health, and wealth.[6] Contrary to the hope expressed in many countries, such as the United States, that increasing racial mixture will eliminate racism, examples from Brazil suggest that mechanisms of racial domination, including racialization processes, shift rather than disappear with greater racial mixture.

Because of Brazil's particular history, race is determined more on the basis of phenotype (physical appearance) than ancestry. High levels of racial mixture in Brazil mean that phenotype varies tremendously throughout the country and even within families. Therefore, although 95 percent of Brazilians are officially classified in one of five racial categories—indigenous (*indígena*), white (*branco*), black (*preto*), brown (*pardo*), or yellow (*amarelo*)—there are over one hundred terms that Brazilians may employ when asked to describe their color (*cor*), reflecting the range and significance of phenotypic variation in Brazilian society.[7] For example, the term *sarará* describes a person with pale or light skin color, African facial features, and afro-textured hair that is very light in color. *Galego* describes a person whose racialized features suggest they are of European descent (*Galícia*): they have pale or very light skin, blond hair, and very light, often blue or green eyes. *Cabo verde* describes a person who has a dark skin color and African facial features, with the defining feature of naturally straight, dark hair and green eyes. *Preto* refers to a person whose hair texture, skin color, and facial features mark them as of unmixed African descent. *Morena* is the most ambiguous term in the race and phenotype lexicon, and it is frequently used. It can define almost any combination of facial features.[8] Researchers have argued that these complex terms function as euphemisms representing "degrees of whiteness," a construction used to perpetuate antiblack racism against individuals who physically and culturally approximate blackness.[9]

It is complicated to analyze how both race and phenotype affect people's lives, but it becomes clearer if we conceptualize these ideas as part of racialization processes, rather than think of them as simply labels. Racialization is the process by which meanings are assigned to physical and cultural traits, and it is "produced and reproduced through ideological, institutional, interactive, and linguistic practices that support a particular construction of Difference."[10] Racialization is important because the meanings that are created and assigned to different bodies sustain racialized social systems like that of Brazil, in which "economic, political, and social advantages are partially shaped by the placement of people in racial categories or races."[11] Thus Ana's quote can be read not simply as an incident of intrafamilial discrimination, but also as a reflection of how racialization affects access to advantages—in this case emotional resources: support, love, and affection in one's own home. The broader implication is that *negros* (those who are brown or black) do not contend only with considerable structural disadvantages. The racial disadvantages that they face in society may be reproduced in verbal interactions, affective exchanges, and differential treatment within their own families.

The Color of Love examines families as critical sites of race-making, racial contestation, and racial negotiation. It explores racial socialization as the process through which racial meanings and boundaries are transmitted and one gains capital and practical strategies necessary to confront life and manage one's positions in society. This book benefits from decades of research that have addressed the role of families in combating racial inequality and discrimination. Building on this rich literature, I aim to extend studies of racial socialization by emphasizing how Afro-Brazilian families engage in practices that simultaneously resist and reproduce racial inequality.[12]

By studying families in which there is significant within-family racial and phenotypic variation, I analyze how individuals within the same family are positioned differently and are socialized with practices, language, and emotions that correspond to their positions in a racialized society. Moreover, I show that families foster the different interests of family members and engage in strategies to assist them in negotiating their future and outcomes on the basis of their appearance. For example, Lilza, a light-skinned, blue-eyed woman who identifies as *parda* (mixed-race) is sanctioned for not using her good looks to marry a white man. I provide examples of family members who may financially support their black-looking family members, yet avoid interacting with them in public in order to preserve their perceived higher social and class status. This book is thus a departure from research on race and family that almost exclusively highlights how families are protective while neglecting their more intricate, even contradictory functions.

I also fundamentally challenge the dominant tendency to study racial socialization across rather than within families. Traditionally researchers have studied racial socialization in families by comparing families to one another on the basis of cultural, class, and racial differences. For example, Brazilian researchers tend to study racial socialization mainly within the context of interracial relationships in comparison to monoracial relationships. They focus primarily on the psychological dimensions, or they frame the structure of black families in a binary manner: organized versus disorganized.[13] In the United States, where racial socialization has been studied more extensively than in any other region, families of color are typically compared to white families. Traditional conceptualizations of racial socialization tend to begin with the assumptions that people have race, that they belong to a family unit of that race, and that they receive socialization that shields them from discrimination and counteracts racism. To be sure, between-family comparisons yield interesting findings, but these contributions are limited because they implicitly (and sometimes explicitly) frame the white family as the ideal, conceive of race as a taken-for-granted status category rather than the product of a racialization processes, or insufficiently theorize intrafamilial differences.[14] In this study, when I asked family members to report on the race of other family members, their response was uniformly, "I don't know. I have never asked them." This suggests the importance of analyzing race as a process rather than a status.

CHALLENGING THE POPULAR MYTH that love can "supersede group differences and render them trivial," this book adds a new dimension to research on race and intimacy by analyzing how in both romantic and familial relationships love and affection can be distributed in accordance to one's race and racial features.[15] In the Brazilian context, there is strong investment in the idea of *amor só de mãe* (a mother's love), which idealizes the unconditional love and affection that women are supposed to have for their children.[16] Destabilizing this idea, I argue that in a racialized society all resources, even love and affection, are symbolic and are unequally distributed, most often (though not always) in ways that benefit family members who most closely approximate whiteness.

I introduce the term *affective capital* to illustrate how differential experiences of love and affection contribute to and reinforce the social relations that sustain a racialized social system. This term refers to the emotional and psychological resources that a person gains from being positively evaluated and supported, and from receiving frequent and meaningful displays of affection. These companionate expressions of love, which significantly shape people's lives, involve "facial expressions, vocal tone, body language, touch, physiological sensations, subjective experience, cognitive appraisal, and behavioral action tendencies."[17] The notion of capital is critical because positive emotions of joy, pride, and love can serve as "enduring personal resources . . . that build psychological resilience, rather than just reflect it."[18] That is, positive emotions generated from affirming social interactions within and outside families can generate personal resources linked to greater creativity, resilience, and emotional well-being.[19]

In a racialized system, affective resources are unequally distributed, with more of these resources often going to phenotypically whiter family members, providing the basis on which they pursue ambitious projects, complete formal education, and are able to avoid the self-esteem issues that can severely hamper family members who are racialized differently. Specifically, I offer examples of how the distribution of affective resources functions among Afro-Brazilians, such as Elise and Dilson, who describe becoming introverted, reluctant to approach people, and hesitant about participating in group activities because they have been ridiculed on the basis of their racial appearance.

There is an important intellectual tradition on which to draw for theoretical grounding on differential treatment of members of the same family. Feminist scholars have revealed how socialization in families functions to reproduce gender inequality. Gender disparities that are reproduced by families "limit opportunities and lead to an inequitable distribution of social resources; the groundwork for those limitations and inequalities begins in childhood."[20] In the same way that notions of gender shape perceptions and emotions even before a child's birth, so might ideas about race, with particular consequences based on gender. Parents often conceive of their children's life chances and even direct the trajectory of their lives on the basis of gender.[21] The same might be said of racialization processes, which have unique consequences based on gender and class distinctions. Likewise, the "patriarchal bargain," a term describing how women engage in negotiations to accommodate patriarchy, might also be relevant to the negotiation of racialization processes.[22] Mindful of the critiques of framing racial negotiations as bargains, I argue that Afro-Brazilians do engage in racial bargains, compromises that are often made ambivalently, in which Afro-Brazilians may comply with racial hierarchies in exchange for perceived payoffs that may be political, economic, psychological, or even affective.

Much like gender, which is an "accomplishment embedded in everyday interaction," race should be conceived as the product of a process.[23] To capture how the intersectionality of race and gender affect people's lives, I focus mainly on how racial bargains differentially affect women and men. Given their vulnerable location in the "matrix of domination," I heavily emphasize the role of Afro-Brazilian women and mothers in this process because they experience more pressure to manage the racial and gendered presentations of themselves and others, and they are more harshly *cobrada* (held accountable) for policing those presentations.[24]

Ana's statement at the beginning of the introduction is a compelling and valuable entry point for rethinking a number of presumptions about how racial hierarchies shape racial socialization in families, but we must also problematize it because it portrays Afro-Brazilian families as monolithic and passive. From even my earliest interviews, it was clear that racial socialization cannot be essentialized as the blind reproduction of racial and phenotypic hierarchies and emotional abuse. Indeed, Afro-Brazilian families exert agency and respond creatively to broader racial hierarchies while simultaneously reproducing racial ideologies. Sensitivity to their strategies of negotiation and racial resistance becomes increasingly important in light of initial discussions of my findings with colleagues, during which they expressed pity for Afro-Brazilians, whom they viewed as lacking true racial consciousness. Uncomfortable with these types of conclusions, I present and analyze data in order to portray Afro-Brazilian families in a nuanced way, highlighting how they contend with structural constraints by relying on an array of practices, discursive strategies, humor, and even ideological innovations. I call the ability to enact this repertoire of negotiation strategies racial fluency, which is learned, cultivated, and continuously developed through the collaborative efforts of close family members and intimate others.

CONCEPTUALIZING EMBODIED RACIAL CAPITAL AND RACIAL FLUENCY

French theorist Pierre Bourdieu uses the term *cultural capital* to describe the predispositions and sensibilities that one learns throughout life that tend to reproduce one's class status.[25] Of the three elements of cultural capital, I engage most with his idea of embodied capital, which suggests that the closer people can come to presenting themselves as possessing and embodying the predispositions and sensibilities of the dominant group (through tastes, accent, language, dress, and mannerisms), the more successful they will be in society.[26]

In this book I use the notion of embodied capital to describe Afro-Brazilians' efforts to manage and negotiate white racial and cultural standards. In a racialized society, economic resources and social advantages are distributed on the basis of one's racial position, which is influenced by physical and cultural traits. Because race in Brazil is based so heavily on appearance, negotiating these strategies often involves managing one's physical body. I conceptualize embodied racial capital as the product of efforts that rely on manipulating the body. It encompasses three major areas: visibility management, navigation of public spaces, and managing evidence of one's cultural affiliations and participation in racialized cultural activities.[27]

With regard to visibility management, I use embodied racial capital to explore how and why families engage in rituals designed to modify racial features, including hair texture and shape of the nose. With regard to navigating public spaces, I emphasize that family members provide guidance about how to negotiate the symbolic and spatial boundaries that designate where Afro-Brazilians can enter or what areas they should avoid. I also explore the types of behaviors that one learns to exhibit upon entering "white" spaces. Finally, the ability to manage one's participation and use of items related to Afro-Brazilian cultural practices is another example of embodied capital. I illustrate how some Afro-Brazilians hide or accentuate their participation in black cultural activities, such as Candomblé or *capoeira*, in response to race-based stereotypes.

I also discuss the multifaceted elements of racial socialization that do not focus exclusively on managing the body. My conceptualization of strategies of "resistance and accommodation" observed in families is informed by diasporic researchers whose work reveals the contours of "everyday racism" and explores how people use their family networks to manage racism.[28] One of the books from which I develop a theoretical concept central to this study is France Winddance Twine's groundbreaking *A White Side of Black Britain*, in which she uses the concept of racial literacy to refer to "perceiving and responding to the racial climate and racial structures that individuals encounter daily."[29] Extending this idea even further, I introduce the concept of racial fluency, which is distinguished from racial literacy in four key ways.

First, racial fluency focuses on how effectively one responds to perceptions of racism. The focus on effectiveness allows the researcher to recognize the moments when racial fluency is incomplete or fails, even though racial literacy is present. Second, racial fluency does not anticipate an outcome that is antiracist, but rather seeks to uncover how racial strategies may intentionally reproduce racist ideologies. This distinction is important because some families do not interpret their socialization as connected at all to racism, while other families socialize their children to directly counter racism, and still other families purposely reinforce racist ideologies.

Third, racial fluency considers the affective realm as critical for transmitting, receiving, and constructing racialization processes. Racial fluency is a type of labor that is developed and refined through routinized actions, discourses, affective sentiments, and concrete strategies.[30] Finally, racial fluency resists privileging unidirectional, parent-to-child socialization and instead emphasizes both the bidirectionality of socialization and the role of close relationships, defined broadly as both biological and non-biological ties, in developing one's understandings of race and racialization processes throughout one's life.[31] Parental-child and romantic relationships are crucial to developing racial fluency, but the interviews for this book also offer multivocality by including diverse perspectives from siblings, grandparents, extended family, and close family friends to explore how those who form part of the extended kinship network participate in socialization and race-making.[32] With regard to racial fluency, I discuss two twin sisters who were separated at birth, with one selected to live with their black mother and the other chosen to live with their white father. Their interviews show how they negotiate race in two different and conflicting contexts in order to ultimately define their racial identity, respond to racism, and negotiate hierarchies of phenotype, particularly related to hair.

I am intentional about clarifying the analytical distinction between race and phenotype because while most social scientists begin with the understanding that race is a social construction, they have struggled to "reach a consensus about how the conceptualization of race as a social construction should guide practical measurement approaches to the study of families of color."[33] I build on the work of researchers who underscore the destabilizing effect that skin color can have on racial hierarchies to suggest that beyond skin color an array of physical and cultural traits shape racialization processes, and each can destabilize hierarchies of race.[34] The term *pigmentocracy*, which is used to describe societies that are organized by skin color, overprivileges skin color and underestimates the role of other physical and cultural traits in driving racialization processes.[35]

Given theoretical debates regarding the way racial systems in the United States and Brazil are converging, it can be useful to understand how physical and cultural traits (such as the increasingly salient factors of behaviors, language, religion, and nationality) contribute to the racialization processes that sustain racialized social systems.[36] If, in fact, the United States is moving toward "Brazilianization" or "Latin Americanization," this research may provide insight into what types of dynamics we might expect to develop in the future in the United States.[37]

MAKING RACE AND NATION THROUGH FAMILY

Racial socialization in Afro-Brazilian families has to be contextualized within the national, regional, and local milieu that shapes it. The trans-Atlantic slave trade beginning in the sixteenth century was a pivotal historical experience that physically and psychologically marked the Africans who were uprooted and enslaved throughout the "New World." Brazil was by far the largest slave society in the Americas, having imported 40 percent of all slaves brought to the Americas, more than any other country.[38] By 1888, after several centuries of racial oppression, slavery in Brazil was abolished. In the national narrative, Princesa Isabel is recognized as having signed the documentation necessary to end slavery. Often ignored in this narrative is that abolition was a hard-fought victory, the culmination of years of organized resistance efforts, growing abolitionist activities, and global pressures.

Though abolition ended chattel slavery, it did not end racial domination. To the contrary, abolition led to the recalibration of the mechanisms of racial domination, and new racial relations became embedded in Brazil's social relations, cultural traditions, and familial relationships. White elites' preoccupation with slavery's stain revolved around their racial anxieties and skepticism about the brown and black population, who they feared might "doom the country to perpetual underdevelopment."[39] These racial anxieties were influenced by the wave of pseudoscientific thinking that swept across the globe in the early 1900s, substantiating the gospel of racial purity and European superiority. Whereas previously the auction block had been the platform on which black bodies were exhibited and dehumanized, now scientific racism nurtured in the halls of the ivory tower provided an "irrefutable" rationale for the subjugation of the "Negroid" race.[40]

These racist ideologies were connected to the eugenics movement and to what would ultimately become known as a racial hygiene project, whose goal was to eliminate racial challenges to modernity. Racial hygienists demanded that populations be ordered on the basis of physical characteristics, and they assigned meaning to certain cultural indicators as well as to previously insignificant physical traits, including hair texture and the size and shape of lips, nose, breasts, feet, and so on.[41] These racial meanings were constructed for the sole purpose of providing evidence for the racial inferiority of Africans and the superiority of Europeans.

Essential to this movement was the notion of racial degeneracy, a condition that could be determined on the basis of "aesthetic criteria," including "protruding jaws, beetling brows, dark skin colour."[42] The significance of aesthetics to racialization processes cannot be understated, as "racist accounts, widely accepted in the time of European colonization and beyond, present the African continent as the metaphor par excellence for physical ugliness and moral decay," which were used to justify the subjugation of Africans.[43] But in this new era of eugenics and racial hygiene, degeneracy was not only inscribed on the body but could be found by identifying certain character traits, such as laziness and hypersexuality. An analysis of these character traits was deployed alongside "sophisticated" methods of craniology, phrenology, and physiognomy to prove African inferiority.[44]

Leading a nation only recently emerging from slavery, white Brazilian elites were eager to disabuse themselves of the nation's ugly race problem, but they were concerned about how this could be achieved, given that its population was composed largely of people of African descent. Appeals to move the nation toward modernity reverberated among the white elites, many of whom "wished to be white but feared they were not" because of their own significant racial mixture.[45] These elites, deploying discourses connecting modernity to whiteness, attributed their nation's underdevelopment to "African barbarism," believing that its population of browns and blacks was "lacking the stimulus of having to maintain a civilized standard of living."[46] Nina Rodrigues, a prominent Bahian anthropologist, earned the dubious title of being one of the most well known proponents of pseudoscientific research. In a twist of racial irony, this popular scientist who spoke of the dangerous degeneration of black and brown Brazilians was himself *mulato*.[47] Although he was not convinced that the Brazilian population could be saved, others who viewed Brazil's presumable racial degeneration as a national ailment believed that the family could be mobilized to advance the "refinement of the race" and achieve "Aryanization."[48]

Strategically, embracing racial mixture or *mestiçagem* was considered the only viable option. It served as a "compromise between the racist doctrines in vogue around the twentieth century and the socio-racial reality of Brazil."[49] Touting Brazil's racial democracy on one hand while actively promoting "whitening" (*branqueamento*) on the other, government-subsidized immigration from Europe was implemented. The efforts to attract white immigrants to Brazil were so substantial that over 4 million Europeans immigrated to Brazil over the span of only three decades.[50] This was more than the number of slaves brought to Brazil over the course of three centuries. Although the government was unwilling to invest subsidies directly in the brown and black populations, the future of the country rested in the wombs of black woman—a group whose sexuality had been used before to support slavery.[51] By the 1930s the nation hoped it could depend on black women's wombs to help usher in a new brighter, whiter future. If appeals to a racial democracy were supposed to be indicative of a society that respected the citizenship and autonomy of its population and families, then legislated whitening policies and anticipation that blacks would become extinct pointed to an alternative hope of a "transgenerational and genocidal de-blackening process."[52]

Among the most popular representations of Brazilian family life are those constructed by Gilberto Freyre, which replaced the nightmarish brutality of slavery with a fairy tale of racial harmony and unity. With its sprinkling of half-truths and its vivid imagery, Freyre's work *The Masters and the Slaves* is a heavily romanticized portrayal of the Brazilian family, singular for its ability to render a compelling version of racial democracy that captivated an international and domestic audience.[53] Promoting a racial project that had been circulating among elites for some time, he suggested that *mestiçagem* was not degenerate, but redemptive.[54] His preoccupation with interracial sexuality featured prominently in the construction of the image of a utopic Brazilian nation—a land of "sexual intoxication" where there was an abundance of nude indigenous women and promiscuous African women with "protruding buttocks."[55] One of the most striking features of Freyre's portrayal of race in Brazil was his descriptions of phenotypically diverse children interacting playfully and indiscriminately under the protection of a white master. Freyre downplayed the violent and exploitative history that often shaped interracial sexual relationships and relied on idealized family portrayals to convey "harmonious" race relations and inspire the global fixation on Brazil's "moreno meta race."[56]

The historical revisionism of Freyre and his contemporaries considerably underestimated the ways that race relations and social norms in slavery "forced patterns of thought and action on slaves and former slaves," some of which have endured and others of which have shifted.[57] For example, the analysis of rates of manumission in Brazil offers overwhelming evidence that mixed-race slaves (*pardos/mulatos*), especially children, enjoyed advantages over African-born and unmixed slaves. Researchers attribute this differential treatment and comparative privilege of mixed-race slaves to "feelings of paternalism and affection," since the mixed-race children were often the children of their mother's master.[58] Yet even with these affective bonds, *pardos* and *mulatos* were often not freed, immediately or at all, and they were rarely, if ever, treated as equal to their white siblings. They were, however, often framed as superior to their mother's unmixed children.[59] Given these dynamics, enslaved women relied on their sexuality, often their only source of capital, to parlay freedom for themselves and social mobility for their children.

Mixed-race slaves were considered privileged to work in the *casa grande*, or big house, rather than doing the backbreaking work in the fields. They were more likely to learn and incorporate white elite mannerisms, language, and customs. Some *pardos* who benefited from an inheritance or the good will of their white fathers went on to own their own slaves and handed out punishments with a brutality that rivaled that of white men. In contrast, some free blacks, *pardos*, and *mulatos* formed mutual aid organizations, helped fugitive slaves, and even supported slave revolts.[60]

Given that white masters were wealthy and that mixed-race slaves were treated better, were much more likely to be educated, and were less frequently and less harshly punished, the possession of whiter physical and cultural traits began to be associated with high status and privilege. So significant were the privileges that *pardos* and *mulatos* enjoyed that many

slaves in the Americas would come to abhor what they perceived as the racial features and cultural traits that had condemned them to their racial
position. Many were more insistent on trying to eliminate their racial features than on dismantling the racialized social system itself. Discussions
of these seemingly contradictory elements of slave life reflect the "pervasiveness and perniciousness of the slave regime and its effects on everyone
touched by it."[61] The new racial relations that developed post-abolition
rely on some of the same hierarchies and compel Afro-Brazilians to engage in familiar racial bargains. Most notably, new modes of domination
have emerged that rely in part on families to "mirror the hierarchy" of the
dominant society.[62]

DIASPORIC STUDIES OF THE BLACK FAMILY

Building on a diverse and diasporic collection of research, this book is
an opportunity for scholars in Brazil and the United States and across
the African diaspora to think more critically about racialization and racial socialization practices in their respective countries. Triangulating my
data with other research that systematically analyzes race, phenotype,
and black families magnifies the centrality of racial negotiations for African descendants around the globe.[63] By making these connections, I do
not discount the regional and national specificities; rather, I illustrate how
European colonialism has engendered hegemonic ideas about whiteness
that drive similar, though not identical, practices, processes, and emotional experiences in all of these regions.[64] This engagement with the diasporic literature moves this book from being a small ripple of research
on Brazil into the potential to initiate more sustained dialogues with diasporic communities about how racialized social systems are maintained
and negotiated.

Making these types of diasporic connections seems inevitable given
that the genealogy of race and family studies in the United States and Brazil dates back to diasporic intellectual debates about "African survivals"
in Afro-Bahian families that were initiated between Franklin Frazier and
Melville Herskovits.[65] Despite these intellectual roots, diasporic connections have not been explicitly made. The breadth of racial socialization
research conducted in the United States is instructive in moving theoretical and conceptual questions about race and family practices forward, as
U.S. researchers have been at the forefront of examining racial socialization. Many U.S. scholars who study black families focus on the "power
of motherhood," the benefits conveyed by extended kinship ties for poor

black families, and the role of socialization in conveying affirming messages of cultural heritage, pride, and racial equality.[66] This emphasis on black motherhood and women in the United States corresponds to research outlining the power of black women as mothers, community leaders, and activists striving against racism in Brazil.[67]

However, I use research from the United States cautiously and critically, by acknowledging that there are important limitations. For example, the role of black women as mothers in both Brazil and the United States is much more complicated and contradictory than researchers have normally suggested as it relates to how they both resist *and* accommodate racism. Moreover, theories of racial socialization from the United States cannot simply be superimposed onto Brazilian families. In fact, U.S. models of racial socialization in families should not be superimposed even onto families in the United States. Bringing together critical race theory and feminist traditions, this research responds to recommendations that family researchers and race scholars engage with one another in order capture how gendered racialization processes, including negotiations of colorism (the awarding of advantages or immunities on the basis of skin color and racial appearance), shape family dynamics in the United States.[68] *The Color of Love* represents an effort to apply these recommendations in a setting that provides ample opportunity to grapple with the intricacies of how racial socialization in families simultaneously manages, contests, and reinforces racialization. Though the study of racial socialization is still an emergent field in Brazil, Edward Telles's monumental work *Race in Another America* provides compelling quantitative data about differential outcomes of family members in multiracial and phenotypically diverse families; it foretells the importance of this qualitative project for the Brazilian context.[69]

THE BLACK SHEEP OF THE NATIONAL FAMILY—SALVADOR, BAHIA, BRAZIL

Nationally renowned for being the cradle of Brazilian culture and the jewel of Afro-diasporic culture, Salvador, Bahia, is a fascinating and enigmatic city. According to the 2010 Census, the city of Salvador is 51.7 percent *pardo* (brown or mixed-race), 28 percent *preto* (black), and 18.9 percent *branco* (white). The term *negro* has increasingly been used by black activists in Brazil as a political term to capture the idea that those who are *pardo* or *preto* are all African-descendants and should be identified as *negros*. These demographics are what give Salvador the distinction of being called the "blackest city in Brazil," as more than 80 percent of its population is Afro-Brazilian (brown or black). Salvador's impressive monikers, such as Black Rome, signify the city's cultural and religious importance in Afro-Brazilian culture and, most important, its symbolism in Afro-diasporic culture.

Salvador enjoys this cultural status because African descendants in Brazil have retained strong connections to West African culture through cuisine, religion, and language in a way that is rivaled by no other diasporic community in the Americas. In particular, the strong presence of the Afro-Brazilian religion Candomblé, which worships Orixás, or African deities, and has ceremonies conducted in the Yoruba language, exemplifies the depth of these connections. These links are attributed in part to Brazil's late abolition of slavery and the bidirectional circulation of people and ideas between Brazil to Africa. So strong are these linkages that Salvador is considered a diasporic homeland for African descendants, many of whom for decades have traveled to Salvador to connect to their African roots.[70]

In light of this history, the high levels of racial mixture, and a rich African heritage, it might seem incomprehensible that one of my respondents would say with a somber expression, "It is harder to be black in Bahia than in any other place in Brazil" ("É mais difícil ser negro na Bahia do que em qualquer outro lugar no Brasil"). In no other place are the contradictions of a racialized system so pronounced than in this city that is populated in large part by *negros*, portrayed as authentically African, but run by a small white elite.

Historically Salvador's rise to preeminence in Brazil is rooted in its role as a center of the slave trade and commerce. Beginning in the sixteenth century, it was at the ports of Salvador that between three to five million Africans were brought in chains to Brazil. The immense profits that resulted from the trade catapulted Salvador to national importance, and as a reflection of its role as the economic engine of Brazil, it was designated Brazil's first capital. The city of Salvador's centrality to the state of Bahia was so great that for centuries after the national capital was moved to Rio de Janeiro, and later Brasília, Brazilians used the term Salvador interchangeably with the term Bahia. The entrance of scores of enslaved Africans to Bahia to work on enormous slave plantations, or *fazendas*, in the area shaped every element of Northeast culture and led to it being the most racially diverse region in the country. To be sure, Brazil's slaveocracy affected the entire country, but its legacy left its most pronounced impact on the racial demographics in the Northeast.

The state of Bahia's contemporary decision to package Salvador as the "Black City: The Most African City of Brazil" marks a critical reversal of white elites' earlier antagonism toward and repression of African culture in Bahia.[71] With the creation of the organization Bahiatursa, the state of Bahia formalized its decision to invest in marketing Salvador as a charming city that is the heart of Afro-Brazilian culture, but it has been only selectively embracing and repackaging examples of African influences as part of this re-Africanization.[72] Instead of raiding and antagonizing practitioners of Candomblé as they had before, Bahia's leaders are now employing Candomblé symbols in their advertising efforts: plastering them to sides of buildings; using them in decorative motifs for expensive restaurants; incorporating them into logos for shopping centers, bus routes, and landmarks; and featuring them prominently in tourist catalogs.[73] Likewise, the martial art form of *capoeira*, which was created by enslaved Africans in Brazil, moved from being framed as a dangerous "sport of ruffians" to being considered the nation's "beautiful sport."[74] *Capoeira* and a musical instrument associated with it, the *berimbau*, serve as unofficial symbols of the Northeast Region that are represented by black men whose sculpted bodies are shown contorted in flexible poses in order to feed an image of Bahian culture that is raced and highly sexualized.[75] Likewise, popular festivals and groups including Carnaval, Lavagem of Bom Fim (Washing of Bom Fim Church), and the Irmandade de Boa Morte (Sisterhood of the Good Death) are now embraced, though they were once criticized or prohibited because of their connections to Africa.

Along the streets, particularly in the tourist regions, smiling darkskinned Brazilian women with gleaming teeth and wearing wide hoop skirts elicit nostalgia for colonial times. Their smiling faces are featured on postcards, souvenirs, paintings, T-shirts, and magnets. Tourists visit Pelourinho, named after the whipping post where slaves were punished, and walk over the cobblestones known as Negroheads as part of their cultural excursion.[76] The perversity of a booming tourist industry based on Afro-Brazilian culture in a city where Afro-Brazilians remain on the margins has been addressed thoroughly by Brazilian researchers.[77]

This cultural milieu is essential to understanding the regional and local context that shapes Afro-Brazilians' lives in Salvador. Being *baiano* (from the state of Bahia) is a core element of how Afro-Brazilians in this study understand themselves. This regional identity is itself highly racialized, as the state of Bahia and Northeast Region of Brazil are objects of racialized caricatures and *brincadeiras* (jokes) that are used throughout Brazil. During my visit to Rio de Janeiro, located farther south, people discouraged me from visiting Salvador, warning that "there are thieves everywhere" and that "*Baianas* are dirty." More subtle Brazilians never directly spoke of Bahia, but they referenced the state in jest, stating that they had committed a *baianada* when they did something wrong, stupid, or absentminded. Still other *cariocas* (Brazilians from Rio de Janeiro) encouraged me to explore Salvador, stating that I would feel right at home and would be able to party often "because in Salvador there is always a party every night" (a coded reference to the stereotype that *baianos* are lazy and do not work). These same *cariocas* warned that though I would have a good time, "não deve mexer na macumba" (do not mess with African religion), a barely veiled (offensive) reference to Candomblé.

Exaggerated constructions of Salvador as completely distinct from and inferior to other cities rely largely on stereotypes of *baianidade* that tend to emphasize "cordiality, tolerance, indulgence, laziness, optimism, humour and characteristic cultural praxes (Candomblé, *capoeira*, extroverted street dancing, fashion, etc.) of Bahian society."[78] Other cities, especially São Paulo, have constructed "white" regional identities that differentiate themselves in clear racial terms from Bahia.[79] In this way, Bahia's darker population serves as a constant and visible reminder of the history that many in the country would prefer to forget, except when there is money to be made. Within the metaphorical Brazilian family, Bahia is the black sheep of the family, receiving less government investment, subject to racialized insults, and striving to construct an identity that is affirming.

Afro-Brazilian families that live in Salvador confront considerable structural disadvantages alongside their conditional cultural inclusiveness. In order to appreciate the significant structural constraints that shape the practices, language, and emotional exchanges that emerge in Afro-Brazilian families, this broader social structure must be considered. Income disparities are high, police brutality against *negros* is so extreme that its effects have been compared to genocide, high levels of violence plague the city, and substandard and underfunded public schools make it difficult for Afro-Brazilians to attain social mobility.[80] Continued resistance to explicitly race-based affirmative action policies designed to address some of these inequalities reflect the ongoing struggle for racial equality.[81] Adding to these barriers are infrequent representations of Afro-Brazilians in television and film (outside of stereotypical characters), beauty ideals that devalue blackness, and day-to-day micro-aggressions, including "elevator apartheid," which separates the largely black servants from the largely white residents in middle-class apartment buildings.[82] These interpersonal practices mirror the types of spatial dynamics that differentiate physical areas in Salvador as white or black, poor or wealthy, marginal or high-class.[83]

These are the formidable challenges that Afro-Brazilians face when constructing their families and socializing their family members. Salvador is an ideal site for this research because of, not despite, the contradictions of its characteristics. In a way that is true of only a few locations, Salvador's history and current social relations make it at once local and global, reflecting the multidimensionality of diasporic communities.[84]

THE STUDY

This research is based on fourteen months of ethnographic fieldwork conducted in Salvador, Bahia, Brazil, between 2009 and 2011, six weeks of follow-up interviews in June and July 2013, and four weeks of follow-up interviews in July 2014. During this time, I conducted 116 in-depth interviews with Afro-Brazilians (blacks and browns) from ten poor and working-class families in an urban neighborhood with a pseudonym of Lua Cheia. The ethnography and interviews center on ten core families, and I also included interviews and ethnographic observations with an additional five families who were the extended family of the core families and lived in other areas of Salvador. I spent nearly a year with the ten core families, attending family celebrations and religious and cultural events, observing day-to-day family activities, and listening to neighborhood conversations. I pursued interviews with extended families only when an invitation was extended. Because the extended families lived in different neighborhoods of Salvador, these interviews provided me the opportunity to observe how neighborhood-specific interactions influence core families.

Interviews were often both formal and informal. The average formal interview time ranged between sixty and ninety minutes. Informal interviews ranged from twenty minutes to six hours.[85] In addition, I conducted informal interviews with Brazilian activists, other residents of Salvador, and various laypeople (beauticians, taxi drivers, teachers, professors, students, and artists). I also incorporate observations from an afro-aesthetics course and seminar offered in a local Afro-Brazilian community. All interviews were conducted in Brazilian Portuguese, digitally recorded, transcribed, and then translated for analysis. I analyzed the data manually using close readings and organizing and coding data throughout the data collection process as detailed in Appendix A.[86]

My relationship with community contact Luana began as a casual, friendly acquaintance when I observed her cleaning an apartment in the building where I lived. After numerous conversations, she invited me to meet members of her family and introduced me to other families in Lua Cheia, an area of the Lower City of Salvador inhabited mostly by large Afro-Brazilian families of low socioeconomic status. Luana helped me to identify the poor and working-class community in the Lower City and served as a central point of introductions between the core families and myself.

Core families lived in close proximity to one another and often interacted daily as part of broader neighborhood dynamics. This means that I was often observing two or more families as they interacted with each other. When there were holidays or celebrations, I would spend several days in the community, sleeping over in Luana's home. I taped formal interviews and informal conversations, and I notated observations in a field notebook during and directly after important events occurred. When possible, I also visited people's places of employment and observed informants interacting with co-workers and customers. Although data from their employment is not discussed here, it provided me with a context in which to understand the lives of the family members. In order to develop a sense of how temporal changes shape families, I observed families approximately one to three times a week for nine consecutive months, returned for follow-up interviews with several families three years later, and visited once more with a few families a year after that.

I initially envisioned conducting observations in a "naturalistic" setting, as an observer occupying a peripheral space.[87] This strategy was untenable in Brazil, where hospitality is prioritized and where people comfortably slip past the blurry boundaries between family, friends, and researchers. Negotiating these social contexts to study racial socialization in families required my own resocialization into the rules and norms that guide these spaces.[88] As a condition of my presence in their homes, families wanted to engage me and wanted me to be involved in some family activities. In fact, my participation and involvement with the families served as the basis on which they trusted me with interviews and observations about private areas of their lives.

LUA CHEIA NEIGHBORHOOD

Lua Cheia is a pseudonym for the small neighborhood in the Lower City of Salvador that is the core site of my fieldwork. The Lower City comprises a fairly large region of the city, and the neighborhood of Lua Cheia is located along the beach in the relative vicinity of Ribeira. The location's designation as part of the Lower City of Salvador is as much a class and racial reference as it is a physical description, to the extent that researchers argue that the rich and poor function in "differentiated and juxtaposed cities."[89] The racialization of space is evident in the fact that the poorer, darker population tends to live in the lower part of the city and the wealthier, whiter population enjoys life in the Upper City.[90]

The demarcation of racial space is evident not only in the description of the Lower and Upper City, but in the changing physical appearance of the area as one moves from one space to the other. Descending from the Upper City to the Lower City down the major street Avenida Contorno, one travels a route that reflects the seemingly effortless idyllic physical landscape of Salvador, with beautifully preserved and gentrified historical areas that are reminders of the city's importance as Brazil's first national capital. Traveling from the Upper City down the Avenida Contorno, on the left is the Bahia de Todos os Santos (Bay of All Saints) and the Bahia Marina, where hundreds of small vessels and cruise ships are docked. The tall, wirelike poles that extend from the boats are often one of the first details visible from the bay, which is framed by a few expensive restaurants offering picturesque views. Hidden directly below this main road is a black community, Gamboa de Baixo, which has been fighting vigorously to reject the urban renewal that threatens to destroy the community.[91]

Near Salvador's oldest Catholic church is a major tourist attraction, the Mercado Modelo (Model Market) and a huge sculpture popularly and colloquially known as the "bunda da mulata" (the mulata's butt). Expansive cruise ships and small vessels now populate the docks on the bay behind the Mercado Modelo; this is where slave ships used to dock during the colonial period—a history that is simultaneously buried and commodified in that market. On the first and second floors of the Mercado Modelo tourist souvenir market, vendors targeting tourists sell a variety of items that commodify Salvador's African heritage, including items related to Candomblé and *capoeira*, black dolls, African masks, African sculpture, and jewelry. Pitch black, grinning dolls, many with large red lips, dead eyes, and hair that stands straight up, are sold by aggressive vendors. Nowadays, it is the image of the African body and the feeling of Africa that are bartered and traded in the market. This is the city of Salvador, and this is the path to Lua Cheia.

In Lua Cheia family and friends interact with each other regularly. The lines separating family and friends are intentionally blurred, and neighbors are more like extended family. In the neighborhood, as in the larger city, residents can often be heard referring to one another as *meu filho* or *minha filha* (my son or my daughter), a hackneyed colloquialism that is used regardless of biological ties. The phrase *minha nega*, derived from the word *negra* (black), is commonly used as a deracialized term meaning honey, sweetie, or dear. The term *negão* or *negona* is often used to refer to a very large or striking dark-skinned man or woman.

Because the homes in Lua Cheia are very small, large families with children spend a significant amount of time outside. The area directly in front of their homes is usually congested with mothers and children, while the *esquina* (corner), located farther away, is a space where mostly males congregate. As is the case throughout Latin America, the bifurcation of social space is an extension of the gendered quality of social domains in which men are "of the street" and wives are "of the house."[92] This spatial separation justifies and fosters the women's responsibility for familial affairs, including the children and housework. Men, on the other hand, enjoy the freedom and independence that comes along with access to broader spaces. Within the confines of the neighborhood, whether at home or on the street, residents express a strong sense of security. Residents proudly brag, "We don't have thieves here; if there are thieves they come from the outside." The framing of an ambiguous "outside" reflects the strong affective ties that community members have with their space and each other.[93]

In Lua Cheia, the gender politics of the neighborhood are such that everything related to the domestic sphere tends to be women's domain: cooking, child rearing, cleaning, and schooling. Although a number of the women in the neighborhood are partnered, their husbands who live with them are often physically present, but emotionally detached. Husbands come in and out of the homes without saying much, without making much eye contact, and without interacting with their children or wives. On the weekends, after a few beers (*cervejas*) everyone is more sociable, and emotional relationships become more apparent.

The core families live in homes that are sandwiched between several neighbors to the left and right. Experts at adapting, large families of over seven people are able to arrange their space in a way that allows for free movement. The outside of the homes directly in front of the door becomes an important space for families with children because there is limited space inside the home to play. Everyone in the neighborhood has a small home of approximately three hundred square feet with two small bedrooms and a kitchen that is attached to a small common area. This area has enough space for a table or a sofa, but not both. Though the bonds of these families begin as neighborly, living in such close proximity fosters relationships that border on extended family and kinship. How these bonds manifest themselves in socialization practices became clear very early in my visits with families.

SECOND SIGHT OR DOUBLE VISION?: DIASPORIC POSITIONALITIES

Renowned American sociologist W. E. B. Du Bois writes about blacks' divided identities in the United States and describes how their "two warring souls" can be a source of tremendous insight, which he labels "second-sight."[94] I had hoped to use my racial positionality in a way that would allow me to fully develop this second-sight, but I would soon discover that my subjective experiences did not represent two warring souls, but rather multiple warring identifications that functioned like an off-kiltered see-saw, shaky and unpredictable. As a researcher, I situate myself as part of the contemporary wave of blacks from the United States who conduct work on race in Brazil. Insights from earlier researchers have played an important role in preparing me for the way I would be "straddling racial categories and disrupting national boundaries, in addition to occupying a 'web of interlocking social categories'" at the same time.[95]

As I prepared for fieldwork, I relied on these insights to understand how my insider and outsider status might both advantage and disadvantage me, how my nested identities would shape my access to information, and how to mute my U.S. lens in order to be able to make new insights and contributions.[96] Yet I was still unprepared for what these nested identities would mean for me practically and the extent to which my race, gender, and Americanness would so thoroughly shape my experiences in Salvador. True to what I had read, I was never simply black, never just a woman, never just a researcher or just American—I never occupied any single identification uniquely. As an African-American woman with dark brown skin, afro-textured hair, and physical features that mark me as *preta*, I discovered that my appearance greatly shaped my experiences in the field. Moreover, how my body and other signifiers were given meaning and interpreted was as much a testament of my colliding identifications as it was confirmation of the centrality of race, gender, and "body politics" in Salvador.[97]

Within my first month I could travel around Salvador and be indistinguishable from natives of the city. I had learned all the major bus routes and schedules (as much as their unpredictability would allow). But the camouflage I enjoyed required linguistic fluency and bodily fluency, the ability to physically incorporate *o jeito brasileiro* (Brazilian style) in my self-presentation. Once this was mastered, I felt perfectly imperceptible on the streets, and without tremendous effort I appeared *baiana*. However, the invisibility of my North Americanness came with an exchange: I was assumed to be a black Brazilian. In this way, my appearance was a double-edged sword, both embodied capital and embodied liability. My cloak of invisibility had a vulnerability: I was sometimes ignored when I walked into stores, spoken to crassly, and disregarded or skipped as I waited in line. Sometimes I was not allowed to enter my apartment building by the doorman, who was "protecting" residents. Yet, these were minor incidents that paled in comparison to many others that I experienced, including the horror of having the military police aim a long rifle at the side of my head and order me out of a car because they suspected I was a prostitute with drugs. In that case, once the officers discovered I was American, they bowed, shook my hand, and said, "Our apologies. When you go back to the U.S. we want you to be able to go back and tell them that the military police treated you with dignity and respect."

It was the ineffable way that people looked at me when they discovered that my blackness was an American (read: better) blackness that reminded me that I was still privileged and most certainly not at home. Despite my solidarity and shared experiences with Afro-Brazilians, my national privilege was a point of difference that I could and did deploy in order to escape the mistreatment that many Afro-Brazilians face without recourse. I could also use this privilege to speak up in numerous situations without having to fear retaliation. Notions of U.S. superiority and status were also instrumental in my access to the community, and this left me feeling ambivalent. Afro-Brazilian families were interested in speaking to me because of my "charming American accent" and also because they had a number of questions about life in the United States, Barack Obama, and popular culture. Often I was objectified and introduced as "minha amiga, uma Americana" (my friend, an American) with my actual name only mentioned later. This introduction provided status to the person who introduced me, but was also meant to let others know to use different rules of engagement, since by virtue of being American I was viewed as a *negra fina* (a refined black woman).

Any initial preoccupations that families may have had about me seemed to erode after my husband came to visit several months into my research. The community was excited to meet him and perplexed that he could not speak Portuguese. After he left, my reception in the neighborhood changed unexpectedly. The children and adults welcomed me with such an unparalleled excitement that it startled me. Children who had not ever wanted to speak with me ran up to me and hugged me, and the difference with the women was also immediately perceptible. Now that they had met the man to whom I was married, they viewed me as safer, more trustworthy, and less threatening.

Children were the most enthralled by and vocal about what they felt were contradictions between my race and my nationality: "But, you look just like us!" one wide-eyed young black girl could not stop repeating. The children often tried to prove that they were cosmopolitan by singing songs by Rihanna, Beyoncé, and Chris Brown.[98] Overall, informants responded in ways that extended U.S. privileges and status to me. Informants accepted me relatively easily and used my racial appearance as a comparison point—by stating that someone is "*morena*, your color," for example, or by explaining that a person is "black like us" or asserting that someone has "bad hair like yours/ours." In addition to racialized features like color and hair, other parts of my body were made topics of conversation—embarrassing for me, but considered normal by my interviewees. My body was at times a point of positive reference, and at many other times a point of critique. I discuss the dilemmas of my positionality in further detail in Appendix A.

The depth of my ethnographic immersion meant that I witnessed and heard about traumatic experiences of abuse and exploitation. Remaining in researcher mode in order to learn from each experience was beneficial but personally challenging. It often meant that I could not jeopardize my research by responding to blatantly racist, sexist, or otherwise offensive comments or intervene if family members were insulting a child or family member. This weighed heavily on me because of the relationships that I had developed with participants. In the same way that Brazilian social interactions are characterized by ambiguity of work and family boundaries, I also struggled with resolving the difficulties that the ambiguity of these boundaries imposed.

Interviews and family observations, paired with my own personal experiences of racism and sexism in Salvador, left me feeling deeply troubled and profoundly anxious about my research. Families welcomed our conversations, and after completing interviews that involved traumatic narratives, they would often thank me for providing them with a cathartic experience. My listening helped those who had never previously spoken about their traumas and abuse, but when the interviews ended, their narratives stayed with me, and with each traumatic interview my anxieties accumulated.[99] For months after returning from the field, I avoided my advisors, shelved my field notes and memos, lost sleep, and above all, refused to replay the interviews. I struggled with having to relive my own traumatic experiences in Salvador, which included not only eliciting painful memories but also observing violent practices in some homes. Along with the anxiety came the guilt that it was the respondents who had entrusted their narratives to me, and yet it was I who needed distance and time to recuperate.

ON LANGUAGE

There have been considerable debates about the use of racial and color terms in Brazil.[100] As Telles explains, there are three acceptable systems of racial classification: official classification, informal classification, and the system of classification used by the black movement in Brazil.[101] Official census data organize Brazilians into five major categories: white (*branco*), brown (*pardo*), black (*preto*), yellow (*amarelo*), and indigenous (*indígena*). Throughout my time in Brazil, an informal classification system was heavily used wherein people were described according to *côr*, which translates as "color" but connotes a person's racialized physical appearance as a whole. I take these informal classifications and identifications seriously and argue that race and phenotype are analytically distinct and should be analyzed accordingly. At the same time, I use the terms Afro-Brazilian and black (*negro*). The latter is endorsed by the black movement as a political racial category for people whose families are composed mainly of those who identify as brown (*pardo*) and black (*preto*). In interviews, speakers often used the terms *preto* or *negro*. Both terms mean "black," but *preto* tends to be used to describe color, and *negro* is often used as a political category in which browns and blacks are both included. When intraracial distinctions specifically within the Afro-Brazilian/*negro* category are important, I make those distinctions known. Otherwise, *negro*, black, and Afro-Brazilian are used interchangeably.

The core Afro-Brazilian families in this study live in neighborhoods that are predominately poor and overwhelmingly brown or black according to the census. I did not categorize families on the basis of my own perceptions of racial identification, but allowed family members to describe their own racial and color categorizations. Despite what census data reveal about race, some family members that I might assume to be *negro* describe themselves as white. Others whom I expect, on the basis of physical appearance, to define themselves as white are adamant about asserting their blackness. In all of the families, the majority of family members with whom I interacted identified as non-white and often black (*negro*). As it relates to translations, I have included the Portuguese only where I believe the original version offers subtleties that cannot be fully captured by English translation.

ORGANIZATION OF THE BOOK

This book explores the creative and contradictory ways that Afro-Brazilian families negotiate racial hierarchies and engage in racial socialization, both resisting and reproducing dominant racial ideologies, often simultaneously. In part I, I discuss the private sphere, focusing on how socialization and stigma affects close family relationships. In part II, I discuss the implications of socialization for the public sphere. I end this section by focusing on three cases of racially transgressive families.

In chapter 1, "What's Love Got to Do with It? Racial Stigma and Embodied Capital," I explore how evaluations of one's racial appearance affect the distribution of love, affection, and emotional experiences in families. I explore critical life transitions, including pregnancy, the birth of a child, dating, and marriage as moments that punctuate the racial negotiations that occur more covertly in daily life. I draw on interviews with and observations of biological and nonbiological family members to illustrate how an array of racial features (nose, hair texture, eye color, and so on) influence interactions and affective exchanges in families. Focusing both on socialization processes and the main actors involved in socialization, I discuss how gendered racism means that black mothers are *cobrada* (held accountable) for producing racially desirable babies and managing appropriate racial displays of themselves and all family members. In this chapter I use the notion of cyclical interactionism to conceptualize the mutually constituting relationship between racialization and racial socialization. I end by linking phenomena observed in Brazil to related secondary data collected from countries throughout the diaspora.

In chapter 2, "Black Bodies, White Casts: Racializing and Gendering Bodies," I illustrate the intrusive and dehumanizing ways that the entire black body has been stigmatized. I argue that Afro-Brazilian families respond to racial stigma in numerous ways, including by engaging in practices that begin in infancy and extend throughout one's life to increase one's embodied racial capital. These detailed rituals, which are elements of what I call the racial bargain, represent Afro-Brazilian families' attempts to exert agency in the face of racial stigmatization. Recognizing the centrality of beauty for women's embodied racial capital, I further examine the gendered aspect of racial bargains by exploring how Afro-Brazilian women manage and negotiate racist aesthetic hierarchies based on whiteness in order to attain beauty and construct their self-presentation. I end the chapter by discussing the emergence of the afro-aesthetic movement and the development of the Instituto Beleza Natural (Natural Beauty Institute) in Salvador, a salon that serves Afro-Brazilian women. I address how these two developments affect families' negotiation of embodied racial capital, and I make connections throughout the chapter with diasporic families.

In chapter 3, "Home Is Where the Hurt Is: Affective Capital, Stigma, and Racialization," I link the practices of racial socialization and differential treatment based on racial appearance to well-being and social psychological outcomes. The chapter operationalizes well-being subjectively, so that it encompasses experiences of and exposure to violence (physical, emotional, and symbolic), impact on self-esteem and sense of belonging, and reports of depression and suicidal ideation. Moreover, negative race-based experiences are framed as important not only to reveal the complexity of interactions in families, but to illustrate that the negative effects produced by differential treatment compound racial inequality by decreasing a person's *affective capital*. Low levels of affective capital lead some Afro-Brazilian respondents to engage in behaviors and make decisions that limit their life chances and reproduce their racial position. By addressing how differential treatment within families can reproduce racial inequality, this chapter deviates from research that focuses exclusively on the protective consequences of racial socialization in families. Addressing gaps in current research, I highlight the traumas of both Afro-Brazilian men and women, while also illustrating how white-looking or privileged family members may intervene to compound or compensate for the mistreatment of other family members.

In the first chapter of part II of the book, "Racial Fluency: Reading between and beyond the Color Lines" (chapter 4), I focus on how family members learn to navigate racial and color classifications. Exploring how racial fluency is developed and executed in social and public situations, I show that racial socialization in families is less concerned with developing a concrete racial identity than aimed at teaching people how to navigate and invoke racial ambiguity. The chapter analyzes how family members engage in socialization practices that have implications for proper racial etiquette, as well as socialization into the uses of complimentary racial terms depending on the context. In this chapter, I explore the process through which Afro-Brazilians arrive at their responses about their racial and color categorizations. The inconsistencies, confusions, and interventions that they experience reveal that ambiguity is the rule rather than the exception. The second half of the chapter explores how *novelas* and popular myths serve as important sources of knowledge about race and Afro-Brazilian history, supplementing racial socialization by family members.

In chapter 5, "Mind Your Blackness: Embodied Capital and Spatial Mobility," I explore how embodied racial capital is used to help Afro-Brazilians navigate racialized public spaces. Racial socialization is both explicit and implicit, with some families relying on strategies that emphasize avoidance of white areas, while others critically question white spaces and encourage their family to transgress racialized spaces. I show that even among the more permissive families, family members are socialized to engage in self-vigilance in order to abide by notions of racial respectability. I also incorporate examples from both working-class and middle-class Afro-Brazilian interviewees in order to illustrate how these class differences affect the racial strategies that are used. In this chapter, public spaces are defined as educational and cultural spaces, so I also examine how family members are socialized to navigate the discursive and physical terrain of education and cultural inclusion.

In chapter 6, "Antiracism in Transgressive Families," I highlight several exemplary cases that illustrate how some Afro-Brazilian families engage in antiracism and sustained resistance to racial hierarchies. Although all families in this study exhibit elements of resistance, these particular families are distinguished for how they creatively develop racial fluency and engage in antiracism through the explicitness of their language, use of affective exchanges, humor, and political mobilization. They also socialize family members to use embodied capital to challenge dominant norms in unexpected ways. The strategies that these families employ are framed as inventive and counterhegemonic, though I illustrate that practices of sustained resistance exist alongside sporadic racial accommodation and internalized racism. This chapter ends by identifying how political and cultural institutions help support sustained efforts at antiracism in Salvador.

The title of the concluding section, "The Ties that Bind," is a reference to both the "tense and tender" ties within families and the diasporic bonds that connect black diasporic families with one another. I weave together key research findings to highlight how racial socialization in Afro-Brazilian families functions in complex and contradictory ways to resist and reproduce the dominant racial order. I argue that embodied racial capital, affective capital, and engagement in gendered racial bargains should be understood as part of a repertoire of similar racial strategies and practices implemented by families of color throughout the world who confront white supremacy. Moving beyond the African Diaspora, I discuss white supremacy as a global phenomenon affecting diverse families.

When bell hooks argues that "everyone must break through the wall of denial that would have us believe hatred of blackness emerges from troubled individual psyches and acknowledge that it is systematically taught through processes of socialization in a white supremacist society," she is referring to the complicity of every major social institution in the reproduction of racial inequality.[102] Because the internalization of racism is systematically learned and families are one of the major sites of learning, this book identifies how white supremacy structures close family relationships in Brazil. Advancing an approach that is multidimensional and cognizant of local, regional, national, and international dynamics, the book explores family as one of many institutions, and yet singular for its ability to simultaneously sustain and resist systems of racial domination.

PART I

SOCIALIZATION AND STIGMA

CHAPTER I

WHAT'S LOVE GOT TO DO WITH IT?
RACIAL STIGMA AND EMBODIED CAPITAL

Our race problems, sometimes they start inside the home.
DONA TERESA, *NEGRA*

LOUD *PAGÓDE* AND ITS MUSICAL COUSIN *FORRÓ* sail out over the houses along the path that leads to the neighborhood of Lua Cheia. This is always a warm welcome, especially after the two long bus rides that carry me here. Before anyone is visible, the music always sets the tone for what the day in the neighborhood will be like. As each step brings me closer, the music pulses louder and the blurry outlines of very light brown to dark brown bodies start to take form.

Corina is always among the first people I see. She is a light-skinned woman with dark hair that falls in subtle waves and facial features that allow her to make tentative claims to whiteness. Today she is outside washing her clothes in an outside sink and pinning the freshly washed shirts and sheets on a short clothesline. She takes pride in her reputation as a good woman who is neat, enjoys keeping things orderly, and can be counted on by everyone who lives in the community. She lives with her two children who share similar features but refer to themselves as *morenos*, and she has an on-again, off-again black boyfriend and a large family of phenotypically diverse siblings who visit during the year.

Two doors down from Corina lives Sonia, a dark-skinned black mother with African features (*preta*) whose six children would all be identified racially as *negros*. She has a chair placed outside the door of her home so she can keep an eye on her children as they play. Her two daughters run by me in their bathing suits yelling "Beeeteeee!!!," and their voices trail behind them.[1] The younger daughter is slightly darker, with African features (described as *morena escura*) and shorter, afro-textured hair. The older daughter has curly, rather than kinky, hair and because she is slightly lighter she is referred to as *morena clara*. Sonia's two older sons are five and eight years old. The younger one is darker than the older one, but they share similar facial features, and their hair is cut so low only the scalp can be seen. They are shirtless, with a faint outline of their ribs showing as they run behind their sisters with their thin arms flailing. Sonia's youngest son, a two-year-old, has medium-dark skin, African features, and no hair. He walks around completely naked (because diapers are expensive), and he hides behind his mother, peeking around her with one eye, as I walk by.

As I make my way closer to the center of the neighborhood, Carolina can often be seen through her open window and translucent half curtains. She identifies as *morena*, and she has medium-brown skin and straightened hair that she wears wet. She is a single woman in her fifties who is seldom without her hips swaying back and forth to the music blasting from a huge, high-tech stereo that she is proud to call her own. She often has a cigarette dangling from her mouth and is casually holding a beer. She lets the strings of her tank top fall down her bronzed shoulders and helps it along with a flirtatious shrug of her shoulders. Carolina's colorful flip flops flap awkwardly as she twirls around at the entrance of her house with her door open, floating in and out to grab an unsuspecting passerby for a few comical seconds of a hip jolting and sensual *forró*—a dance from the interior.

Damiana is the self-proclaimed neighborhood beauty, with light caramel skin and a flawless complexion, thin lips and nose, and naturally straight hair. She is a businesswoman who is seven months pregnant when I meet her. She is often carrying groceries, selling beers from her home, or making a snack that she can sell to her neighbors. Her pregnant stomach seems larger than life, a protruding bulge in vibrant summer dresses that tightly hug her stomach. Her growing belly is an indication to her excited neighbors that her delivery will be soon. Damiana's daughter Regane has the same caramel complexion, but has coarser, curlier hair. She is often running around the neighborhood with Sonia's daughters or playing with other young children in the main plaza. Today Regane must have had a late start; she walks out of her house stretching her arms, wearing short shorts and a tight half top that reveals her entire stomach. "Hope you aren't going out like that!" her mom yells, laughing, as she stands either cooking or washing dishes in the kitchen.

These are the moments. Diverse Afro-Brazilians appearing to interact seamlessly, sharing a common space, ostensibly without regard for race, color, or phenotype. Everybody is smiling, happy, and cooperative: Corina offers her neighbors delicious coffee with cookies, others later offer to buy each other beers at the neighborhood bar, and Damiana offers a freshly made fruit salad to quell the heat of a scorching day. The women laugh with each other, telling stories about the past week, giving advice on what to cook during the weekend, and otherwise making small talk about the daily happenings. They have a rich life and perceive that race is merely one dimension of it.

On the other hand, this one slice of Lua Cheia does not show that Corina is in a bitter family rivalry with her siblings, who resent her because she is white. Damiana and Regane are anxious about the racial appearance of the unborn baby. And Luana languishes in an alcoholic haze to dull the pain of mistreatment in her family. The cheerful ambience is seductive, but Corina reveals within just hours of meeting me, "I am laughing on the outside but inside I am suffering." This is a poignant commentary about life in Salvador, and it is a sentiment that would be echoed by a number of respondents who live in the neighborhood.

The common notion that "there is no place like home" is a product of lasting memories, experiences, and, most important, positive feelings that are associated with the idea of home. Yet as early as the colonial encounter in the Americas, it became evident that by manipulating close bonds of love and trust in families, domination could be "routinized and rerouted in intimacies."[2] The "family gaze" might be used to describe the way that families determine the well-being of family members by evaluating their appearance; however, rarely do researchers identify how the family gaze can reproduce a racist gaze, where racial features are identified, evaluated, and exchanged for emotional resources as well as for economic and social opportunities.

This chapter examines how routine comments, practices, and affective exchanges create an environment that naturalizes racial stigma. When individuals possess racialized features that deviate significantly from an idealized or even relative whiteness, the responses to their devalued appearance can produce and reproduce stigma. Racial stigmatization emerges from the ways that broader ideas about whiteness become mapped onto the body and reverberate throughout a family.[3] The data presented in this chapter is testament to the persistence of hegemonic whiteness: even in the absence of a physical colonizer, social relations are structured by a dominant ideology that often reproduces white supremacy.

The extent to which race plays a role in affective interactions can vary significantly throughout one's life, but critical life transitions, including the onset of dating, impending marriage, and the birth of a child, heighten the racial tensions and anxieties that are present as at least a subtext of familial concern. The confluence of race, phenotype, and gender means that entering motherhood is anxiety-inducing as well as exhilarating. Messages, practices, and emotions demonstrated as early as pregnancy may carry the suggestion of racial stigma and foreshadow the way these concerns will matter for the child's entire life. Because families not only are permeable to racial hierarchies but help produce and validate racialized meanings, the relationship between socialization and racialization is one of cyclic interactionism. Ultimately, the "tense and tender" ties that characterize love and affection in families are the stuff of racial domination.[4]

Knowing that differential treatment and inequality "begins in childhood, even in our pre-parenthood anticipation of the children we may someday have," I begin with a pregnancy and discuss the importance of racial appearance throughout the life course.[5]

THE HAND THAT ROCKS THE CRADLE: MOTHER-CHILD RELATIONSHIPS

You have some that were just asking to be born ugly, just asking to be born ugly. Look, I am realistic. Some ask to be born ugly. [*Elizabeth: What do you mean?*] They are poor, black, and ugly, . . . and they don't like to study. (Mauro, 19, unemployed)

In Afro-Brazilian families, high levels of racial mixture have led to the presence of such a wide array of phenotypic combinations and features that there are over a hundred categories to describe racial appearance. So central is the body to socialization that the family has been described as "the most intimate and inescapable realm where one's physical appearance is interpreted and classified."[6] Racial socialization in phenotypically diverse families provides an opportunity to analyze the role of the family as the first site of reproduction of dominant racial hierarchies.[7] Contrary to research emphasizing the sacred notion of *amor só de mãe*, the unconditional love that mothers have for their children, affective resources can be unequally distributed in families on the basis of racial features.[8] That a similar saying does not exist for fathers is indicative of the gendered expectations of parenthood.

Among the first women whom I meet in Lua Cheia is Damiana, a pregnant twenty-eight-year-old who is married to Márcio and has a nine-year-old daughter, Regane. She is tall, slender, and caramel-colored with naturally straight black hair. When Luana initially introduces me to Damiana, as "minha amiga americana" (my American friend) who is interested in studying black families, Damiana responds, "Well are you going to interview me? I'm a *mulher negra* (black woman), right?" I was uncertain about how Damiana would identify because her racial phenotype might allow her to claim another category, so I am pleasantly surprised that she identifies as *negra* and wants to be interviewed. She talks extremely quickly, which makes our initial interactions difficult, but after a while I get used to her fast-paced speech pattern.

Damiana's family has opted for a sofa instead of a table in their small home, so against the back of the kitchen sink they have placed a long, orangish-brown living room seat, which faces an entertainment center that holds the most reliable source of diversion: a large television set.

Despite the domestic sphere being the space of women, Damiana's pregnancy does not inhibit her ability to circulate around the neighborhood. Early in the morning she can be found washing and hanging clothes or walking to the neighborhood market and returning with heavy bags full of fruit, juice, and other sundries. One day as I spot Damiana returning home from the market with large grocery bags, I rush to her side and insist that she allow me to carry her bags. I grab the bags out of her hand, and she laughs at what she considers my unnecessary pampering while we walk the uneven path back to her house.

One day Damiana asks me to sit outside of her house and peel mangos so that we can talk while she makes the fruit salad that she sometimes sells. The front of her house has no porch. There is only a small square slab that sits outside of her door. She has a yellow plastic table and several plastic chairs, which look very similar to the chairs found at the local bars and restaurants. In fact, they are clearly marked with the Skol beer brand name and logo. While we chat and peel fruit for the salad, Damiana asks Regane, her daughter, to bring me the family album. She is proud to show me that she is the prettiest of her sisters, the only one who was born with naturally straight hair. As I flip through the pictures and she cuts mango, Damiana reveals that she has a strained relationship with the women in the neighborhood, in part because of rumors that her husband was caught cheating with her neighbor's young niece, Cinthia. In addition to the rumors about her husband, the more damaging whispers are those alleging that Damiana is an adulteress who sleeps with men while her husband works, and is (allegedly) also sleeping with young Cinthia behind her husband's back.

This is standard *fofoca* (gossip), a reflection of how the neighborhood women are often watching, monitoring, and policing behavior that is not befitting of their community. Extramarital affairs are discouraged for married women, although when single women bring men into their homes, the neighbors are aware and sometimes avoid knocking in order to offer privacy. When the couple emerges from the house, there are light-hearted jokes from the neighbors to convey their support for the relationship. The physical proximity of neighbors means that secrets seldom remain secrets. Neighbors are privy to and also greatly influence some of the most intimate elements of family life.

Unfortunately for Damiana, although many women find friendship with one another, she does not enjoy close relationships with any of the other women in the community. She believes they are jealous because of her long, naturally straight hair, and indeed, neighborhood conversations suggest that some of them are. Although not all the women consider themselves her friends, Damiana's pregnancy organically shifts the casual conversations among the women to questions of families, babies, and socialization. Their sense of shared motherhood and womanhood leads to hours of lively conversation.

One morning Damiana awakens excited to share some of her vivid dreams of her unborn child.

> I have dreams about what she will look like. Sometimes she is white and sometimes she is *morena*. I hope she gets her nose and straight hair from me. That's why I sit here all day and watch *gente bonita* (pretty people) on television. If an ugly person walks by I try not to even look in their direction (*laughs*).

These initial remarks and Damiana's constant commentary about her own features reveal that beauty and racial features are a central preoccupation for the pregnant mother. The baby's skin tone might vary between white and brown, but her references to skin color suggest that it is not a major concern. Instead, the baby's nose and hair are the *indicações* (racial markers) that she constantly discusses and that will be most decisive. They are the focal points because they are viewed as more easily correctable than skin color. Though research suggests that racial features for women are key in influencing their future marriage prospects and job opportunities, it is uncertain how much Damiana is thinking about the baby's prospects. At this point, it appears she is more concerned with the personal recognition or status she might enjoy for having a baby who meets racial expectations.

I spend a significant amount of my time in Damiana's house, sitting on her sofa watching the *gente bonita* (pretty people) who appear on Brazilian variety shows and *telenovelas* (soap operas), which she watches as a preemptive measure so her baby will not be born ugly. As she watches, she comments on the actresses' beauty, focusing on their hair and noses, and her observations continue even during commercials. Damiana promptly dismisses the beauty of a dark-haired white woman wearing an ornately sequined Samba costume with the accusation that the actress uses a blow dryer to straighten her hair, unlike Damiana herself, who has naturally straight hair. Soon after, Ivete Sangalo, a white Brazilian and popular Bahian songstress, appears in commercials promoting her music. Damiana comments on Sangalo's beauty, positively evaluating her nose shape, as well as the straightness and length of her hair. In a reflection of the gendered nature of these evaluations, her comments of this type do not extend to the male celebrities and television personalities.

Damiana's decision to actively pursue opportunities to watch *gente bonita* on television and to avoid ugly people on the streets might initially be interpreted as a nonracial activity, except that the phrase *gente bonita* is often colloquially understood to mean "white people." Therefore, her comments express the normalization of whiteness and the conflation of beauty with whiteness.[9] Seemingly race-neutral phrases like "pretty people" mask the racial and gender dynamics that are inherent in constructions of beauty, and in doing so give racist evaluations that privilege whiteness an objective character.

Regardless of these preemptive efforts to influence the racial appearance of the baby, curious neighbors who are already circulating rumors about Damiana's sexual history also whisper that she may have a *barriga suja* (dirty womb or stomach). These whispers only exacerbate her anxieties about the baby's racial appearance.[10] *Barriga suja* is a pejorative phrase that describes a woman's tendency to produce dark-skinned babies, but it is not used for all mothers. Instead, it is applied specifically to women who could possibly have a lighter child because one person in the couple is significantly lighter than the other.[11] This phrase normalizes gendered racism by comparing blackness to a birth defect and placing blame on the woman for being responsible for the "defect" by having a dirty womb. Objects are considered dirty because they are useless or have no value; the rhetoric of dirty and clean wombs resonates with the concerns about race and cleanliness that were articulated during the eugenics era.[12] Damiana does not respond to the sexist and racist comments in a way that challenges the whispers, but she continues her daily television ritual, hoping that, in fact, she does not have a dirty womb.

While Damiana does not problematize the phrase *barriga suja*, not all families accept it without critique. A father and several mothers whom I interview recall hearing the phrase used in reference to another family member or even themselves. Two interviewees illustrate how they resist such comments:

> [They say] "Oh, she has a clean stomach. Look at the color of the baby! They [the parents] are really dark and he came out white." Now he really was white and fat (*referring to her nephew*). People said this (*laughs hard*). Oh my, what ignorance! Imagine how ignorant it is to think that if a woman is black and her husband is lighter that if she has a clean stomach the child will be born white and if her stomach was dirty it will be born dark. Lord have mercy! (Rebeca, 51, retired teacher)

Critiquing what she refers to as "ignorance," Rebeca finds humor and absurdity in recalling the way passersby viewed her nephew and focused on his color to make determinations about whether his mother had a clean or dirty womb.

Similarly, Daniel reports that he is very familiar with the term:

> I have heard this many times as a child and as an adult. [*Elizabeth: What do you say?*] Well, they say this and I say, "No, nobody has a clean or dirty stomach. Everybody is born like God wants and it is good." (Daniel, 57)

With a very stern look, Daniel reveals that he is bothered by the idea of clean and dirty stomachs and relies on universal ideas about humanity to substantiate his claim that we are all equal. Daniel would be viewed as white in Bahia, and his wife is *preta*, a very dark-skinned black woman with African features. His frustration with the racist and sexist terminology is connected to this personal experience, as he reveals later.

These moments of resistance offer little relief to mothers because both they and their children will be judged on the basis of racial phenotype. For this reason, fears of racial stigma are encoded early on in the mother's and family's expectations and desires. Upon the baby's arrival they come to shape the family system, ultimately influencing a mother's interactions and affective responses to her other children and her baby.

Damiana went into labor on a day that I happened to be traveling to another area of Salvador, so I did not get to witness the delivery-day happenings. I was hoping to accompany Damiana to the hospital to see the process of registration and observe how everyone responded to the newborn. This was a potentially important space, according to what other Brazilian respondents had told me and what researchers have written about hospitals being a "site of surveillance" as it relates to policing race.[13] For example, when she is pregnant with her youngest child, Alberta, of the Fernandes family, recalls the joy of delivering her baby boy, whose appearance was the talk of the maternity nursing staff:

> Girl, Leo, he was born with the perfect nose! I mean the perfect nose. (*She turns her head to show her profile and then slides her finger down the bridge of her nose and taps it at the end*.) All the nurses came to see, and they all said he was born with the perfect nose. You should have seen it! Even now, my son has the perfect nose. (Alberta, 42)

According to Alberta, the moment her child was born, the nurses were talking about and clamoring to see the child with the "perfect nose." Of course one wonders what happens when a baby does not have perfect features. Because race and phenotype are so unpredictable in Brazil, delivery day can be disappointing for mothers hoping to win the racial lottery, especially if they have taken all the necessary precautions. Taynara, who has a medium brown complexion and naturally curly hair, and who identifies as *negra*, reveals that when her daughter was born light skinned, relatives and friends exclaimed, "Você pulou a fogueira!" (You jumped over the fire!). This statement is as much about framing whiteness as an accomplishment as it is a suggestion that birthing a visibly black child is comparable to being burned by fire.

Lilza's interview also reveals how the internalization of racial hierarchies can create feelings of disappointment when children are not born with highly valued racial features. Lilza says with regard to her mother's best friend, Jani:

> Well, when I was born she [Jani] died of envy because her daughter was born *mulata*. She is light and her husband is black, . . . but he had good hair, kind of good hair, you know, better hair. His hair is straight and her hair is coarser but she is white, she is light. Who is white here in Brazil? There isn't anybody who is, right? So then she has a daughter that was born a true *mulata* with coarse hair, dark skin, black (*negra*). And, the daughter of my mother, despite her being a black woman, I was born white with light eyes. So then, she looked at my mom and she said, "I wish that my daughter had been born blonde with blue eyes." And, still

to this day, she compares her daughter to me. Do you understand? Even when I started college she said that she didn't want her daughter to go because it was full of pot smokers. That college was a place for drug addicts. Because the truth is she felt uncomfortable.[14]

In this example, Jani explicitly expresses her disappointment that her daughter was born with features that are less highly valued and convey low status. Her daughter was born a "true" *mulata* rather than white (*branca*) or even *morena*. *Mulatas* are sexualized in comparison to white and *morena* women, who are more likely to be called beautiful without the baggage of hypersexuality.[15]

Jani's emotional response of jealousy in relation to her best friend's daughter Lilza is evident in her disappointment that her dreams of having a white child have gone unrealized. The competition between the two parents extends to the college level, when Jani is forced to save face for her daughter's inability to enter college. Although Jani could seek the assistance of organizations committed to the enrollment of Afro-Brazilian students in college, she rejects the possibility and instead she reconceptualizes college as an endeavor that is not worthwhile. In this way, Jani's refusal to fully embrace her daughter's racial categorization affects her daughter's educational trajectory.

In the quote Lilza describes the racial phenotype of Jani's partner in order to illustrate the basis on which Jani was initially hopeful about her child's potential racial appearance. Jani's husband possesses racialized features, such as "better hair" that compensate for his dark skin color and position him slightly higher in the phenotypic hierarchy. The notion of "better" or "good" hair reflects racist aesthetic hierarchies where straighter hair is indicative of whiteness and hence is more highly valued. In addition, Lilza's question and laughter about whether it would be proper to refer to any Brazilian as white are a reflection of her own racial anxieties related to her white-looking appearance. This theme will be further developed in chapter 4.

With children, public visibility and displays of the body are pursued or withheld on the basis of a racialized system of worth.[16] These are the considerations that cause Damiana to feel euphoric when she delivers a baby girl who is unanimously viewed as pretty: the baby has white skin and straight hair. Damiana passes out very small plastic white baby dolls with little ribbons attached to announce the arrival of the newborn.

After the delivery, Damiana eagerly invites me to take a stroll around the neighborhood as she displays her baby to the community. Her insistence that I accompany her is a gesture that strongly resonates with classic studies of Afro-Brazilian families in Bahia noting that when babies were born lighter and with white features they are strapped to the front of the mother's chest, while those with stigmatized black features are hidden on mother's back.[17] The walk down the crowded main road in the hot sun strikes me as an informal yet emotionally laden act involving the interplay of surveillance, display, and a desire for validation. As we walk, Damiana asks me if I would like to hold the baby, and my perhaps irrational fear of dropping the newborn keeps me from accepting the offer. When I realize that my refusal is starting to seem offensive, I reluctantly accept the tiny infant in my arms and clutch her close to my chest for extra security. Damiana chuckles, apparently amused by my awkward struggle to find a natural position for the baby in my arms.

After only a few minutes I return the baby to Damiana because she is heavier than she looks. But not before friends, family members, and unknown passersby peak over the receiving blanket to steal a glance at the newborn. Strangers and passersby are very comfortable offering unsolicited comments about the *gordinha* (chubby little baby), which is the same type of monitoring extended to women's physical appearances, as well.[18] Although some passersby glance quickly and smile, others more aggressively take a closer look before rendering their verdict of approval or disapproval.

THE NEIGHBORLY GAZE

What might be considered the family gaze in Brazil can be applied to neighbors who function as an extended family, participating in racial socialization by policing racialized bodies, legitimating colorism and phenotypic differentiation, and reproducing racial stigma. Throughout the diaspora parenting is viewed as a community activity shared between "bloodmothers" and "othermothers," who shape ideas about race and racial features.[19] Notions of private and personal physical space are limited in Brazil, and these dynamics affect more than housing arrangements and public space. Extended family members serve a crucial socializing role because their concurrent distance and closeness allows them to socialize family members in ways that might otherwise be deemed unacceptable.

Explaining why family friends are able to speak so harshly about the children of their neighbors and friends, Lilza refers to her mother's best friend, Jani, and states: "It's that she's been my mom's friend since they were young. . . . That's why she can talk to her so shamelessly." ("É que minha mãe é amiga dela desde novinha, . . . é por isso que ela fala tão descaradamente.") The general license that people have to judge and comment on women's bodies extends to intimate associates such as neighbors, coworkers, and church congregation members. In response to the looks and comments from the passersby, Damiana suggests that we walk until we find *fitas*, or colorful ribbons, from the Igreja do Bonfim (Bonfim Church), which she claims will protect the baby from the *olho grosso* (fat eye) of jealous passersby, including friends and family.

While Damiana's neighbors dote on the newborn baby, they express their racialized concerns. During our stroll through the neighborhood, we stop at a supermarket where Damiana used to work. Inside, two cashiers press their hands to their cheeks and leave their registers to congratulate Damiana and catch a first glimpse of the baby.

> She's beautiful! . . . But you know you really have to do something about that nose (*laughs*), that wide nose (*nariz chato*) of hers. You will definitely have to fix (*afinar*) that nose with a clamp (*pegador*). You need to pinch it down. There's no way around it. (*Everyone nods and laughs loudly.*)
> (Marta, 34)

The compliment about the baby's beauty is immediately diminished by advice about how to modify her problematic nose. According to the neighbors' commonsense evaluations, a wide nose is an objectively undesirable characteristic. At the same time, their comments are ambiguous because they are delivered in a humorous tone. Due to this ambiguity, I figure that perhaps the comments have been made in jest, to mock antiquated ideas about black racial features.[20] As we are leaving the store, a male store worker clamps his nose with his fingers and laughs as he repeats that Damiana needs to buy a clamp for the baby's nose. Damiana waves goodbye and is still laughing as we exit. I worry that asking about this interaction might be viewed as naive and insulting, but I muster the courage to ask whether she will buy a clamp for the baby's nose. She replies as though the suggestion is preposterous: "No, Elizabete, there's no way I'm going to buy a clamp for her nose! . . . I'm just going to use my fingers!"

At the risk of inhibiting the baby's breathing, Damiana follows the advice of her friends and does engage in a ritual in which she pinches and holds down the baby's nostrils for a few seconds daily with the hope that her nose will become thinner. I become aware of this through Damiana's young daughter Regane, who reports this practice to me in a private interview. Regane has decided to confide in me because she is concerned that the baby cannot breathe and fears that her mother might be hurting her baby sister. As Regane describes the process to me, she pinches down her nostrils and uses her free hand to count to five. She giggles as she completes the demonstration, informing me that her mother does this to the baby several times a day.

Damiana's decision to engage in the ritual is not based on mere individual preference, but is connected to community reinforcement and an entire system of racial norms that require mothers to "discipline the bodies" of their children on the basis of racial, gender, and phenotypic hierarchies.[21] Not only do neighbors suggest that the ritual is important to eliminate black-looking racial features, Marta explains that it is part of her role as a good mother: "A mother has to take care of it."

Modification of a wide nose was reported as a practice that mothers are both aware of and participated in within four other families. Some mothers explain that babies have skin that is more pliable and flexible, so pinching serves as a type of "conditioning" that can reshape it. In other families, modifying the nose involves a more extreme process:

> I remember my mom doing this to my sisters. She would light a small candle and warm her fingers over the flame, and then she would pinch the baby's nose and hold it. They said it would correct the nose. Who wants a wide nose? I remember the women, our neighbors, would shout to us from their windows: "Don't forget to pinch her nose!" (Tais, 49, retired teacher)

Engagement in this dangerous practice involving fire reflects the embodiment of race and the embeddedness of notions of racial stigma in family practices. The purported success stories that the women discuss are considered reasonable motivations for at least exerting the effort to "correct" this devalued feature. As Marta, a light-skinned woman with two daughters, informs Damiana:

> I have two children and I did it, and my mom did it to all of us so they wouldn't have *o nariz que o boi amassou* (a nose that the ox stepped on). (Marta, 34)

Not only does Marta offer evidence suggesting that the process works, but she employs a common phrase that frames a wide nose as looking as though it has been stepped on or damaged by an animal to remind Damiana of the consequences of not participating in the practice. With the popular consensus that a wide nose is to be negatively evaluated, Damiana feels compelled to intervene so her daughter does not have to be the target of such comments and so she herself will be viewed as a good mother. Given Damiana's previous comments, in which she praised her narrow nose and those of other women, it is clear that the baby's nose has aesthetic value that also reflects on Damiana.

Yet, there are some mothers who reject these racial rituals. Dona Lara, a mother of three who identifies as *preta* and *negra*, says that she has personally observed nose modification but refuses to engage in the practice in her own family. In an interview that turns into a boisterous family conversation, she explains her position:

> DONA LARA: Oh, yeah, that's something that people used to do in the interior. My mother did this with my young sisters.
> ELIZABETH: Where is it done? In the kitchen?
> DONA LARA: No, it was not anything that was hidden, she did it right there in the living room. Get a candle, pass your finger through. . . . It was said to improve the appearance of a baby.
> DILSON (HER SON): What? Are you serious?!
> DONA LARA: Yes, they said it would improve the appearance——
> DILSON: (*cuts off his mother's statement*) Then why didn't you do it to me! (*The room fills with laughter.*)
> ELIZABETH: (*once the laughter subsides*) Why did you decide not to do it?
> DONA LARA: Because, because I don't have these issues with beauty. I think blacks are beautiful. . . . It doesn't work anyway. It was not even just the nose. They used fire to try to give the baby dimples, because people thought dimples were pretty. It was the same thing.

All families are aware of the stigmatization of black features, but they do not all internalize these ideas and attempt to modify their children's racial appearance. Still, Dilson jokes that his mother should have used the technique on him. Although everyone laughs, his own experiences with racial stigmatization suggest that it may not be just a joke (see chapter 3). Similarly, Dona Lara's response that the procedure "doesn't work anyway" suggests the ambivalence with which parents approach these practices. Would she have tried the technique if she believed it worked?

An unexpected element of the conversation is Dona Lara's revelation that mothers attempted to use the same process involving fire to create dimples on the cheeks of babies. Though dimples are not a racialized feature, a baby with dimples is more likely to be considered beautiful than one without them. Again, mothers are faced with the stigmatization of racial features and the emphasis on beauty in Brazilian society, so they employ these rituals to try to manage these pressures and maximize a child's embodied capital as best they can.

A nose is viewed as correctable in infancy, but some other features are viewed as unsalvageable. Dona Elena, a sixty-eight-year-old black woman, describes the birth of her daughter whose nickname is Neguinha (translated as Blackie or little black one):

> When Neguinha was born she was totally black, I mean really black. When I came home from the hospital and her father saw her, he said, "Ugh! Where did you get that black baby? Take her back!" (laughs)
> (Dona Elena, homemaker)

In this case, the delivery of a very dark-skinned baby has the emotional consequence of dampening a normally joyous occasion. Though both parents describe their race and color as black (negro and preto, respectively), their child's even darker appearance leads to a negative emotional response. Although laughter is used to deflect it, the husband's repulsion is consistent with his internalization of the broader meanings and values attached to a very dark skin color. From birth, their daughter Neguinha, now thirty-seven years old, has been exclusively referred to by this nickname so that very few community members even know her legal name. Her skin color has come to define a large part of her identity. Neguinha is one of the few people who refused to be interviewed for this study.

Even when there is resistance to the rituals, neighborly advice—"don't forget to pinch the baby's nose"—reminds mothers that their children's bodies and their own worth are on display. Furthermore, reinforcement from neighbors that frames the ritual as a necessary corrective practice constructs a broad nose as a legitimate, even medicalized problem that needs to be fixed and forces a mother to act so she will not be viewed as neglectful.[22] If there is any doubt that correcting a wide nose is a racialized practice, the prevalence in Brazil of what has been explicitly labeled "Negroid nose surgery" should resolve it.[23]

Nonbiological mothers—or "othermothers," neighbors who engage in the family gaze—convey messages and behaviors through their affective responses that have considerable ramifications for Afro-Brazilian families. Neighbors' comments and their racial surveillance continue throughout the life course and can be a source of tremendous anxiety for mothers and siblings. A number of respondents reported that their phenotypically diverse family was the source of scrutiny and surveillance by neighbors. Deborah, who has five siblings, states:

> In my family there are only two people who do not have straight hair: my younger brother and sister. And this thing comes up when you have family portraits and people from the outside often ask, "Does everybody have the same dad?" We felt really uncomfortable because they often asked this. (Deborah, 26)

The comments received from nonbiological extended family members are often consistent with the messages received within biological families. Lidia recalls her father interacting with his grandchildren in ways that transmitted ideas about racial hierarchy and phenotype:

> My father, God bless him, he cannot stand to see a nose. . . . My sister has a big nose and she got it from my father, but he has a big nose that is kind of narrow (*afilado*). My father talks so much about it that he seems to be racist. He forgets that he is black! We tell him, "Dad, you are black, you just have light skin. Do you remember your dad's nose? Your dad had a nose, it was flat, and your daughter got it from him and got it from you. Your nose is narrow but it is enormous." When a grandchild is born he says, "Hey, look, he's going to clean the race, clean the race." And when he says it we let him have it. And we say, "Don't laugh and smile too much because when they are one year old and this color, at two years old they end up *pretinho, pretinho* (black, black)." This can only be to bother us. It's not possible for him to be racist, right? (Lidia, 54, retired domestic worker)

The notion of "cleaning the race" bears traces of the language of racial contamination that was popularized through the racial hygiene concerns in early twentieth-century Brazil. In Salvador, where families are phenotypically diverse and whiteness is overvalued, socialization practices develop with the goal of repositioning on the phenotypic continuum. Although whiteness may not be attainable, a phenotype that approximates the image of *morenidade* is increasingly popular.[24] *Morenidade* is considered an attainable approximation of Western whiteness characterized by light brown skin (rather than white skin) and soft brown hair that bounces. At the same time, some researchers argue that the idea of *morenidade* is simply an updated version of *mestiçagem*, which uses the allure of racial mixture as a way to either eliminate blackness or accept versions of blackness that approximate whiteness.[25] Lidia's struggle to understand what she perceives to be internalized racism on the part of her father is also significant, as it reflects the difficulty in processing these comments when they come from family members. Although she and her sister "let him have it," others simply do not know how to respond when their loved ones make what are perceived to be racist comments.

In other cases, the importance of race and phenotype is manifested not in how mothers treat their children, but rather in how mothers treat others. As Liliane recalls,

> My mother did not like *pretos*. She never lied about it to anyone. She thought the saddest thing in the world was for a black child to step foot in front of her. She would say "take it away, take it away." She had [black] children, but she did not like *pretos*. If he is black, he is not a person, take him away. She did not like them. If I were to invite you to her house now, she would say, "Oooh, child what a beautiful woman you are," stuff like that, hug you. But as soon as you left, [she would say] "You bring that black devil around here?" (Liliane, *parda*, 48, searching for a job)

The negative affect that Liliane's mother expresses toward dark-skinned black children is clear to her own children, who are exposed to the disdain that she feels for *pretos*. In addition to the studies that suggest that negative emotions affect siblings and children, observations of a mother rejecting black children is a powerful image that may potentially shape how her own children view themselves and others.[26]

The most substantial element in Liliane's quote is that not only is blackness devalued, it is dehumanized to the extent that a *preto* is "not a person." As someone classified as *preta*, I would be considered not a person but a devil. I was inserted into a hypothetical situation in order for Liliane to show how racial etiquette and cordiality promote scripts of interacting that are often at odds with people's true feelings. Consistent with this, Afro-Brazilians often stated throughout the interview process, "O racismo no Brasil existe, mas no Brasil é muito mais velado" (Racism in Brazil does exist, but it is much more hidden). The veiling of racism is partially a result of Brazilians effectively managing the rules of racial etiquette and relying on front-stage behaviors that respect the rules of cordial race relations. Feigned pleasantries are used alongside coded language and racist humor in order to reproduce and normalize dominant racial hierarchies.

MAMA'S BABY IS DADDY'S MAYBE

In a patriarchal and racialized society, mothers are often considered to blame when children are born with black-looking features, as though blackness were a defect. In fact, Western societies more broadly "hold mothers responsible for child outcomes and thus for the health of families, future citizens, and the nation."[27] Blame for a child's phenotype is closely connected to the honor/shame complex in which a women's sexuality is embraced, yet monitored for its adherence to sexist rules of behavior.[28] In Brazil, women are framed as more sensual than women of other nationalities. But a woman's sexuality is labeled good so long as it is expressed after she leaves the home of her father and as long as it is limited to the confines of marriage.[29] As an extension of this idea, wombs are good or clean as long as they produce a baby with light or white features, in line with the implicit and explicit appeals to improve the race.[30] Hence, women are not only defined by their sexuality but are also judged and defined as good or bad by the racial product of their sexuality. A mother may suffer from intense sexual stigma or be considered sexually suspect if a baby's appearance is not consistent with expectations.[31]

Over coffee and cookies in her home, Corina provides an example about how her in-laws responded to the racial appearance of her eldest child, and she describes the material consequences of her son's possession of a racialized feature: black ears.[32]

> You know that when a baby is born it is sometimes born a little dark (*pretinho*) with really dark ears. The day his grandmother came to see him, she asked, "Why does my grandson have these black ears?" And I say, "Because in my family there are *morenos*, my grandfather is *preto*. This comes from my family. My daughter is *morena* because she got it from my mother's side of my family." They thought he was someone else's son because he was born with black ears. I guess she was used to seeing white ears, I don't know (*laughs*). I didn't understand. The first thing that she said in the hospital when she saw my son, she said, "Why are his ears black?" She was angry about his ears. So he [her partner] waited for two years to register him. (Corina, 56)

In Corina's situation, the child was born lighter, but his dark ears carried the suggestion that he might turn out to be darker than Corina or her partner. In an effort to save face with his family, her partner decided not to officially recognize the child as his own, which stigmatized both her and the baby. Corina expressed her sense of relief when her partner finally decided to give her a "dignified name"—to marry her and recognize their son. The suspicion that results from having a light-skinned baby with black ears jeopardized Corina's respectability and compromised her moral and economic status. Dependent on male validation to recuperate this lost honor, she was grateful when her partner decided to marry her and restore her social standing.

Dona Elena's situation involved similar sexual suspicion when her grandson was born:

> The first thing people look at is the color to see if the baby looks like anyone in the father's family. This one right here, his mother (*pointing to her grandson*), he was born really, really white. And his [father's] family said, "Ah no, it's not possible! It is not possible, this boy right here is not yours." But as he got older he became darker, darker, and darker. (Dona Elena, 68)

When a baby is delivered, features are immediately evaluated, and racial features are a particular source of suspicion. Dona Elena's experience suggests that even when a woman produces a baby with an appearance that is considered racially or phenotypically desirable, a mother's sexual fidelity is subject to scrutiny if the child does not match expectations. Hence mothers who might otherwise be focusing on preparing their homes for the entrance of a baby experience stress and anxiety over racial features they cannot control. This is not merely a question of aesthetics: these anxieties reflect the intersectionality of racialized and gendered expectations on both symbolic resources (moral status) and material resources.

RACIAL ROULETTE AND SIBLING RIVALRY

Analysis of racial socialization practices is often conducted across groups and across families, and has rarely considered favoritism and differential treatment within families to make broader arguments about how racialization affects family systems, processes, and inequality. According to the family systems paradigm, the differential emotional responses of a mother to one child can be learned by other family members and affect sibling subsystems, influencing the "quality of sibling interactions, relationships and adjustment."[33] Although studies that illustrate this have typically approached differential treatment as it relates to age, birth order, and gender, racialization processes may also be the basis of differential treatment.

Parental favoritism of children on the basis of racial appearance can be a source of lifelong strain in sibling relationships.

Regane is a precocious nine-year-old girl with a beaming smile and effervescent personality. She identifies as *morena* when I ask, and later she hesitantly states that she is *negra*. Hearing her mother's dreams of having a white baby with straight hair leads to a series of behavioral changes. Regane begins to neglect her hygiene, refusing to comb or wash her hair at all. In response, her mother punishes her by roughly combing her hair outside the door of their home while loudly exclaiming, "I hope the baby's hair isn't like this!"[34] This is a significant event, as researchers suggest that hair-combing experiences between daughters and mothers in the diaspora "contribute to the formation of enduring aspects of the young girl's personality, gender, and racial role formation, and to self-concept and self-esteem."[35] Regane is already teased by neighborhood kids for having hard or nappy hair (*cabelo duro*), and she is visibly embarrassed by this event. Her mother's constant comments about the hair of the white women who appear on television make Regane even more self-conscious about her hair, and this exacerbates her negative feelings.

Regane is excited when she finds a bright orange piece of fabric lying around the house. In an act of limited agency and self-affirmation, she ties the long, tattered piece of orange cloth around her head and pretends that it is her long straight hair. She runs and smiles, twirling around in sheer happiness as she enjoys the orange scarf, which blows over her shoulder and transports her to a world where her hair bounces and she is beautiful. Her enjoyment is short-lived. She has to run from the neighborhood boys, who eventually manage to snatch it off, and the teasing begins once more.

Damiana, her mother, chuckles as she informs me that upon seeing the newborn baby for the first time, "Regane cried all day." Given studies that emphasize differential treatment on the basis of age, this is a quite natural response to the uncertainty of the entrance of a new sibling into the family. However, Regane's interview clarifies that her concerns are rooted in a specific issue:

> ELIZABETH: What happened yesterday? How does it feel to have a sister?
> REGANE: (*pauses, looks down*) I ran in the house and cried all day.
> ELIZABETH: Why did you cry?
> REGANE: Because I am afraid of losing the love (*carinho*) of my parents (*whimpers*).
> ELIZABETH: Why do you think this will happen?

REGANE: (*looks at me incredulously*) Because of the baby! You saw her, didn't you? She was born *limpinha* [clean] and with straight hair. I'm afraid they will love her more. . . . Her hair won't give them as much trouble. . . . Everybody is saying it. She will get everything and I'll have nothing (*covers her face with her hands and sobs*).

Even as a young girl, Regane understands the value of racialized features and how readings of her skin color and hair texture may lead to a change in the affective treatment that she receives. Her reference to the baby's light skin as *limpinha*, or clean, illustrates that she has also internalized the conflation of whiteness with cleanliness. Worst of all, from her perspective, the baby's hair is straight and will not be considered a problem. Though this interview takes place after the baby is born, Regane is still visibly shaken.

The same day as my interview, Regane's fear that she will be compared to the baby is substantiated when we hear her mother agree with a family friend that although the baby has a wide nose, "at least the baby's hair didn't turn out like hers" (pointing at Regane and frowning). Regane refuses to talk and is inconsolable for days. In response to Regane's angst, I interview her mother, Damiana, who once more explains her peculiar way to assuage Regane's anxieties: "I tell her, Don't worry, she [the baby] will get darker." Rather than reassure Regane that the love she feels for her will not change, Damiana makes an ambiguous statement suggesting that if the baby does not become darker, perhaps Regane will need to worry.

Weeks after the baby's birth, Regane resents the baby and obsessively monitors any changes in her sister's skin color or hair texture. Damiana chuckles as she tells me that Regane seems upset that she is not perceiving any changes in the baby's racial features, but to Regane, this is no laughing matter. The echoes of several influences, including her mother's racialized desires for the new baby, her mother's emphasis on her own beautiful straight hair, taunts by the neighborhood kids, and the images of *gente bonita* plastered on the streets, in magazines, and on television are all powerful forces against which Regane attempts to construct her sense of self. The idea that her younger sister might approximate the idealized white appearance that has been elusive for her is scary and anxiety-inducing for the nine-year-old. Despite these fears, over several more weeks, I catch Regane holding her sister and looking at her with a loving gaze. She tickles her, calls her pet names, and coos at her like an adoring older sister. These are the bonds that lead her to expose to me what she perceives as the dangerous nose-pinching ritual that her mother performs on the baby. In these ways, Regane's relationship with the baby represents the "tender and tense ties" of family relationships.[36]

Regane initially fears that the *carinho* (affection) she receives from her parents may change because of her skin color and hair texture. It is too early to tell whether what she fears will materialize. Unfortunately, the family moves to Rio de Janeiro only months after the baby arrives to be closer to family there, so I am no longer able to follow the developments. But in other families phenotypic differences between siblings remain, and some Afro-Brazilians perceive the distribution of affection as unequal.

These experiences of unequal treatment or differential levels of *carinho* are not limited to early childhood but can extend into adolescence, when a child's racial appearance continues to be a status symbol for a mother and father. News that an American researcher is studying families travels fast, and Juliana, a fifty-two-year-old white mother, insists that her family be included in the study. I had spoken to Juliana previously when she told me she was married and had two daughters. She is excited that she has run into me again on this day, and walks me over to a group of girls to eagerly introduce me to her teenage daughter Adrielle. While complimenting Adrielle's light skin and eyes, she encourages me to stroke her daughter's hair—"Go on, touch her hair!"—I smile, but feel very uncomfortable with the awkward request. Juliana proceeds to share with me Adrielle's age, her year in school, and her hobbies. She continues by smiling broadly and bragging: "She doesn't even look Brazilian does she?" I find the boast unusual, but continue listening to the mother's adulation.

Among the group stands a brown-skinned, wavy-haired teenager with her head lowered and her hands folded across her chest. Though she is standing close enough to Juliana and Adrielle to suggest that they know each other, the girl is completely ignored. At the end of our conversation, as I am walking away, I turn back to inquire about who the young girl is, and Juliana replies indifferently with a swipe of her hand, "Oh, her, she's my other daughter." The markedly different treatment of the two girls exemplifies the idea that "beautiful things . . . are rarely called beautiful but . . . they are shown to be so by the constructed [centers] of care in which they are presented."[37] Juliana's other daughter's value is clearly articulated as inferior; even without words, the dismissive hand swipe reinforces her devalued status in the family.

It is sometimes difficult to uncouple beauty and race, and I argue that they should not be uncoupled because they work together to influence the affective interactions that unfold within families. Stated differently, Adrielle is valued because she is beautiful, and she is beautiful because she is white. References to Adrielle's lack of an authentic Brazilian appearance reflect the ways that both racial and national hierarchies privilege whiteness. She is beautiful because she is so light that she does not even look Brazilian (nonwhite).

Even if they have brothers or male cousins, the reference groups for young girls are usually not males but other young girls or female relatives.[38] Nonetheless, males are also subject to aesthetic evaluations and may experience differential treatment. Lilza, whose mother's best friend has clear preferences among her children, reports:

> LILZA: Her [Jani's] son was born with green eyes and with light skin, and then this son, my God, he was the one that she liked the most. All of the boys [Jani's sons] came out with light eyes. He was the one she valued. So then you even have that.
>
> ELIZABETH: In what ways, what do you mean?
>
> LILZA: In everything, even the way they were treated was different. She would say he was the prettiest, in everything that she said. Yes, yes.
>
> DILSON (LILZA'S HUSBAND): The care she gave, yes, she even took care of the other one better (*O carinho, sim, cuida melhor do otro*).
>
> LILZA: And now her son is dating a black woman. She was disgusted by it. And even her daughter is with a black man and her grandson is black. So then she says, "No, he's not black, he is *moreno*. He is *moreno*. He is *moreno* and pretty," *cabo verde*, right (*laughs*), and it goes from there. So yeah, there is a lot of prejudice.

This is not merely a question of favoritism. In this case Jani's affection and level of care is reportedly influenced by the racial appearance and relative attractiveness of her light-skinned and light-eyed son. Moreover, her negative racial affect toward black features makes her unwilling to call her grandson black, and instead she uses the term *moreno* and encourages others to do the same as a strategy for recovering his status. Even the term *moreno* is not sufficient: Jani feels compelled to qualify the term by referring to him as a pretty *moreno*. In this way, the grandmother can be proud of her grandson, but only after she negotiates his racialization and places him a category in which he does not have to be considered black. Though it is difficult to convey from the quote alone, when Lilza uses the term *cabo verde*, a phenotypic descriptor for a person of African descent who is dark skinned with naturally straight hair and green eyes, she does so mockingly to illustrate her exasperation with people's efforts to create other terms for black.

Although the child is a boy, these phenotypic distinctions are important to his grandmother, who feels disappointed that her children, who fall in the mixed-race categories, have squandered their phenotypic capital by marrying *pretos* (dark-skinned people with African features). She considers their marriage to *pretos* an act that has undone her labor to lighten the family by marrying their father.

Dilson, Lilza's husband, finds the differential treatment disturbing, but tries to rationalize Jani's behavior:

> I think that it is unconscious, a mother is not going to treat her child in a way that is not equal to the other, . . . you know, deliberately, but I think that it is a thing that comes from within her. I don't think that it is deliberately.

Dilson refuses to believe that she deliberately treats her light-skinned son differently from her other children. The only way he can make sense of the relationship is to suggest that she has a psychological impairment or problem that "comes from within her." He believes in the sacred idea of *amor só da mão* (a mother's love), and as a result, he is convinced that mothers are incapable of intentionally engaging in differential treatment. But some mothers and family members do treat children differently, and when they do, they are responding not to individual quirks, but to a broad racial hierarchy that clearly devalues proximity to blackness on the ideological level and rewards proximity to whiteness on the material and symbolic level.

SHE'S JUST MY (PHENO)TYPE!:
RACIAL BARGAINS AND ROMANTIC LOVE

Despite Brazil's global reputation for its racial mixture, research suggests that interracial relationships in Brazil are not as prevalent as one might expect. Only 30 percent of marriages—including both common law and formal marriages—occur across color categories.[39] According to these statistics, the overwhelming majority of married Brazilians are in a relationship with someone from the same color category. Levels of interracial relationships are even lower if browns and blacks are aggregated into the category of *negro*.

Throughout my time in Salvador, the issue of romantic love and sexual pairings was the theme about which Afro-Brazilian men and women spoke with the most passion, conviction, and relative ease. Often they would introduce the subject before I had a chance to broach it myself. To help me understand the role of phenotype in romantic relationships, Thiago, who is thirty-four years old and identifies as *preto* and *negro*, decides he should explain what would happen if he brought a woman home to his family who looked like me (a dark-skinned woman with African features):

> THIAGO: If I were to take you to meet my family, they would say, "I didn't like her." If I ask why, they would say, "No reason," but it's a lie. It's because you are black, with hair like mine. You won't have anything to offer (*laughs*). You won't have anything to offer me. You have to have something to offer. Either you need to have *boa aparencia* (good appearance) so that the family can be more . . . more . . . more well-accepted (*bem vista*), or. . . . They are not looking at the human part, the part about love and care or the fact that the person wants to start a family with you.
>
> ELIZABETH: If I were rich, would it be different?
>
> THIAGO: It would be different. In this case, you would be able to help out, so they would try to win you over (*conquistar você*). Even if they have no money at all, they would say "Oh, she's coming to our house." They go and buy a pizza and fish, they don't even have money to pay their light bill and it is about to get cut off, but they will make a feast (*banquete*) for you, . . . wanting to know about your life: Where do you live? In the United States? (*He covers his mouth, pretending to gasp as his family might do upon discovering this information.*) Because if you have money, they will say, "Wow, I liked her." Once you say where you work and how much you have, people start asking you for things like you have an obligation (*laughs*).

An analysis of this example reveals that in some families, *pretas*, or black women with afro-textured hair and African features, are not considered marriageable partners unless they can compensate for this with other characteristics, such as Americanness or wealth. Thiago's response to my question about class status illustrates the complexity of racial bargains, which cannot be understood without consideration of the intersectionality of race, gender, and class. Ultimately, in a patriarchal society, the value of all women is greatly determined by their appearance, which explains the preoccupation with appearance in this study. Given their devalued position, *pretas* have to provide other evidence of their value because otherwise they are perceived in some families to "have nothing to offer."

Thiago's example shows how racialization is a concern not only for black-white interracial relationships, but for relationships among people who identify as *negros*, as well. Given the statistics about the proportion of interracial relationships, it is important to understand how racialization functions to shape social exchanges in both intraracial and interracial relationships. This does not mean that all relationships can be understood as the product of such calculations or exchanges, but that everyone makes decisions in a social context in which these calculations are expected and have consequences.

Some of the social exchanges that occur within the context of an interracial relationship are complicated negotiations involving exchanges of beauty and whiteness for loyalty.[40] In the example below, a black partner provides unconditional love to his white partner even after he finds out she cheated on him and has a child from another man. His daughter tells his story:

> For years I thought that my dad was a fool. He lived with her like he was her slave for years. But he did not want to separate from her. He was so in love with her. She was light with very long black hair. He was very much in love. And my brothers, none of them are married to black women. Even though they are unhappy and they complain about their lives, at least she is white. (Liliane, 48 years old)

Liliane's suggestion that her father was her mother's slave offers a persuasive metaphor for how beauty can be exchanged for "greater diligence, devotion, class status or other benefits provided by the dark spouse."[41] Her father's preference for white women has also influenced his sons, who Liliane contends have tolerated being mistreated and unhappy in exchange for the status that being married to white women affords them.

Unlike black men, who might rely on economic status as a good that can be exchanged in the marriage market, black women, particularly dark-skinned women, have much less symbolic or economic capital available. Given how both patriarchy and racism function, they have fewer options for marriage or commitment; instead they are viewed as ideal sexual partners due to racist stereotypes about their "primitive sexual impulses."[42] In the tourist areas of Salvador, such as Pelourinho, it is very common to observe very dark-skinned Afro-Brazilian women with white, European men. Márcio explains this phenomenon, stating, "For black women, for them to have an opportunity it has to be with a foreigner. Foreigners love black women." In these relationships, a black woman's attractiveness and blackness may be attached to her being viewed as an exotic other. These types of relationships in Bahia may be either casual or long-term, but they rarely lead to marriage.[43]

Women are not the only partners who are judged on the basis of phenotypic features. Subtle insults provide evidence of how racialization processes shape evaluations of romantic relationships for men as well. Consider the following conversation between Vânia and her boyfriend Paulo:

> VÂNIA: My family on my mom's side is racist. My mom is not because she married a black man, right? But they [her mom's family members] are prejudiced. For example, they didn't want my mother to marry my dad because he is black.
>
> PAULO: She [Vânia] went to introduce me to her grandmother and I sensed it.
>
> VÂNIA: I didn't say anything to him about it. I hadn't said anything. But you know, when my grandmother saw pictures of him she said he is a *moreno bonito, bonitinho* (cute). Well, if he were white she would have said, wow, he is beautiful (*lindo*)!
>
> PAULO: [She would have said] What a beautiful man (*homem lindo*)!
>
> VÂNIA: But she did not say what a nice-looking black man or what a nice-looking *moreno*.
>
> PAULO: But she said, he is a cute one (*ele é bonitinho*). It is always in the diminutive. You are always less.
>
> VÂNIA: I really like my grandmother and my godmother.
>
> PAULO: Look, I like your grandmother too, but she is really racist (*they laugh nervously*).

Vânia notices how the interactions between her partner and family clearly illustrate that her family views him as less ideal than a white partner and perhaps as less overall. An ineffable feeling, a sense that something is awry offers the first indication that he is being evaluated differently.

Both Vânia and Paulo are aware of how discursive strategies in Brazil function. They recognize how the use of the diminutive and slight changes in words are tied to significant differences in meaning.[44] But Vânia's ambivalence in criticizing her family is apparent as she follows an example of her grandmother's racial prejudice with an assertion that she "really likes" her grandmother. It is Paulo who makes the distinction that regardless of the love she feels for her, the reality, as Paulo sees it, is that she is racist. They laugh in agreement, and while the humor helps to diffuse the tension, it ends the conversation ambiguously.

Researchers have demonstrated that emotions, particularly negative affect, can be used to control the actions of family members.[45] Liliane's family's reaction to her boyfriend is disgust: "For them he was ugly, he was black (*preto*)." Likewise, in Márcio's family, as well as others, there is a standard agreement that the ideal partner should not be someone who has three strikes against them: "preto, pobre e feio" (poor, black, and ugly). Though these are stated as independent characteristics by many families, the terms are understood to be essentially synonymous. A similar construction has been used in the United States, where a family member may be warned not to marry a dark-skinned person who is "blackandugly," as though these qualities were inextricably tied or synonymous.[46]

Similarly, Ivone reports:

> In my family, the majority of people are black. I was told I could not date a *negro*, I had to date a *branquinho* (little white guy). But I fell in love with my boyfriend and he is *negro*. He is beautiful and he is black. I got home and I introduced him to my mom and my grandmother. My mom loved him. It was not her, it was my older aunt who said "ok" with a look of disgust. She waited for him to leave and then she said, "Oh, Ivone you left milk to be with coffee with milk?" And I said, "Yes, it is because I discovered that coffee with milk is better than plain milk." Her response, "You are a disgrace." And I said, "A disgrace is a person who does not realize that it is not a person's color or their job that matters, it is who the person really is." (Ivone, 23)

Despite being part of a family where "the majority of people are black," Ivone was socialized to avoid black partners because she is very light skinned with long wavy hair. The backlash that she receives is not vocalized from her mother, but it comes from her aunt, who is disappointed about the decision. Ivone is called a disgrace not only because she does not agree with these racist views, but because she articulates a forceful counterargument that is evocative of black male sexuality. Though Ivone's statement strongly challenges her aunt's debasement of her partner, it relies on stereotypes of black male sexuality to do so. Ivone's mother is silent during the conversation, which makes her position on the matter ambiguous. Her father is completely absent from these discussions since they occur within the realm of women's talk.

Beyond directly undermining relationships by making explicit comments, family members also convey disapproval and reinforce racial stigma in more subtle ways. Most surprisingly, Lilza laughs at the irony that "*até nas orações*" (even in their prayers) class and racial distinctions are evident. She describes her two black cousins, Maiara and Sueide, who are sisters dating men of different backgrounds. Lilza reports that Maiara's boyfriend is studying medicine, and so when they go to church, family members pray, "Que o casamento deles dê certo" (Let's hope their marriage lasts). In contrast, Sueide's boyfriend is described by the family as "a nobody," so in church they pray, "que Deus veja ai que é melhor" (Let God decide what is best). This is not merely a commentary on class. Sueide's boyfriend is "a nobody" both because he is black and because he has a low-status profession. If he were white and in medical school, or simply white, she suggests, the prayer might very well be different. Lilza laughs and continues by explaining, "The introduction of a black person is always more difficult when he arrives by himself. When he is a nobody and he is black, it's really hard." (*A apresentação do negro sempre vai ser mais difícil quando ele chega só. . . . Quando ele não é ninguém e quando ser negro é difícil*).

Lilza explains that concerns about partnering do not merely affect her cousins but shape how her family responds to her marriage to Dilson, a thirty-two-year-old security guard who is among the darkest-skinned people I interview in Salvador. Dilson has a wide nose and thin lips, he wears his hair cropped so close to his head that he appears almost bald, and he has a slight gap between his front teeth. Although both of his parents, Dona Lara and her late husband, are dark skinned with African features, Dilson is much darker than both of them.

After the recent marriage of Dilson to Lilza, Dona Lara decided to move in with the newlyweds to help support their family. She had recently become a widow, so the marriage of her son had come at an opportune time. The newlyweds assist her through her grieving, and in return she provides them with limited help around the house, cooking and cleaning. Her son and daughter-in-law get along well with her and enjoy the help that she provides them. Lilza sometimes works ten hours a day, and as a security guard Dilson has long, often unpredictable hours. Dona Lara welcomes the opportunity to help her hard-working son and daughter-in-law in their home along the beach, while also anticipating the eventual arrival of a grandchild.

Because Dilson and Lilza are among the few couples whom others identify as being in an interracial relationship, I grow increasingly curious about how their racialization shapes their experiences. By all standards, Lilza is considered a great catch because she well-educated, with a graduate degree, and she is personable—*gente boa*. From a racial perspective, she is considered the ideal woman: fair with blue eyes and light brown hair with blonde streaks. She is often read as white and is considered very attractive. In fact, Lilza at one point reveals to me that a friend *tomou um susto* (was shocked) to hear that her mother is black. She did not believe it. Dilson, on the other hand, would not be considered conventionally attractive. Many would consider him *um homem feio* (an ugly man) simply because he is *preto*.

Given these dynamics, I ask Lilza how her mother responded to their marriage. She asserts that her mother had no problem with the relationship, but that the comments of her extended family are often a source of contention:

> LILZA: When I got married, several people said like, they said that because I was white I was supposed to end up with something better. They said this primarily to my mother: "How are you going to let her—how could you let her?" And my mom would come and tell me. And I would say, "Ask her if she wants me to marry a white man . . . who is shameless, drunk, just like her husband." She never said anything to me, she said this to my mother and my mother told me everything. She said it like this, "But if at least he were a doctor or a lawyer!" (*laughs*)
>
> DONA LARA: Compensating for being black! (*laughs*)
>
> DILSON: Black, but . . . (*voice trails off; laughs*)

Through this conversation, it is clear that relatives and close friends who are *de consideração* (considered family) rely on mothers to serve as intermediaries to accomplish at least two goals: police racial boundaries and ensure that family members are aware of how their offspring should wield their embodied racial capital in the marriage market. Comments filtered through Lilza's mother suggest that it would be a grave mistake for her to marry Dilson because she would be wasting her phenotypic capital when she could get "something better." Their concern is that she has potential to use her whiteness to "trade up" rather than marry a lower-status black partner. While the notion of marriage markets, trades, and social exchange are suggestive of an impersonal commodity exchange, the discourse about family members needing to "compensate" with their profession speaks to how relationships are approached as racial bargains.

Their laughter adds a curious element to the conversation as it comes in response to some of the most offensive elements of their narrative. This "emotional aesthetic" provides the family with a way to be critical of their own, but to do so in good form and with cordiality.[47] Both Dona Lara and Dilson understand all too well that Dilson is considered an undesirable mate unless his blackness can be counteracted or compensated for by an additional quality or status. Consistent with Dilson and Dona Lara's analysis, researchers argue that whiteness is used as a valuable commodity, or symbolic capital, that can be exchanged for love, fidelity, or economic security.[48] As Thiago's comments about dark-skinned women or *pretas* illustrate, those whose bodies do not conform to racist aesthetic hierarchies have much less symbolic capital to exchange in a patriarchal and racialized society. For this reason, in this study long-term romantic interracial exchanges are often framed and critiqued by respondents as mostly occurring between wealthy black men and white women of any class status.

Critical of the overvaluation of whiteness in romantic relationships, Sonia explains:

Like this, today you see a big business owner who is *negro*. He is not going to marry a *negra*. He is going to marry a white woman. And why would a white woman marry him? Because it's obvious, he has money and he is a business owner, because if he were like this black without money she would not marry him. Her? She is beautiful, blonde, white, you think she is going to marry him? I think in situations like that, that is not love. And him, he is prejudiced against himself. Her, well it is not that she is not prejudiced. I think it is very rare for a white woman to fall in love with a black man. It happens yes with many, but it is rare, but mainly if he has money. Because nowadays money really does count, right?

Both women and men who were interviewed cited interracial relationships between wealthy black men and blonde women as examples of racism, dismissing these romantic relationships as superficial negotiations of economic status and whiteness. They rarely mention the way that similar negotiations of phenotype and status occur within intraracial partnerships. Alberto, much like the majority of respondents in the study, expressed skepticism about these relationships:

Sometimes they are really attracted to each other. Sometimes they are not even looking at color. Sometimes there is chemistry and they become involved with each other. There is chemistry between a man and a woman. You know, opposites attract and that is it. Or it may even be a co-incidence. But many times, I think it is about status. As though a white woman represents status. (Alberto, 48, janitor)

Narratives or experiences related to marriages involving black women and white men are particularly rare. Given research suggesting that women exchange their beauty for status, black women's location in the aesthetic hierarchy immediately decreases their chances on the market unless they are considered exceptionally beautiful.[49]

The case of Marcia and Daniel represents one example of how these negotiations unfold in a couple that many consider to be interracial. Marcia is a dark-skinned woman with African features who is overweight and chemically straightens her hair. She is married to a very light-skinned man, Daniel, who is also overweight and identifies racially as *negro*. He complains that most people consider him white. They are one of only four married couples I met in which the wife is significantly darker than the husband. Daniel refers to his wife lovingly as *negona* and is proud of her achievements, often bragging about her education and credentials, which include two college degrees, in technology and history. Daniel drove me to Marcia's workplace so I could see her nice office, her computer, and the certificates mounted on the wall. Meanwhile, Daniel works as a janitor and admits over the course of our interviews that he has had and continues to have sexual affairs with other women. The example of Marcia and Daniel might be an example of how whiteness can be traded for devotion and license to engage in these type of extramarital relationships. However, more evidence should be collected to determine the extent to which this happens more broadly in families.

Cecilia's black sister, Gabriela, believes she can engage in a romantic exchange on the basis of her exceptional beauty, but ends up disappointed:

I have a sister who is *negra*. She went to work in a store where she was hired on the spot. The owner of this store liked her but she told him that she was just interested in the experience. He was a black man and had a beautiful color. But she was also pretty, I mean really pretty, very pretty face, you should have seen her. To go forward in her career, she depended on him. He fell in love with her. He was *preto*, so that was the end of that. She ended up meeting a manager of one of his stores who was my color, not even. He was not white. . . . She chose him because of his color. I am certain of it. She did not even have to say it. She has had boyfriends that were bank managers. Why did she choose him? It wasn't passion. Now

she is suffering. She was a virgin when she met him, ended up pregnant
and found out he was already married. Now she is fat and cannot afford
to get in shape. I think the worst thing in the world for a person is the
pain of regret. (Cecilia, 37)

In this case, Gabriela could have exchanged her attractiveness for a relationship with a well-to-do black owner of several stores. Instead, she pursued the much lighter but lower-status manager, who welcomed a sexual
relationship with her. When she discovered that she had lost her virginity
and become pregnant with a married man, she was devastated. The pregnancy resulted in the loss of both her moral reputation and her status.[50]
Her beauty might have been exchanged for status, but according to her
sister, she was manipulated and lost both. Now that "she is fat and cannot
afford to get in shape," the likelihood of her exchanging her good looks
has significantly decreased in a society that overvalues beauty as the primary capital of women.

Chinyere Osuji's recent research on black partners in traditional interracial relationships in Rio de Janeiro offers findings that point to the importance of racialization processes in romantic partnerships. She suggests
that black partners may be welcomed into a family, but this acceptance
may require some negotiation. One of her interviewees stated that she was
accepted by her partner's white family, but "they don't want to see me as
negra, because they think that negros are ugly."[51] Rather than outright rejection or acceptance, there is a negotiation process whereby the white
family reframes the black partner's racial identity so she can be acceptable
to them. Even a negotiation process that leads to acceptance is thus structured by racialization based on a belief in black inferiority.

For all of these reasons, I am curious about Dilson and Lilza's relationship and whether there are indications of a similar social exchange. Although I had spent time with the Barán family, napping on their ham-
mock, sharing meals, and interviewing several family members, Dilson
has been extraordinarily quiet and distant. In our conversation, I ask him
about his experiences and opinions about interracial relationships. As he
talks, he avoids eye contact with me:

Here in Brazil, you feel that image of a black man who wants a partner
as white as can be. So, then, he marries a white woman or whatever. And
then this comes from the more radical blacks really, a racist black person in regards to whites: "You married a white woman? You are black.
You should marry a black woman." It comes from the more radical peo-

ple. You know? And then there are others that have a different vision because of the soccer players. They ask you, "You think you are just like the soccer players by marrying a blonde woman?" But you can see that in the back of that commentary is an idea that really is racist. That you are not highlighting or looking for a good person whom you like, you are looking for a person with a different skin color than yours. It is a way to self-discriminate, or it is a way for the white person who does not have a chance for mobility. It is not really because they like the person, but it is because they want to take the place of that black person.

In Dilson's opinion, racist, radical blacks are those who interrogate other blacks about their choice in nonblack partners. Indeed, given that romantic relationships between black people have been framed as retarding the civilization and modernity of Brazil, the black movement encourages "black love" to reinforce racial affirmation and as a critique of whitening (branqueamento).[52] At the same time that Dilson is critical of "radical" blacks, he also senses that there is some truth in the concern about people marrying out of interest rather than out of love. I found particularly interesting his belief that a white person may marry a black person as a way to take the black person's place. That is, a white person who has been unsuccessful in society can use whiteness to marry someone who is black and successful. It is only because whiteness is viewed as symbolic capital that this type of transaction is conceivable.

With a graduate degree, Lilza is one of the most educated people I interviewed in this research, and she exudes confidence about both her decisions in life and her future. She and Dilson have been discussing the idea of having children and are currently *fazendo os cálculos* (doing the calculations) to decide on when to do so. Although I expect Dilson to be more vocal now that the conversation is shifting from being about Lilza to being more directly about them both, he stays relatively quiet on the issue. However, Lilza reveals:

So yeah, there is lots of prejudice like that. I know that my child will be born *negro* and many people are going to think that he is adopted. They are going to say it, and I am going to have to go and say to them: He is beautiful being black. The end. That's it. Do you understand? He has to be proud of his color. It's a beautiful color. It's the type of color that you don't need to sit under the sun all day putting on all that sunscreen. You understand me? He is going to be like him (*leans towards her husband*). A pretty color. Now, that question about being ugly and being pretty and stuff like that. It's a thing that, well who dictates that?

This comment suggests that Lilza is already preparing for possible encounters with passersby who might make assumptions about or apply racist stereotypes to her future child. Not only has she already decided that her child will be *negro*, she is already preparing to foster his racial self-esteem and combat the influences of neighbors. In her mind, her child will be black and beautiful, not beautiful despite being black.[53]

DIASPORIC AND GLOBAL CONSIDERATIONS

The affective interactions, racial bargains, and racial rituals that I present in this chapter resonate with studies of families of color across the African diaspora. In this chapter I have incorporated only a few examples of diasporic connections; there is much more to be said about how the "web of diasporic identities" links these communities.[54]

Traversing boundaries of language and culture, the commitment to *limpar a raça* (clean the race) that has been seen in Brazil is reflected in desires to *adelantar* or *limpiar la raza* (advance or clean the race) in Spanish-speaking Latin America.[55] These ideologies have direct consequences for racial socialization in families, in terms of both family formation and the day-to-day interactions of family members in the Americas.

In her analysis of dark-skinned women with African features in families in Spanish-speaking Latin America (a group referred to as *Latinegras*), Lillian Comas-Díaz notes that it is less acceptable for lighter men to marry black women because a child having a "visible Latinegra mother is a clear sign of her children's mixed racial ancestry, reducing their opportunities to *adelantar la raza* (improve the race), and thus limiting their attractiveness as potential spouses."[56] She adds that when a lighter-skinned woman marries down (marries a black man), it is less threatening because fathers are rarely present; people would be less likely to see the black (*Latinegro*) father and stigmatize the baby.[57] Concerns that evidence of African heritage can reappear in the fifth generation (from a great-great-grandparent) manifest as the fear of *requintar*, which helps explain the near obsessive anticipation of and vigilance over a baby's features in some families in Spanish-speaking Latin America.[58] Writing about black Puerto Rican women, Angela Jorge posits, "Her negative experiences are not only from outside groups but from her own community and family that judges her dark skin and African features harshly."[59]

The shared history of slavery means that the French-speaking Caribbean has also been part of this system of white supremacy and whitening. Frantz Fanon offers insight into the phenomenon with an interview with a black woman in Martinique:

Mayotte loves a white man to whom she submits in everything. He is her lord. She asks nothing, demands nothing, except a bit of whiteness in her life. When she tries to determine in her own mind if the man is handsome or ugly, she writes, "All I know is that he had blond hair and blue eyes and a light skin and that I loved him." It is not difficult to see that a re-arrangement of these elements in their proper hierarchy would produce something of this order, "I loved him because he had blue eyes, blond hair and a light skin."[60]

Here, Fanon illustrates that whiteness ideologies influence perceptions of love. Does she love a man who is white or does she love a man because he is white? The respondents in this study sometimes struggle to determine how to answer this question, which is a reflection of how deeply the emotional realm is structured by racial ideologies.

The desire for whiteness is replicated in the strong racial dimensions and ideologies that shape the tensions between Haiti and the Dominican Republic, the latter having been described as a "negrophobic" nation even though its population is largely descended from Africans.[61] In the 1960s, during the height of the civil rights movement in the United States, a student activist wrote a letter to her mother that was published in the Student Nonviolent Coordinating Committee newspaper. In it she critiqued her mother for promoting antiblack prejudice:

> I remember many years ago, being told over and over to pinch my nose every once in a while to make it sharper. It was strongly emphasized that I should find a husband as light as possible and with the straightest hair imaginable so that when we had children, they could "pass for white."[62]

Nose pinching has been practiced in Brazil, in the United States, and throughout the Caribbean, where it has been taken to such extremes that "a young girl was taken unconscious to the hospital emergency room after using a clothes pin to close her wide nose in order to make it narrow and thus to look less Black."[63]

In the United States researchers have written at length about the ways in which differential treatment based on skin color has shaped family dynamics. Looking beyond romantic relationships, researchers in psychology and the social sciences have produced some of the most extensive research addressing how skin color affects sibling rivalry, favoritism, and differential treatment within the same family.[64] Recent research suggests that parents of dark-skinned children may "scapegoat" them and hold their lighter-skinned children in higher regard, and that they may also intentionally and unintentionally project a wide range of characteristics onto their children.[65]

Throughout this chapter, I illustrate that laughter and humor is used in diverse ways to lighten racial slights, critique obsolete family practices, and encourage racial modification. In this, Donna Goldstein's work on the presence of an emotional aesthetic is influential. She describes how humor is used among residents in poor communities in Brazil to deal with traumatic experiences and their harsh daily realities.[66] In terms of humor, racial jokes called *brincadeiras* function very closely in Brazil to racist comments spoken *en forma de broma* (jokingly) in Puerto Rico.[67] In Mexico and Peru, racial humor occurs on the "front stage," and "individuals are expected to 'go along' with racist jokes and humorous name-calling" or risk being labeled "overly sensitive."[68]

DISCUSSION

Certain life transitions, including the birth of a child, entering a romantic relationship, and marrying, tend to precipitate explicit conversations about race and phenotype among intimate family members and neighbors. During these transitions, concrete practices, use of racialized language, and affective responses that reflect racial and phenotypic hierarchies mean that emotions and feelings transmit important messages about racial stigma. Seemingly visceral responses to race and racial features are central to the socialization of racial affect, whereby family members, through a naturalized process, internalize ideas about racial stigma and reproduce social interactions on the basis of them. That is to say, emotion circulates through families and shapes relationships and racialization processes.

In families light skin color and phenotypically white characteristics are not a "neutral standard, but something that functions as a symbol of status in Brazilian society,". elusive but nonetheless aspired to.[69] Consistent with the way that material resources are unequally distributed in a racialized social system, family members who are considered the blackest looking are disadvantaged and receive less affective resources vis-à-vis their lighter family members. Families do not merely respond to racial hierarchies, they "do race" and may help reinforce inequality by reproducing it. Jani's decision to discount the idea of college for her daughter illustrates just one way that racial socialization in families produces inequality, rather than merely reflecting it.

Women, including mothers, daughters, and extended female family members, are central to practices of racial socialization that involve the evaluation of gendered and racialized bodies. The emotional investment in racial rituals is further heightened for women because not only are they the subject of intense scrutiny, they are required to scrutinize others as an indicator of their commitment to good mothering practices. Critiques by other women are the impetus for and reinforce practices that manage the racial appearance of children.

In all of the families I studied except one, the father plays a secondary role in children's upbringing and racial socialization. However, fathers do make their presence known as evaluators of the mother's racial product and as the protector of the mother's perceived fidelity, which they determine in part by assessing the racial phenotype of their children. In this way, racialized language, affective responses to racialized features, and concrete practices that respond to race all have a decisively gendered element.

Although mothers are central to socialization processes, racial socialization occurs in the context of a wide array of family relationships: mother-child, father-child, sibling, and extended family (both nonbiological and biological), as well as in romantic relationships. I highlight this broad range of relationships to reveal the pervasiveness of hegemonic whiteness and to show how a whiter racial appearance can lead to higher levels of affection (Jani's son and Regane), exposure to more positive evaluations (Adrielle), and experiences that foster positive affect (Lilza). Similarly, in romantic relationships racial bargains and social exchanges occur in which phenotype functions as symbolic capital that can be exchanged for the promise of love, loyalty, and status. The intersection of hegemonic notions of beauty, status, race, and gender means that *pretas* (dark-skinned women with African features) are severely disadvantaged in these romantic and familial interactions.[70]

Language also emerges as an important factor that promotes the socialization of racial affect. The use of racialized terms and phrases, including *barriga suja* (dirty womb), *limpinha* (clean), *limpando a raça* (cleaning the race), and *gente bonita* (beautiful people), and even the use of the diminutive form of adjectives to describe the attractiveness of a black person, serve to conflate whiteness with cleanliness, goodness, and attractiveness. This is an extension of historical concerns about racial hygiene and the contemporary relevance of a "whitening sentiment," which are still very present throughout Brazil and the Americas.[71] These terms normalize the racial stigma associated with blackness and legitimate the use of racial rituals designed to correct racial features.

In conclusion, an analysis of the affective interactions within families, in nonromantic and nonsexual relationships, provides a broader lens through which to theorize the mechanisms of domination. Researchers tend to focus very little on how emotion affects racialization and racial socialization processes, and they give insufficient attention to the intersectional dimensions that shape the unique pressures for mothers and daughters. Although mothers are responsible for disciplining racialized and gendered bodies and mothers are the actors who engage most visibly in differential treatment, their hands are tied because they act within the constraints of significant social pressures.

Examples from across the diaspora illustrate that black families are complex, contradictory, and often conscious of their limited options, and they make the best decisions possible for them. This does not suggest that such decisions and actions should not be problematized, but rather that they should be contextualized. Many mothers and women engage in racial bargains with ambivalence or reframe their use of racial rituals, such as nose-pinching, as helping rather than hurting family members.[72] Some mothers describe their engagement in racial rituals as resistance or agency in a society that uses the racialized and gendered body as a tool of power and oppression. Ultimately, in response to the provocative question posed in the title of this chapter, "What's love got to do with it?," this research suggests that in many families there is love, but what love looks like often depends on what you look like.

CHAPTER 2

BLACK BODIES, WHITE CASTS:
RACIALIZING AND GENDERING BODIES

Hoje é da moda ser Negão . . . é verdade! (Nowadays, it's in style to be a really black man. . . . It's true!) ALBERTO, 46

AMONG DONA LARA'S EARLIEST MEMORIES is of a white store owner who followed her as she walked through a corner store. After she paid for her things, he taunted her until she reached the exit, using a racist insult that she will never forget. Visibly hesitant to reveal what the store owner said, she hedges around my inquiries until with sad eyes she finally reveals that he kept repeating, "Negros fedem, negros fedem!" (Blacks stink, blacks stink!) She cannot explain what prompted the white store owner to respond to her in this way, but she remembers every other detail, including the exact location of the store, its name, and a description of the store owner. Her son, Dilson, is in the living room listening to her recount the story to me, and he is surprised that she has never shared it with him.

She describes this experience as *marcante* (striking), then tells me about some of her most memorable and positive experiences involving schooling. She takes great pride in having been a star student and brags that because of her rigorous *formação* (training) she still remembers all the country capitals; she even dares me to quiz her. As a child she especially loved the holiday events and "always dreamed of being a beautiful angel in the Christmas play . . . and [wearing] a beautiful white dress." She recalls wondering why she was never selected to be one of the Christmas angels and that one day she asked her mother. She explains:

> The teacher never chose me to be an angel. I asked my mother why I was never chosen to be an angel. And she looked at me and said "because black angels don't exist." Just like that. I was really young so I sat and thought about that, I mean I really thought about that thing, and after a

while I said to myself she was right (*nods slowly*). There really is no such thing as a black angel. Who ever heard of a black angel?

Despite having shared a number of good memories from her childhood, these two memories she recalls as critical moments when she realized that her racialization as *preta* (a black woman) had implications for her perceived beauty, morality, and worth. As black Brazilian sociologist Alberto Guerreiro Ramos writes about whiteness in the Brazilian context, "Deus é concebido como símbolo em branco, em branco são pensadas todas as perfeições" (God is conceived of as a white symbol; everything that is perfect is thought of as white).[1] If the most sacred and holy beings are beautiful in a society where racialization is based on the assumption of black inferiority, indeed, there can be no black angels.

Using an intersectional analysis, in this chapter I analyze how racializing and gendering bodies has unique implications for Afro-Brazilian women, as they both are subjected to "hegemonically defined standards of beauty" that privilege whiteness and must serve as their enforcers in their families.[2] Building on the significance of emotion and affect to racialization in families, I emphasize that the internalization of beauty norms is insidious because a racist aesthetic hierarchy becomes naturalized: it comes to feel universally and naturally true. I recognize the sharp feminist criticisms of gendered and racist beauty ideals, and at the same time I take seriously women's desire to manage and present their bodies in accordance with dominant norms because it feels good to be seen as beautiful (affective capital) and because it is associated with material and economic advantages (embodied capital). I further develop the theoretical concept of embodied racial capital, which captures what is at stake in accommodating normative rules of racial appearance. Rather than blindly reproducing racial hierarchies, Afro-Brazilians may rely on *critical accommodation*: they may temporarily accommodate racial hierarchies with the goal of ultimately challenging inequality. Gendered racial bargains represent the complex, contradictory, and creative ways that Afro-Brazilian men and women work to reposition themselves in a society that devalues blackness and objectifies them.

PRETTY HURTS: RACIALIZATION, GENDER, AND BEAUTY

Toni Morrison once wrote that beauty is one of the "most destructive ideas in the history of human thought." It "originated in envy, thrived in insecurity, and ended in disillusion."[3] When she wrote this, she was referring not merely to how the physical human body is evaluated, but also to the pernicious way that the naturalization of systems that designate people and objects as beautiful has been used to determine that others are worthless and disposable. The danger of beauty is linked to the way that notions of beauty foster an oppressively narrow set of dichotomies: goodness and badness, Christianity and secularity, cleanliness and dirtiness, morality and immorality.

In its most destructive act of all, beauty has been invoked to make determinations about who is human and who is not. Historically the emergence of white supremacy depended on this dichotomy, which has been violent to those who have been racialized as the black other. Early discourses about Africans' "ugliness of appearance," and the supposed clear proof of their "stupidity" connected physicality to aesthetics and moral deficiencies to justify enslavement.[4] This institutionalized system of racial evaluation illustrates the "extreme devaluing of Afro-Brazilians and the way in which black people's bodies have been *abjectified* as bad or unpleasant and identified with 'nature' and 'primitive sexual impulses.'"[5]

The symbolism of color firmly embedded in European religious notions of morality only bolstered claims that the dark, African body was inferior, dangerous, and potentially evil.[6] Less known are the social norms that were enforced on black women's bodies in order to maintain these boundaries. Enslaved *negras* in Brazil were denied the right to use certain colors, prohibited from adorning themselves with colorful headscarves, and denied the right to wear shoes or clothing that was considered above them.[7] Controlling the representation or appearance of the "other" is a vital element in the construction of whiteness and beauty, as it is only by making black ugly that white can be beautiful.[8] Intentional efforts to deny black women access to beauty offer an important historical context for understanding black women's contemporary emphasis on beauty.

Researchers have increasingly studied whiteness not as a racial label but in terms of how it functions relationally as a source of power and capital.[9] In a society where whiteness was once one's ticket to humanity, whiteness was priceless—except when it had a price. In Spanish Latin America free slaves (*libertos*) could purchase whiteness by buying a document, the *Real cédula de gracias al sacar*, which gave them access to privileges reserved for white people.[10] In contemporary Brazil, Bernd Reiter notes:

> Whiteness is a highly desirable good to all those that are able to claim it with success. Because of Brazil's long history of associating whiteness

with civilizational potential, whiteness has developed into the strongest marker of elevated social status. It symbolizes education and holding a regular job. Additionally, most Brazilians almost automatically associate it with being middle-class, having money, owning a car, and having access to other private services, most importantly private education.[11]

Beyond the purported biological superiority of whites, whiteness functions as a good and as a symbol of potential and attained success. It was a valuable good during slavery and remains a valuable good now. This is a reality against which Afro-Brazilian families contend in the socialization of family members.

Though the colonial gaze is less looming in the postslavery and postcolonial era, black Brazilians are socialized to police themselves and emotionally invest in the legitimacy of dominant racial hierarchies. The pressures to conform in Salvador are considerable, as stares and direct commentary communicate: "There is no need for arms, physical violence, material constraints. Just a gaze. An inspecting gaze, . . . which each individual under its weight will end by interiorizing to the point where he is his own overseer."[12] Whiteness shapes social and racial relations in Brazil, engendering new ideologies and concrete practices that reinforce racialization based on black inferiority. These ideas are beyond ideology because they become coded in language: whiteness is associated with morality, so "what is dirty is associated with Black, with color, and with Black men and women. Gestural, oral, and written language institutionalize the deprecating meaning of blackness."[13]

Pinho describes how black racial features are degraded and stigmatized, noting how noses and lips are described not as full, but as *grossos* or *grosseiros* (vulgar or crude). A nose is not wide but is a *nariz chato*, with the adjective *chato* meaning not only wide, but also boring or dull. Likewise, racial stereotypes that blacks have a repugnant body odor and "bad" hair carry an obvious negative connotation and also suggest that blackness is repulsive and needs to be tamed. When I ask Dona Ceci, "Do you know what *catinga* means?," she quickly shushes me, puts a finger over my mouth, and pulls me to the side. She looks around uncomfortably, checking to see if anyone has heard me say *catinga* aloud, then she leans in close and angrily whispers:

Where did you hear that word?! Who said that word to you? Tell me! *Catinga* is a horrible, horrible word that describes the smell of a dead animal that has been rotting for days, but people use it to describe the way that they think blacks smell. *Catinga* . . . it's a horrible smell. They say that is how blacks smell. Never say that word again.

A putrid bodily stench is used as a defining feature of blacks. It fits alongside other racist representations that historically portray blacks as repulsive, wild, and subhuman.

In contrast, whites are constructed as the *gente bonita* (pretty people), with *cabelo bom* (good hair), *pele limpa* (clean rather than white skin), and a *nariz fino* (fine nose). Racialization processes are thus embodied and mapped onto the linguistic framework of a nation. It is for these reasons that researchers argue that though the numerous color categories in Brazil give the impression of boundless fluidity, the extensive vocabulary used to capture race and color reflects the "bedrock reality of racial polarization and opposition," anchored by whiteness on one end and by blackness on the other.[14]

Afro-Brazilian women are not only responding to a white gaze; the male gaze is also omnipotent and vocal. Men assert their masculinity in public areas by hissing and making unsolicited comments, calling women "linda" (beautiful), "gostosa" (tasty or sexy), "morena," and a favorite, "Deusa de Ébano" (Ebony Goddess). The shouts from construction workers, bus drivers, and passersby reinforce the objectification of women and remind them that their bodies are on display and available for evaluation.[15] Out of respect for other men, these unsolicited comments do not usually occur when women are accompanied by men. From interviews, I learn that girls begin to hear these comments and experience street harassment from men at an early age. Twelve-year-old Teresa remembers exiting a bus on her way home from school at the age of ten and hearing a man whisper "gostosa" as she walked by. She ran all the way home and told her mother about the comment. Her mother explained that she was now a woman and that from now on she should expect these comments but ignore them. Mothers are at the forefront of socializing young girls about self-presentation, instructing them on the importance of managing their racialized and gendered sexuality, and attempting to protect them from unwanted advances. Entrance into womanhood is not a biological process but a social one, based in part on the male sexual gaze.

Given the centrality of the body in influencing access to economic and educational resources, the body is considered an important terrain on which to negotiate inequality. Embodied capital—achieved by manipulation of the body in order to maximize access to the resources normally allotted to the dominant group—is considered a pathway to social mobility. Encouraged by the "mothering voices" around them, women practice visibility management to maximize their embodied racial capital or decrease their embodied liabilities. Naturally, access to resources also affects the way embodied racial capital can be negotiated. In Brazil, white, middle-class women openly discuss plastic surgery in terms of what work they had done, whereas poor, Afro-Brazilian women speak frequently about what work they want to have done. If it is true that "not one part of a woman's body is left untouched, unaltered. No feature or extremity is spared the art, or pain, of improvement," black women's bodies would have to succumb to endless modifications in order to achieve the ideal body.[16] The quest to understand how racialization, gender, and beauty function together leads me back to the beginning: babies.

CHILD LABOR: PRACTICING RACIAL RITUALS ON BABIES

They say this little black boy has such fine features. And I say, what do you mean *fine* features? (Daniel, 57)

Insistent on better understanding the local meanings attached to some of the practices I had observed in Afro-Brazilian family life, I consult with Nancy da Souza e Silva (Dona Ceci), a well-respected leader, practitioner of Candomblé, and one of my most significant research mentors during my time in Salvador. In our conversations we discuss race and phenotype in Brazil, but it is woven together with her riveting stories about the Orixás and Candomblé religious traditions. One of our many conversations reveals the elaborate system of what I call racial rituals, practices that families use to police and modify one's racial appearance.[17] Racial rituals are examples of how hegemonic whiteness moves from ideology to embodied practice. Dona Ceci begins our conversation by confirming matter-of-factly that she is very familiar with the nose modification practice:

There is a history that when a baby is born with a flat nose that the mother early in the morning before giving the baby a bath has to light a candle, heat her fingers close to the candle flame and place it over the baby's nose three times. Three times. Three times over the nose of the baby pulling it so that it will be thin (*fino*) like a white person's nose. What happens is a type of quote-unquote physical therapy. If you have any type of problem and every day you massage that area, eventually it will start looking different. So it is the same thing, every day, every day.

Not only does Dona Ceci offer confirmation of this practice, but she explicitly links it to racialization and the desire to approximate white features. Her framing of the practice as physical therapy or massage suggests that the practice and technique are medicalized as a necessary intervention to address a legitimate problem.[18] That this process needs to be repeated three times speaks to the routinized aspect of these rituals.

After Dona Ceci discusses noses, her commentary quickly progresses to lesser-known rituals of the "black community" that discipline the body. She moves along to the hands of the baby:

> They take the baby when the baby is born. They do this. . . . Give me your hand *(she takes my hands and looks at my palms)*. Look right here *(tracing the inside of my palms)*. If this part is dark, he will be born black. So they look and they say, "Ah, this one is going to be black." And it goes on from there. Well you know that generally this happens more for blacks than for whites. Whites have to conform much less but the black has to. But this is real. This happens a lot in Brazil.

Dona Ceci's insights are valuable because she articulates the connection between the scrutiny of racial features and the pressure to achieve racial conformity. This pressure reflects the influence of broader ideologies and hierarchies that privilege whiteness, but are also perceived to be associated with material benefits. Michael Baran's ethnographic studies reveal a similar preoccupation with interpreting early indicators of race. He notes that his informants "remarked on how a baby's skin color changes, how they are born with light skin that darkens with age. To tell what color a baby's skin will turn out to be, you have to look under the fingernails."[19] Dona Ceci's insights are consistent with and expound on such findings from previous studies.

From hands, she moves on to feet:

> DONA CECI: Oh! What about the feet? The feet! Closed-toe shoes so they do not end up with long feet like a black person's foot.
> ELIZABETH: Wait, what is a black person's foot like?
> DONA CECI: They say it's long and wide, and the white person's foot is thin *(uses her hands to illustrate)*.

In this case, closed-toe shoes are used to prevent growth to what might otherwise be the excessively large size of a black person's feet. The racial associations of large feet reinforce other racist portrayals of black features, including lips, nose, and sexual organs, as exaggerated, vulgar, or grotesquely large.[20]

Dona Ceci continues:

> So the child is born, the father is black, mother is black, and the child is born white. It is white, but it is not really white. It is just that he is born really light, really light. So they turn him to see if on his butt there are these little things (*negoçinhos*), to see if he has black marks on his bottom.

Previous researchers have written about how the presence of dark spots on a baby's buttocks are used to predict whether a child will develop a darker or lighter skin color.[21] This is considered an important ritual because a black baby's initial skin tone can be drastically different from its final skin color. When a child is the product of two black parents, there may be concern about how dark the baby will be, so further examination is needed.

Finally, when I think there is nothing left to scrutinize, Dona Ceci suggests that a baby boy's penis can also be problematic:

> There is another thing too! If the baby is born with a large, dark penis, really dark and big, they say to take the baby and face it toward the door. On a Friday you say this. You put your hand over the penis three times and say, "Comegato, comegato, comegato" (Cat eater, cat eater, cat eater).

I cannot contain my confused laughter, and I ask her to repeat the ritual because surely I have misunderstood. She laughs a hearty laugh and replies, "I do not know what to tell you. I do not know what to tell you. I am tired of seeing it done!"

These rituals are important because they demonstrate the importance of physical features in the determination of one's categorization and evaluation. Beyond one's categorization, the presence of certain racial features can translate into attributions of competency and be perceived as predictors for future behavior and success. E. S. Cavalleiro notes how racist readings of the black body are used to justify racial prejudice. An interview with a teacher reveals the following belief:

> Racial prejudice, if you think about, generally it's all about body odor. A black person, their skin, the melanin makes it so that their smell is much stronger. Nowadays this prejudice is decreasing because there are modern products—deodorant, creams. These types of antiperspirants take away

the odor. When the odor is gone, there is no longer a reason for whites not to talk to blacks and vice versa.[22]

Reproducing these absurd ideas while simultaneously hoping to challenge them, black respectability politics in the 1930s in Brazil focused on cleanliness and addressing body odor as a way to "help blacks" avoid racism.[23] Not only does this approach frame racism as an individual issue and discount the relationship between white supremacy and unequal access to power and resources, but the circular and nonsensical argument frames blacks as responsible for their own oppression.

In one family there was a strong belief that lighter babies do not cry as much as dark-skinned babies.[24] In this case, lighter babies are considered not only more beautiful, but also better behaved. One is left to wonder whether the stereotype that darker babies cry more is related to them being treated more harshly. This phenomenon is not limited to Brazil: Comas-Díaz notes that racial attributes assigned to babies are common in Spanish-speaking parts of Latin America, where "a colicky baby may be described as *esa prieta majadera* (that bothersome Black female baby), while a non-Black colicky baby may engender concern or be identified as a *majadera*, without any allusion to her color."[25] Other diasporic researchers offer evidence that lighter-skinned mothers and grandmothers may project fewer expectations on darker-skinned family members.[26]

There are generational factors to be considered when situating these racial rituals in the context of contemporary Salvador. I directly observed only one of the rituals (nose pinching), but other mothers confirmed their participation in various rituals, and Dona Ceci has observed several of them herself. Dona Ceci's familiarity with the rituals suggests that practitioners of Candomblé, who deeply value African traditions and worship African deities, are also exposed to these pressures. Though respondents suggest that the rituals are becoming less common, their existence provides insight into how invasively the black body is dissected, catalogued, and subjected to endless evaluation.

GENDERED RACIAL BARGAINS: SEXUALITY, HAIR, AND BODY

Beginning in infancy and continuing into adulthood, racial features are markers on the basis of which Brazilians are evaluated and afforded access to valuable resources. This has unique implications for Afro-Brazilian women. Distinctions between *mulatas*, *morenas*, and *negras* are often articulated through meanings inscribed on readings of hair texture, skin color, facial features, and the size of buttocks.[27] In a casual conversation in the Fernandes home, a mother and daughter, *morenas*, with straighter hair and lighter skin than their black-looking family members humorously lament that they are *secas*. This term literally means dry, but it is often used colloquially to mean lacking in curves and having smaller hips and buttocks. Alberta, who can be described as a *figura* (comical and animated person), proceeds to tell me in a joking fashion:

> Girl, it's true. Not everyone can be a *negra gostosa* (sexy black woman). So, look, see this is why I put . . . (*she unbuckles her shorts and pulls them down in back to reveal her padded underwear*) just a little something here, and now look at my *bunda gostosa* (sexy butt). (*She struts around the room in an exaggerated, sexy fashion. We all laugh.*)

These patterns are relevant across the diaspora, though they manifest themselves in different ways depending on the context and historical moment. For example, in the United States and the Caribbean, the "shape and size of the bottom" are considered black racial features, so that when a white or nearly white woman has a large butt, it is seen as "a sign that the person has 'black blood' in her ancestry."[28] What is unique about contemporary Brazil is that large buttocks are increasingly associated with the image of a Brazilian woman, and Brazilian women of all racial categories feel pressure to embody and express a certain type of Brazilian sexuality.[29] Alberta's desire to wear a butt pad in order to be a *negra gostosa* reflects these pressures. The mother uses the term *negra* rather than *mulata*, which suggests that she believes having a nice butt is a trait applicable to all black women, and not just *mulatas*. Notably, though isolated body parts that are stereotypically associated with blacks may be viewed as attractive, this does not destabilize the racial hierarchy. Instead, by eroticizing black women it both reinforces patriarchy and promotes racial objectification.

The time and attention that some Afro-Brazilian families invest in embodied capital is not merely about preferences; it is shaped by structural and practical implications. Some interviewees describe a direct connection between aesthetics, perceived competence, and opportunity. Lilza explains:

> This happens, this really happens! I have experienced this! When I was younger, we were really poor, we lived in the favela, Brotas in Salvador.

But one day my teacher in class pointed to all the white children and said that "You, the pretty ones, the little white ones you are all going to college," and the others would have to figure out something else. It was not surprising because my uncle said the same thing about my cousin, Victoria, who was much darker than me. And, she was in my same class. So, she heard that at school and at home. My uncle didn't think that a black person would succeed in college. And you know what, he is black!

According to Lilza, not only does a teacher assume that only the pretty and white students will be successful, but a black father echoes these sentiments and doubts that his black daughter will ever enter college. Unable to interview Victoria, I ask Lilza to provide more details about what happened in her life. Lilza describes Victoria as a *batalhadora* (hard-working woman; go-getter). The negative comments that she heard from her father convinced Victoria to study even harder, and she recently graduated from college. Lilza quickly scrolls through Facebook on her cell phone and shows me pictures of Victoria's graduation. Both Dona Lara and Lilza roll their eyes as they describe the reaction of Victoria's father at her college graduation party, because they heard him telling others, "Well, this is what happens when you invest in your child."

In no other way does the evaluation of racial features surface in Brazilian and diasporic black families than by the evaluation of hair. In the shared history of these societies, "African hair was deemed wholly unattractive and inferior."[30] Connected to the broader ideology of African inferiority, hegemonic standards of beauty are transmitted "as grooming practices by relatives" both in the form of direct commentary and by the "reactions and expectations of adults."[31] These emotion-laden reactions play a significant role in the internalization of racial hierarchies, which become mapped onto the body. When informants are asked to discuss hair texture and its significance, *they are all* knowledgeable and provide remarkably consistent responses. This common sense is so strong that respondents laugh because they do not understand why I am asking such obvious questions. The responses below best capture the high level of consistency on comments related to good and bad hair:

Bad hair is black people's hair. Our hair, your hair is bad hair. (Sonia, 31)

Bad hair is your hair. Your hair is bad. Black people's hair is like this, so you have to value it because it is different. (Daniel, 57)

Good hair is really, really straight, white people's hair. Bad hair is hair like mine. (Marcos, 26)

Good hair is straight hair, is it not? In my case, I have bad hair. Good hair is white people's hair. There is good hair and there is bad hair. (Luisa, 52)

It is not that the niceties normally extended to me as a researcher from the United States fall by the wayside in conversations about hair. It is simply not considered a violation of racial etiquette to refer to my hair as bad hair, which hints at the widespread commonsense nature of ideas about racial features.[32] The use of "good" and "bad" terminology is an extension of the historical and rigid dichotomies of black and white, tightly coiled and straight, African and European, wild and civilized. Even though there is a continuum of hair texture, in Bahia if hair is not straight it is not good hair.[33] It is difficult to ignore the diasporic connections, as the construct of *cabelo bom/cabelo ruim* finds itself reproduced in English as good hair/bad hair and in Spanish as *pelo bueno/pelo malo*, all of which are based on ideas of African inferiority.[34]

Gendered racism overemphasizes beauty for women everywhere, but in Brazil, where "a beleza abre portas" (beauty opens doors), hair can be a significant impediment for black women's economic mobility.[35] Racialization of features is thus not merely a question of aesthetics, it is a reflection of power, of the authority to name and judge, and to determine who should have access to what resources. On the basis of ostensibly objective standards, *negras* are excluded from television and even from beauty pageants, even those that specifically focus on capturing the beauty of Bahia.

In describing the most beautiful women in Brazil, three Afro-Brazilian young men clamor to explain the criteria:

CARLOS (*pardo*, 23): The prettiest women in Brazil are light skinned or white. It's rare for a black woman to be considered pretty.

MARCELO (*negro*, 26): Unless she's like, like, what's her name? Like Tais Araújo!

LUIS (*moreno*, 19): Yeah, but she is like an improved black woman (*they laugh*).

Tais Araújo is a black Brazilian woman who is considered attractive. This is in part because she has light brown skin, "fine" features, and a thick, long mane of spirally, loose curly hair. Representing what some researchers refer to as "domesticated blackness," her physical features approximate white hierarchies of beauty despite her *negra* identity.[36] Even still, she is considered abnormally attractive, a fact that only further reinforces the abjectification and degradation of black women. Though the young men laugh in the interaction, their comments are spoken as critiques of the way that *negras* are represented, rather than reflections of their own personal beliefs.

During an interview, Lilza, who identifies as *parda* but is viewed as white, complains that when she tells people she is an African-descendant they "laugh in my face." She takes pride in embracing her racial heritage and counters any challenge to her racial authenticity by offering, "eu também passo creme no meu cabelo" (I also use cream in my hair). At the same time, Lilza feels uncomfortable confronting the privileges that she receives on the basis of her embodied racial capital. Responding to my direct question about whether family members or others treat her differently on the basis of her appearance, she states,

> Oh, yeah, when you are pretty, people are nicer to you, they say nicer things about you. People treat you better when you are pretty, they think that you are nicer, and they are nicer to you. If I go to work wearing jeans, people will treat me different. [Elizabeth: But, what about color?] And then on top of that if you were white, they accept you better, faster. This is why a good appearance (*boa aparência*) is important.

In previous research and in conversations with other respondents, *boa aparência* is described as an ostensibly racially neutral phrase used to describe the white features and straight hair that are preferred in employees. As one respondent explains plainly, "*Boa aparência* means not being black and being pretty. Either you straighten your hair or you do not get the job." The phrase *boa aparência* is a racist euphemism used by employers to exclude Afro-Brazilians from professional opportunities on the basis of seemingly objective measures.[37] These connections elude Lilza, who instead frames *boa aparência* as a question of race-neutral principles, such as being *bem-arrumado* (well-groomed), wearing professional clothing, and using professional hair-grooming practices. Only when further questioned does she assert that *cabelo arrumado* (well-groomed hair) is by definition straight hair in Brazil and that one's racialization does have practical consequences.[38]

Dona Lara, Lilza's mother-in-law, is present during this conversation and hears Lilza further minimize the comments of blacks who, Lilza says, blame racism too much for job discrimination. Dona Lara, who is sick on the day of this conversation, becomes visibly upset and starts to tremble. She grabs my arm and states firmly:

Yes, yes, yes. It's, it's, it's the truth! They say it because it is the truth! White people say it doesn't exist, but we blacks know. Ask black people. We know because we live it!

She squeezes my arms and comes closer as she recounts how just two years before she was passed over for a position that she had legitimately earned. Though she had the highest score on the entrance exam for a training program, she was initially told that she had failed because the test administrators did not believe someone who looked like her could perform so well. Perhaps more noteworthy than the memory itself was the way in which she seemed to come alive during the interaction, speaking quickly, furiously, eager to tell what had happened to her. She loves her daughter-in-law, but disagrees with Lilza's framing of blacks as hypersensitive. She admits, with a hint of embarrassment, that after feeling "decepcionada pela experiência" (disappointed by the experience), she decided not to pursue the training program further. This was a conspicuously upsetting situation for her, and the emotional drama of it all left her feeling that it was not worth pursuing. In situations like these, the weight of negative experiences can compromise affective capital, leading a person to withdraw from the very opportunities that might help them.

Dona Lara is certainly not the only woman who has been passed over for a job because of her racialization and assumptions about her competency. In her work on women in Brazil, Doreen Gordon writes "blackness and poverty are gendered," which, she argues, partially explains why employers are reluctant to hire black women for positions that require face-to-face interaction.[39] I noticed throughout my time in Salvador that black women were absent in certain service-oriented positions. Restaurants and culinary services are among the only public places where black women were allowed to have a presence, and even this was limited by the type of restaurant. Fast-food restaurants (*restaurantes a quilo*), for example, would often have black women cooking and replacing the food in the buffet line. At up-scale restaurants, including expensive steakhouses (*churrascarias*), not only was it much less likely for a black woman to serve, but women were less likely to be working there. Thus not only do racialization and gendered inequality lead to differential opportunities, but inequality is produced or reinforced because of differential access to money.

Although researchers in Brazil and Latin America often discuss beauty and *boa aparência* as it relates to women in the workforce, rarely do they explore how these questions affect men's experiences. Alan is a black professional who wears his long natural hair either in braids or in a style that allows his thick curls to reach his shoulders. He has been successful in school and currently works at a prestigious public university in the Northeast. His styling choices are intentional, shaped by his desire to "combat stereotypes" about race, hair, and competency. As we talk, he scrolls through his phone to find a faculty picture taken at the university where he works, in which he is the only black person and his face is framed by the halo of a loose, coily afro. He explains that his family supports, or rather tolerates, his decision to wear his hair this way because they realize that they cannot convince him to cut it and because he has been able to gain a position at a prestigious university. He believes his aesthetic choice will positively influence the self-esteem of black students and change people's minds about the perceived correlation between hair texture and competence. As a man, he has more aesthetic flexibility than black women, who are often expected to present themselves as capable and attractive, which often precludes having unstraightened hair.

THE ROOTS OF RESISTANCE: AFRO-AESTHETICS

Interviews and observations make it clear that hair is a more decisive feature in determining racial categorization for women than other physical characteristics. Moreover, previous studies have noted that "Black women's hair is a key site for mapping and reflecting internal struggles and transformations related to race and gender," particularly for women who assume their blackness (*negras assumidas*).[40] Despite the potential economic and social consequences, several *negras assumidas* in the study refuse to straighten their hair because they consider it the physical manifestation of their racial identity. Moreover, two *negras assumidas* critique the constant vigilance and hair maintenance schedules of their friends and family members, whom they characterize as being addicted (*viciada*) to the chemicals and hair-straightening practices, as though they were a drug.[41]

Barbara, a *negra assumida*, shares that when she is offered a once-in-a-lifetime opportunity to work for the 2014 FIFA World Cup games as a representative, she is disheartened to learn from the training manual and orientation that she must straighten her hair to participate. Having recently cut off her previously chemically straightened hair as a reflection of her racial consciousness, Barbara is torn about what to do. In a quintessential example of gendered racial bargains, she decides that by blow-drying her hair straight, she can meet the standards of good appearance (*boa aparência*) in a way that will transform her curls only temporarily.

The economic and social significance that hair plays in the lives of Afro-Brazilians means that there is no dearth of new technologies designed to address their hair "problem." But how women choose to wear their hair reflects the creative and contradictory ways in which they negotiate the symbolic and material implications of racial appearance. In Brazil, researchers have increasingly addressed questions of embodiment and inequality, focusing on how Afro-Brazilians use their hair to affirm their racial identity and even improve their self-concept.[42] Adding to this research, I analyze how everyday women, most of whom are not *negras assumidas*, negotiate their bodies and work to maximize their embodied capital.

Per Brazilian beauty protocol, I walk into a local beauty salon for a manicure and pedicure. This was not originally part of my research; nor is it part of my normal beauty routine. But I had been reprimanded twice for violating beauty standards. Sonia, a mother of six, saw that I had chipped toenail polish and exclaimed, "Elizabeth, come here! I never want to see you walk out of your house like that again. Let me repaint your toenails!" That my chipped toenails were such an important detail in a country and community where families struggle to pay their rent and buy food spoke volumes about the importance of body, beauty, and gender in Salvador.

As I wait to be attended at the salon, a light brown woman with long, straight hair and features that mark her as *parda* (racially mixed), sits in the adjacent room in a salon chair, having a hair relaxer applied. After the cream has been applied, a light brown beautician with short, straightened hair circles the client's head with a space-age-looking bright blue laser. Instantly intrigued, I ask the beautician what the laser does. She smiles and replies, "it makes the hair look prettier, straighter." When the beautician finishes, the women in the salon look at the young lady approvingly, nodding and offering compliments. This procedure is known as "Photo Hair," which uses a laser to accelerate the absorption of hydrogen peroxide by the hair strands, shortens straightening time, and most importantly, makes the straightening last longer. The beautician, relying on a reading of her client's hair through a racist aesthetic lens, clarifies that straight hair and pretty hair are synonymous.

In Brazil, the emergence of an afro-aesthetics movement represents an ambitious effort to create new models of black beauty to recuperate blackness, by establishing Africa and African culture as points of pride rather than shame. In Patricia Pinho's preeminent piece on afro-aesthetics in Bahia, she notes that the movement is "one of the major realms for the production of new representations of blackness, reversing the nefarious meanings previously attributed to skin colour, hair texture, and facial features into signifiers of beauty and pride."[43] By challenging over three hundred years of racial degradation, the afro-aesthetics movement confronts the formidable task of redefining a collection of symbols and re-inscribing them with African cultural meaning. One strategy is to promote the incorporation of colors, patterns, and styles that are associated with Africa into the aesthetic realm. The end result is the creation of stylistically new products: afro-hair (*cabelo-afro*), afro-clothing, afro-makeup, afro-jewelry, and even afro-nails, which are called *afro* because they draw on patterns and color motifs that reflect the notion of a unified African identity.[44] New stores owned by blacks display patterns and fabrics that highlight notions of Africa and are emblazoned with images of women wearing their hair in afros. This all builds on the decades of cultural organizing that groups like Ilê Aiyê and Olodum began in the 1970s with the objective of affirming blackness.[45]

Afro-aesthetics' wide-reaching impact on culture in Salvador is most visibly seen in new hairstyles, including hair braiding and dreadlocks, and in the growing market for products designated as "afro."[46] Black activists, who for decades have been emphasizing the importance of self-acceptance, hope that the afro-aesthetics movement can foster revised notions of blackness. To do so, the afro-aesthetic movement draws on its diasporic links and embraces the "Black is beautiful" slogan from the United States and iconic imagery of Jamaica's Bob Marley to create products that foster racial pride and racial resistance.[47] Through its intentional appeal to fashion and the embodiment of blackness, the movement aims to highlight the symbolic realm where what is considered an authentic cultural "blackness" is explicitly linked to Africa.[48]

On the streets, on buses, and in public areas, black hair styles (*cabelo-afro*) can be easily observed. The movement addresses both hair texture and hairstyling because both have been historically important. Graciana reveals,

Me, I am seventy-one years old, and I felt it in my own skin. My mother never braided my hair when I was younger, and I would love to see the children with braids who were blacker than me. She would say, "No, that is *criolo*, it is *criolo*. I don't want it!" They were the small braids, you know. But no, my mom would curl my hair so it would look like Shirley Temple. Just like Shirley Temple. I felt this. I remember my father didn't let me comb my hair with his comb. Because he said that I had black people's hair.

Certainly times have changed since Graciela was a young girl, but what have been enduring are the negative associations attached to afro-textured hair and items related to African culture. Because braids have a historical association with Africanness, they were not an option for Graciela; her mother called them *criolo*, a derogatory term used to describe blacks in Brazil. Instead, the idealized image of beauty and femininity was the young, white Shirley Temple from the United States. Yet even with a "white" hairstyle, Graciela could not escape perceptions of the inferior quality of her hair, of which her father's actions reminded her.

Although this negative racial affect still exists, elements of the afro-aesthetics movement have slowly become incorporated into the socialization practices in some families. *Blaque pau* (pronounced Black-EE Pow), originates from the phrase *Black Power* in the United States and refers to hair worn in its unstraightened, naturally curly, or kinky state. In Brazil, the hairstyle has been gaining popularity. Fernanda, a college-age *preta* who wears bright headscarves and does not straighten her hair, states that just a few years ago when she would board the public bus, she would never see anyone else with natural hair. Now, she says, it is common to travel around Salvador and see black women proudly wearing their naturally curly or coily hair or even elaborate *amarrações* (head wraps).

Though *Blaque pau* is typically used to describe hair styled as an afro, it has been used to describe other aspects of art and culture as well. Walter explains:

Blaque . . . when we say Blaque here it is not only a question of color. Blaque is a way of . . . it is a style that the person has. How they do their hair. That loose hair, that full hair, that is the Blaque style. Nowadays many people want to have an afro but they can't. (Walter, 19)

Walter also is proud that his hair can do what other people's hair cannot. For him, *Blaque pau* is about a hair style, but it is also about one's personal style more generally. He has a penchant for theater and an increased consciousness about race because of the afro-aesthetics movement, and this has led him to adopt a race-specific artistic nickname:

My creative name is Blaque. I love my color and I like afros. When I went to make my brand . . . when I was taking a class, a teacher told me that I had to choose a trademark. At that time, I was wearing my hair a little longer on the top and there was a song that had just come out that was saying afro hair and braided hair were great. So I like my afro, but I did not like the idea of talking about *negros* and *pretos*. I named myself Blaque and everyone knows that it means black.

Walter is inspired by songs that affirm his emerging afro-aesthetic, and he incorporates that aesthetic into his artistic identity. A major struggle for black activists in Brazil is convincing Afro-Brazilians to *assumir-se*, or assume their blackness, so Walter's act is potentially progressive. However, the remaining part of his quote substantiates the fear that the movement will be co-opted or reduced to stylistic preferences without political grounding.[49] Walter wants to adopt the hairstyle and the aesthetic, but he admits that he does not want to discuss race or racism. Although co-optation is sometimes viewed as the inevitable conclusion to an aesthetics movement, ideally it occurs after considerable political mobilization has occurred and gains have been made.[50]

As I participated in a seminar on afro-aesthetics in Salvador in July 2013, one young Brazilian participant excitedly asked me if I could tell her whether her colorful nails were, in fact, afro-nails. Her sincere question about the authenticity of her nails exemplifies both the successes and the limitations of the movement. As afro-aesthetics gains momentum and popularity, there is always the danger that it will be co-opted and divorced from the movement's political foundation. When such co-optation happens, objects, styles, and preferences reflecting the notion of Africa and Africanness are reduced to mere fashion items. As one respondent declared when critiquing what he perceived as the superficiality of elements of the movement and of the movement's impact in Brazil, "Hoje é da moda ser Negão. . . . É verdade!" (Nowadays, it's in style to be a really black man. . . . It's true!).

The effectiveness of the afro-aesthetics movement at fostering racial consciousness is further challenged by Edna's perception about how black hairstyles are used in her family:

You see people wearing their hair in braids more during the time when Carnaval is coming. After it is over, everybody goes back to straightening their hair. (Edna, 36)

Thus, even when Afro-Brazilians wear their hair in braids, they do not necessarily internalize a political racial consciousness, or they may view it as an enjoyable but temporary racial performance. That blackness is considered suitable to be performed only one week out of the year reinforces the exploitation of blackness as a commodity, which connects to broader ways in which blackness is superficially incorporated for monetary gain.[51]

Another element of the afro-aesthetics movement is thick braids that are created by weaving synthetic hair into plaited sections of one's own hair in order to produce a style that is shoulder length or longer. The use of these braids offers a visual aesthetic that counters gendered and racialized aesthetic hierarchies. But hearing Afro-Brazilian women discuss why they have elected to use synthetic braids reveals the more complicated meanings attached to these styles. Some black women report using synthetic braids primarily as a way to avoid doing their own "bad" hair, rather than out of any specific interest in afro-aesthetics. Others report that braids provide them with a way to achieve the bounce that is responsible for the appeal of "good" hair. Across the diaspora the complaint can be heard that "our hair never moves"; in Brazil, hair is not good hair unless it bounces.[52] But even as I problematize these perspectives, I am cautious about recognizing how Afro-Brazilians are negotiating their racialization alongside gender hierarchies. The hegemony of whiteness means that the introduction of alternate hairstyles that decenter whiteness makes an intervention that challenges white normativity. When hair styling and grooming are viewed as questions of embodied capital, the decisions that women make can be more clearly framed in terms of symbolic and material power, rather than matters of self-hatred. But these ideas are not mutually exclusive; rather, they function concurrently. That is, Afro-Brazilians may feel as though their natural hair needs to be improved, but they are also seeking a way to achieve beauty that feels authentic. Thus the use of alternative hairstyles, with or without a specific political consciousness, illustrates that Afro-Brazilian women are actively participating in negotiating and redefining beauty hierarchies within the constraints of their social locations.

The goal of the afro-aesthetics movement is to convince all Brazilians, but Afro-Brazilians specifically, to reevaluate normative aesthetic standards and to embrace other types of beauty and styles that reflect Brazil's racial and ethnic diversity. The message of accepting and valuing oneself takes on even more urgency in light of the puzzling and disturbing interactions I observe among children at a local community center. As I sit in on an art course for children, I observe Afro-Brazilian girls stroking the straight hair of their white and straight-haired peers during instructional time, during classroom breaks, and during lunch. Even as they participate in conversations with peers and teachers, they continue running their fingers through the straight hair of their white classmates.

During breaks, these young Afro-Brazilian girls run to the bathroom and douse their hair with water in order to achieve a look that is wet and wavy, rather than dry or "bad," and then they return to class. Their straight-haired peers, the objects of their attention, do not respond to the attention, and everyone acts as though this is a normal part of their daily activities. Straight hair is considered desirable and valued, and the young black girls, many of whom cannot attain it themselves, seem to be trying to grasp it physically by stroking the hair of other young girls. These young black girls and the girls in the core families I interviewed are all very aware of standards of beauty and how they do not fit them, so they struggle to figure out how they can attain or navigate unrealistic aesthetic hierarchies that seem to only accentuate racial differences.

Community centers may be permeable sites for racial inequality, but they can also be spaces that, like families, resist racial hierarchies. As part of a course on afro-aesthetics at the same community center, I attend six classes in which a talented hair-styling instructor trains a group of between ten and twenty black women, using a large doll head similar to the type used in cosmetology courses. The instructor, Carla, is a striking black woman with dark skin and African facial features, and she often wears beautiful, colorful head wraps that match her afrocentric style. Having previously been selected as the queen of Ilê Aiyê in a black beauty pageant organized by the cultural group Ilê Aiyê, she has had several years of experience styling hair and designing clothes. During the class, Carla demonstrates the correct way to braid using synthetic hair. She circulates the doll head so we can all take turns practicing her technique by plaiting and weaving in the braids. The end result is a white, blonde mannequin head filled with *tranças* (braids) of all different shapes, colors, and sizes. It is an odd sight to see black Brazilian women weaving synthetic hair into the blonde mannequin's head. This becomes less strange when one considers that many of the women view this class as providing professional training that may improve their financial situation as hair braiders for foreign (presumably white) clients.

Carla does not just train her students on afro-aesthetics; she insists on spending the entire first hour of each three-hour class meeting discussing aesthetics as it relates to cultural affirmation and racial identity. At one point, a black, female psychologist she has invited to visit the class brings copies of the bell hooks article "Straightening Our Hair" in Portuguese ("Alisando os nossos cabelhos") in order to have a deeper discussion about racial identity, hair, and self-esteem for black diasporic women. In this way, the community space provides a way for black women to develop skills that can lead to their economic empowerment, access to an alternative form of embodied capital based on afro-aesthetics, and a forum for discussion of the challenges related to their hair and racialized bodies that many of them face within their homes.

Throughout the course, the women sit in a large circle and share narratives about how their decisions to wear their hair naturally was a point of contention in their families. Moving beyond hair, these discussions often initiate broader conversations about race, particularly about the way families have internalized racism in ways that affect these women. One student confesses that her mother not only doesn't support natural hair, she doesn't believe that blacks should be doctors. Others reveal that despite being humiliated in public because of their hair, they have decided to continue wearing it naturally. Still other students remain quiet, hoping to learn the technique but uncertain about wearing braids themselves and unsure whether to assume their blackness.

The quest for self-affirmation leads some women to wear synthetic braids or a *Blaque* (afro), and others to use a chemical relaxer or Mega Hair (long, straight, natural-looking extensions). But since 2010, Salvador has offered another alternative: the Instituto Beleza Natural (the Natural Beauty Institute).

INSTITUTO BELEZA NATURAL:
THE MCDONALDSIZATION OF BEAUTY

In 2010, coinciding with my fieldwork, the Instituto Beleza Natural opened a franchise in Salvador. The Instituto is a salon created by Zica, an Afro-Brazilian entrepreneur, black hair guru, and former domestic worker. One of the first black multimillionaires in the country, Zica experienced a meteoric rise to fame in Brazil as a result of her hair technique. Her original inspiration for Beleza Natural was a vision of providing a natural hair solution for women that did not require hair straightening. With Zica's trademark technique, the salon promises to transform frizzy hair into defined curls. With over 300,000 Facebook followers, the salon offers high-demand services that it markets with a colorful and modern website featuring young, smiling faces of Afro-Brazilian women who upload before-and-after pictures along with testimonials about how much the hair treatment has changed their lives.[53]

Instituto Beleza Natural is easily the largest hair salon in the city. Strategically located in the center of Liberdade, the largest black neighborhood in Salvador, it has had a considerable impact on the way Afro-Brazilian women negotiate beauty norms and embodied racial capital. Researchers have only begun to analyze the salon as an important site of racial contestation and identity negotiation. I draw on their work as well as on observations from my own visits.[54] Having been handed fliers advertising the salon and having heard both compliments and criticisms of it, I visited the salon three times and listened to two formal presentations by the local and regional managers.

What becomes immediately clear upon entering the three-story Instituto is that the hair treatment is merely one element of its business model. The enormous building is nothing short of luxurious, and it accommodates over a hundred employees and thousands of customers who enter each month. Aesthetically appealing, the inside of the building is designed with glass doors, large open waiting rooms, free Wi-Fi, and unlimited water and coffee for visitors.[55] The salon still shows signs of newness, with bright recessed and studio lights that reflect off of the shiny white ceramic tile floors and enhance the already pristine appeal.

Smiling faces of black women with long curly and treated hair can be seen on all of the reading material and on the walls of the salon. But the most persuasive models for the services are the black female consultants, who must all undergo the chemical treatment as a requirement for employment.[56] The Instituto is one of the finest examples of Ford-style assembly-line production that I have observed in Brazil or anywhere.[57] The salon is separated into four major areas, for washing, chemical application, drying, and styling. It also has a special upstairs area to accommodate VIP customers and large caravans of Afro-Brazilian women from across the country who travel to Salvador to receive the trademark hair treatment.

Upon arrival, each client receives a free, private introductory session with a consultant in which her unique hair needs are assessed. During this session, the hair consultant determines whether hair is healthy enough to be treated and also discusses the relationship between hair and self-esteem. If the client is approved, she schedules the chemical application, choosing either the *super-relaxante* (super relaxer) or the *relaxante* (relaxer) treatment.

The hairstyle that is achieved at the end of the process looks similar to crimped hair or dry, elongated curly hair, depending on the client's original hair texture. The treatment, including required hair products, costs approximately $R50 to $R70 in Brazilian Reais and must repeated every four weeks; this amounts to roughly 10 percent of the monthly minimum wage in Brazil.

Beauty salons "can be analyzed as a site where hegemonic gender, class, sexuality, and race tropes simultaneously are produced and problematized."[58] Though the Instituto Beleza Natural caters primarily to Afro-Brazilian women, it intentionally uses color-blind language in marketing, never mentioning race and instead focusing explicitly on the way that hair grooming practices can help women overcome class barriers. Instituto creator Zica thus contributes to a racial ideology that silences any questions that deal with race and body and replaces it with a color-blind and class-based rhetoric.[59]

Additionally, Beleza Natural's use of a language that focuses on treatment or improvement seems to exploit the racial anxieties of black women. It suggests that afro-textured, coily hair is acceptable but needs to be improved by undergoing a chemical process. On the other hand, the meanings that women themselves attach to their beauty practices must also be considered. Women can take creative measures to accommodate the dominant ideologies while simultaneously carving out a space to challenge the same hierarchies.[60]

Many clients claim that the services offered by the Instituto Beleza Natural, despite the cookie-cutter end result, the cost, and the use of chemicals, have provided them with the confidence they need to be successful in the job market. That Afro-Brazilian women are willing to spend a handsome proportion of their monthly income on this beauty ritual is a reflection less on Beleza Natural than on the value of beauty in Brazilian society. For many of these women, beauty is money, and they view the treatment as the quickest and most effective way to increase their embodied racial capital without having to subscribe to straight-hair standards. The women who frequent the Instituto Beleza Natural and invest in this service are no different from others who desire to exert agency in the face of constrained options. By articulating the close connection between hair and economic opportunity, the salon does not promise racial affirmation, but instead focuses on access to the job market, social mobility, and even improved affective relationships.[61]

Newsletters produced by Beleza Natural suggest that black men are increasingly being targeted as potential clients. Though their experiences at the salon will not be discussed here, their experiences do shed light on the relationship between racialized ideas of good appearance and perceived economic mobility. The labor that men exert to fit aesthetic standards and to maximize their embodied capital often goes undertheorized even though there are compelling reasons to consider the barbershop politics that illustrate how black men embody their identities.[62]

Fernando, who self-classifies as *negro*, explains that his family has never supported his decision to grow out his afro-textured hair. He says that their wishes are a reflection of their internalization of racial hierarchies as much as their concern about whether he would be able to get a job. He tells how his long hair affected his job search:

> I graduated from the Federal University. I applied for a competitive job as a public servant. I passed the test (*concurso*), and I had to go in for an interview, a meeting with a psychologist, and [a meeting with] the human resources person. She told me that I would need to cut my hair if I wanted the job. Well, she did not tell me I had to cut it, but that if I wanted the job, it would be best to cut it. So, I cut it off. It was longer than this before (*pointing to his full afro*). I got the job, and then I let my hair grow again. They cannot fire me now, even if they wanted to! (*laughs loudly*).

Fernando delights in his critical accommodation, having temporarily adopted racist aesthetic requirements in order to achieve his professional goals, only to later grow his hair out again. But most Brazilians, let alone most Afro-Brazilians, do not have jobs that offer the type of security and freedom from termination that public servants enjoy. For people in other fields of employment, the decision to straighten or chemically alter their hair cannot be understood as a simple case of self-hatred or self-denial. Beleza Natural, which promotes unstraightened hair but requires expensive chemicals to treat curly or coily hair, is an important though not unproblematic intervention for black women who have been rendered invisible and devalued by popular beauty standards.

HIDE MY ROOTS! AFRO-AESTHETICS AND CULTURAL MOVEMENTS AT HOME

How do families in Salvador respond to changes in how Bahia is being portrayed abroad, to the growing emphasis on Afro-Bahian culture in the rest of the world, and to the afro-aesthetics movement? Data suggest a significant disconnect between international portrayals of Salvador and the lived experiences of poor and working-class Afro-Brazilians. On a Saturday night, twenty-two-year-old Conceição (black) and her cousin Paulinha (white) are getting ready to go to a club. They have been dressing and undressing all evening trying to figure out which outfits are the best to wear. I sit on Paulinha's bed as they unabashedly take on and off their dresses, comparing their breast sizes and complaining that their breasts are not big enough. Paulinha's young brother Leo is also in the room, but he appears to be accustomed to their nakedness and barely responds. After Conceição gets dressed, her cousin slowly runs a heated flat iron through her hair. Hoping to straighten the hair at her temples and behind her ear, Conceição holds her ear down and flinches a little while laughing and demanding, "Girl, even if it burns me, hide my roots!" She prides herself on her hair and brags that she can get any man because she is *negra com cabelo índio*, or black with Indian hair.

Although natural hairstyles are common on the street and among some college students, in the core families I am studying, this is not a popular choice.[63] For families in this study, the Afro-Brazilian cultural heritage that is promoted at an international level and heralded by the tourism industry in Bahia is not viewed in the same way in their homes. Few cultural practices are consciously marked or discussed as black, African, or Afro-Brazilian. Cultural celebrations, including the Festa de Iemanjá, which theoretically celebrates the Candomblé goddess of the sea, are enjoyed by many as a secular holiday and reframed as Brazilian rather than Afro-Brazilian. In the Festa de Iemanjá parade that accompanies the celebration, Iemanjá is represented by an enormous statue that is carried down the street, and often she has white skin and very long, straight black hair. Even the practice of making an offering to her is performed out of tradition, not religious conviction. In fact, many of the respondents who celebrate the festival of Iemanjá wince when Candomblé is mentioned or respond with looks of disgust and fear.

Likewise, although black dolls are sold in bulk to tourists in a number of stores around the city, they are almost completely absent from the Afro-Brazilian homes I visit. When I introduce coloring books and crayons, the young girls do not color the faces brown. When they do decide to outline a face in brown, they insist on using yellow crayons to color the hair. This is no surprise considering how proudly they show me their book bags, which bear the image of a blonde-haired, blue-eyed Barbie or Cinderella. In shopping centers and stores, I rarely see a black doll. The only black dolls I observe are the very dark-skinned dolls and figurines intended for tourists, not for children in Salvador. In 2010, when there was an international Barbie exposition at Salvador Mall, I figured it was a must-see event. A large area in the mall was cordoned off with life-size displays of Barbies from around the world. I asked a colleague to take my picture as I posed near the African Barbie, who stood alone as the children seemed to be less interested in her than in any of the others.

Despite these limitations, black women in Lua Cheia do incorporate some aspects of afro-aesthetics into their beauty routines. Some respondents use synthetic braids and enjoy having me put twists and natural braids into their hair, but only for fun. One of the young girls, Janete, is an aspiring hair stylist who practices her trade on her friends in the community. Given that tourists enjoy having their hair braided as part of the Brazilian experience, Janete's mother is very encouraging of this career goal. At the same time, the majority of the adult women in the study maintain their monthly appointments for hair relaxers or have their hair blow-dried straight. Hair salons seem more ubiquitous than grocery stores in Salvador, and Luana, who struggles to pay her rent each month, prioritizes her hair appointments. I am careful about how I interpret this in light of research that suggests that self-care and beautification offer a way for black women to express a "sense of entitlement to economic, emotional and social well-being and an effort at its attainment."[64] Consistent with this, Luana says that she needs to go to the salon because otherwise she feels run-down (*acabada*); in other words these beautification efforts are investments in her affective and embodied capital. Her monthly hair care visits make her feel better about herself, which is as much about race as it is about gender.

DIASPORIC DIMENSIONS

Baianos are certainly not alone in facing the pervasiveness of hegemonic whiteness. Racialized notions of beauty and the abjectification of black bodies relates to babies, hair, and aesthetics in societies across the diaspora. The common use of the phrase *buena presencia* (good appearance) in Spanish-speaking regions of Latin America closely parallels how *boa aparência* functions to eliminate people of visible African ancestry from job opportunities in Brazil.[65] *Boa aparência* and *buena presencia* are manifestations not merely of an ideology but of a racial system in which one's racial location, specifically one's proximity to whiteness, is rewarded with material and affective advantages. In the United States there are no longer signs and policies indicating that blacks need not apply, but nebulous terms such as *fit* and *professionalism* are often code words for racialized behaviors and physical characteristics.[66]

The deconstruction of a black body illustrates that no feature is left above reproach. Though in the study no families directly mentioned the way that lip size is racialized, researchers provide examples of mothers and family members in Latin America who warn blacks to "Cierre la bemba!" (Close your *bemba*!). *Bemba* is an offensive term used to describe thick lips, so the demand is an abrasive and offensive admonishment to control one's racial features by closing one's mouth so one's bottom lip does not hang down.[67] The pervasiveness of whitening might suggest that skin color is the major target of embodied practices, and it certainly can be in some regions. However, what this chapter illustrates is that the entire body is racialized and mapped with ideas about whiteness.[68]

Responding to similar phenotypic hierarchies, but never observed or even mentioned in these families, skin bleaching provides a "unique lens through which to view the workings of the Western-dominated global system as it simultaneously promulgates a 'white is right' ideology."[69] In Jamaica, blacks' use of skin bleaching or "brownin'" has precipitated a broader debate about whether these products should be regulated and whether their use is a symptom of self-hatred. Critical of those who frame skin bleaching as simply a reflection of self-hatred, some researchers argue that bleaching in Jamaica has elements of transgression because it "destabilizes popular conceptions of blackness" and allows women and men to play the race game more effectively.[70] But if playing the race game involves excising and erasing multiple parts of one's body and internalizing ideologies of whitening, I argue that gendered racial bargains are dangerous because it is difficult to play the game without also getting played yourself.

DISCUSSION

In Brazil, concerns about body and appearance dominate every aspect of social life. How can they not do so in a country where social interactions are based on being able to quickly interpret and respond to racialized and gendered bodies? For all Brazilian women the relationship between gender and beauty is a trap that heightens their self-consciousness and compels them to engage in some level of self-surveillance and self-modification.[71] But for women who identify as *negra* or whose racial features do not approximate aesthetic norms, the level of surveillance and modification involved is significant, as are the perceived potential rewards. Aesthetics and hair grooming are not simply about vanity. They represent embodied capital, symbols of power, and the gateway to attaining valued social resources. Considering that businesses implicitly make hiring decisions using criteria of *boa aparência*, some argue that access to free plastic surgery should be a right for Brazil's poor population![72] Intense pressures to conform to beauty norms and sanctions against those who do not comply, as well as the material outcomes related to attaining beauty standards, explain, in part, why Brazil has the second highest rate of plastic surgery in the world.[73]

Afro-Brazilian women find themselves at a crossroads, seeking to find validation as women and also aspiring to counter the negative stereotypes associated with the racialized meanings attached to their bodies. The afro-aesthetics movement has in some ways given a voice to these racial and gender dilemmas and provided visibility to black cultural forms, as well as created alternative avenues for black women and men to negotiate beauty hierarchies on their own terms. Though it has had limited success at raising the racial consciousness of all who partake in it, the visibility and accessibility of new aesthetic possibilities are considerable contributions given the history of abjectification of blackness and degradation of black womanhood more specifically.

Additional considerations must be taken into account to determine why the styles of the afro-aesthetics movement have not become more widespread. During my time in Salvador, none of the employees at banks, and few government officials or major television personalities, adopted afro-styles. Though these styles are becoming a more popular choice as an expression of cultural diversity, they are still viewed as threatening and unprofessional, and they can potentially threaten one's economic mobility. Re-Africanization is embraced discursively and on a limited cultural level to entertain an international audience, but this does not necessarily apply to black Brazilians in their day-to-day professional lives.[74] On the other hand, the growing interest in natural hair among racially conscious and upwardly mobile college students has contributed to increased opportunities for Afro-Brazilian women to become entrepreneurs and start their own businesses capitalizing on afro-aesthetics, including hair braiding and other hair-styling options.

The development of Instituto Beleza Natural and the broader afro-aesthetics movement has an important but complex role in challenging hegemonic whiteness in Brazil. While the Instituto should be problematized for framing curly and kinky hair as needing to be improved, it simultaneously provides an alternative model of beauty that is not based so squarely on the standard white aesthetic of straight hair. Though this "natural" process is achieved with chemicals, the end product is more defined curls, rather than the elimination of curls. Perhaps the development of this salon is a normal step in a successive process of black liberation. In the long run, the availability of hair-straightening products and techniques may lead to the development of "natural" aesthetic interventions. As Afro-Brazilians feel more empowered to shape and mold their own image, the development of more counterhegemonic aesthetic practices may emerge. The question is whether Afro-Brazilians can remain vigilant and critical of the ways in which even resistance efforts can reproduce dominant hierarchies.

When black women and families with babies engage in visibility management that performs mainstream notions of beauty, they increase their embodied capital and may be rewarded for it economically and affectively. The goal of the afro-aesthetics movement is to present an alternative path to embodied capital that challenges dominant images of whiteness. In the vision of the movement, embodied capital and affective capital are maximized when people can express their authentic selves, rather than being alienated by oppressive and unachievable models of beauty and culture. Considering the political foundation of the afro-aesthetics movement, the best measure of whether the vision of the movement has been achieved may rest less in aesthetics than in its ability to encourage Afro-Brazilians to organize for structural equality and visibility beyond the cultural realm. The movement's demise may be the best indication of its success if it fosters internalization of a new ideology at the national level that proclaims, "Eu prefiro ter cabeça do que cabelo!": What is in my head is more important than what is on my head!

CHAPTER 3

HOME IS WHERE THE HURT IS:
AFFECTIVE CAPITAL, STIGMA,
AND RACIALIZATION

We cannot value ourselves rightly without first breaking through the walls of denial, which hide the depth of black self-hatred, inner anguish, and unreconciled pain.
BELL HOOKS, *BLACK LOOKS*

LIVING IN A RACIALIZED SOCIAL system, Afro-Brazilians are inundated with racial images, dehumanizing messages, and structural inequality, which when paired with negative experiences in their homes, have significant material and emotional consequences. Social psychologists in Brazil have used phrases such as "social humiliation" and "traumatic conflictive situation" to convey the omnipresent psychological threat that results from living in a society where access to basic necessities is denied, where one is socially invisible, and where there is chronic exposure to various forms of social inequality and systematic exclusion.[1] These terms have been used to describe how stressful social conditions undermine black women's mental and physical health in Brazil.[2] As much as Brazilianists explain the nuances and complexity of the phenotypic continuum, this flexibility offers very little consolation for those who are situated at the extreme racial pole of blackness. Stated most succinctly by interviewee Nina, "Dark-skinned black women (*pretas*) are the most rejected group in Brazil."

These negative social psychological outcomes are connected to sociologically informed concerns that examine the mechanisms through which racial hierarchies gain legitimacy and affect day-to-day interactions and experiences. Racial features have been described as personal attributes that may function as a "deeply discrediting" stigma and may lead to a negative or "spoiled" social identity.[3] Over time, the members of a society who possess stigmatized features are vulnerable to structural inequalities—including historical exclusions, media misrepresentations, and discriminatory treatment—and negative interpersonal relations that concretize associations between the possession of racialized features and stereotypes.[4]

The socialization of racial affect that occurs in families is critical because "negative parental affect in childhood and adolescence can create a 'successively contingent process'" whereby early disadvantages lead to and compound later disadvantages.[5] These have significant developmental implications, yet the unique consequences of negative affect produced through racialization or racial socialization in families remains understudied.[6] This chapter explores how racial and phenotypic differentiation influence Afro-Brazilians' self-esteem, sense of belonging, experiences of psychological distress, and exposure to traumatic experiences.[7] Using a theoretical conceptual frame of affective capital, I discuss how the unequal distribution of affective resources in families leads to differential experiences of support, love, and encouragement, which has a lasting impact on one's life chances. The resources gained from having high levels of affective capital is what helps people to develop positive self-esteem, drives them to pursue ambitious projects, and allows them to pursue relationships that are beneficial to them.

INCOG-NEGRO: ABANDONING BLACKNESS

Research suggests that negative racial socialization within families can lead to an "alienating symbolic reality" and "identity fragmentation," particularly among women.[8] These experiences can lead a woman to actively assume a black identity, but they can also lead both women and men to pursue a trajectory of racial distance and abandonment of one's own family and even children. The latter trajectory is more common than the path to racial and gender activism, at least among respondents in this study.

The Pereira family is composed of a father and his three daughters, all of whom have features that mark them as black. Their life history offers a cogent example of how the internalization of racial and phenotypic hierarchies compromises the quality of familial relationships and leads to abandonment and exploitation. Fifty-four-year-old Tânia and her sisters offer a riveting account of why their father abandoned them, in part because of his racial ambitions:

> My father was really bad. Just horrible! He drank a lot. . . . When my mother died, he started staying out late with a lot of different women. As little as we were, little girls, he left us at home by ourselves. He decided to

marry one of the white women he was dating, so he split us up and gave us away to other families so he could have children with her. I was six years old. . . . The new family treated me like a slave. He didn't take care of us but he took care of his new white family.

In this example, the pursuit of forming a white or whiter family led a father to callously distribute his three black daughters to different families around the city. If it was unclear whether race and phenotypic differences were the driving force behind his abandonment, they were convinced of it when they observed him with his lighter-skinned progeny, praising them by pointing and saying, "Look, now he's *limpando a raça* (cleaning the race)!" For these sisters, their father's desire to form a whiter family did not simply undermine their relationship with him, it affected their sense of self-worth and led to years of vulnerability and abuse.

As a result of their father's abandonment, Tânia and her two sisters endured several years of exploitation and physical and emotional abuse as *filhas de criação* (raised daughters) in families that informally adopted them. This practice is not uncommon in the Northeast of Brazil. Afro-Brazilian girls are regularly informally adopted and live as raised daughters in the homes of wealthier, often lighter or white families, where they provide labor in exchange for food and shelter.[9]

Tânia was sent to live with a wealthy couple, Benedita and Antonio, who were married and had no children. Rebeca, her older sister, was informally adopted by a married couple who had a toddler, a young baby, and plans for more children. When she first entered her new home, Tânia was asked to call her new family members aunt (*tia*) and uncle (*tio*); similarly, Rebeca was asked to call the matriarch in her new family godmother. The naming process was an important step in their socialization because it created the impression that they were full members of the family. However, they soon learned that these names were given to foster the illusion of family and to mask the power dynamics that drive these relationships.[10]

When Tânia is asked to provide details about her childhood as a *filha de criação*, she states:

The truth is, . . . if I were to speak honestly I did not have a childhood, I did not have an adolescence. I considered myself an adult ever since I was a child because of the type of life we had. [I did] everything, everything, everything! I washed, ironed, cooked, cleaned, and went grocery shopping.

Tânia rattles off the list of responsibilities effortlessly, vividly recalling the hefty tasks that were assigned to her as a nine-year-old. She recalls that her responsibilities began immediately upon her arrival in the home and that they were all-encompassing, leaving little time for enjoyable activities. She recalls being required to go to school, but only because her *tia* disliked uneducated people. Tânia's education was encouraged not because it was considered a basic right but because it fulfilled the whim of her *tia*. Even though schooling provided opportunities for both education and socializing, Tânia was required to come straight home after school and was prohibited from having friends or dating until she was well into her thirties.

Elaborating on her feeling of having lost her childhood, Rebeca describes what it was like to raise her adoptive family's children beginning at the age of ten years old:

> I wanted to study, and my godmother didn't really let me. . . . Back then Anastasia was a baby and Anastasia's mom said, "No, you are only going to school only once you have put Anastasia to sleep." So, I went to school after I put Anastasia to sleep. If she didn't go to sleep, I didn't go to school. My responsibilities were to take care of them [Anastasia and her brother]. They slept with me. I woke up in the middle of the night to give them *mingau* (porridge). When Anastasia cried during the night I had to get up to warm her up a bottle. [Her mother] She slept. It was me who had to get up. I was an adult-child (*criança-adulto*). I went all around Salvador with Rafael and Anastasia, and I had to do it all.

Not only was education viewed as a privilege rather than a right for Rebeca, but she was also socialized to prioritize servitude over her basic education. When she prepared the older children for their naps by bathing them and dressing them, she remained uncertain about whether she would be allowed to go to school. Rebeca laments having had to negotiate competing role expectations, and is visibly angry as she recounts how she sacrificed her childhood raising Anastasia and Rafael while their mother rested soundly at night. When asked to speak about the specific ways that she was treated differently, Rebeca focuses on her extensive list of domestic chores:

> I had to clean the apartment, sometimes at night after Rafael went to sleep. I had to clean the bathroom. When it was time to sleep I was cleaning the bathroom. We would have to wake up at 4 or 4:30 in the morn-

ing to carry water, clean the house, clean up after the dog, and everything else. It was me and Tânia when we lived close to each other.

Rebeca resents having had to fetch and carry huge barrels of water as a child. She recounts how she and her sister crossed several roads very early in the morning to bring water from a community well so their adoptive families would have water for baths and cooking. Rebeca is perturbed when she recalls that though everyone needed the water, the adults slept or sat on the porch watching as the girls took several grueling trips to the well to retrieve water. Moreover, even though she and Tânia provided the water, they were permitted to bathe only if there was water left after everyone else had finished their baths.

When she is asked to explain the differential treatment that she experienced, Tânia focuses on the emotional and affective realm. She deemphasizes her labor at home and focuses more on abuse, isolation, and her feelings of extreme sadness:

> You feel the distance in the way that you're treated, the way you are insulted and humiliated. All of this stays with you. Humiliation in front of other people, cursing at me, hitting me, . . . it really leaves you with your face on the floor. What stands out most are the things that were said. The words, the insults, like "find your lowly position," "tramp," phrases [like] "you have nothing," "you will never have anything." You realize that you are really property. I can beat my property, I can ask it to do anything, I can do anything to it.[11]

Tânia's chilling statement that she is "property" illustrates how her personhood has been undermined, her desires have become irrelevant, and she has come to feel that her existence is merely to serve others. This resonates with why scholars have linked the practice of informal adoption to slavery.[12]

Quite different from Rebeca, who was called an "ingrate" by her adopted family because she left the family after she became engaged, Tânia continues to live with her "aunt" Benedita. Tânia's narrative of violence, abuse, and exploitation is even more devastating because she has endured the relationship for over four decades. Throughout our interview, Tânia works to resolve the contradiction between being told that she is an "adoptive daughter" and feeling exploited. Tânia subversively rejects being called an adoptive daughter in public and refuses to forget the pain that has been inflicted on her. She states:

It's very easy to open your mouth and say: "She is my adoptive daughter." But you're not treated as a daughter. I think that to feel that you have to feel affection. You have to receive affection, get attention, like a daughter! I don't feel that. I don't feel it because you can't change the way you think or the way you see the things that happened to you and what you heard and then place a cloth on top of it and say, "No, she is my daughter."[13]

For both Tânia and Rebeca, but particularly for Tânia, membership in a family is not simply about a title but about love, affection, and sincere feelings of belonging. It is the emotional neglect and the complete dismissal of her emotional needs and personhood, more than the exploitation, that is so devastating and enduring to Tânia. As a result, she has a difficult time trusting people, is still a virgin, and has determined that she deserves this treatment.

There were several cases of *filhas de criação* among the families in this study, but only one other situation in which a family's decision to send their child away was shaped by race and phenotype. In sixty-seven-year-old Camila's narrative about her mother's life, she reports that her mother was sent away from her biological family because of her race:

When she was six years old, they sent her to live with another family. You know what my mom was? Her father was Spanish and she was born with white skin. She couldn't stay in the community where she lived because it was in a *quilombo* [a runaway slave community]. So she went to live in another family to give the children in that family company. She lost the notion of what it meant to be black because she was not raised with blacks.

Camila's mother was displaced for racial reasons and went to live as a playmate in a family with white children. Her mother did not choose to abandon blackness, but perhaps it can be said that blackness abandoned or expelled her. Not only had her mother "lost the notion" of blackness because of this experience, but, Camila recalls, her mother socialized her to avoid blacks and cultural practices that are associated with black people.[14]

These examples illustrate the psychological aftermath experienced by Afro-Brazilians who are abandoned by their families because of phenotypic considerations. In some families there is not physical abandonment but a lack of support, low levels of encouragement, and feelings of inadequacy. Thiago and Arivaldo, who identify as black, insist on being interviewed together because they grew up as close cousins on an island outside of Salvador. Thiago explains how the lack of support and encouragement that he received in comparison to his white siblings affected his life:

> THIAGO: So, my mom was always saying why couldn't we be more like our white brothers who lived in Salvador. We needed to be rich and successful like them. Except with our dad, who was a cowboy and poor, . . . she kept saying we needed to be like them. And when they came to the island we would have the table all set for them. They sent the money but we had to make a feast (*banquete*) for them. They always discriminated against us in our own family. She always repeated that "you need to be more like your brothers in Salvador, you act like you don't want anything," things like that. So, then you start to realize that. When they came to eat, we didn't eat the same food, they would eat these big fish and we would eat what was left. My brothers never had to work because they went directly to Salvador to go to school. And now I'm sure they see us as *marginal* (criminal). Because all of them had jobs, they have their children in school. They lived in Salvador studying and growing while we remained here working. They don't help us. They recognize that we are brothers, they come here to the island to visit but they act like they are lords. My mother never treated them in the same way.
>
> ARIVALDO: She was always discouraging you all, like you couldn't do anything. But she never talked that way about her sons in Salvador.
>
> THIAGO: They could come to Salvador with gifts for her, and what did we have? We couldn't give her gifts. All we could give her was trash, maybe food that we could give to the pets (*laughs*). The fruit that maybe someone threw away we could bring back (*chuckles*). At home my mom would say, "nunca vai ser gente" (you will never be people). I understand it now but that's why I left my house because I didn't feel good there.

In this exchange, Thiago explains that not only are the lighter children of his mother from a different partner viewed as superior, but he was socialized to treat them in a manner befitting their higher status. In this case, differential treatment is explained as a matter of both class and skin color: the white siblings were able to pay for the food and bring gifts to their mother, which the black children were not able to do.

Rather than acknowledge the structural advantages that the white siblings enjoy, including private education, life in Salvador instead of on a remote island, and financial stability, their mother framed Thiago and his black siblings as lazy. This is true despite the fact that they divided their time between working in the fields and attending some of the poorest schools in the region. With low investment in his affective capital, the toll of these constant comparisons was so great that Thiago left his home as a teenager because he "didn't feel good there." Leaving his home meant that he would be vulnerable to other dangers, but he decided to follow this course hoping that though he would never be considered a person at home, perhaps he could find support elsewhere. Indeed, he did find another form of family through his involvement in *capoeira*. Unfortunately, others in a similar position are not as successful, and they never recuperate from differential treatment.

For other Afro-Brazilians, racial abandonment is not a result of being rejected by their families. As Larissa notes, it is a conscious decision made in hope of acceptance among whites:

> A friend of mine was like that. A racist black person. She was black but she only liked whites. So much so that I was not very close with her. She felt rage (*raiva*) at her own race, you see what I'm saying? My friend was like that. She would always say that she did not like her color, and no, she did not like her color and she always said it. She was my color. She always hung out among white people and they accepted her. [Elizabeth: Where do you think she got these ideas?] I do not know. Sometimes it's from your own family? We don't talk anymore since she left school. You can often find blacks who do not like other blacks. (Larissa, 12)

Examples like the one above are common narratives that respondents provide when asked to provide examples of racism. These comments are consistent with previous research that frames blacks who hold anti-black attitudes as suffering from shame and rage at their race.[15]

WHEN RACIAL ROULETTE IS VIOLENT

The internalization of racial hierarchies can also have consequences that lead to physical violence in families. David is very light skinned, but with facial features that would be characterized as African and European. He informs me that he often has to correct people who refer to him as white, which is also why he wears his hair in cornrows or braids. Consider David's narrative about his brother Augusto:

There was always tension. It's always there between brothers, you know. But my father kicked my brother out of the house when he was only twelve years old, and I think it had a lot to do with him being dark. They never got along. They always fought. My mother was white and my father was black. I don't think he wanted dark children. He treated my brother very differently.

When they were young, David reports, he and Augusto often would get punished for misbehaving, but Augusto was always beaten and punished more harshly. In this family, internalized racism led a father to reject his darker son, which not only destroyed both the parental and sibling relationships, but also had significant material and psychological consequences. Augusto became homeless, did not receive an education, and became involved with illegal activities. David explicitly links the beatings and the constant fighting to his father not wanting a black child. David has since graduated from college, while Augusto struggles to meet his basic needs: a place to live and food to eat. In contrast to Thiago, who was able to find an alternative family structure that supports him, Augusto was left to fend for himself and ended up having a very different life trajectory.

Arivaldo points out that relationships between siblings are marked by cruelty and closeness, and that relationships can be especially strained in extended families among family members who are racialized differently. With regard to his two sisters, he notes:

> In the family, there are some people who have fine hair because of the racial mixture, a little from Portuguese, Indians, and so you have that mixture and so those that are *puxou do lado dos índios* (pulled from the indigenous side). For example, even though they are black, but with straight hair, *tiravam onda* (they showed off), saying, "No, I have good hair. I'm superior." And then there are others who are born lighter who say, "Oh, I'm lighter, I'm white, I'm lighter and you are black." So, we have to confront this. My sister—I have two sisters and two brothers, and the two sisters are younger than me—the one who is thirty-two years old is lighter, and she always told my sister who is thirty years old, "You were found in the trash. You are not my sister." (*Você foi achada no lixo. Você nao é minha irma.*) This is why our country is like this. The one who steps on the black, is the black himself. (*Quem pisa no negro é o próprio negro.*) It begins in the family.

In this case, a dark-skinned sister represents the reflection of her sister's blackness, which is "a painful mirror" that the lighter sister would prefer to avoid or deny rather than claim.[16] As Arivaldo notes, these types of ideas are not limited to his sisters, but extend to other family members, who rank each other on the basis of their positions in the phenotypic hierarchy. Their internalized racism leads to them enact symbolic violence against their siblings, reflecting and producing a number of emotions, including shame, guilt, and anger.[17]

There are also narratives of physical abuse against lighter or white-looking family members. However, the emotions that shape this treatment reinforce notions of racial hierarchy based on white supremacy. Corina confesses that she was involved in a racial rivalry with her siblings because she is white and her siblings are not, but as I ask for more details, I learn that the rivalry did not emerge simply from differences in racial features, but from the fact that Corina's mother abandoned the three black children and moved to a different city with Corina. Corina has a white father, and her siblings have a black father. Devastated by their mother's decision to marry a wealthy man and abandon all three of them while taking Corina, the three siblings have not spoken to Corina in decades. Corina reveals that there was much more occurring behind closed doors:

> My mother mistreated me. She always mistreated me. She would hit me all the time. Whenever I did something, . . . even a small thing, she would slap me across the face. . . . I'll never forget the day (*long pause*) . . . when she punished me by throwing scalding hot water all over me. I asked her, "Mama, why do you do these things to me?" (*pauses to cry*) But I knew why. I had the color of father's skin, his straight hair. I was white and she hated me. She was jealous of me, her own daughter. . . . For my birthday. . . . What do mothers usually buy for their daughter's birthday, Bete? Well, she brought me a tight dress and high heels because she wanted to prostitute me out to an old man from São Paolo. That's how she saw me, a prostitute. (Corina, 56)

This example is critical because it reiterates that in a racialized society, all members participate in the reproduction of and resistance to racial hierarchies. Although the immediate victim in this narrative is the lighter-skinned family member, Corina is brutalized and nearly exploited not because her mother is ashamed of her, but rather because her mother is jealous and is ashamed of herself. Corina is punished at home by her mother, and she is estranged from her black siblings because their mother chose her over them.

Corina explains that her mother went through a period of not speaking to her after she decided not to accept the invitation to travel to São Paulo with the older man. She explains how she coped with her mother's treatment:

> When my father would come over he would ask me how I was doing, and I would start to cry because my mother mistreated me. Psychologically, I don't know why I didn't go crazy. This is really interesting. Because today if you were to analyze things, everything that you say to a person, if you compliment one without complimenting the other it creates trauma. It creates trauma. It creates trauma so I think it has to be equal.

In an effort to reconnect with her darker siblings, Corina contacts them and invites them to have lunch and meet her family. On the day her siblings visit, Corina hosts a full house of family members and hardly has enough chairs to accommodate them. Corina's house has a kitchen table with chairs instead of a sofa, so her family members have to bring in extra chairs from outside. Rather than sit in on this private sibling reunion, I stop by only long enough to say hello. They are drinking festively and interacting as though all of the issues have been resolved.

The next day, I speak to Corina, who informs me that she explained to her siblings the reasons why their mother left with her rather than with them. She explained that her mother did not want to leave them, but her partner (who was white) required her to leave the darker-skinned children behind. Corina's siblings did not accept the reasons that she provided as valid, but they were in agreement that their sibling relationship should no longer suffer. Corina is excited to put this behind her or to work to mend these relationships. However, the more that I speak with Corina, the more it appears that her siblings' anger and jealousy may also be connected to how they are differentially treated outside of the family.

Uncritically, Corina complains about the difficulties that she has in finding a job as a maid:

> The woman, who was blonde, did not want me to work in her house because I am white. Because I was white she did not want me to work there. She couldn't accept it because I was same color as she was. So I think that was prejudice against me because she said I had a face more like a madam than a maid. She said I don't have a face of a maid, . . . that I had another

type of posture, a way of speaking. She said all of this in the door of her house, she didn't even let me in. I swear to God. My mom and my children know this, that somebody discriminated against me. It is not just blacks that are discriminated against. I always thought it was just blacks that were discriminated against. But the fact is that in my family there are black people (because my grandfather is black, my mom is *sarará*) because my mom comes from a family that is black and white. So, I thought at that moment when she said I had a face that was more a madam than a maid that I would never go back to trying to find a job as a maid in a family house.

Many dark-skinned women would welcome the opportunity to be considered for jobs outside the area of domestic service but are trapped in positions that are low-status and involve hard labor, long hours, and very low pay. Corina sees herself as a victim of this system, and while she is certainly discriminated against, she never acknowledges how her embodied capital makes her ill-suited for low-status "black women's work." In fact, Corina's light skin may have been considered threatening to the blonde woman looking for a black woman to work. Framing Corina in this way corresponds with a common saying in Brazil: "a white woman to marry, a mulatta to have sex with, and a black woman to work."

This construction of "black women's work" is important because it drives the decisions that some lighter or whiter-looking women make about their employment. For example, in a discussion about future mobility, one light-skinned respondent, Railda, mentions that she does not want her employer to sign her worker's registration card because being officially listed as a domestic worker would dirty her worker's registration card (*sujar a carteira*). Railda is willing to forgo receiving benefits at her job, if it means she does not have to list domestic work on her employment record. This language of contamination is connected to the way that this type of work is devalued as black women's work and connected to a history of slavery.

DEPRESSION, TRUST, AND TRAUMA

Differential treatment in one's private family life can lead to internalized racism and racial resentment that has negative consequences for perceived well-being as it relates to depression, trust, and trauma. As John Burdick eloquently notes in his examination of the relationship between race, color, and family, "it is precisely because of the strength of emotion present in families, of the high expectations within them for love, unconditional acceptance, and affection, . . . that experiences of differential treatment within them create deep psychic wounds."[18] For Yasmin, experiencing differential treatment in her family as a child and then later being confronted with similar issues as an adult has led to depression:

> I was entering into a depression, and by luck I happened to discover that from a person who was close to me. I felt really cold. I didn't know the symptoms of depression included feeling sleepy. So my friend who works in the area of health called me and she said, "You have to get out of this. You are entering depression." I entered into depression. I thought that I was going to go crazy. I did not have any friends outside of my family. My family was everything to me, they were the people that I loved the most. My family was everything for me. The truth is, they were not anything. They only wanted to destroy me. Everybody was against me. (Yasmin, 41)

After experiencing decades of mistreatment in her family because of her racial appearance, Yasmin reports, she went through a period when she distanced herself from her family and stopped leaving her house. She struggled with reconciling why she was an outcast and how it was possible for the people who she thought cared about her to betray her. Even though she managed to survive her depression, her experiences in her family shape her encounters with others:

> I don't want any more friendships. I just want the ones I have to last. I don't trust anyone anymore. I don't want to invite anyone in my house ever again. Where I live I say good morning, good afternoon. People call me stuck up but I don't care. Whenever I walk by, I greet everyone. I do my part by treating every person like a citizen.

Negative affect and differential treatment in her family has created such a deep sense of distrust toward others that Yasmin is reluctant to pursue friendships or let others get close to her. Similar to Yasmin, several women reveal how the negative psychological consequences of differential treatment based on race or phenotype in their own families has led to suicidal ideation and feelings of worthlessness. Three women express that they have felt as though death would be a preferable option to their current lives:

> There were times when I said, "Oh, God, I am going to give up." But I have a friend that says that God does not give you more than you can

bear. Everything that you are going through is because you have to go through it. I had such a great attachment to my family. With all the suffering that I had gone through, I wanted to leave but I didn't have the courage. (Raquel, 44)

Why am I even living? I sometimes ask God why did he make me (*pause*). Sometimes I just want it to be over. I do, Bete, sometimes I wish I could just end it. (Ana Cristina, 52)

If I did not have my religion I do not believe I would be alive. So many people could never go through what I have gone through. They would have ended it: thrown themselves out of a window. I have thought about how I would do it. (Corina, 56)

While none of the women succumb to suicide, the fact that differential treatment in their families pushes them to this point reveals the depths of their pain and despair. They all frame their ability to overcome by highlighting their religious backgrounds, as each of their statements suggests that religion is fundamental to helping them cope with these emotional difficulties. Throughout the interviews with these women, Catholicism, Spiritism, and, more rarely, Candomblé are mentioned as inspiring their will to live. Consistent with past research in Brazil, the interviews suggest that religion serves as an especially important source of support and racial affirmation for black women.[19]

Arivaldo also observed differential treatment of phenotypically different siblings in his extended family. He discusses the emotional impact:

I never saw this type of different treatment in my [immediate] family. But in my family I saw this within my aunts, uncles, and cousins. Buying clothes for one but not for another. Taking one to sign up for a course to be successful, but not spending as much on the other one in the same course. [Elizabeth: Do they explain why?] They don't explain why. They do it, but they don't explain it. It creates a trauma especially when it's done in front of everybody. But, it wakes you up. You can't blame them though.

Differential treatment in families can lead to material consequences as some family members receive more education and training, or receive better-quality clothing. This treatment also can shape a person's self-esteem and undermine the bonds that might otherwise develop among family members. Arivaldo mentions that it is the silence around unequal treatment that creates trauma as the blackest-looking family members try to understand the source of their family's decisions and differential investments in the absence of direct commentary. Most intriguing is his comment that he cannot blame his family, which is a position he takes because he believes that they are merely reproducing the ideas with which they were raised.

Whereas Arivaldo's coping strategy is to not blame the family for differential treatment, in other families a favored child may actively exert efforts to repair the damage that has been created by differential treatment, as Corina did when she tried to recreate the sibling bonds that were destroyed by her mother's decision to leave her darker-skinned siblings. Along these lines, Dona Lara explains what happened when her first cousins were treated differently in their home. Everyone in her family witnessed the two sisters, one light and the other darker, being treated differently, but no one said or did anything, until one day at school.

Dona Lara attended school with the darker cousin, who one day asked her to return a book to her teacher's classroom. Upon returning the book, Dona Lara explained that it belonged to her cousin, and the teacher replied, "Ah, it is such a shame, all of the things that that poor girl has gone through with her mother being dead and her father having abandoned the family. Poor thing." Dona Lara was shocked and explained that her cousin's mother was not dead; nor had her father abandoned the family. They determined that the cousin had lied about her entire life as a way to deal with the trauma of differential treatment. Dona Lara explains:

> Imagine (*Dona Lara speaks just above a whisper*), this child was so mistreated that to her it was like her mother was dead and her father had left the family. Imagine what would be going on the mind of a child to say something like that. The teacher told me not to tell my cousin that I knew about the lie that she had told. The teacher talked to her mother about it, and she was put into therapy for several years because of that trauma. To this day, she still doesn't know that we all know what she told her teacher. [Elizabeth: Did her sister ever find out?] I think so, but I'm not certain. But everybody could see that their mother treated them very differently. But her sister really takes care of her now. She pays for her children to go to good schools and does everything for her. You know, to try to make up for it.

In this case, a child who had been traumatized by differential treatment received therapy for years to confront some of the trauma. The favored, lighter-skinned sibling felt guilty about the treatment and spent many years and a significant amount of money to recuperate the relationship and compensate for the favoritism.

There are also Afro-Brazilian women like Barbara and Ismara, who claim to "walk between both worlds" of black and white and who have to recover from some of the trauma that they experience in their families. My initial conversation with Ismara is in some ways serendipitous. Traveling on a ferry from the island of Itaparica to Salvador, I strike up a conversation with Ismara, who is witty, spunky, and gregarious. With a smile that has been perfected by braces and an intellect that has been sharpened by her time in college, Ismara joins me in a conversation that smoothly transitions from economic disparity to hair and back to labor policy and domestic workers in Brazil. Ismara spends much of the time of our journey recounting memories of her childhood and her struggles to accept her blackness. She is bubbling over with narratives that she wants to share, and we have less than an hour on the ferry, so she excitedly accepts my invitation to be formally interviewed and agrees to speak with her sister about the prospect as well.

The only set of twins in this study, Barbara and Ismara spent nine months developing in their mother's womb side by side, only to be separated at birth and to live apart until they were teenagers. Born to a young interracial college couple, a white man and a black woman who could not take on the responsibility of raising the girls, Barbara was sent to the home of their black maternal grandmother, and Ismara to their white paternal grandmother. Barbara and Ismara are fraternal twins who closely resemble one another. They have a light brown complexion with curly hair rather than coily hair and dark brown, almond-shaped eyes. The main physical difference that I perceive between them is that Ismara is heavier than Barbara. Ismara also makes a point of mentioning that her hair texture is different from Barbara's. She says that her sister has a looser curl pattern and what would be considered better hair. Barbara disputes the charge and, sincerely perplexed by the suggestion, asks me to offer my opinion on the comparison. Given everything I have learned, I decide it is safer not to enter the debate about categorizing hair textures.

Ismara self-identifies as *negra* but was raised with the white side of her family in a rural part of Bahia. She chuckles and responds with a definitive "No, never" when I ask if her white family ever discussed race. To illustrate the subtle ways that race impacted her life, she explains that as a child, she had a white friend named Helen. Sometimes while playing with Helen, she would be asked to go to the store to buy bread or lollipops.

As a child, Ismara did not question it. She delivered the bread and candy and resumed her playtime with Helen. But as an adult she wondered why she was always asked to walk to the store alone and Helen was required to stay in the house. Reflecting on the experience, she reveals that there was an important yet subtle difference between how she and Helen were treated. Helen was seen as needing "protection from the world" while she was seen as being "of the world." Families would be "willing to run the risk" of sending Ismara out, while Helen was considered more delicate. Ismara's family never contested or questioned it. They accepted the practice without any explicit discussion of race. Perceptively, Ismara states:

> It is only in retrospect that, you know, I can think about it and really understand what was going on. I did not have words for it, but . . . but it's like you could feel the difference, you know? Back then I didn't see myself as *negra*, I would have said I was *morena*. I called myself *morena*, but I felt I was different.

Though Ismara does not discuss this with me, her twin sister, Barbara, reveals that the lack of conversation about race in the family made Ismara emotionally vulnerable to the slights she experienced in school. Barbara explains that Ismara did not understand why she had no friends or why her *coleguinhas* (young classmates) did not invite her to play or to their parties, so she internalized the rejection by overeating. As a loyal sister, Barbara is hesitant to reveal this, but is also sympathetic to her sister's struggle.

The white side of the family was the wealthier side, and Barbara remembers playing in Ismara's room and thinking that she did not have nearly as many toys as her sister. Barbara also remembers that Ismara was not used to getting spankings and that Ismara had to adapt to this whenever she visited her mother's side of the family. In addition to not attending the same quality of schools (Ismara attended an exclusive private school), they also had a different cultural experience during their childhood. Barbara recounts that her aunts (who were *negras*) would enjoy braiding her hair for school. She smiles as she remembers how every week her aunt would send her to school with new creative hair designs and colorful bows. This contrasts with Ismara's struggles with her hair and with either silence or complaints about its texture in her family.

Raised in a white family that did not discuss race openly, Ismara struggled to make sense of the relationships that shaped her life and to understand her own racial identity. Ismara's traumatic experiences in an all-white context sparked her interest in understanding more about the interpersonal racial slights that left her feeling unsettled, but about which she never spoke. This search for answers ultimately led her to join a community organization in Salvador that gives her the historical foundation to better understand race and racial inequality. As a result of what she has learned, she has developed a more political-oriented racial consciousness and considers herself a *negra assumida*.

Excited about her knowledge about how racial inequality shapes Brazilians' life chances and about her new perspective on racial classification, Ismara attempted to recruit her twin sister into the fold. This took some effort, and they both laugh when they think about the multiple heated disagreements they had when Ismara tried to explain that racism exists in Brazil. Barbara remembers dismissing the conversations about racism as *besteiras* (foolishness). Ismara persisted over the course of nearly a year and finally succeeded at resocializing Barbara. Both are now *negras assumidas* who have graduated from high school, have entered college, and are on their way to what they hope will be successful careers in which they can make a difference.

Rarely do such narratives of resocialization have a simple ending. Barbara explains her resocialization as a process and says that she is still learning to see herself with new eyes. She confesses that she has never considered herself pretty and that she is working to embrace her beauty. She reveals that a year ago she even had her doubts about dating her current boyfriend because of his "hard hair" (*cabelo duro*). She reveals this reluctantly, but she does so to illustrate that she is still learning to liberate herself from internalized racism. She did overcome her initial hesitation about her boyfriend, and in retrospect she feels embarrassed that she ever felt that way about him in the first place.

PRETTY PLEAS: BEAUTY AND SELF-ESTEEM

Se pudesse pedir uma coisa, pediria ter cabelo grande, loiro e olhos azuis. Mas não quero ser branca, não. (If I could make any wish, I would wish for long blonde hair and blue eyes. But I really don't want to be white.) (Regane, 9)

The white beauty norm for Afro-Brazilians is dangerous because it can "build a distorted image that will seek refuge from its physical reality and stimulate mechanisms of negation and compensation."[20] For young girls, "identity fragmentation" is exemplified in how they come to construct a sense of self through interactions with others. Beauty is inevitably at the center of their constructions of self because it is central to constructions of both race and gender for women.

February 2, the Festa de Iemanjá, is one of the most sacred days for Candomblé practitioners because it is the day they pay homage to Iemanjá, Mother of the Waters. No longer limited to religious followers, the celebration has been "transformed from a community practice into a massive cultural project," attracting a broader domestic and international audience.[21] With limited transportation, residents of Lua Cheia find it difficult to access Rio Vermelho, where the main celebration occurs. Nonetheless, the neighborhood is in an excited mood as residents prepare to make small offerings to Iemanjá at the nearby beach. In addition to making offerings, it is customary to ask Iemanjá to grant a wish. As everyone is walking toward the beach to make their offerings of soaps, flowers, and candles, I indifferently ask Damiana's daughter Regane if she will ask Iemanjá for anything. She responds in an exasperated tone, explaining that every year she asks for the same thing, but her prayers have gone unanswered. She wishes that Iemanjá would grant her blue eyes and long, blonde hair that grows all the way to her butt.

Over the preceding weeks, as the resident hair braider I have enthusiastically combed Regane's hair, twisted it, braided it, and styled it in ways that have garnered compliments and even made her smile when she looked in the mirror. Admittedly against my normal approach, with Regane I offer words of affirmation: "You know, I think you have great hair and I like braiding it." She turns and looks at me with a slight frown and confused eyes. Her head is slightly tilted to the side as if she is trying to figure out why I am lying to her. In light of her socialization, my admiration has to be a lie. It challenges everything she has seen and heard and everything she feels about "cabelo bom" (good hair) and "cabelo ruim" (bad hair). It is an implausible suggestion that the messages she is receiving from her family and society are wrong. That simply cannot be.

As an example of just how embedded notions of good and bad hair are in Brazilian society, Raíssa, a *negra assumida*, provides a gripping example of how these ideas shaped her life as a young girl. She vividly remembers struggling to accept her naturally curly hair, which was considered bad hair in her family. She starts to chuckle as she begins to tell a funny story, and eventually is laughing so hard that it is difficult to understand what she is saying:

(*Laughing*) On my birthday, my uncle gave me a wig. [Elizabeth: Your uncle bought you a wig?] Yes, he did (*laughing*). I put it on to go to church, but when I got to church (*laughing*), I was scratching (*laughs harder*). I couldn't take it. I screamed, "It itches, it burns!" My head was hot! (*laughing*)

Raíssa's laughter is contagious, and tears start to well up in her eyes. But as the laughing subsides, Raíssa has a look on her face of anguish, and the sadness in her eyes stops me cold. I stop laughing, realizing that laughter is the only way that she can handle the absurdity and pain of this experience. Instead of her uncle trying to convince her to love her own hair, he purchased a ten-year-old wig to hide it.

Throughout my time in Lua Cheia, young girls consistently report that they secretly—or not so secretly—wish for longer and straighter hair, including nine-year-olds Natalia and her best friend Zica:

> ZICA: If I could change anything about myself, it would be my hair. I would love to have really, really long hair, to the floor (*pauses*). So long that ten people would have to help me with my hair just so I could walk!
>
> NATALIA: Well, I would want long hair too, but it doesn't need to be *that* long, just a little longer than it is now and brown. A little lighter than it is now, . . . and in waves.

For Zica, who would most likely be considered *preta* because of her dark skin and her African facial features, the desire for long hair is attached to a Rapunzel-like fantasy. As she describes the fantasy, she smiles widely and seems to enjoy pondering what having long hair would be like. She would like to have the longest hair of anyone in Brazil, hair that would require the assistance of an entire entourage.

Natalia's fantasy is not as extravagant as Zica's. It represents a more realistic compromise and perhaps an effort to partially resist aesthetic norms. Natalia is lighter-skinned with features that suggest she is mixed-race. Interestingly, Natalia does not want blonde hair, straight hair, or an immediate transformation. Instead, her desires are framed as small modifications, but one modification leads to another as she says that she wants her hair to be "browner," a "little longer," a "little lighter," and "in waves." With each descriptor she moves farther away from what she looks like now and closer to the idea of what she thinks she should look like.

Although these fantasies reproduce ideas about beauty and whiteness, the girls are also articulating a nuanced approach to beauty. To describe how black women negotiate beauty hierarchies, researchers use the phrase "Lily Complex," which involves "altering, disguising, and covering up your physical self in order to assimilate, to be accepted as attractive."[22]

But while these girls are certainly responding to racial hierarchies, their goal is not to be lily white. Even in their pleas for prettiness, as Regane's comment makes clear, they want to change their hair texture and color, but not their skin color. In fact, Regane follows up her wishes to Iemanjá with a frown and a near diatribe about how pale white skin is completely unattractive. Natalia wants longer hair, but not straight hair. Though a far cry from racial affirmation, this does illustrate their negotiation of oppressive hierarchies rather than wholesale adoption of these ideas.

Joana, a dark-skinned black woman with straightened hair, is under no illusion that her racial appearance will change with a wish to Iemanjá. She has a lighter-skinned boyfriend and looks embarrassed when she admits that her friends and people on the street have stopped them and matter-of-factly asked, "What does he see in you?" When I ask Joana if she thinks that she is pretty, she pauses to think and responds, "I am nice." When I ask her again about her attractiveness, she shrugs and repeats that she is nice. Her use of *simpática* to describe herself is at best a very weak and ambiguous way to compliment herself, as *nice* is often used euphemistically to describe an unattractive person. She has exclusively dated lighter-skinned men. This could be a coincidence, but her responses to other questions suggest that her preference in boyfriends may be rooted in something deeper (see chapter 6).

With shy, 18-year-old Elisa, who describes herself as *negra* and actively participates in cultural activities related to afro-dance and afro-aesthetics, our weekly conversations revolve around mundane issues. Tentative about being recorded, Elisa often gives short answers, and her soft, soothing voice requires me to listen more attentively. After I have met with Elisa and her family and developed a closer relationship with them for months, one day we discuss the notion of racial trauma, which seems to be a trigger for her reflections about her upbringing. She immediately replies with an uncharacteristic eagerness and a series of unexpected narratives that encapsulate the relationship between the embodiment of race, gender, and shame:

> ELISA: My family used to always congratulate me on my good grades—"Good job, Elisa, good job!"—but it was like I had to get good grades because I was black and ugly, . . . so it was good that I had good grades to compensate for it. You know? My aunts and cousins would say these things. I have never told anybody about these things before, . . . never. I used to be ashamed of being *negra*. I used to want to be white with long hair. . . . It was my dream, and I felt embarrassed of myself. I think that's

why I'm so shy now. For so long I have been so ridiculed that now I'm just shy and I can't bear being in front of people. That day we were hanging out, I wanted to dance so badly but I made up every excuse not to go up to dance. I could have made a way but I just couldn't do it.

ELIZABETH: You think that you being shy has to do with these experiences with race?

ELISA: I think so. . . . The way that people were talking that I was black, that I was horrible, I hid myself to avoid being ridiculed.

We have known each other for several months by now, and this is the first time we are having a conversation about these types of intimate family issues.

The dance to which she refers was a community event in which people were called up to dance in a large group. Elisa and I had taken dance classes together, so she had practiced the routines that were being performed. Yet still, she could not bring herself to perform because of the prospect of being seen and judged in front of a large audience. She blames herself, saying that she could have made a way, but she could not bring herself to do it. The shame and embarrassment that Elise feels is an example of how racial and gender hierarchies can lead to a "humiliated self-esteem."[23] Even the support that her family offers for her to complete her education is a double-edge sword, a reflection of their resignation to her being unmarriageable and their belief that she can best spend her time becoming more educated.

Elisa desires to be white and to have long hair because it seems to be the only solution to her shyness, her shame, and her belief that she is ugly. Elisa believes that the marriage market is a game of social exchange for which she may never have enough to compensate for her racial phenotype and perceived ugliness.[24] When she completes her statement about her "traumas," we continue to walk silently side by side, heading toward an ice cream vendor. We change the subject as we eat our ice cream, and over the next months we continue our dance classes, but I cannot bring myself to return to the topic.

SELF-ESTEEM, BEAUTY, AND MASCULINITY

Aesthetics and esteem questions are often discussed only as they relate to women. This emphasis is understandable given the way that evaluations of beauty have historically been used to control women by linking their worth to their beauty. However, it is critical that black men are not rendered invisible and that researchers study how similar, though not identical, considerations affect their lives.

Dilson, who is married to Lilza, becomes nervous in our interview as I begin to shift the conversation to address self-esteem, beauty, and race. His body language, which reflects a great deal of tension and tightness, is as intriguing as his answers to my questions. Before he begins to talk, he looks down often and then picks up a nail clipper that happens to be on the living room table. He nervously begins fiddling with it and begins to clip away at his nails, avoiding eye contact with me while explaining:

> DILSON: In my youth, well yeah, in my youth I never was the type of guy, I was never the type of young person, I was never the type, maybe because of the church, that had a lot of girlfriends and stuff like that. You know? (*He pauses and looks down at his hands, with his shoulders clenched in close.*) But I had that image that people were saying that a black person was ugly, that you are a monkey, that you look like a monkey, that you are an ugly color. . . . Those type of things leave you feeling sad (*starts to fiddle with the nail clipper*). So, when I went out I didn't want to be the center of attention, because if I were to be the center of attention it would be the center of negative attention. You know? (*looks up at me*) If I were to be the center of attention it would be because they would be saying, "Oh, look at his hair, look at that nappy hair of his, look how big his nose is." That type of thing. You understand? Look how ugly he is. You are black and you are ugly. You are black and ugly. And so it's difficult in relation to, . . . I mean even during that time like just getting along with the girls. When a girl came up to me in biology class or something to ask me a question. I was always doubting whether they were really interested in me or if they wanted to make fun of me in my face or something. You know? Even if they were saying, "Oh, you are *bonitinho* (cute)," I thought it was just for them to mock me (*fazer chacota de mim*). You know, that they would just be playing around, like it was a joke. I never believed in what they were saying because of my physical appearance, with regard to beauty or anything like that with another person. I just didn't believe it. I thought I was ugly. This was the force of the prejudice that I was dealing with in my own mind.
>
> ELIZABETH: So, when did you overcome this, . . . or is this a process?
>
> DILSON: Exactly. I don't think, . . . I don't want to say it like I have already overcome this. This is something that I think I will also have to confront for the rest of my life.
>
> LILZA: (*interrupting*) Even now he thinks he is ugly (*laughs*).

ELIZABETH: Is that right?

DILSON: (*displays an embarrassed smile and looks down*)

LILZA: Yes, it is! Because I say he is good-looking, and he still doesn't believe it. He keeps saying . . .

DILSON: (*chuckles and interrupts*) Look, I think this way, with regard to being black. Those who are black, those who have really, really dark skin, will have to deal with this for a very long, long time. I don't think we will ever do away with this. For this to disappear, there, there would need to be . . . something more, I don't know.

The exchange with Dilson reveals the depth of the psychological distress that young black males may experience as they try to cope with racial hierarchies and sexual expectations in a period of their lives that is already complicated by the awkward phase of adolescence. In Brazil men are expected to flirt with and approach women, but Dilson felt limited and threatened by the very prospect because of his racial appearance. Given the negative comments that he had received in the past, there was always a fear of rejection, fear that he would be the butt of a joke.

The internalization of racial hierarchies is most evident in Dilson's self-doubt, which did not allow him to believe that girls could be genuinely interested in him. There are clear similarities between Dilson's position and that of Regane, for whom it is inconceivable that her hair is beautiful. As we talk, Dilson's body language and use of the nail clipper distract from the conversation and provide a reason to avert his eyes, which I also interpret as a sign of shame. This affect has been best articulated by Frantz Fanon: "Shame. Shame and self-contempt. Nausea. When people like me, they tell me it is in spite of my color. When they dislike me, they point out that it is not because of my color."[25]

Dilson's devastating honesty provides insight into the intersection of race, masculinity, and aesthetics. That there are not more studies of these types of male experiences is not a reflection of their lack of importance to men; rather, I believe the articulation of these insecurities is rare because they can undermine notions of masculinity. During two family debriefings, family members expose their male relatives for chemically straightening their hair to attract women. Though these revelations are made in a joking fashion, with all family members laughing, it is important to understand how men grapple with reconciling the dilemmas that emerge from their negotiations of aesthetic hierarchies, masculinity, and expectations of sexuality.

Black men in this study often articulate alternative ways of recuperating their self-esteem in the face of differential treatment and phenotypic differentiation in families. Both Thiago and Arivaldo wear their hair in dreadlocks, and when I ask if women like their hair, they respond by sucking their teeth and in unison giving an emphatic, "Não, de jeito nenhum!" (No, no way!). Because men's worth is less connected to their beauty and more connected to their status, which can be attained in numerous ways, men can pursue a wider variety of strategies to increase their status. At the same time, these strategies are structured by inequality and racial stereotypes.

Arivaldo and Thiago agree that their involvement in *capoeira* provides an alternative family structure in which they find support and a philosophy of life that focuses on the equality of all people, a sense of purpose, and the importance of resistance. For all of these reasons, it also provides a way to increase their affective capital and sense of self-esteem. Thiago is the more outspoken, explaining:

> We can only get our self-esteem through our performance, and when they applaud our art and performance, this helps our self-esteem. This never happened within our own families. When we heard applause from those who see us, that's when we knew we were doing something really important. It's in this way that we were looking for, using art to accomplish things. Despite everything that happened in our family, we realize that our culture is a rich one, with its values and everything. The stories that we heard from our family, that's how we started identifying with our art.

Thiago insists on recognizing the limitations of his family upbringing, but also illustrates that the strong foundation forged by his family is what generates his interest in pursuing *capoeira*. But, it is from the response of the audience, an external validation, that Thiago derives his self-esteem. That both Thiago and Arivaldo link *capoeira* and self-esteem is a critical point to recognize in the context of Salvador's booming tourist industry, which is driven in part by images of *capoeira*. Black men with limited options and faced with structural exclusion, superficial cultural inclusion, and the day-to-day microaggressions that reinforce their devalued status may pursue *capoeira* as a way to regain their self-esteem and to assert their masculinity.

Arivaldo and Thiago participate in Angolan *capoeira*, the traditional form of *capoeira*, which is played more slowly and closer to the ground and explicitly connects *capoeira* to the struggle for racial equality in Brazil. However, regional *capoeira*, which is the more popular, exported version of the art form, has increasingly grown in popularity around the world.

Its elaborate gymnastic moves, including kicks that are similar to those in karate, and its more upright position are more consciously performed in a way that is less connected to the philosophy of Angolan *capoeira*.[26] Respondents frame regional *capoeira* as attractive to black men because it provides them a way to be visible and applauded while taking part in an activity that has both domestic and international relevance. They are applauded both because of their abilities and because of their blackness, a combination that for some makes their performances more fulfilling.

To be sure, understanding how art forms and behaviors provide capital does not mean that these same strategies cannot be problematized. However, a perspective that recognizes black agency within structural constraints provides a space to reveal how people negotiate inequality, as well as how inequality can be produced in noncoercive ways. Afro-Brazilians may welcome the opportunity to participate in *capoeira* or to be actors in the tourist machine because they have limited choices, but also because they perceive that their participation offers material and affective payoffs. Men who participate in *capoeira* have access to embodied capital because learning to play well gives them the ability to embody Bahianness and even Brazilianness for a foreign audience that is willing to pay for and celebrate such representations. The image of a *capoeirista*, alongside sexualized notions of dark-skinned black men (*negões*), presents a way for black men to use their embodied capital to access symbolic, affective, and economic capital.

Other black Brazilian men hoping to engage in embodied performances as a strategy to deal with their racial and masculine identities embrace a style called *brau*.[27] Drawing from a wide range of discourses and styles, *brau* is adopted by "lower-class youth engaged in experimenting with the soul-brother style in Bahia." Men who adopt this style wear clothing associated with blacks from the United States "so as not to take on directly a look that is considered white."[28] In this way, black Bahian youth draw on and reinterpret transnational discourses in order to refashion themselves on their own racial terms. *Brau*, which is about dress, self-presentation, behavior, and race, "performs a subversive and disruptive corporeality" that challenges racial etiquette and normative ideas about black masculinity.[29]

WE DON'T BELONG TOGETHER

One of the critical psychosocial benefits of family membership is the feeling of belonging and security that it provides. These are the same emotions that a nation tries to produce in its citizens because these emotions lead to the development of affective bonds and foster loyalty. From a developmental perspective, differential treatment from parents has the potential to significantly affect sibling relationships and family members' well-being.[30] Given that sibling relationships are the longest-lasting relationships that people have, among the consequences of compromised sibling relationships is a diminished sense of belonging in the family and an inability or reluctance to develop future relationships with others.

Because of the stark phenotypic differences between them, Liliane states that her darker-skinned sister Margarete struggled with her color and would often ask her mother, "Why was I born this way?" The question was not posed merely because of phenotypic differences but also because of the antipathy with which her mother talked about blacks. In retrospect, Liliane claims to now understand the tension in their relationship and forgives Margarete for her cruelty by matter-of-factly stating:

> She is a bitter, bad person, and an angry person. And it is because she never had love. She never had love because my mother never liked blacks.

When Liliane talks about blacks, she does not use the term *negro*; she uses the term *preto*. This is an important distinction because while all of her family is *negro*, *preto* is a term used to describe the darkest-skinned family members. Not only did Margarete disproportionately feel the wrath of her mother's disdain for dark-skinned blacks, she experienced differential treatment even when she was with her sister in public. Liliane remembers:

> When we would go shopping together and we wanted to go into a store to look at things, she would be like, "Excuse me, do you have that in this color?" And the salesperson would say, "Did you see the price?" And then she would say, "I did not ask you for the price, I asked you if you had this color." She experienced things like that. Why did they ask her the price? Because they thought that she couldn't pay for it. She has gone through this in my presence.

These negative experiences of racism reinforced in public and private spheres only heightened the tension between them. One option might have been to completely reject her mother's racist comments, but Margarete internalized these ideas. Now that Margarete has started her own family with a black (*preto*) man, Liliane anticipates problems:

> My sister hates blacks. Unfortunately, all of her kids are black (*pretos*). She married a black man and had black kids. I asked her, "Why did you

marry a black man and have a black child if you know you do not like blacks?"

One wonders if or how racial rituals will come to shape her interactions with her own children, particularly her daughters.

Though a compromised sense of self and belonging has been studied as a phenomenon most relevant to women, men too must negotiate racial hierarchies, and the consequences have implications for subjective feelings of belonging. Corina reveals that in addition to the two *moreno* children who live with her, she has another older son who is black. I did not discover she has another son until months after we met. She explains that he has emotional problems:

> My son has psychological problems because sometimes he says, "Why was I was born with nappy hair (*cabelo duro*)?" and my daughter was born with straight hair. It's been a few years since I've talked to him about it, and he first started to accept it and like it. I said to him, "That isn't what's important. What's more important are our feelings" (*sentimentos*).

As Corina provides details about her son's issues, she mentions aesthetics as part of the issue, but she frames his "psychological problems" mostly as being related to feeling that he does not belong, particularly when he is standing near her and his other siblings. His mother's reliance on a universal message, "What's more important are our feelings," to console him seems to miss the point that he *is* speaking about feelings: how he feels about himself and how others feel about him. In Brazil, concerns about hair are deeply rooted in a racialized affective framework, where evaluations or feelings of others influence racial categorization, attributions of attractiveness, and one's life chances. Corina's strategy of denying the importance of hair texture in order to foster a sense of belonging may not be the most effective strategy of addressing her son's problems.

Similarly, for João, surveillance and vigilance from the neighbors about his skin color contributes to his insecurities. As a result, both of his parents, Claudia and Andrés, report having to work to get him to "accept himself." Claudia reports:

> One day I was going to Andrés's mother's house and ran into a friend whom I hadn't seen in a long time, and she said, "Ah, Fábio looks just like his dad, but João does not look anything like him." This is because João is darker than Fábio, who looks more like his [Andrés's] dad. His dad is darker than your hair. To get him to accept this about himself, we have to

tell him that his grandfather, his father's dad, was really dark, and he took after his grandfather.

To foster self-acceptance, this family affirms that the son gets his looks from another family member. In doing so they hope to convey a sense of belonging and pride, but the reassurance for the son is not that he is beautiful or attractive, but instead that there is a genetic reason for his racial appearance. In this family, the question of belonging is much more significant than the question of attractiveness or beauty.

Lilza's upbringing was a complicated one, in part because her parents, Fátima and Affonso, have never been married. In fact, Fátima has been Affonso's mistress since before Lilza's birth, so Lilza's relationship with her father has been one of holiday visits and half-secret meetings (though Affonso's wife knows about the elicit relationship). Complicating this even further is the psychological distress that Lilza undergoes not only as a result of being the love child of an affair, but because of the obvious phenotypic differences between her and her mother:

> When I was younger, she didn't let me tell people that I was the child of her lover. I would tell people and she fought with me about it. She would say, "This is my life and I don't want you talking about it to anybody." And I would say, "But Mom, it's my life, too." I didn't know better, and I would tell people that my dad was married to someone else. And for the longest time I thought that I was adopted. Really, I did. I looked nothing like my mother. Everyone always commented on this. I even thought to myself, my God, maybe they are right, maybe I am adopted. I had that in the back of my mind for a long time. I only came to really believe I was really my mother's daughter when my brother was born and he came out very, very light just like me.

Lilza manages to chuckle as she recalls the years of feeling as though she were adopted. It was a quest for truth and candor that compelled young Lilza to try to openly talk to others about what she knew about her father.

Although it is easy to idealize interracial and phenotypically diverse families, a rarely studied side of these families is the feelings of detachment and compromised sense of belonging that may result from not seeing yourself reflected in your parents and siblings. For Lilza, only with the birth of her younger brother did she have confirmation that she was not adopted. But in other families this never happens; questions of paternity always linger and lead to anxious family interactions.

DISCUSSION

Racial hierarchies in families lead to the unequal distribution of emotional resources, and differential family interactions may influence perceptions of support, love, and belonging. The narratives highlighted in this chapter give voice to some of the daily experiences and lifelong trauma associated with socialization into racial affect on the basis of white supremacist ideologies.[31] Perhaps the phrase "everyday wounds of color" underestimates the extent to which experiences of differential treatment are internalized not merely as wounds but as recurring traumas.[32] Respondents' narratives illustrate how mothers and fathers may abandon their children, deliver implicit and explicit messages that are symbolically violent, and mistreat or physically abuse family members on the basis of their internalization of racial hierarchies. Though studies of favoritism exist in research on families, they are often disconnected from the power dynamics and sociological conditions that create and reproduce differential treatment. And the emotion-laden experiences of racial socialization are crucial not merely because they help us to learn about how families make race and participate in racialization; they are significant because differential treatment leads to unequal access to affective capital.

Not only do these experiences shape a person's affective state in the moment, the resulting feelings shape how a person confronts the world and future relationships. In this way, positive emotions generated from self-affirming social interactions within and outside of families can generate personal resources linked to "greater creativity, resilience, and emotional well-being."[33] Unequal access to these positive emotions and experiences decreases self-confidence, increases personal insecurity, and engenders emotional boundaries that can hinder one's life. Thus a person's location in a racialized social system, or proximity to whiteness, not only influences distribution of material resources, but also dictates the distribution of affection, which can be considered an internal family resource.[34]

The life histories of Tânia and Rebeca, the *filhas de criação*, offer a riveting and compelling illustration of how phenotypic differentiation can initiate a trajectory of lifelong suffering and exploitation. Not only does exploitation within the context of adoptive families lead to a compromised sense of well-being, but the women's reports of losing their childhoods, wasting their lives, and suffering emotional and physical abuse is evidence of their severe trauma. In situations where adoptees are able to leave their adoptive families, many retain ties to the adoptive family because of an external and internalized sense of obligation and gratitude, a lack of biological ties, and a desire for love. Researchers argue that "negative parental affect including rejection, hostility, and reduced levels of parental support and warmth" can function as a chronic stressor and source of "identity disruption."[35] For all the reasons that family can function in a profoundly positive way in fostering pride, belonging, and a sense of community, it can be devastating when positive emotions are absent or replaced by consistently negative experiences and emotions.

When bell hooks argues, "We cannot value ourselves rightly without first breaking through the walls of denial, which hide the depth of black self-hatred, inner anguish, and unreconciled pain," she is referring to many of the emotions and interactions that I have analyzed.[36] Internalized racism and the effects of racial socialization in families "explicitly identify individual selves, families, and subaltern communities as permeable sites (rather than sources) into which racism, as both a structural and ideological force, penetrates."[37] Individuals who are phenotypically different from family members can experience a number of negative outcomes, but parents and siblings can and do combat disadvantage in ways that protect family members. Throughout this chapter, I provide examples of siblings working to repair the damage caused by differential treatment, and of efforts to use therapy to deal with its aftermath. Family members step in to style the hair of young girls, which contributes positively to self-esteem. Moreover, individuals demonstrate their agency by proactively searching for mechanisms to cope with the discrimination they face in their own lives. Religion is a coping strategy often used by women, *capoeira* is one used by men. Although everyone is part of a racialized social system, everyone does not passively reproduce inequality. The strategies used even by people within the same family are variable and evolving. But as Dilson notes, "Those who are black, those who have really, really dark skin, will have to deal with this for a very long, long time."

PART II

RACIAL SOCIALIZATION AND NEGOTIATIONS IN PUBLIC CULTURE

CHAPTER 4

RACIAL FLUENCY: READING BETWEEN
AND BEYOND THE COLOR LINES

Education either functions as an instrument which is used to facilitate integration of the younger generation into the logic of the present system and bring about conformity or it becomes the practice of freedom.
PAOLO FREIRE, *PEDAGOGY OF THE OPPRESSED*

SHIFTING SOMEWHAT FROM EXAMINING how racial phenotype shapes differential treatment in family relationships, in this chapter, I explore how Afro-Brazilians develop the racial fluency necessary to navigate Brazil's complex racial/phenotypic lexicon, manage tacit racial rules and etiquette, and negotiate racial commonsense.

Paulo Frere discusses the possibilities and pitfalls of education, explaining that it either breeds conformity or facilitates students' ability to deal "critically and creatively with reality and discover how to participate in the transformation of their world."[1] Here I illustrate how socialization in Afro-Brazilian families relies on social learning and racial education that accomplishes both simultaneously.

STRATEGIC SEMANTIC AMBIGUITY
AND RACIAL INCONSISTENCIES

Significant racial mixture (*mestiçagem*) in Brazil means that color inconsistencies and racial confusions within families occur frequently, especially when members are asked to categorize themselves. Past research might lead one to reasonably anticipate that racial socialization takes on an important role in the development of a clear sense of racial identity, but in Brazil racial socialization often fosters ambiguity and inconsistency rather than crystallization.[2] My seemingly direct questions of "What is your race?" and "What is your color?" lead to a series of unexpected conversations in which the majority of informants have to arrive at their final response through a process that involves contradictions, family interventions, and corrections. The confusions do not mean that there is no dominant racial logic or that Afro-Brazilians have no racial consciousness. To the contrary, the slipperiness of the terms is precisely the rule that drives social interactions.

Given the diverse ways that both color and racial categories are used in Brazil, a number of studies have focused on deconstructing racial terminology and examining the internal logic of color classifications.[3] At one end of the spectrum are the researchers who suggest there is an almost completely situational quality of color classification. They argue that race varies depending on place, time of day, familiarity, degree of relatedness, desire to show respect, age, and generation.[4] While this extensive variation in color term usage was not observed in this study, I argue that strategic semantic ambiguity does occur as Afro-Brazilians exercise agency in determining when and how to use racial and phenotypic terms in certain moments.[5]

For decades researchers have studied the nature of racial logic and racial rules, but I was more interested in analyzing how children, young people, and adults develop fluency in these intricate matters. *Racial fluency* is a term that draws comparisons between the management of racial symbols and the ways humans develop language; it seeks to answer how socialization teaches Afro-Brazilians to confront their position in a racialized system with creative strategies that manage, reinforce, and contest their placement in the racial order. Thus racial fluency is as much about the diverse strategies people use to identify and manage racial situations as it is a reflection of the different ways that people define themselves and others.

Racial socialization includes the role of phenotype and color consciousness in Afro-Brazilians' lives, as well as the ways family members racially classify themselves and the extent to which they discuss these classifications among themselves and consider them important. Evaluating this involves two seemingly straightforward questions: "What is your color?" and "What is your race?" Table 4.1 details how informants answered the first question; 72 percent identified their color as either *moreno* or *negro*. When asked their race (see table 4.2), 65 percent defined themselves as *negro*, and 18 percent described themselves as *pardo*. Despite previous claims that Brazilians use hundreds of color categories, respondents used fourteen different color terms throughout the time I spent in Salvador.

Table 4.1. Answers to "What is your color?"

Color Category	Percentage	Frequency
neutral (*moreno*)*	42%	49
black (*negro*)**	30%	35
white (*branco*)	11%	13
brown (*pardo*)	7%	8
black (*preto/pretinho*)	3%	4
other***	6%	7
total (percentage rounded)	100%	116

*Variations on *moreno* include *moreninho, morena escura, morena clara,* and *morena total.*

**Negro* is a political term that refers to anyone who is brown or black. However, use of the term *negro* for color or racial classification does not necessarily imply high racial-identity salience or a particular racial consciousness.

***Mestiço, sarará, torradinho, india negra, caboverde, mulato.*

Table 4.2. Answers to "What is your race?"

Racial Category	Percentage	Frequency
black (*negro*)	65%	75
brown (*pardo*)	18%	21
white (*branco*)	9%	9
black (*preto*)	2%	2
other*	8%	9
total (percentage rounded)	100%	116

*"I don't know," human, Gemini, *mestiça, moreno,* and so on.

More relevant than informants' final responses about race and color are the intense deliberations often involved in arriving at them.

FROM THE MOUTHS OF BABES

Children and adolescents in the neighborhood are the source of some of the richest data, and I marvel at their ability to process, question, and defy the etiquette of racial cordiality. Among this group, racial fluency is still very much in its nascent stage of development. My interview questions bring to the surface issues that many have been curious about, but have never fully thought through or articulated aloud. As a result, my interviews with the youngest participants are full of racial problem solving and efforts to grapple with the meaning of color and race, first steps that will ultimately give way to racial fluency.

Natalia and Zica are two young girls in one extended family from Lua Cheia. An invitation to attend a party for Natalia's aunt's pet dog, Zequinha, is what leads me to their neighborhood, located on the other side of the city. Having never attended a dog party, in the United States or in Brazil, this is an event that I refuse to miss. The location of the party is Natalia's aunt's terrace, which is built on top of her uncle's house, which sits atop her grandmother's house, which is built on top of her great-aunt's house. For residents of the favelas (shantytowns), where there is limited room to expand horizontally, this type of spatial arrangement saves both space and money. The party is not unlike others in Brazil: there are *cervejas* (beers) all around, plenty of *feijoada* (bean stew), loud music, and lots of dancing. There was even a special chocolate dessert—*brigadeiro*, a popular Brazilian birthday dessert—just for the dog. Later in the evening, following the party, several of us—Natalia and Zica, their mothers and aunts, and a few young neighbors—sit outside of the houses on the severely cracked sidewalk, singing popular North American songs and joking about the absurdity of a dog party.

As we laugh, a young man approaches from the left, carrying a rifle almost as tall as he is. He sends a bolt of fear through me. These families live in a neighborhood that is considered one of the most dangerous regions in Salvador, often the target of televised police attacks and shootings. As he approaches, Natalia glances over at me, concerned that I will not understand that we are not in danger. The armed teenager finally reaches where we are sitting and simply passes by as if we are invisible. Natalia and her mother chuckle nervously, assuring me that there is no need to be afraid—he is simply waiting for the police.

Not long after the young teenager passes by, we decide to call it a night. I plan to sleep over at Natalia's house, at the invitation of her mother, Mona. They live in a one-bedroom house shared by four people and built directly above Natalia's uncle's bar. Their bathroom is not working properly, so I have to walk down a flight of cement stairs to shower, using a bucket of water that has been heated on the kitchen stove. Natalie stays with me, making small talk while seated in a chair outside the dark, makeshift shower, whose shower curtain is barely long or wide enough to ensure my privacy. The shower curtain is so short, in fact, that we both burst out laughing during my awkward attempt (and failure) to discreetly reach out of the shower to grab my towel from her.

After I finish showering, Natalia leads me back up into the bedroom, and I am invited to sleep in her bed, a twin-size bed that is surrounded by a sea of blonde dolls—not one black doll in sight. Natalia, Mona, and Damian, Natalia's brother, sleep in the larger queen-size bed in the same room. Each of the children has a corner in which to keep special toys for organization's sake. Before bed, Natalia smiles as she sifts through her box of belongings to show me her best doll, another blonde Barbie wearing a short skirt and high heels. Too tired from the evening to ask questions, I decide that a conversation about the dolls will have to wait for a later time. I dust the sand off the bottom of my feet, lay my head down, and pull a bright pink comforter over me that bears the same image as the pillow on which I rest my head. It is the last image I see before closing my eyes and the same image Natalie sees before she closes her eyes every night and in the morning when she awakes: Cinderella.

The next morning I wake up, return to the terrace that was the location of the party, and notice that Natalia and Zica are playing the hand-jive games that I taught them the night before. Having developed somewhat of a rapport, I play a few rounds with them, and soon after, we begin to have a serious conversation in which I ask them to tell me about themselves, their lives, and their country. Not long after, the conversation turns to race and color:

> ELIZABETH: What is your race?
> NATALIA: (*hesitates, shrugs her shoulders*) *Mestiça*? I don't really know.
> ELIZABETH: What is your color?
> NATALIA: *Morena.*
> ELIZABETH: Ok, so your race is *mestiça* and your color is *morena*?
> NATALIA: No, no (*giggles*).
> ELIZABETH: But that's what you said (*smile*). Oh, ok, what is your color?
> NATALIA: *Morena.*
> ELIZABETH: What is your race?
> NATALIA: (*silence*)
> ELIZABETH: (*awkward silence*) It's just that you described yourself with several different words, and I want to make sure I understand. What is your race?
> NATALIA: (*fiddles with her hands and giggles nervously, then speaks slowly and softly*) *Negra.*

When I ask the first question about race, Natalia not only responds that she does not know, she shrugs her shoulders and has a blank facial expression as though the question is irrelevant. She is familiar with color categories, so she initially uses the most ambiguous term to define her color: *morena*. When she is prompted to resolve the incongruence between her answers, Natalia's nonverbal behavior and her lowered voice convey her reluctance to say that she is *negra*. Afro-Brazilians' reluctance to self-classify as black has been previously documented by researchers, but this interaction is unique because I observe Natalia shifting answers and grappling to reconcile her own perceived contradictions.[6]

Natalia's four-year-old brother, Damian, is present during our interview, and he is growing increasingly frustrated with the questions and all the attention that I am giving the girls.[7] Damian is a preschool-aged boy with a tiny frame and a sweet, friendly demeanor. He is so light skinned that his mother, Mona, refers to him as white. He has large dark brown eyes, very light brown hair, and what are considered African facial features (wide nose and full lips). Since the very first day Damian and I met, he has hugged me tightly and called me his *tia* (aunt). His mother laughed when she noticed how attached he was to me, as he is to other women that she said he finds sexually attractive. I assume his response is less a question of sexuality and more a result of my attentiveness, as he enjoys the mundane questions I ask him and is excited to tell me about his day.

So Damian has never called me Elizabeth or Bete (as I am commonly known); for him I have always been *tia*. I do at times share close quarters and personal space with Damian, which I opine might cause him to mistake me for family. However, I soon realize, I am not Damian's only *tia*, but rather one of many. In fact, I am slightly disappointed when I realize that there is nothing particularly special about being called his *tia*. The word can be used almost indiscriminately to refer to any woman. The term *tia* may suggest familial intimacy, but it is merely a construction that allows children to engage in conversations from an early age that blur family and nonbiological relationships. Other kids in the neighborhood call me *tia* if they want to know if I have seen Natalia, if a stray ball has come my way and they want it back, or if they want to tell me I have dropped something. It is a way to say "hey you" to an adult woman rather than anything more. *Tia* can also be used by strangers when speaking to a woman as a sign of respect.

But for the moment, I am interviewing Natalia, and Damian is circling our table trying to remain quiet but approaching sporadically when the temptation to touch the funny little metal object that sits in the middle of the table (the voice recorder) is too much to resist. Our conversation continues, with Natalia fumbling with her fingers and seeming uncomfortable answering questions about her race. I decide to shift the questions and ask Natalia and Zica to help me understand what my race and color are in Brazil. I preface this shift by explaining that in the United States things are different. This excites Zica, who responds:

> Yes, I know! Because in America they have neighborhoods for black people and for white people. Don't they? The blacks cannot go to the white people's neighborhood and the white people are not allowed in the black people's neighborhood. I saw it on television! There's a lot of racism there, huh? One day I want to go to the U.S. What would it be like? (*smiles broadly*)

Apparently, Natalia and Zica have learned from television that this is the racial reality in the United States. Their comments are similar to those of many adult interviewees who say they have seen the movie *Mississippi Burning* and as a result express pity that I live in such a racist country. When I redirect the girls and ask them to help me understand my color, they assert that I am *morena*. Damian, no longer able to contain himself, states in a loud voice, "*Preta*! Tia, you are *preta*! You are *preta*, tia, *preta*!" He walks over to me with his tiny fingers reaching for my face and is proud that he knows what he perceives as the correct answer to the question.

Horrified by Damian's vocalization, Natalia pops his hand and tells him to go away. To her dismay, this only makes him more committed to answering the question, and with innocent confusion he whimpers and obediently walks to a chair, but not before making his last plea: "But she *is preta*." We continue our conversation, discussing movies they have seen about the United States, when suddenly Damian, unprovoked, spontaneously shouts "*Preta*!" while pointing at me. He then covers his mouth and laughs.

I am fascinated by Damian's unabashed commitment to identifying me as *preta* and by his sister's embarrassed reaction to his violations of racial etiquette. Damian is too young to have internalized racial rules and does not understand that *preta* is generally an unacceptable term and is certainly an offensive term for someone considered a high-status guest.[8] If someone were to have asked me, I would have stated, "I am *preta* and I am *negra*." Little Damian's "racial literacy" is accurate: *preta* is how someone who looks like me is classified. But the resistance that he receives from his sister is the same resistance I face when asserting my own color and racial identity with adults in Brazil. He has perfect racial literacy, in that he reads my features well and understands how I would be racialized in Brazil. But he lacks *racial fluency*, which is the ability to master the nuances of the context in which this knowledge should be wielded. To frame this interaction as a question of whether Damian is right or wrong would be misguided. It is far more complicated than that. The question is one of developing the fluency to understand and apply the rules of proper racial etiquette, a lesson that, according to Natalia, Damian fails miserably.

Natalia, as the older sister, is the enforcer of racial etiquette, but her efforts are futile because Damian is too young to understand and quite confident that I am *preta*. I ask the girls again to explain why I am *morena* and they are *negra*. I am curious about how they will reconcile this with the fact that I am darker than both of them, I have afro-textured hair that is more coily than either of theirs, and my facial features would be classified as African. They look at each other, giggle, and muster a reply that is nonsensical: "it is because our parents are *negros* so that makes us *negras*." When I explain that my parents are also *negros*, they look back at me with blank faces. Of course, the assumption that phenotype is a necessary and sufficient basis on which to determine race is faulty. In social settings I understand that my status, my gender, my age, and my nationality are all important determinants, and even though Natalia and Zica cannot or will not articulate these nuances, because of their racial fluency they know how to employ the rules in practice.

Leo, a light-skinned nine-year-old boy with straight hair and features that mark him as white, responds slightly differently. He replies confidently that his color is *moreno*. However, when I ask, "What is your race?" he is appalled and, with a frown, responds, "What? Race? You mean like a dog?!" In Brazil, the term *raça* has historically been defined as breed. However, contemporary developments, including growing research on racial inequality and the black movement in Brazil, have emphasized the social significance of race in society. Brazilians now increasingly associate the term *raça* with a social construction that is quite different from an animal breed.

At nine years old, Leo has not learned what race means; nor can he provide a response about his racial classification. I assume this means that he has low racial fluency and that he receives little racial socialization at home, but I am wrong on both accounts. Leo's family, the Fernandes family, is among the largest and most phenotypically diverse families in the study, with members who fall everywhere on the racial continuum and represent several points on the phenotypic continuum. They range from very light-skinned to dark-skinned members, with hair textures ranging from straight to very coarse and curly, and some possess racial features that are difficult to categorize.

Leo's mother, Alberta, and her brother, Clovis, are very light skinned with what is described as "almost good" hair. Straighter hair and hair that looks like white people's hair is considered good. Hair that needs to be moisturized or chemically treated is considered bad hair and associated with being of African descent. But Alberta has another brother, Guilherme, who has a slightly darker, light-brown complexion and hair that is wavier than their "almost straight" hair.

Although Leo's earlier responses suggest that he has never heard of the notion of race before, his mother and Uncle Clovis talk about race frequently in the house and in his presence. Both self-identify racially as black (*negro*), even though they define their color as brown (*pardo*). Over dinner in a casual conversation with Leo and me, Alberta states:

Look, my skin is this color (*taps her forearm*), but I am black! We are black. I put cream in my hair if I want to comb it too. So, girl, I am black! I can't stand racism. If there is one thing I cannot stand, it is racism! It is the biggest ignorance. (Alberta, 42)

Alberta is confident and outspoken about her blackness. According to her, the fact that she applies hair products before combing her hair is much stronger evidence of her race than her deceiving skin color. She deploys her political position against racism as additional evidence of her authentic blackness, and later discusses her support for the quota system that guarantees a percentage of positions at universities and schools for African-descendants. Leo is present during this conversation and continues eating dinner without looking up, as though our conversation does not concern him. Her racial consciousness has not been passed on to her young son, as one might expect. Despite Alberta's explicit and relatively radical racial and political consciousness, when Leo is asked if there is anybody in his family who is *negro*, he replies:

My mom's brother [Guilherme] is *negro* and his wife is *morena* and they have two that came out really black and the other that came out white. Two took after him, and one took after her.

He does not acknowledge that his mother or Uncle Clovis are *negros*. His Uncle Guilherme, whom he labels *negro*, is only slightly darker than Leo's mother and older uncle, but has wavy hair and is currently serving a prison sentence. He also does not have the same economic resources as his two siblings. When asked why his Uncle Guilherme is *negro* when his mother and other uncle are not considered *negros*, Leo explains that it is because of skin color. However, Guilherme is actually lighter than his wife, whom Leo refers to as *morena*. Leo illustrates his racial fluency by effectively negotiating racial rules. Though he is unable or unwilling to articulate how his uncle's prison sentence affects his racialization, he seemingly naturally places his uncle's wife, a business owner, in the neutral color category.

Conversations about race take place in his home, but Leo's racial identity is not intentionally cultivated. His confusion about how his family understands their racial heritage becomes evident in a conversation about ethnic diversity in Brazil. While I am sitting at their kitchen table, Leo runs into the house, excited to share that his class is moving on to a new unit.[9] With his backpack still on his shoulders, he begins:

LEO: Do you know what we are learning in school? (*Before I can answer, he continues.*) We are learning about African-descendants! (*smiles widely*)

ELIZABETH: That is pretty interesting, especially because I am an African-descendant.

LEO: What? *You? You* are an African-descendant? (*He looks at me with a huge smile and surprised eyes.*) Now maybe I can interview you (*laughs at himself*).

ELIZABETH: Well, yes, I am! (*I also laugh at the comment and his facial expression, because the rest of his family has spoken about their African heritage, and his mother identifies as negra.*)

LEO: I can't believe it (*smiling broadly*). I know an African-descendant! I actually know an African-descendant.

ELIZABETH: Leo? You know that I am not the only African-descendant around here?

LEO: (*his excitement and smile beginning to fade*) What do you mean? (*slightly frowns*)

ELIZABETH: Leo, I think you know many other African-descendants.

LEO: Wait, what do you mean? You, you don't mean in *my* family do you? Because my family is from Europe, that's what I always heard (*poking his chest out and rolling the "r" in Europe*).

ELIZABETH: Oh, ok.

LEO: But wait, do you think? . . . No, Elizabeth, I'm not. I'm going to ask! (*Leo runs into the living room, where he finds his mother, a cousin de consideração, and his great-aunt.*)[10] Are we African-descendants?

PAOLA (*his great-aunt*): Yes, we are African-descendants. Your great-grandfather was *preto*!

LEO: But, but grandmother always said that she was a beautiful Indian!

PAOLA: Well, that may be, but . . . (*her voice trails off with a chuckle*).

VANESSA (*darker-skinned cousin de consideração*): Child, of course you are an African-descendant! We are all blacks! Our skin color may be different but we are all black.

In this interaction, Leo reveals that he has, in fact, received some socialization about his heritage, and he has strong affective attachments to his understanding that he is European. Despite his deceased grandmother's assertion that she was a beautiful Indian, he strongly identifies as European. His great-aunt laughs, and I surmise that it is because she understands the tendency of families to highlight Indian heritage instead of African heritage as a way of lightening, if not whitening.[11] But Leo's anger is initially puzzling to me because he has already informed me that there are *negros* in his family, so I have assumed he knows there are African-descendants in his family.

I observe this disconnect in conversations with other children and many adults, and I learn that often blackness is not understood as being connected to Africa. Although respondents understand that slavery occurred and that *negros* were slaves, it is not clear to them where slaves originated or how that history is related to them.[12] Despite the presence of a tourism industry based on the connection between Bahia and Africa, many families did not understand or fully appreciate the connection.

Although Leo has not internalized his mother's racial consciousness, this does not mean that he has learned nothing about race. His racial and color descriptions of his Uncle Guilherme and his wife demonstrate he has an understanding of racial nuances. Not merely responding to class, status, or behavioral cues, such as Guilherme's prison record, Leo labels his aunt in a way that is consistent with racial etiquette. Research suggests that gender and class play a role in the willingness to define other family members as *negro*, and Leo has the racial fluency to manage those differences handily.[13]

At a later point, the precocious nine-year old begins to mimic what he perceives as my odd questions and expresses an interest in becoming a researcher himself. To begin his training, he decides to ask me about my race, and I indulge him. I respond that I am *preta* and *negra*, a reply that he finds unacceptable:

> No, no you are not *preta*. Elizabete, you are not *negra*. You are *morena*. (*He pauses, looks at my arms, and glances up at my hair and face.*) Well, . . . you are *morena escura*, but you are not *negra*. Now your husband (*pauses*), he is a little bit black. (*He leans in with a lower voice and holds his two fingers close together in a near pinch.*) But you are not black, Elizabete! Black is the color of, . . . black is the color something like that (*pointing to my field notebook*). You don't look like that. You are not *preta*!

Through this interaction, Leo illustrates his familiarity with racial etiquette, but his comments suggest that his racial fluency is still developing, and he encounters a minor hiccup as he tries to situate me. Initially he rejects my identification as *preta* and identifies me as *morena*. But having recently revealed that he is *moreno* and having taken inventory of my skin color and other features, he recognizes the significant differences between us and finds a compromise by asserting that I am *morena escura*—a wonderfully ambiguous intermediate term that exists in his racial toolkit. This allows Leo to acknowledge that I am darker than he is (*escura*), while still allowing me to remain in the ambiguous, safe, and respectable realm of *morena*. Leo is a confident child, which is why he corrects me with no hesitation. He accepts that I am an African-descendant and recognizes that I am dark skinned, but the term *negra*, even though it is not perceived as strong as *preta*, is still not available to me.

Edward Telles argues, "Brazilians may seek to avoid offending dark-skinned women of high status by labeling them as black. . . . To refer to a woman as *preta* is especially demeaning and nearly inconceivable in the case of a high-status woman."[14] Leo's resistance to accepting my self-identification as *negra* and *preta*, as well as his careful articulation that my husband is "a little bit black," is consistent with previous research highlighting that strongly racial terms are avoided when they refer to women and high-status individuals. My husband is *negro* and *preto*; he is often mistaken for being African in the United States because of his dark skin and other features. Leo wants to acknowledge that my husband is dark skinned, while also responding to his impression that we might feel or should feel ashamed of being black. These negotiations echo another informant, who states frankly, "We call ourselves *morenos* so that we do not have to say *negro*." Leo resolves his dilemma by engaging in complimentary color categorization, a reasonable compromise that allows him to recognize my husband's blackness politely. He is just "a little bit black."

Dona Lara of the Barán family is a *negra assumida*, a black woman who assumes her racial identity. Indeed, she explains that she never really had a choice in the matter because her appearance made it impossible for her to refer to herself as anything but black. She recalls an experience with a close friend whom she encountered when she was on a stroll with her young sons:

> One time a person, a friend, in reference to my son, said, "Your son is a pretty *moreno*." And I said, "*Moreno*? No, please don't call him *moreno*. He is black." And then she said, "But that is such a strong word," and I say, "No, it's not strong at all. They are really black, indeed!" (*Uma vez uma pessoa, uma amiga se referiu ao meu filho disse, "Seu filho é um moreno bonito." E eu disse, "Moreno? Gente não, não chama ele de moreno não. É negro." É ela: "Mas esta palavra é tão pesada," e digo "Não, não tem peso não. Eles são negões mesmo!"*)

Dona Lara proudly recounts this moment in which she refuses to accept *moreno* as an appropriate or adequate term for her children. Her insistence that *negro* be used is both an expression of her own identity and a result of her understanding that this will be the basis on which her sons will be treated.[15]

Young Leo does not avoid the term *negra* altogether. He uses it to describe his cousin *de consideração* (one who is considered a cousin) though she is several shades lighter than I am and has straighter hair. When I ask him to explain why she and I are categorized differently, he cannot say why, but then he explains, as though it were a separate issue, that his cousin was poor and came to live with his aunt when she was young. Even though he does not state it explicitly, her class and status are both factors in his decision to label her as *negra*; this is consistent with racial rules.

Other children in this study also report not discussing race with their parents and describe their own families in terms very different from those their parents use. All of the children provide answers to questions of race and color, but none of them answer questions about race confidently. They are more confident, though not certain, about color classifications. Some change their answers, and others simply say that they do not know their race. Roseane, an eleven-year-old brown-skinned girl with wavy hair in the Matos family responds to the question, "What is your race?" with the most creative and unexpected reply. After thinking about the question and asking me to repeat it, she shrugs her shoulders and replies, "Gemini?"—her zodiac sign. Roseane's mother, on the other hand, has very clear notions of her own racial identity. Without me asking a question, she refers to herself as *negra*.[16] This racial consciousness has not been transmitted to Roseane, who is confused by the very term race (*raça*).

In seven of the ten core families, family members vacillate between color and racial categories and often answer my questions with questions. Even when a family member is certain of their race or color classifications, others seem to be completely unaware of theirs. As a result, there is seldom consensus. With regard to race, there are eight racial terms used by informants, but 85 percent of them identify as either black or brown (see table 4.2). Racial categorization is less a source of debate among adults than color categories are. The extensive use of racialized and color nicknames suggests the prominence of such terms in everyday life in Salvador. Respondents are heard referring to themselves and one another as:

black (diminutive): *neguinho* or *pretinho*
black/honey: *nego/nega*
big black man/woman: *negão/negona*
toasted or burnt one: *torradinho*
black (offensive, used towards black women): *negrinha*
black from Candomblé (offensive): *preta do bozó*
very white (offensive): *branquela*
very white (nonoffensive): *branco*, with heavily rolled *r*
pretty people: *gente bonita*
ugly people: *gente feia*
milky (offensive): *parmaleitisinho*
coffee with milk: *café com leite*
milk: *leite*
very white, or big white woman: *brancona*
purple: *lilais*
deep red: *jambo*

Overall, children's responses are drastically different from the responses of adults and teenagers. Almost all of my informants over the age of thirteen understand the concepts of color and race, even if they are not certain how to classify themselves. Adults show less uncertainty than children about their racial classification, and occasionally they show bold pride. Despite her physical appearance, Lilza is insistent that she is not white:

> Look at me, am I white? I'm not white. White people don't have this skin and they don't put cream in their hair. If I don't put it in my hair, my hair is coarse.

Reflecting on her mother's racial identification, Lilza reveals:

> My mother, . . . for years she has not considered herself black. She is going to say that she is *morena . . . parda*. But she is not going to say that she is. . . . She may even say that she is Indian color. She does not characterize herself as black. If you were to ask her, she is not going to say that she is black. She is going to say that she uses product in her hair so that her hair doesn't stay coarse. She is going to say that. You understand? But it doesn't stay like that. Your hair [texture] does not change just because you put product in it. (*Lilza and her mother-in-law laugh.*)

Given her mother's conflicted ideas about race, Lilza was uncertain of how to identify when she was a child. She confesses that this is something she and her mother have never really discussed and most likely never will. It was only after Lilza was hired to work for the Brazilian census as a teenager that she determined she could not be easily placed in either a white or black category. Hence she concluded that she is an African-descendant and she is *parda*.

Daniel, a fifty-seven-year-old taxi driver and father of three responds to questions about race and color in the following manner:

> ELIZABETH: What is your color?
> DANIEL: *Pardo. Pardo* on the outside, *negro* on the inside!
> ELIZABETH: What is your race?
> DANIEL: *Negro!*

Daniel is another representative of those who even while using an intermediary color category identifies racially as black—or, as Daniel states, "*negro* on the inside." Daniel assumes his blackness, even though he mentions that on the basis of racial appearance others consider him white. He later reveals that his wife is *negra* and offers the fact that he has always been more attracted to *negras* as evidence of his racial loyalty. As mentioned earlier, his marital fidelity is not as strong as his racial loyalty: he confesses numerous extramarital affairs to me during our interview. He justifies this by explaining that his father maintained three separate families when he was growing up. In the neighborhood, Daniel is known for having *filhos bonitos* (beautiful children), and he has passed his racial consciousness on to both of them. Giselle, his daughter, is very light skinned with wavy hair, and she has stopped straightening her hair because she is active in the black movement. She is both a college student and a *negra assumida*, which is a significant decision for Brazilians who might otherwise be read as not black. Expressions of racial pride like Daniel's are rare. It is much more common for there to be confusion when people are asked questions about color and race, to the extent that other family members are often called in or asked to intervene to reconcile the answers.

FAMILY INTERVENTIONS IN RACIAL CLASSIFICATION

Over the course of several weeks, I have the opportunity to meet with Jocelia, a light-skinned woman with short, black, wavy hair who is amused by my "peculiar" questions about race. She is the host mother of an American student, Stephanie, a friend of mine who is living in Brazil and conducting research on another topic. In fact, my visits to see Stephanie often include long conversations with Jocelia about Brazil, the United States, and any other issue that interests her. Stephanie does not speak Portuguese very well, and it appears that Jocelia requested to be a host mother because she enjoys the company of someone with whom she can chat. While this certainly has its benefits, whenever Stephanie and I have plans to attend a scheduled event, I call her when I am downstairs to avoid the unpleasantries of abruptly cutting short my conversation with Jocelia. Otherwise when I visit, I enjoy a warm reception: Jocelia always offers me several drinks, fruit, and sometimes dinner. She is curious about and even amused by what I am doing in Brazil. Upon initially hearing of my interest in race and family, she replies, "Oh, Bete, if you are interested in studying race why did you come to Brazil?" The suggestion is that race does not exist in Brazil.

On one evening when I am feeling particularly bold, I muster the courage to ask Jocelia about her racial identification. She asserts confidently, "I'm white, but I have a sister who is *parda* and a brother who is *moreno*." We continue talking as I recount what I have been doing over the last few weeks. Our conversation ends only when there is a knock on the door. Jocelia excuses herself to answer the door and returns with a woman who looks very familiar. Jocelia laughs at my emotive facial expression and introduces the woman at the door as her sister, Ariane. I am shocked because Jocelia and Ariane look as though they could be identical twins. Their height, skin color, hair texture, and facial features are all the same. The only difference that I perceive is that Jocelia is much heavier than Ariane, but otherwise the similarity is uncanny.

Hardly able to contain my curiosity, but cautious about seeming overly interested, I ask with a pretense of indifference why Jocelia is considered *branca* and Ariane *parda*. Ariane stands silently for a few awkward seconds, and her eyes drift upward in a pensive manner. Her response is as though she has never thought about this before. Seconds later, almost angrily, she responds, "Why am I *parda* and you *branca*? . . . Why would dad do this?" Jocelia chuckles nervously and responds, "If Ariane were to apply for college, she would be eligible for quotas, but I wouldn't because I'm white." Jocelia takes pains to place extra emphasis on the fact that she is white and proud of it. For clarity's sake, I ask Jocelia to explain once again why she is considered white even though she has light brown skin and appears to be Ariane's identical twin. She shrugs her shoulders and says, "Because my *cartão* (identification card) says so."

This encounter reveals how ambiguous official racial categorizations can be and the way in which structural processes such as birth registration are implicated in these complexities. Initially I am concerned about having created a family problem where none has previously been, but it later becomes clear that this is not the first time the sisters have discussed this issue. That Jocelia relishes her official white status even though she understands that it might mean not being eligible for some opportunities is a strong statement about the psychological benefits she enjoys from her legal racial status. The process of registering a child requires and reinforces inconsistencies and serves as a space for racial whitening.[17]

Though she initially laughs about it, seventy-year-old matriarch Dona Lara offers an important explanation for why Afro-Brazilians use legal birth documentation to declare whiter categorizations:

> But why is the black person like this? He was so devalued. So much so that people themselves. . . . On my birth certificate, you know what color it has on it? (*pause*). *Morena. Morena*! It's, it's, it's like it's offensive to call someone black. (Mas por que o negro é assim? Era tão desvalorizado.

Que as pessoas mesmas. . . . Na minha certidão de nascimento, sabe qual é a cor que tem? (pause) Morena. Morena. E, e, e, como é de ofender chamar de negro.)

Dona Lara's clear and concise explanation reveals that it is her understanding that parents hope to use the birth certificate as a means of legal or official whitening. As she argues, the tendency to whiten children on documentation is a legacy of slavery and a reflection of the way that blacks had been devalued in society. The act of attempting to subvert racial categorizations with registration transmits a tacit message that negative racial categorizations can and should be manipulated. Of course, it also reinforces a strategy that supports social mobility and improvement of life chances through whitening rather than through direct contestation of the devaluation of blackness. However, Dona Lara reveals that having the term *morena* listed provides none of the advantages hoped for because "when people see you they know your race, they know your color."[18]

In cases in which family members are not clear on how to answer questions about race and color, family interventions are sometimes necessary, and these conversations sometimes reveal the extent of racial and color inconsistencies among both educated and less educated respondents. In a one-on-one conversation about color and race, Walter, a very dark-skinned, nineteen-year-old high school student with college ambitions who wears his hair in an afro, reveals the confusion in his family:

ELIZABETH: What is your color?
WALTER: My color is *negro . . . preto.*
ELIZABETH: What is your race?
WALTER: No, my color is *preto*, my race is *negro.* On my dad's side, I have an uncle, and he and my dad look just alike except my uncle is white. My dad is bald, around this height (*uses his hands to indicate height*), but my uncle is white. So they look just alike, even their beards. It's only in their skin color that they are different. (Só pela côr que se vê a diferença.)

Initially confused about differences between race and color, Walter attempts to show that his family has a variety of phenotypes and that many are not *preto* like him. He then provides unsolicited information about the phenotype of his father and his uncle. He attempts to explain the racial identity of his uncle and father, but finds himself hedging, stuttering, and pausing consistently throughout the discussion. In the end, his answer is almost unintelligible. With reference to his uncle, he explains:

I . . . I . . . I don't know. I would say that he . . . if you are looking . . . I
think . . . I don't think he would say that he is black. He would say something else. It's that you never know what a person might say. One day they
say one thing, the next day something else. What color is my mom? This
thing is tricky. She is *preta* (black) because *parda* brown doesn't exist. She
is *negra* with a lighter skin tone. On my birth certificate it says *pardo*. On
my mother's birth certificate it says *parda*. I don't know if it stayed *parda*
or not. I could check it for you. It's something so variable that I cannot
say that a person who is darker is going to be *negro* because it's so variable. This business of *pardo* is pointless. My professor says that *pardo* is
the color of "papel da bunda" (*literally translated as "butt paper," a vulgar term for toilet paper, which is a gray color in Brazil*).

Particularly interested in how young people understand race and color,
I allow Walter to continue his response in order to hear him work through
his racial questions and doubts. His reply that categories are completely
variable is consistent with the dominant narrative about racial fluidity in
Brazil, which has come under intense scrutiny.[19] Yet, even while he recognizes the situational and variable quality of color and race, his understanding of race is black-and-white; as he views *pardo* as a "pointless"
category.

Walter initially confuses his race and color, does not know how to
classify his parents and relatives, and adds that his birth certificate states
that he is *pardo*. His is the quintessential example of how Afro-Brazilians
struggle to reconcile mixed messages about race and color. When he asks
his mother to intervene and find his birth certificate, she begins deconstructing their family history again, focusing on the nonblack relatives in
her family and her Portuguese ancestors. But to the questions about her
own color and race, she answers *preta* and *negra*, respectively.

Similarly, when twelve-year-old Larissa, who has dark, caramel-
colored skin, light-brown hair that has been chemical straightened, and
facial features that define her as black, does not know how to respond to
questions about race, her lighter-skinned brother intervenes:

ELIZABETH: What is your color?
LARISSA: *Morena*.
ELIZABETH: What is your race? (*Paulo, her brother, walks into
the room.*)
LARISSA: Huh? *Raça*? What do you mean?
ELIZABETH: Whatever it means to you.

LARISSA: (*pauses; shrugs shoulders*) Um, um (*thinks for a few seconds*), I don't know.

PAULO: (*interrupts as he grabs a drink from the refrigerator*) You are *negra*! We are *negros*. Me, you, and Elizabeth! *Negros*! Black hair, black skin, white teeth! (*We all laugh.*)

LARISSA: Well, *negra* (*chuckles again*).

This interaction further illustrates the incongruity in how family members classify themselves. It is not that race and color are difficult issues to discuss but that they simply are not considered important enough to discuss explicitly. In this family as in others, racial socialization is characterized by ambiguity and a de-emphasis on rigid racial and color categorizations. Paulo is surprised that his sister does not know how to answer the question about her race, and his intervention becomes a teaching moment.

It may seem like an arbitrary joke when Paulo adds an extra phenotypic signifier of race by referencing our white teeth, but this happens often in interviews and is an important detail. Several informants use white teeth as a phenotypic signifier for blacks, especially if they want to characterize someone as an attractive black person. Racial categorization is never based solely on skin color; color is considered in conjunction with other physical and cultural traits.

In Brazil, one is not objectively black, but one becomes black or discovers one's blackness through a racialization process that varies. Thirty-three-year-old Thiago, who strongly identifies as black, explains the process of discovering his blackness:

I discovered that I was black since I come from a mixed family. My sister is lighter and my father is really dark skinned. My grandfather was even darker. He had like straight, . . . well, straight hair. He had hair that was good, a little better and different than us. We have bad hair and he had good hair. Well, in their viewpoint he had good hair. It was then that I realized that I have to value who I am. I had to value our color because my grandmother showed that though she was eighty-six years old, she didn't even look her age. She prayed, she gave us advice, she was a lucid person. I knew I was black because of the roots and heritage of my parents and my grandparents. I knew it was important. I knew that I could work hard without getting tired, when they got old they didn't look their age, we had this wisdom and knowledge. That's how I knew. One of the differences between me and other people is that I believed in what my family did. They were hard-working agricultural workers; they were blacks. As blacks they worked harder, they had an ability to take care of kids, the family, and the animals. This comes from blacks. For us, color was not as much of a big deal. I realized that skin color might vary, but the personality and heritage, the knowledge of where you come from, your values remain, and the family is much stronger united.

For Thiago blackness is a question not merely of phenotype, but of values, traditions, and heritage. His racial pride emerges from essentializing blackness and relying on stereotypes about work ethic, graceful aging, and blacks' connection to nature. It was by being part of a phenotypically diverse family that he came to the realization that blackness should be defined less in terms of how one looks and more in terms of cultural and behavioral traits.

WILL THE REAL WHITE PERSON PLEASE STAND UP?

The importance of racial features to racial classification emerges in a number of interviews. Larissa distinguishes between her white friends by referring to them as *branco* (white) or *branco de cabelo liso* (white with straight hair). Interviewees use these distinctions to emphasize the difference between someone who is "legitimately" white and someone who has very light skin but is understood as white only by Bahia's standards.

Similarly, but much less often, the phrase *preto de cabelo duro* (black with hard hair) is used to describe a distant relative, such as a grandparent or great-grandparent, when there is a desire to emphasize a slave heritage or authentic blackness. When Walter's mother is called to intervene in a conversation about race and color, she describes his great-grandfather as "black, black with nappy hair, a legitimate black" (*preto, preto de cabelo duro, negro legítimo*). The additional modifier suggests that it is hair that ultimately determines that a particular ancestor is indisputably black, or *negro legítimo*.

Even these claims to legitimate blackness are complicated by the diverse uses of nicknames based on skin color. Afro-Brazilian families often refer to the lightest members of the family in white color terms, while offering a disclaimer that by *white* they are referring to skin color rather than race. In other families the darkest member of the family is sometimes referred to as *negro* or *preto* even if everyone in the family is considered white. That is, in a family of medium- to dark-skinned *negros*, the family member who is lightest could be called *branco* and the darkest might be called *preto*, even though the entire family is structurally situated as nonwhite and categorize themselves as *negros*. Marcelo, a man with a light to medium complexion and self-described "bad hair" explains that in his family being the *neguinho* (blackie) was a good thing:

> In my family I was called Neguinho. But wait, wait a minute, it wasn't like a racist thing! (*laughs*). It was just my nickname; it wasn't anything racist. I was the *neguinho* of the house. That meant that everybody loved me, everyone treated me well. I was the *neguinho*.

The relative use of these terms resonates with analyses of alternate meanings of the same words based on context and use of the diminutive. Of course, the term *neguinho* still has a racial origin.[20]

On the other hand, lighter-skinned informants who might be read and treated as white on the basis of their racial appearance fiercely maintain and patrol strict boundaries for classifying who is a real white person and who is not. Even when they use the term *white* for their own racial classification, these respondents often make it a point to qualify their whiteness or dismiss their legitimate claim to whiteness and distance themselves from the privileges that come with it. In fact, most of the white Brazilians I interview (outside of the core families) resist asserting their whiteness altogether and sometimes prefer to call themselves *morenos*.

Twelve-year-old Jorge and his wealthy white family invite me to a local outdoor steakhouse (*churrascaria*) in order to show me around Salvador. He and I have a few minutes to chat while the adults search for meat and beer. We begin the conversation with questions about how I am enjoying my time in Brazil, and our chat slowly evolves:

> ELIZABETH: So, I am studying race in Brazil, but I'm trying to understand how it works.
> JORGE: Oh, you are studying race in Brazil?
> ELIZABETH: Yes, and I'm trying to understand it. It's difficult for me. For example, what is your race?
> JORGE: (*pauses, smiles, and looks at his arms*) Moreno (*shrugs*).
> ELIZABETH: Oh, ok. Well, do you know how many races there are in Brazil?
> JORGE: Oh, ok, let me see. . . . Ok, there is black, white, wait, we learned this in school! There is like a whole bunch, like have you heard of *caboclo*, *zamba*, it's like a mix between white and Indian, . . . or black and Indian, . . . or something like that. Then there is, . . . uh . . . *mulato*! We have all of this in Brazil.

ELIZABETH: Yes, that's a lot. So, if you had to fill out something to tell your race, which would it be?

JORGE: Well, . . . I would, . . . well, I think . . . I put *moreno*.

ELIZABETH: Oh, ok. I didn't know that *moreno* is really an option, is it? You didn't say *moreno* when you listed races. Is *moreno* a race?

JORGE: No, well, . . . ok, then if, . . . ok, I am white. But, I'm not really white. Look my skin is not all that white like white people with blue eyes in the United States (*looks at his arms and compares them to mine*). But it's . . . ok, I would put I am white, but I am not that white.

By the age of twelve, Jorge has internalized racial etiquette, referring to himself first as *moreno*, and only later as white when he is forced to reconcile what he has stated earlier with the list of races that he has told me. On the basis of his facial features and skin color, he would be consistently classified as white in Bahia, so I am interested in how he uses the *moreno* category. For him, true whiteness means having blonde hair and blue eyes, which he does not possess. He feels uncomfortable owning his whiteness, and even once he acknowledges it, he relies on ideas about North American whiteness to suggest that he is not really white. This interesting juxtaposition is common for the white middle class in Salvador, who frame whiteness and racism as a U.S. problem. Jorge is darker than most whites in the United States, but because whiteness is relational, he receives all the privileges that come with whiteness in Brazil.

These racial negotiations are not unusual in Salvador. Andrea, a white mother, struggles to confront questions of whiteness as it relates to herself and her mixed-race daughters. She is married to a black man and has two light-skinned daughters who have "almost straight" dark hair and white facial features. Andrea herself is considered racially white by everyone in the neighborhood: she is very light skinned and has very light brown, naturally straight hair. She describes her daughters as white, and then the following conversation unfolds:

ANDREA: My daughters are white.

ELIZABETH: What does it mean to be white?

ANDREA: If I were white, I would have eyes that were blue or green, and I should be blonde with blue eyes and blonde hair. But I'm *morena*. Well, I am not *morena*. Am I *morena*?

ELIZABETH: I don't know.

ANDREA: I am not *morena*. And my daughter, well, she isn't either. I think that she is not white, she is brown (*parda*). She is not white, she is *parda*. Wait, I was wrong. Here in Bahia it is called *mulata*. No, *mulata* is darker, so it is not that. What is it called? (*pauses while she is thinking*) Ok, there is black, white, brown. Did you know that there is even *ruivo* (redhead). You know what that is?

Her discomfort and shifting responses are a function of her position as the white wife of a black man who lives in a popular black neighborhood. For all of these reasons, she would rather not assert her whiteness and racial privileges and instead decides to classify herself as *parda*. When others in the neighborhood are asked to classify her, they uniformly describe her as white.

Andrea shifts among terms—white, *morena*, *parda*, *mulata*—until she shifts the conversation altogether. Ultimately she does not reconcile the racial classification of her daughter and attempts to introduce red-haired as a racial category in order to avoid answering the original question about her race. Her strict criteria of whiteness include blue eyes and blonde hair, which few people in Bahia have. All of this allows her to downplay her discomfort with her own whiteness, but it may also represent her sincere connection to the black community. This is consistent with other findings suggesting that white mothers sometimes adopt alternative meanings of whiteness once they partner with black men and have mixed-race children.[21] In fact, Andrea holds strongly critical views of racism, which she articulates through structural arguments about how racism affects education and labor market inclusion in ways that systematically disadvantage blacks.

THERE ARE NO WHITES, WE ARE ALL BLACK!

In Salvador, families rely on a number of color and phenotypic terms to describe themselves and others, but they are much more consistent in their racial categorizations. Many Bahians use a racial logic that is based on a black-white conceptualization of race.[22] This is so even though Brazil has a sizeable indigenous and mixed-race population. Liliane argues:

> In society a white person has to be white. Either you are white or you are black. Either a person is white or in society he is black. (Liliane, *negra*, 48)

Some respondents adopt the position that "*negro* is a race, and within that race is a variety of colors." Others self-identify as black by default, without the often associated political consciousness; they report that they are black simply because their features make it obvious that they are not white.

Racial classification is a distinct process from racial identification, which implies the internalization of a racial consciousness. In the most extreme cases, respondents classify everyone in Brazil as *negro*. Informants articulate this formulation of race in a number of similar ways:

> For me no one is white. Here, everyone is black. (Vânia, *mestiça*, 31, call center worker)

> Brazil doesn't have whites. We are all African-descendants. (Sandro, white, 48, mechanic)

The discursive and ideological shift away from the notion of "We are all Brazilian" to "We are all black" is significant, particularly if it is observed outside of Bahia. But, the question still remains of what it means to assert that everyone is black, when those who make this argument are more likely to identify themselves in the intermediate or white category.

Evidence suggests that although everyone is racially mixed, those who are racialized as white enjoy significant advantages. Previous researchers have referred to the tenuous claims of whiteness held by those who are considered *brancos da Bahia* (Bahian near-whites); their claims to whiteness might be challenged once they leave the region.[23] One black activist in Salvador explains the way claims to whiteness function in a regional context:

> There is a joke that people in Brazil ask themselves, "Who is white?," most of all in Bahia. But this is a false discussion because the idea that all of us are mixed . . . biologically, actually, we all are. But, socially, which is what counts, we are not. And so it is this that we are accustomed to saying in Bahia that those who are considered white in Bahia do not manage to pass the airport security screening at the Guarulhos Airport in São Paulo. Because in São Paulo they say, "Here, we know who is white." But this does not lessen the importance of social and racial hierarchies in Brazil. Because there is also a system known as a pigmentocracy. The lighter that you are, the greater your chances of social mobility.[24]

In families, the way that this pigmentocracy functions is difficult to confront because it requires people in the same families to acknowledge privileges and advantages that they unfairly receive. Rather than confront this, some family members remain silent, while others internalize these ideas and engage in practices that may further lighten the family. In other families, the hierarchies on which the pigmentocracy is based are rejected altogether and replaced by an alternative ideology of race.

RETELLING NATIONAL TALES

Considering how racial fluency in Afro-Brazilian families responds to constructions of race and notions of Brazilianness, one must consider how racial perspectives are informed by people's understandings of Brazil's history. For example, the disconnections I observed between blackness and Africanness might be related to what Brazilians learn about the period of colonization and postcolonial development in Brazil. National tales, including the dominant narrative of Brazil's discovery and representations of slavery, socialize Brazilians to accept national accounts about race that trivialize the brutality of slavery and portray all Brazilians as equal members of a larger national family. Stories are political, and historical storytelling and personal narratives "often reproduce power relations, as the specific stories we tell tend to reinforce the social order."[25]

While historical narratives are different from racial stories in that they involve historical rather than personal experiences, the historical narratives that respondents provide can be analyzed for their role in promoting a particular reading of historical events and contemporary conditions. Gilberto Freyre's historical revisionism played a fundamental role in downplaying racial stratification in order to reinforce the image of Brazil as a racial democracy.[26] Hence national tales can be fundamental to perpetuating racist ideology, but the content of the stories is only one aspect of a more elaborate "interpretive repertoire consisting of frames, styles, and racial stories" that once analyzed can reveal how racial ideologies influence the recreation and interpretation of events.[27]

Respondents report learning about the history of race and slavery in Brazil from *telenovelas* (soap operas), and the historical knowledge they gain influences their consciousness and shapes what they believe about their own origins.[28] In response to my request, "Tell me about the beginning of Brazil," several informants begin in an almost scripted manner with the following phrase, "In the era of the great voyages, Pedro Cabral . . ." The formal and nearly identical phrasing of their historical accounts suggests that they have memorized or internalized a similar storyline of exploration and discovery. Though the specific details of their narratives vary, their approach to the question is one that idealizes discovery, rushes through slavery, and focuses on the postabolition creation of a new raceless Brazil, with Princesa Isabel as the adored heroine. Both the precise details and the style of their historical storytelling reveal much about some Afro-Brazilians' affective ambivalence toward this history.

The youngest respondents consistently report not having learned or discussed Brazil's history with their families. They often state that they are educated by the *telenovelas* (watched mainly at home) and from lessons at school. When Tati, an eleven-year-old, is asked to explain the beginning of Brazil, she offers the following historical account:

> TATI: The Indians came first and then whites, blacks, and then racism. Whites came here on ships and boats. Blacks came in cells at the bottom of the ships. That's where the white people tossed them. They were here to work for whites and did not receive money. After slavery ended, life was easy for blacks, and there are many wealthy blacks now.
>
> ELIZABETH: Where are they?
>
> TATI: I don't know, in various places. Like Helena and her godmother.

Tati offers a historical narrative that correctly acknowledges that three main groups have played a major role in Brazilian history: blacks, whites, and indigenous groups. She does not suggest that their initial encounter is a friendly one. Instead, she associates the encounters of the groups with racism and highlights the harsh way that whites "tossed" (*jogaram*) blacks into the ships and exploited them when they arrived. However, Tati's pace in telling the story is worth nothing. She rushes through the uncomfortable first three sentences and continues with a sense of relief once she reaches the point where "slavery ended." Her rapid progression through the narrative parallels how popular representations of Brazil's history briefly acknowledge the horrors of slavery then emphasize a postslavery era of racial equality. According to how she understands this history, the end of slavery signaled the beginning of a new era and what she calls an easy life for blacks.

The absence of legal segregation or Jim Crow laws in Brazil after slavery has been used to suggest that racism was and is less brutal there than in the United States.[29] Tati's story concludes with an assertion about Brazil's racial egalitarianism, which she establishes by referencing the presence of wealthy blacks. The two wealthy black people she mentions, Helena and her godmother, are fictional characters on a popular *telenovela* called *Viver a Vida*. To this eleven-year-old the two fictional characters on the show are real, and it is difficult for her to separate reality from the fictional dramas of the *telenovela*.

When the precocious Leo, a nine-year-old boy, is asked about the beginning of Brazil, he starts with the common story line and in a loud voice, "In the era of the great voyages." He continues by elaborating on the motivations behind the voyages, focusing on the exciting search for gold, jewels, and spices. He is particularly interested in talking about shiny objects, and the majority of his historical account involves describing the large rubies and colorful jewels that the explorers bring back to the royal family.[30] In Leo's narrative the beginning of Brazil does not include a history of slavery. He does not mention blacks until I directly ask him, "How do blacks enter into the history?" Leo offers a sophisticated reply for his age:

> Blacks arrived here through slavery. In the past, the whites had more power than blacks and more money. So they took blacks from a place called a chapel, I mean the slave quarters (*senzala*). That is where he got blacks and put him to work. The *negros* didn't get paid anything, and if the *negro* didn't want to work they would tie him up to a stick and beat him. But time passed and Princesa Elizabete [*sic*] appeared. So Princesa Isabel, thought, thought, and thought, and with Don Pedro II decided to end slavery. After this, they [blacks] started to earn money, their life started to become a little easy, they started to build houses, get married, have children. Before they just went out, they weren't able to get married.

Like Tati, Leo is familiar with Brazil's history of slavery and frames the past as though it is drastically different from the present. He states that back then, "whites had more power than blacks and more money." In his narrative he acknowledges the physical abuses of slavery and excitedly offers to show me what it was like for a slave to be beaten. I decline the demonstration.

In both Leo's account and Tati's, the violence of slavery is used to show the extent of Princesa Isabel's benevolence. She magically "appeared," and after a moral epiphany ("she thought, thought, and thought"), she made the generous decision to end slavery. There is no indication of black resistance, no black agency at all in the abolition of slavery, only a morally upright, white princess who became the savior of the passive, oppressed black masses. But it is Leo's request to recreate the beating of a slave that resonates with me because it illustrates how popular depictions that dehumanize slaves lead a child to think of slave beatings as part of a fun game that I might enjoy reenacting.

Other children have less sophisticated accounts of history and can offer only brief snippets of their understandings of Brazil's beginnings. According to Regane, blacks were not slaves. She states: "Blacks sailed on ships to get here. They were sailors." Ana Luzia, an eleven-year-old, argues that blacks were not brought over as slaves. Rather, "blacks and Indians lived here together until white people came." I expect to hear varying accounts of Brazilian history from children, particularly because of how slavery is portrayed in the *telenovelas* and because it is only partially addressed in schools. However, adults also offer varying accounts of Brazil's beginnings. Some demonstrate limited historical knowledge, and others provide accounts that challenge dominant narratives.

Sonia, a mother of six, is uncertain of how to answer questions about Brazil's history. This becomes increasingly evident during our interview:

> ELIZABETH: What did you learn about how blacks came to Brazil? What do you know about this history?
>
> SONIA: What they say in the books, you know, blah, blah, blah (*we laugh*).
>
> ELIZABETH: How did they arrive?
>
> SONIA: Um . . . sheesh . . . um (*pauses several seconds as she is thinking*).
>
> ELIZABETH: What I mean is how do you understand this story?
>
> SONIA: Let me see, . . . well, like this, . . . let me see, how will I tell you? . . . Wait a minute, my brain is slow today (*laughs*). You want to know how blacks arrived in Brazil? (*pauses*) I don't know.
>
> ELIZABETH: Did you learn about this in school?
>
> SONIA: It's like this. . . . You mean like this when the Portuguese came and blah, blah, blah (*in a singsong voice*).
>
> ELIZABETH: Yes, that's what I mean (*we both laugh*).
>
> SONIA: You mean like, ok. In the 1500s blah blah and the negros blah blah and Princesa Isabel gave them freedom with the Golden Law. Yeah, yeah so they freed them (*in a singsong voice*).
>
> ELIZABETH: They freed them? They freed whom from what?
>
> SONIA: From slavery, because according to blacks they were slaves. Well not according to blacks, according to everyone, the slaves, the books, everyone, the people talking, the soap operas. The blacks were the slaves. So maybe blacks are ashamed because in the past the black was a slave. Right? And now today they don't accept themselves, maybe one thing has to do with the other (*I prepare to ask another question*). All right, Bete, that's enough for today.

Sonia stumbles uncomfortably as she tries to piece together a historical narrative about the beginning of Brazil and the arrival of blacks in the country. She repeats the question, stutters, and laughs nervously as she realizes she does not have a clear response. Between her long pauses and uncomfortable laughter, she reveals the little that she has internalized about the dominant narratives of history, but it is the way that she offers the details, the sing-song type of voice she uses that suggests there is an accepted story line that she is supposed to know, and even without all the details, she identifies the major elements. As in other respondents' narratives, not only are black agency and resistance unrecognized, but blacks are not even initially acknowledged as slaves until I ask for additional information. Her omission is symbolic of how blacks have been erased from the story of discovery and even of slavery and abolition.

It is the end of Sonia's narrative that offers the most poignant insight. After she recounts the history of slavery, she links it to a previous part of our interview in which she had discussed the question of blacks who do not want to be called black, which she says comes from something "inside of the person themselves." After relaying this narrative about slavery, she begins to ponder the possibility that the negative associations with blackness may have something to do with slavery. Before she can fully think through the possibility, she abruptly ends the conversation by stating that she has had enough for the day. Never one to end an interview early, I interpret the abrupt ending as an indication that she feels uncomfortable with our conversation or needs time to think through the revelation she has just made.

Some adults also offer a more subversive account of history. Felipe, who is thirty-four years old and works with computers, states:

> FELIPE: For me there was not really a discovery. Pedro Cabral and the rest came, and really they were looking for other places, but they stayed here. There wasn't really anybody living here. It's like this, the countries and places that superdeveloped are the direct result of the exploitation of other regions. The captains divided the land because there was all this land that wasn't being used. The Indians, they didn't last long doing hard labor, so they targeted Blacks.
>
> ELIZABETH: Where did blacks come from?
>
> FELIPE: Good question. . . . I think, I think they got blacks from Europe. Where did they get blacks from? (*he laughs*).

Felipe's account of the Portuguese explorers as confused travelers challenges portrayals of them as knowledgeable and brave voyagers. Moreover, he provides a sophisticated critique of Brazil that is reminiscent of the arguments of prominent scholars who emphasize the superexploit-ative relationships between core and periphery countries and populations. However, though Felipe says that the Portuguese targeted blacks, he does not use the language of slavery to describe these relations. He also reveals that he does not know where blacks lived before they were brought to Bra-zil. In this way, his account challenges the dominant narrative of discov-ery, but it also has historical inaccuracies and reveals his unfamiliarity with how Africa figures in this history. Felipe's mother, Dona Elena, is a practitioner of Candomblé, and in our conversations it becomes clear that it has been important for her to pass on this more critical version of Bra-zilian history to her children. She has been successful, at least partially, in the case of Felipe.

Surprised about how seldom respondents mention Africa in their re-sponses about Brazil's beginnings, I begin to ask, "Where did blacks live before they were slaves?" My informants' answers are amazingly diverse. They include "Portugal," "Europe," "Spain," "quilombos," "I don't know," and "Blacks and Indians always lived in Brazil." Only ten infor-mants identified Africa as the continent where blacks lived prior to com-ing to Brazil. Despite their differences, the most striking commonality of all of the story lines and historical narratives is that everyone knows how the story ends: Princesa Isabel freed the slaves and ended slavery. Leo re-flects on the history and calls it a "happy story" due in large part to Prin-cesa Isabel's actions. In fact, the national tale that he relays is a happy story that is totally disconnected from the harsh reality that many Afro-Brazilians face.

DISCUSSION

The racial fluency that Afro-Brazilians develop through the course of their lives involves not only the acquisition of a diverse lexicon of racial terms, but the development of flexible racial schemas to understand how context, status, and phenotype work together to influence racial catego-rizations. In addition to learning from the ways the adults around them speak, children also learn from being sanctioned for violations of racial etiquette and racialized codes of conduct. As they develop racial fluency, they have a number of tools in their repertoire, including strategic seman-tic ambiguity, complimentary color categorizations, and expectations that they will engage in the proper racial etiquette. One of the most impor-tant findings is that they do not complete this development in childhood; rather, achieving racial fluency is an ongoing process. Little research has been conducted in Brazil to understand the developmental stages of racial identity, but the analysis of racial fluency suggests that this would be a fruitful research area.

Racial socialization is sometimes framed in terms of explicit messages, conversations, and practices that help family members learn about who they are, how they are situated in their society, and what they can expect from the future. This framing of racial socialization suggests that researchers can directly observe and catalogue intentional moments of racial instruction. In the field these moments of explicit, intentional instruction are rare. The explicit racial socialization model that has been associated with child rearing in the United States simply does not characterize the development of racial fluency described in this chapter.[31] However, there are critical ways that family members are educated about race that are perhaps more effective because they are implicit.

The goal of racial socialization for many black families in Brazil is not developing a distinct racial identity, but learning to manage and master racial flexibility. Racial fluency in Brazil is based on accepting that race and phenotype are moving targets and that one need not fit nicely into any of the boxes. In fact, the goal is to remain difficult to pin down, and to manipulate the racial, color, and phenotypic lexicon rather than finding a definitive space within it. One may be *negro*, but there are numerous color terms available in order to not have to be described as black. When parents are not explicit overseers of the way children understand race and their history, *telenovela* characters and other figures, including siblings, foster an understanding of race that contributes to the development of one's racial education.

An emerging discourse that respondents used was the idea that "We are all black," and that "There are no whites" in Brazil. A large number of informants are insistent on recognizing phenotypic differences while asserting that everyone is black. Whiteness is a social construction. It has a relational quality so that one need not be considered white elsewhere in order to receive the privileges of whiteness in Bahia.

In the Bahian case, this is further complicated because sometimes it is unclear whether the "we" in the statement "we are all black" refers only to Bahians or to Brazilians more broadly. One of the major goals of the black movement in Brazil has been to transform the racial consciousness of Afro-Brazilians so they will unite under a broader *negro* identity.[32] This effort is reflected in the development of public campaigns in Bahia that discourage Afro-Brazilians from identifying as white on the census by insisting, "Não Deixa a Sua Côr Passar em Branco: Responda Com

Bom C/Senso": Don't let your color go blank (white): Respond with good (census) sense.[33] However, using *negro* as a universal term may also unintentionally obscures the very dynamics that the movement seeks to highlight: racism and pigmentocracy. If everyone in Bahia who has a distant African ancestor is classified as *negro*, this conceptualization ignores the structural differences between those who have a proverbial "foot in the kitchen" and those who, as a respondent aptly phrases it, have their "entire bodies in the kitchen."[34]

CHAPTER 5

MIND YOUR BLACKNESS:
EMBODIED CAPITAL AND SPATIAL MOBILITY

The Negro is unaware of it as long as his existence is limited to his own environment; but the first encounter with a white man oppresses him with the whole weight of his blackness.

FRANTZ FANON, *BLACK SKIN, WHITE MASKS*

KEISHA-KHAN PERRY STUDIES race, gender, and spatial exclusion in contemporary Salvador, with an emphasis on the role of Afro-Brazilian women in organizing against black removal from the neighborhood of Gamboa de Baixo. For the black women activists who lead the movement, their resistance is about land rights, but it is also about spatial politics and their right to occupy space as an exercise of their full citizenship. By linking their resistance to the successive removal of black women and families from several poor neighborhoods (*bairros populares*) across Salvador, Perry's study illustrates how "spatialized racial restructuring" affects the livelihoods of poor black communities.[1]

Building on Perry's assertion that "urban development is the spatial dimension of the whitening project," I explore additional ways that racial hierarchies shape spatial mobility in Afro-Brazilian families."[2] Though none of my respondents participate in the grassroots movements Perry studies, the spatial dimensions of race in Salvador orchestrate seemingly mundane decisions in their lives, including where they shop, where they go to the beach, where they pump gas, and where they sit in church. In this chapter, I explore how families approach the dangers and possibilities of transgressing racialized and classed spaces, and discuss how family members deploy embodied capital in their negotiations of spatial mobility.

TUDO NO SEU PRÓPRIO LUGAR
(EVERYTHING IN ITS PLACE)

In Salvador, strategies to manage spatial mobility serve several purposes: they reinforce racial hierarchy, challenge racialized boundaries, and protect Afro-Brazilians from dangerous and potentially uncomfortable situations. Omnipresent physical barriers, heavy policing and surveillance, messages from media and schools, and a racist gaze together ensure that people "do race" properly in physical and representational spaces.

Barbara, a twenty-one-year-old, reveals that her grandmother socialized her about how to negotiate white spaces with the idea that "I am black and I respect myself" (*Sou preta e me respeito*). For her grandmother, respecting one's blackness includes avoiding public humiliation by respecting rather than transgressing racial boundaries. Barbara explains that this perspective informs other advice that she receives from her grandmother: only go to stores with inexpensive clothes, marry a lighter or whiter person, and do not dress in bright colors. With regard to the latter, her grandmother believed that "blacks should not call attention to their dark skin color and should not wear red because they [would] look like devils." Weighing her grandmother's advice against her own ambitions, Barbara ultimately rejects her grandmother's advice in order to stake her claim to equal citizenship.

For Taynara, the relationship between race and space emerged at an earlier age in her observations of the spatial arrangement of her neighborhood in urban Salvador. She explains:

> Despite not being a part of the black movement back then, we lived in what were called urban *quilombos*. These were places where after slavery black families stayed. Where I lived there was just all blacks. There was still the big house on the hill. The neighborhood had a *casarão* (a big house) and had little streets where black people lived. Dona Linda was a fat white lady who lived there. Now it [the house] has deteriorated and gone down. We did not have any formal education, but we had a sense of blackness and whiteness, even though we did not understand it. We had Motown and Michael Jackson. We knew that Dona Linda did not want us playing with her children.

Even after slavery, black families continued to live in spatial arrangements that were extensions of the master-slave relationship. The spatialized racial aspects of Taynara's living arrangements, which she associates with the separation of the master's big house and the slave quarters, were central to the development of her racial consciousness. Although she could not articulate it, residents like her felt spatial marginalization in their skin (*na pele*). Both the distance that blacks maintained from Dona Linda *and* the rules about who black children could play with helped construct racialized space. Such insights from residents themselves expand the contours of the debates surrounding race and space and lend support for studying how racial inequality occurs even within shared multiracial spaces.[3]

Beyond the external organization of neighborhoods, spatialized racial dynamics are reflected in other ways as well. What Telles coins "elevator apartheid" reflects the idea that when blacks transgress white spaces there are conditions to their presence.[4] Service workers in middle class apartments are limited to using the service elevator rather than the social elevator. As an extension of this, small rooms called *dependências* are built into most middle-class apartments in Salvador. These tiny, closet-sized rooms are designed for live-in maids (mostly *negras*) and symbolize the exclusion and isolation of domestic workers, who work there. Arguably these rooms function as modern-day upgrades of the slave quarters, reflecting the *"gendered racial logic of spatial exclusion,"* which makes the second-class status of poor, black women part of the trappings of a middle-class lifestyle.[5] Taynara's references to Motown and Michael Jackson indicate the importance of seeking U.S. black cultural references for Brazilian blacks who have historically been spatially excluded and marginalized from the cultural realm.

Given the tacit rules of spatial mobility, Afro-Brazilians may feel a sense of security when they circulate in spaces in which there is relative race or class homogeneity. As Felipe states:

No one ever talked about discrimination or racism, ever. Because, . . . it is really because, . . . well, the places, . . . today it's possible that discrimination exists since we are part of, . . . well, in the past we didn't go to places where whites were because we did not even have money to go to those places. But now you have this [racism]. But as children we did not have this because we only went to black places. But today, no, it's different. (Felipe, 34)

By only going to events where there were other *negros*, Felipe and his family were able to effectively avoid interpersonal racism. However, now that his family is earning more money and has moved into the middle class, they occupy a different location, which has forced him to deal with experiences and situations in which he is racially isolated and targeted.

Entrance into the middle class means transgressing symbolic racial boundaries. As Angela Figueiredo suggests, "the experience of being in the middle class seems extremely important" for the recognition of class and racial differences because blacks feel "out of place."[6] Rather than remain silent, Felipe reports that he now discusses with his family some of the racist situations he has encountered both in college and in his previous job as a computer technology specialist. He reveals:

> At work, they would say things like "Ah, that *Neguinho* doesn't know how to program." Things like that. In college I have had experiences with professors who said things like, "that dumb Blackie." But because I was paying to go there, I reported him to the college administration because he treated me in a discriminatory way, saying, "That dumb Blackie does not know anything."

In Felipe's job and at college, racial insults are trivialized as jokes (*brincadeiras*), and these racist social situations and the negative feelings they elicit contribute to some Afro-Brazilians' active avoidance of encounters with whites in certain spaces.[7] When the protection of a majority black space is no longer available, Felipe's shifting class status exposes him to racism in ways that he has never had to experience.[8]

For Felipe, what makes the situation worse is that at his job, he feels that he cannot and should not respond to racism:

> I sat there and didn't say anything. Because if I would have said something I may have lost my job. The boss wouldn't think that I was right, plus my boss was white! (*chuckles and shakes his head*)

But Felipe's silence does not reflect his passive acceptance of his racialization. He reported his college teacher who made racist comments toward him. He decides to remain silent in the context of his current job because he fears there will be no recourse or protection for him.

Interactions between blacks and the white elite are limited not simply because of class differences, but also because of strategic efforts by members of the white elite to avoid spaces that are coded as black or low class.[9] Throughout my time in Brazil, white, middle-class Brazilians insulted and avoided locations that they considered *baixa estral*, or low class, a designation with racial overtones.

One of the most obvious places to observe the racialization of social space is Iguatemi Shopping, a large mall located in Salvador's business district. The spatial arrangement of the mall, similar to the distinction between the Lower and Upper areas of the city, has symbolic and racialized meanings. As one moves up from the ground floor to the top floor, the stores become more exclusive and more expensive. Moreover, as one ascends, the clientele becomes predominately white, though *negros* may be present as salespersons (if they are light skinned) or custodians. In a conversation about how much she hates racism, fourteen-year-old Paulinha, who is white, recalls feeling angry at seeing police follow and harass a group of *moreno* teenagers in Iguatemi mall. She explains they were targeted because they did not appear to be dressed in nice clothing.

In spaces that are known for their wealthier and whiter clientele, blacks, and particularly black males, are considered suspect regardless of their clothing. This even applies to seemingly mundane spaces:

> You can go to the gas station, there is one in [the neighborhoods of] Amaralina and Pituba. Blacks do not go to the one in Pituba. . . . It is not that none go there, but they do not use it often. They go to Amaralina instead because they know that everyone here is of the same class and they will not be discriminated against. White people, it is like this: when you are poor—90 percent of blacks here are poor—whites like to interact with blacks when they are their *empregados* (employees) or with a black women when she is beautiful, they want to just use her, . . . like for sexual pleasure. (Breno, 35)

For Breno, both class and racial considerations shape a decision as mundane as where to pump gas. The two stations that he refers to are located only minutes apart, but the clientele is drastically different. Similarly, in the city of Lauro de Freitas, outside of Salvador, it is common knowledge that Villas do Atlântico beach is the white beach, while Buraquinho is considered the black beach. There are no explicit signs or legal codes, but rather a tacit social rule that blacks are to "mind their blackness" and remain in socially acceptable spaces. Afro-Brazilians may eventually internalize these rules of spatial negotiation to the point that their decisions about where to pump gas, enjoy the beach, and live seem like personal choices rather than decisions structured by race or class.

At the same time, following these rules is not merely a matter of convenience or custom, and it does not guarantee that one will not be targeted. Nonetheless, Lúcio believes that it is his responsibility to preemptively address racism by controlling what he wears:

I never encountered that type of thing because I always presented myself . . . well dressed. You know, like a nice shirt and pants. I mean you
can't blame people for discriminating against black people. If you see a
black guy walking around with old jeans and shirt, what are you going to
think? We all do it.

Lúcio, who identifies as *negro*, not only naturalizes racial profiling, he justifies it, suggesting that one should expect to be treated poorly if one is
not well dressed. But even when blacks dress according to the dominant
norms, they are still considered suspicious because "blacks are not supposed to look well groomed—the ones that do are considered suspect by
definition."[10] There is an additional gender component that overlays this:
when black women are dressed too nicely they are assumed to be prosti-
tutes. I experienced my own such racist and sexist encounter with military
police, as I describe in the introduction.

It is also a question of safety to avoid encounters where violating a tacit
rule of racialized space could mean being viewed as threatening or suspicious. During my research period, a college student and research collaborator named Matheus was beaten by the police, arrested, thrown in jail,
and beaten several times more once he was incarcerated. He remained in
jail for weeks before being released and found innocent of the charge that
he had robbed a tourist while visiting an island.[11] He was in the wrong
place at the wrong time with the wrong color. Afro-Brazilian families are
cautious about certain public spaces because encounters with the police
can be dangerous and deadly, particularly for black youth and adults. In
fact, the state of Bahia has among the highest rates of police killings of ci-
vilians in the country. This reality speaks to the high stakes involved for
blacks when they occupy racialized spaces, and it explains why some families rely on embodied capital as a survival strategy.[12] Urban violence and
police brutality are increasingly framed as problems affecting the direct
victims, overwhelmingly young men, as well as the mothers and wives
who are left to support their families in the wake of these traumatic and
violent experiences.[13] While I was in Salvador, protests against the genocide of black youth were held to raise consciousness about racialized violence and police brutality in Brazil.

OUR KIND OF PEOPLE:
RACE, CLASS, AND SPATIAL MOBILITY

When her brother Paulo interrupts our conversation to interject that on
the basis of our skin color and white teeth, Larissa and I are black, he

is demanding that she assume her blackness and that all of us recognize ourselves as *negros*. But in spite of Larissa's uncertainty regarding how to answer my question about race, she is racialized as *negra* and treated accordingly in her extended family. Larissa's cousin, Paulinha, is very light-skinned *branca de cabelo liso* (white with straight hair). Three of Larissa's black cousins, her brother Alberto, and I are invited to attend Paulinha's fourteenth birthday celebration at a local restaurant. As we walk in together, everyone takes their seats, including Paulinha's school friends who have met us there. Paulinha attends a private school and has very few nonwhite friends at the school. Most of her friends are *brancas de cabelo liso* like she is, and some might also call them spoiled, wealthy kids (*filhos de papai*).

Larissa enters the restaurant with her best friend, Monick, who is light skinned with traditional African features (*sarará*) except that she has reddish hair, which looks to be very damaged by harsh chemicals. Larissa and Monick sit at the end of a very long table with space separating them from Paulinha and her friends. The phenotypical differences that separate Larissa and Monick become insignificant as they are clearly demarcated as the *negras* of the group, phenotypically and socially. Paulinha and her friends laugh with each other, reaching over the table to tease each other and joke. Larissa and Monick, at the other end of the table, cower into one another and glance nervously at the group. Their efforts to find a way into the conversation by laughing and smiling are not acknowledged, and the group continues to interact while ignoring them.

I observe Larissa and Monick continually adjusting and readjusting their straightened hair and constantly pulling down their bangs. I am also placed at the end of the table with them, along with their black-looking cousin Lúcio. The gulf that separates us from the lighter group is immense, though it was established with no harsh racial words or contestation. All of the dark-skinned relatives are placed at one end of the table, and despite the privilege that sometimes comes with being a black North American, my place is there too. Regardless of Larissa's refusal to classify herself as *negra*, the rules of racial and class interaction clarify her racial position.

Similarly, in Lua Cheia Sonia's neighbors, especially the women, have been discussing Sonia's birthday celebration for weeks. They complain about having to bring their own meat to be grilled during the barbecue (*churrasco*), but they agree to do so. On the day of the party, all of the neighbors dance and take pictures until a large group of eight white people, who are referred to as *gente bonita*, arrive. Upon their arrival, special chairs are set up in an area separate from everyone else. There are no whites-only signs, no tense exchanges of racial epithets, no written rules, but there is a tacit understanding that a special section will be arranged just for them. The residents become uncomfortable interacting with the white family, who are not biologically related to Sonia, but include the godparents of several of her children.

I watch as the adult Lua Cheia residents slowly dip back into their homes and shut their doors. I am curious about what is happening, and I begin asking questions. I visit Corina, who defines herself as white in interviews but clearly feels the weight of her tenuous claim to whiteness in this situation. When I knock on the door and peek in to ask her why she is not outside, she cracks her door and says, "You see all those *gente bonita* that Sonia invited!" She ducks back into her house and closes the door quietly. Not all of the neighbors completely retreat from the outdoor party; others continue to dance but keep their distance from the white partygoers.[14]

These spatial considerations are informed by race as well as class: *gente bonita* are both white and of perceived high social class. Not only are they deserving of special chairs, they are intimidating to some of the neighborhood residents. But similar dynamics may occur within families of the same racial group when they are of different social classes. In fact, class differentiation in some black families can be more devastating than phenotypic cleavages because class is considered an acceptable basis for explicit discrimination. Dilson explains that he would sometimes visit his paternal uncle's house to watch television because his own family was poor and did not own a television. One day he decided to visit, and when he entered, he took a seat on the living room floor to watch what his older cousin was watching. He describes the encounter:

> When I sat down, he [his cousin] looked at me with a face this big (*holds his hand out beyond his face*), he turned off the television, and went back into his room. He didn't want me to be there. It was like my presence bothered him. In fact, I never went there again. Now, if we had been in a different economic situation, if my father had been a businessman or something, they wouldn't have ever let me sit on the floor, they would have told me to sit on the sofa. All of them are black, but they have a financial situation better than us. Even with me sitting on the floor, it was like this.

In this case, Dilson entered his uncle's house understanding how racialization and class function, and he did not even attempt to sit on the sofa. He links these spatial negotiations to class status rather than race because his cousins are also black. However, their shared blackness made race even more relevant because it compelled his cousin's family to work harder to differentiate themselves on the basis of class. Even though Dilson followed proper protocol and recognized that his place was on the floor, his mere presence bothered his cousin.

This incident might have been considered an exceptional occurrence except that on the other side of Dilson's family, his maternal aunt does not even allow him to come inside her house. He explains:

> My uncle's family, the brother of my father, the one who worked in construction, they were well-off. They always had a really good life, they always had cars and houses, and they never wanted to mix themselves with people in the family because we were poor and black. They also went to our church, to the same church. But they did not want to mix with us. You understand? They didn't want to have contact with us inside of the church in order to maintain appearances. You know? They would say, look at you with shorts on and sandals or whatever. And then they would tell my mom that she needed to dress me better. As a child, I didn't really understand what was happening. When I would go to her house [his aunt's], she wouldn't even open the door to us. She did not open the door. She did not even open the door. If I was sent to her house with a package or something important, I would have to go there, drop it off and leave quickly. But as time went on things got better for us. We earned more money and then things started changing, but so did our outlook. We still didn't go to their house anymore because we knew how they had other interests and prejudice. In this case it wasn't an issue of color, it was a question of class. She would say that we were inferior, that my mother was envious of her because her kids studied at private schools. She said all of that. As a child you aren't really able to process all of that, you see the good in everything so when something like this happens, it makes you see the world with different eyes, especially when it happens in your own family. It's complicated.

Through these reflections, Dilson reveals the dilemmas of being poor in a family of wealthy or even middle-class blacks. In this narrative, Dilson's aunt is a gatekeeper monitoring symbolic and physical boundaries at church and at her home. That they would purposely try to avoid Dilson's family in church in order to maintain appearances speaks volumes about how expectations of racial solidarity can falter under the weight of class solidarity. The cruel way that his aunt refuses to receive him in her home shapes how he interacts with her part of the family—now only minimally.

Most revealing of all, when I ask Dilson's mother whether there is any tension among her siblings, she shakes her head no and reports that she had never heard what her son experienced until now. It is her daughter-in-law, Lilza, who encourages Dona Lara to tell me about how her siblings ignore their family when they go to church services. After reassurances of privacy from Lilza and me, Dona Lara reluctantly admits that her siblings avoid sitting next to them at church so that people do not think they are related. Not wanting to upset Dona Lara, Lilza changes the subject and conveniently offers to take me to see the sunset before it gets too late. As Lilza and I walk out of the house, she reveals that she wanted to take me for a stroll in order to speak with me privately. She says:

> Elizabete, you have to understand, Dona Lara will never say a bad word about anybody because she's just like that. But her sister, there have been several times when she has not invited us to family events. She purposely does not invite Dona Lara to some of her events. It's true. There is something there between them. She would never tell you this because she is such a good person, but it is true.

Dona Lara finds herself in an irreconcilable situation. On one hand, she is grateful that her brother and sister have helped her financially when her family fell on tough financial circumstances. She remembers fondly that her sister helped her sew her wedding gown, pictures of which Dona Lara proudly shows me. Out of loyalty she is understandably reluctant to criticize how they treat her family at church or to admit that they exclude them from social events. These family relationships are complex because they are not always marked by cruelty; they involve generosity and moments of happiness. But it is because these family bonds can be enjoyable and beneficial that challenging racism and classism is difficult to do. This type of differential treatment in families has significant consequences. In addition to causing family members to see the world with different eyes, as Dilson states, it changes the way they see themselves.

RACIAL RESPECTABILITY, SPATIAL INCLUSION, AND EMBODIED CAPITAL

In an unexpected conversation over a delicious plate of bean stew (*feijoada*) at an outside table at a beach house, Raíssa and Taynara, two *negras assumidas*, both college-educated and mothers, destabilize my conceptualizations about racial socialization in Brazil. I attribute this fortuitous conversation to their class status, their education level, and—an important detail—the fact that they are both religious practitioners of Candomblé. Historically, Candomblé houses of worship (*terreiros*) have served as a space for blacks, especially black women, to feel culturally affirmed, spiritually grounded, and politically empowered.[15]

As I explain my research and some key findings, Raíssa and Taynara nod their heads in agreement, then offer insights of their own about how they approach racial socialization. Their experiences resonate with what researchers have written about some of the major goals of racial socialization in the United States. Most of the racial socialization literature focuses on the types of messages conveyed in families, which researchers group into four main categories: egalitarianism, racial group pride, racial barriers, and participation in African American culture.[16] With the slight modification of the fourth category from African American culture to Afro-Brazilian culture, these are the goals that shape how Raíssa and Taynara are raising their children. While in most Afro-Brazilian families that I interview, messages connecting prejudice and discrimination to racial inequality are rare, Raíssa and Taynara are committed to socializing their children with a central goal of ensuring that they know they are racially equal and, most important, that they will engage in behaviors that actively demonstrate and embody their racial equality.

For Raíssa and Taynara, Candomblé is not folklore, it is part of their everyday spiritual life. For both of them, teaching their children the values of traditional, Angolan *capoeira* is an important element of socialization into a racial outlook and understanding of history that they hope will positively guide their children's racial identity. Raíssa also describes how she transmits embodied capital to her son, a laborious task requiring self-surveillance and vigilance about how one's physical and behavioral qualities influence impressions about blacks as a whole.

Raíssa is a professional writer with a penchant for critically deconstructing systems of oppression. She reveals that although there are a number of problems with the way she was raised, she feels that nowadays Brazilian children lack respect and the morals of the past. Our conversation begins with this critique and develops into suggestions about best parenting practices for black children. Raíssa explains that she sees one of her major roles in her son's life as socializing him into behaviors that show that he is educated and that will allow him to avoid situations where he might *passar vergonha na familia* (cause shame to fall upon the family).

This concern with avoiding family shame and humiliation is central to her socialization messages. To this end, her racial socialization focuses on developing her son's embodied capital so that he learns to present and move his body in ways that help him manage and combat racial stereotypes.

Meals and formal events are spaces that represent opportunities for him to exhibit his embodied capital. Raíssa explains that she teaches her twelve-year-old son, Murilo, the proper way to hold a fork so if he is ever in a position to eat in public he will be prepared. She explains painstakingly that when Murilo sits at the table to eat, he also is instructed not to hover over his food and is told to eat it slowly. The etiquette related to food not only encompasses the way in which one eats, but also whether one eats in public settings. Raíssa explains:

> If we are eating out or going to an event, I make sure that he eats before we go so that he is not hungry when he arrives. That way, he does not have to ask for food or be hungry. Otherwise, it seems like we don't feed him at home (*laughs*). Also, if he is invited over to someone's house or even is in the street, I tell him, "You do not ask for anything and you do not accept anything." When he is invited over to someone's house, he is not to ask for anything. He may only ask for water and permission to go to the restroom. And under no circumstances is he to ever to open someone's refrigerator or walk into someone's bedroom, open up their personal things, no nothing like that. No way!

I am intrigued by Raíssa's diligence with these details, but also curious about the level of preparation and self-surveillance this approach requires. While on the surface this may seem like traditional middle-class socialization, this conclusion would be short sighted, ignoring the ways in which the particular history and treatment of Afro-Brazilians informs these practices. Adopting appropriate etiquette during meals has more nuanced and explicit meanings for Afro-Brazilian families who have been framed as uncivilized and wild. Raíssa teaches her son these values because she does not want him to "*passar vergonha na família*" which has implications not only for his primary family but for his racial family. These practices and values are specifically what she calls "things of the black family in Brazil." I refer to them as part of the repertoire of racial rituals that black families develop.

Throughout our conversation, she implies that the mistakes Murilo makes and the humiliation he experiences are not merely his own but are projected onto blacks as a whole. They take on even greater importance because as middle-class blacks they are often isolated or in situations in which they are considered racial representatives.[17] This is the current reality for Raíssa because she is the only black person in her workplace, and she anticipates that this will be the same for Murilo.

Raíssa's concern about her son's embodied capital in public spaces is also evident in how she polices the way he dresses and the lessons she teaches him about being conscious of his cleanliness. When he goes to participate in sports, including *capoeira*, she always tells him to wear clean white socks. She explains:

> One day I saw that he came from school directly and headed to his *capoeira* practice. When he took off his shoes and I saw his dirty socks, I walked him all the way home so that he could put on clean socks.

Her concerns with cleanliness are not coincidental, but rather function to help her son counteract the racial stereotypes about blacks as dirty. Not only must he wear clean socks, he is not allowed to leave the house with *cuecas folgados* (baggy underwear), "in case something happened in the street and he needed to go to the hospital."

Taynara nods her head throughout the conversation and offers affirmations and other examples that complement Raíssa's emphasis on countering racial stereotypes through one's behaviors. Taynara explains that when her daughter is invited into someone's house, she is told not to touch anything, ask for anything, or accept anything. Both of the mothers are clear that under no circumstances would their children ever leave the house with old, torn panties (*calçinhas rasgadas*). Raíssa tells a funny story about how she followed this rule religiously, and the one time in her life when she had not, when she was pregnant, she went into labor. A normally soft-spoken women, she laughs loudly as she reveals that to her horror she had to be rushed to the hospital in her dreaded old underwear.

Brenda, a twenty-one-year-old black woman, admits that she has been socialized in the same way. As a result, she separates her underwear into two categories—underwear that she wears daily and underwear that she puts aside for special occasions. Brenda laughs as she admits that because she has internalized the rule about not opening refrigerator doors, she is uncomfortable opening her boyfriend's refrigerator even though they have been dating for over a year.

Apart from how Murilo presents himself at formal events, one of Raíssa's goals is concerned with teaching him how to manage and influence the impressions of others, especially in the context of school. She explains one situation in which she had to intervene:

> Several Christmases ago, Murilo's class participated in a secret Santa. One of his classmates, a white girl, realized that he had pulled her name, and she cried and made a scene because she did not want him to get her a gift. She thought that by him being black, it meant he would not give her a good gift. The teacher eventually asked Murilo to choose again and he chose a male classmate. But when he came home to tell me what happened this really upset me. So you know what I did? I went to the mall, and we bought him a skateboard, the nicest skateboard I could find. I bought one for Murilo and one for him. Do you know how much that skateboard was? (*laughs*) It was $150 reais, and I had to pay for it over several months! It was not even about the gift, it was about the principle. It was more to show the teacher. They never seem to hear or do anything when it comes to things like this.

In this example, Raíssa takes seriously the humiliation that her son faces and invests handsomely in reminding students that their racial stereotypes do not apply to him. In this case the lesson also includes the idea that using racial stereotypes to judge a person's economic resources is wrong. She explains that she was willing to make the investment because making her point was worth more than $150 reais; it provided a foundation for the future treatment of her son in this class and sent a message about racial stereotypes to her son's negligent teachers. Raíssa continues with additional details of her son's home training that all relate back to cleanliness, good manners, pride, and protecting family honor.[18] While on the surface these are simply middle-class values, they have a distinct racial element for middle-class blacks like Raíssa, who "are looked upon with curiosity when they participate in middle-class social activities."[19]

Discursive space is important to consider as it relates to race and navigating racialized public spaces. Both Raíssa and Taynara explain that under no circumstance are their children allowed to interrupt an older adult. That behavior would result in a "slap in the mouth." They both laugh as they reminisce over moments from their childhoods when they suffered the consequences of violating this rule. Taynara refers to herself as the true black sheep of the family (*a veradadeira ovelha preta da família*), which is a position that she proudly occupies and negotiates by enforcing her own rules of racial etiquette. She is the oldest of her four sisters and the only one of them who identifies as black. In a family of phenotypically diverse sisters, Taynara is conscious of influencing her sisters and holds them accountable for racist commentary. Drawing on her authority as the oldest in her family, she monitors the discursive spaces that her sisters use and reprimands them for their racist comments.

In contrast to the way that racial etiquette often uses strategic semantic ambiguity and complimentary color categorizations, Taynara's racial etiquette is anti-racist, rather than anti-race:

> My sister says she is white. With a nose this wide and thick lips, how can she say she is white? They try to use racist language around me, try to say that Maria [Taynara's daughter] has "good hair," but I don't allow it. There are times when my sister is describing somebody and she says "the little blackie with nappy hair" (*aquela neguinha com cabelo duro*). And, I say, "You mean she's black with hair like mine?" (*She states this in a strong accusatory tone.*) When we are together and we are watching television, if a commercial shows a black person, I turn like this to show them I'm watching and listening in case they say something. (*She turns her head slightly and cuts her eyes to show the way she monitors her sisters.*)

For Taynara, monitoring the discursive space and limiting her daughter's exposure to racist commentary is a conscious effort to reject racism and foster a positive racial identity. Against the grain, she has assumed her blackness, and now she must constantly negotiate a sense of self that affirms blackness, which for her also includes an embrace of her natural hair, despite her family's objections. When I ask if it is difficult to speak up when her sisters say something that is racist, she explains, "How can I not do this? This is what I do every day when I teach my students to have pride in who they are. I cannot say this in school and not speak up when I am at home. I do it every day, so it is natural." In this way, Taynara sees the personal as the political and chooses to extend the lessons about racism that she teaches in the classroom to her family members who have internalized these hierarchies.

The racial politics that shape the lives of Taynara and Raíssa allow and even require participation in black cultural forms, including *capoeira* and Candomblé. Historically, *capoeira* was initially considered an innocuous art form played or performed by African slaves, but by the nineteenth century in Brazil, it was vilified, in part because it was considered "a tool that enabled slaves to commit offences and criminal acts against their masters."[20] Not only was the game itself vilified, but the *capoeiristas* were criminalized as troublemakers who made it difficult for elites to eliminate what they considered outdated and obsolete African traditions. These stereotypes were promoted so successfully by the ruling elites that although *capoeiristas* were revered among many black communities for their agility and talents, black families began to accept the portrayals of *capoeiristas* as dangerous.[21] In these two middle-class families, *capoeira* is used as an alternative form of embodied and cultural capital that gives their children the ability to connect with their culture and racial history in a deeper way, rather than reproduce hierarchies.

In other families *capoeira* is considered a waste of time and even a liability. In the families of Arivaldo and Thiago, racial socialization centered around avoiding or downplaying any connection to *capoeira*. Despite becoming *capoeiristas* and ultimately creating an organization that assists at-risk youth through *capoeira*, their families were adamantly opposed to their participation in the art form. Arivaldo explains that his family's response to his interest in *capoeira* was swift and unequivocal:

> They always said this in our family, that *capoeira* doesn't have a future, *capoeira* is for bums, *vagabundos*. Why don't you do something else? Whenever we did anything that was related to *capoeira* it wasn't valued by them. They were afraid because of the lives that they had. They wanted us to work so that we could be considered decent people (*dignos*). For them decency meant working, and you could not get decency through *capoeira*.

Arivaldo's family's resistance to and framing of his participation in *capoeira* can be directly linked to the construction of *capoeira* as a worthless career choice. An important emotion that drives these messages is fear—fear that because of their involvement they may not be successful and might lead criminal or dishonest lives. Thiago points out that he had to confront other issues as well:

> For me, it was even harder because of my parents being religious and things like that. They had no consciousness at all of *capoeira* as an art form. So they would cut up my *capoeira* pants. So then I had to leave my clothes at the *capoeira* school. And if I got injured in *capoeira*, I would have to sleep in someone else's house because they wouldn't allow it. They would say, you got injured doing *capoeira*, then you need to go to *capoeira* to get well. *Capoeira* will have to get you medicine, so I would go to the streets. So no, they never liked it. My *capoeira* clothes and my instruments were stored at the *capoeira* school or someone else's house.

Thiago goes on to explain that his deeply religious evangelical family is distrustful of both *capoeira* and Candomblé, cultural forms that are heavily influenced by African culture. His family is part of a growing Pentecostal and evangelical movement in Salvador that often and erroneously frames Candomblé as devil worship. Some evangelical Christians have adamantly protested the display of imagery of Orixás (Candomblé deities) in the city of Salvador because "they attributed power to them, arguing that they would unleash a negative force in the city and could even cause physical illness to viewers."[22] That these groups perceived dangers just from having one's gaze fall upon the sculptures in public spaces illustrates the harsh resistance that both men faced in their families and from the broader society to African-influenced cultural practices.

Thiago explains how negative views about the Orixás and Candomblé affect the decisions that he makes about the public spaces that he visits:

> Even going to Candomblé ceremonies is something that they don't believe in. There are a number of things that I have to do secretly, even now. So many things that I have to do secretly. If they see me going to a Candomblé ceremony they think I'm doing something bad. You know, evangelicals have that type of prejudice. So I had to explain that there is nothing bad going on here. But for them it has been planted in their mind that it is bad, it was done as a way to take culture from our people. Because without culture, our people die.

Despite the public visibility of Candomblé in Salvador, many Brazilians continue to hold negative stereotypes about the religion, which is why Thiago must hide his participation. As recently as May 2014, federal judge Eugênio Rosa de Araújo caused an uproar when he asserted that Afro-Brazilian religions such as Umbanda and Candomblé "não contem os traços necessarios de una religião" (do not have the necessary characteristics to be considered a religion).[23] This cultural degradation of Candomblé should not be viewed in isolation because it is an extension of the devalued status of other physical and cultural features that are racialized as black or African.

Perhaps most compelling are Arivaldo's and Thiago's reactions to their strict childhood socialization and the lack of familial support. To fully convey the struggles he had growing up with his grandfather, Thiago states:

> You know sometimes I would sit and think that maybe my grandfather was never a child, because he was so hard, so it seemed like he was never

a child. This is just to give you an example of how much we suffered with him. It seemed like he didn't even have a heart. There was no way of satisfying him. He always thought we were wasting time, not taking life seriously, so it made us feel that way.

Rather than expressing resentment, both frame their harsh upbringing and the discouragement of *capoeira* with deep sensitivity. They contextualize their socialization as a product of the racist belief systems that were "planted" into their families, as well as their parents' experiences of a pervasive racial inequality. Thiago states:

> What I think was good in all of this is that with little education, they didn't have much education, they gave us basic things. That I have a lot of pride, that my parents did this with all of these struggles that they faced. Despite everything that I went through with them I can't fault them for it. I had to understand without agreeing with them. I wanted to show them that *capoeira* was what gave me dignity and made me the man that I am. I was not going to *sujar a imagem da família* (ruin the family name).

Similarly, Arivaldo forgives his family for discouraging his participation in *capoeira*, and he expresses understanding of their position, given the oppressive context of his parents' lives:

> My mom was in agriculture, a slave on a plantation. So they had a really difficult life, no electricity, no internet. They didn't have transportation, not even a car in that time. I understand for them being illiterate, not being able to read or write and growing up here. For them, all you had was your character and how well you worked. In addition to raising us, they took in other kids to raise as well. So they shared with everybody so we saw the other side. We saw the social side, the human side. They never had a methodology to raise us, you have to have an opportunity for that, but they didn't have it. So, they were strict so that we would have a better future. So that's why they always said you have to work and study, work and study. So, that's what I did. At nine years old, I would go to school at night because I needed to work during the day.

Throughout my conversations with Thiago and Arivaldo, they emphasize the notion of human dignity and unity, both ideas fundamental to the philosophical foundations of Angolan *capoeira*. Indeed, the way they understand their own family life is a reflection of how they view *capoeira* as "a way of life" that encourages players to value the history of African resistance and treat people as equals. Their public participation in *capoeira* reframes success so it is not about material success and social mobility, but about how much one can contribute to the advancement of black, at-risk youth in Brazil. Their ability to contextualize yet not support the positions of their families exemplifies how defiance against socialization is possible and successfully pursued by Afro-Brazilians.

UNIVERSAL LESSONS OF RACIAL EGALITARIANISM

Unlike the examples from Raíssa and Taynara, who explicitly discuss cultural and racial identity as part of their racial socialization, in core families in the study, conversations tend to largely revolve around the idea of universal equality. The statements from mothers below are examples of how other families teach their children to navigate racialized spaces or racial encounters.

When Diana is asked about what she teaches her children about race, she responds:

> I also always tell them not to lower their heads and never stop chasing your dreams, do not let people insult you or discriminate against you because that will leave you feeling run-down. (Diana, *negra*, 40, married woman with three children)

For Diana, racial socialization is not viewed as something that needs to be explicitly addressed. Her socialization is couched as universal, but it has clear racial undertones. Like her, other mothers report instructing their children to stand up for themselves in public situations where they feel they have been discriminated against. In four families mothers framed this lesson in the exact same way, stating, "we should never lower our heads" (*a gente não deve baixar a cabeça*). While not explicitly so, this message is racial socialization, as the imagery of lowering one's head is connected to the embodied, deferential behaviors that blacks displayed towards whites during and after slavery to illustrate submission. Hence the mothers offer a message with content that gestures toward race and slavery but does not directly mention it.

Diana's insistence that her son not let anyone insult or discriminate against him is also vague. She instructs her children to have a positive attitude but gives them no indication of how not to let themselves be discriminated against. Without further discussion about strategies or even about the types of discrimination that they might face, it seems unlikely that they will be prepared for. However, her son Sergio recounts that he confronted an older white woman who made him "feel like trash" when she clutched her purse after he asked her for the time. He directly links his response to socialization from his mother and what he learned about not allowing people to insult him.

Similarly, the instruction that Larissa receives emphasizes not feeling inferior to others. She reports what her mother teaches her:

> Never feel lowered. Each person has their own abilities. To never lower oneself means never to feel less than other people. (Larissa, 13)

For Afro-Brazilian families that have relatively light or white children, their socialization messages have little to do with responding to racism and are sometimes more directed at their children's potential role as discriminators. One white mother, Andrea, replies that this is what she teaches her two daughters who have black fathers:

> I tell them you don't have to discriminate against anyone. Never discriminate against anyone because we are all equal, right? In the eyes of God, we are all equal and we are brothers. (Andrea, 62)

Andrea's racial socialization is also universal, but it reflects her anticipation that her daughters will be potential discriminators, rather than the victims of discrimination. She feels no need to teach them not to feel lowered because their relative whiteness precludes them from experiencing this in the way that it is expected for dark-skinned blacks.

Universal messages are not reserved for messages that convey racial egalitarianism but are extended to conversations related to self-acceptance. In the front of their house, eight-year-old Dania, Sonia's daughter, a dark-skinned girl with very curly hair, is whining and begging her mother to straighten her hair. I am surprised by her tantrum because in a previous conversation she told me that she has never wanted to change anything about herself, especially not her hair. Today, I discover that she lied to me and has been begging her mother for months to straighten her hair. Referring to a previous conversation she has had with me about the importance of transmitting positive messages of self-acceptance to her children, Sonia proudly states:

> See, this is what I mean. She wants me to straighten her hair. But, I tell the girls to accept what you have and what you look like. God made you

like he wanted to, your hair, everything. Don't try to change these things. But Bete, you really should straighten your hair. Haven't you ever thought about it? Don't you want straight hair? I could do it for you. (Sonia, 31, homemaker and mother of six)

While there is an explicit message of self-acceptance that is important for Sonia to convey to her daughters, implicit in her comments about my hair is that self-acceptance is reasonable only up to a point, and my hair surpasses the threshold of acceptance.

Sonia does not view her comments as contradictory; rather, they illustrate how women "hold themselves to a different standard of attractiveness" than young girls, who occupy a different position.[24] While the natural hair of a young girl can be accepted and even embraced, this acceptance is in part because of the assumption that they are not responding to the "male gaze" in the same way as an adult woman. That is, entrance into adulthood signals an important transition that is heavily organized by a type of racialized gender socialization into dominant aesthetic rules and hierarchies.[25] Hair straightening and trips to the salon mark "the transition from 'innocent' childhood to 'sexual' young womanhood."[26] Sonia offers affirmation about the importance of acceptance to young girls, but at the same time, she offers a message that it is not appropriate for grown women. I graciously but firmly decline the offer for her to chemically straighten my hair.

EDUCAÇÃO É A SALVAÇÃO: EDUCATION IS SALVATION

In all of the families, formal education is highly valued as the key to social mobility and future success. Thiago appreciates the deep level of commitment that his parents had to his education despite being illiterate themselves. The mantra that his family lives by is "Educação e formação é transformação" (Education and formation [training] is transformation). He learned this lesson very well, and he regrets that his father didn't live to see him accomplish significant milestones: entrance to and graduation from college and the construction of his new house.

Dona Elena offers a pithy version of this idea by socializing her children into the message that she received from her father: "Educação é a salvação" (Education is salvation). She teaches her children to fight against racism and discrimination by acquiring as much education as possible. This advice provides little consolation for her son, Felipe, who after receiving his college degree still faces significant racism. Other mothers who socialize their children to take advantage of educational opportunities echo Dona Elena's approach. Sonia reports that she socializes her six children to:

> Never give up on your dreams, study because today public school is not much. And if a student is not really interested, sometimes he doesn't learn anything at all. So, with this little instruction that the government provides they have to take advantage of it. Because if we had money to put them in a private school (*escola particular*) they would not be in the government one. Government schools are very weak. The fundamental base, literacy, there is no base, so it falls on the parents to reinforce. Those with money put them in private school.

Mothers believe that education is one of the best ways for their children to achieve mobility. They specifically link education to class mobility and often downplay explicit references to racial disparity or barriers. This is the case even though they recognize that their children attend some of the poorest-funded schools in the city. Class consciousness is much stronger than racial consciousness, and, due to the prevalence of the belief that racism is simply an individual problem, class mobility through education is viewed as the solution.

Studying and excelling in school are articulated as being important for boys and girls, yet in six of the ten core families' homes there are no books in the homes. Although the families have few resources, the importance of education is internalized, particularly among the girls, who are often interested in incorporating educational games into their play. One evening five of the young girls in the neighborhood ask me to play school with them. Curious about what this means, I cheerfully agree. They enthusiastically scavenge through their houses to find a book that they can use to read. When they cannot find a single book, they suggest taking turns reading from my field notebook, which for obvious reasons is not a viable option. Eventually they find a book to read: a tiny green pocket Bible with tattered pages and minuscule print. Everyone huddles around the small green book, passing it around to read. They each read their favorite passages, stumbling over words, asking what words mean, discussing what they think the passages mean, and applying parables to comical real-life situations. There is such passion and desire to read and improve their skills, but the lack of a single book except the small Bible severely undermines their efforts and puts into the perspective the huge challenge it will be for the young girls to realize their dreams.

Eleven-year-old Bruna, Sonia's oldest daughter, hopes to be a civil engineer, a career plan that she still firmly asserts three years later in a follow-up interview. The other younger girls would like to be doctors, singers, and dancers. Regane, who is full of surprises, reveals that she plans to be all three: a doctor, a singer, and a dancer. When Bruna questions the feasibility of her ambitious plan, Regane looks sad but then perks up as she finds a solution. She says that she will sing and dance while she is studying to be a doctor, and focus on being a doctor when she graduates. I admire their aspirations and their passion, but I am also aware of the tremendous struggles that lie ahead of them.

Even while parents, particularly mothers, transmit strong lessons about the importance of education, schools can be a difficult space for black students, who are often the target of racial insults from their peers and racialized name calling from teachers. This is exacerbated by the common use of racial terms to refer to the students, which in the context of the pervasive racial hierarchy in Brazil can be distressing.[27] Moreover, teachers are known not to respond to reports about racial insults, and their silence signals a tacit acceptance of racism.[28]

In Brazil, students often only spend about four hours a day in school, with the option of attending class in the morning or the afternoon. The majority of the children in the study attend class during the 7:00–11:00 a.m. period. In a small focus group involving five of the girls in the community, all report being called racist names or hearing them, including *nega do cabelo duro* (nappy-headed black girl) and *cabelo de bombril* (brillo head), as well as hearing a number of terms and phrases that reference race and phenotype. But the worst schoolyard insult is one that references racial features alongside African cultural blackness: *preta do buzó*. *Buzó* refers to the offerings that are made as part of Afro-Brazilian religious rituals, and *preta* refers to a dark-skinned black female. As Bahian activist Rodrigo suggests when I ask him to deconstruct this insult, he explains, "There exists a scale of insult: *branco* is good, *preto* is bad, and *preto do buzó* is even worse." The stigma of cultural blackness in the form of practicing Candomblé is so great that attaching *buzó* to an already offensive racial insult adds another layer of injury.[29]

Regane is particularly affected by the phrase *cabelo de bombril* because it builds on the anxieties she already has as a result of her mother's comments about her hair, facial features, and skin color. Yet even after having participated in interviews in which she was brought to tears by revealing how badly her friends tease her about her "bad" hair, as I am walking through the neighborhood, she runs up to me and asks, "Have you ever considered cutting your hair and selling it as a scouring pad?" She then laughs loudly and runs off. I am confused and saddened that Regane is doing to me exactly what the other kids in her neighborhood do to her. She is using the very same language that made her cry to jokingly insult me. She does so, in part, because the texture of my hair makes me the only person against whom she can use the words from a superior position. She relishes the joke, proud that on the basis of the rules of the racial hierarchy, her hair is "better" than mine. This is a powerful commentary on the internalization and reproduction of racism.

Despite the racially hostile environment in schools, parents hold very tightly to the hopes of what education can provide for their offspring. They hope that education can help their children avoid future racism, but most do not address the racism that the children currently face in the schools. Sonia is the exception. She claims to engage in racial socialization as it relates to preparing them for the future. When asked how she prepares her six children for racism, she states:

> Everyone is prepared for this. Of course everybody has to prepare. By talking like this: nowadays blacks are . . . everyone is prejudiced, the majority of people. Large companies and business people are made up of white people because they think that only white people are rich. But their blood is red just like a black person's blood. His blood is not white, so this is ignorance. For me, that's it.

Sonia frames racism as an individual problem of ignorance, but she reports that she discusses racism with her children. While her intentions may be well placed, none of her six children report having talked about racism or discrimination at home.

WHAT IS RACISM?

Discursive spaces are not physical locations, but they are liminal areas where certain themes are considered off limits or taboo and others are openly discussed. In Brazil, discussions of racism that are structural and link claims about racism to solutions that involve public policy or a societal approach are off limits. In families, racism is defined using an individual or prejudice model as though it is a sickness that exists within individuals. Therefore, examples of racism are almost always connected to interpersonal relationships rather than structural inequality. Family practices and racial socialization are products of dominant racial hierarchies and reflect how family members both define racism and understand its role in organizing their lives.

The core families define racism in three main ways: racial name calling, racial self-hatred, and disagreeing with a marriage or marrying someone because of race. The following are typical statements about racism:

> My family on my mother's side is racist—very racist. They are prejudiced. For example, they didn't want my mother to marry my father because he is black. (Vânia, 31)

> [Racism] comes from inside the person themselves. (Nora, 48, mother of five)

> [Racism] comes from the family, home training, education level. In the high schools they don't really touch on this issue. Racism blocks them from thinking in a different way. They are raised with these ideas. (Selton, 26)

Racism is defined as an individual or family-derived problem, so rarely do interviewees describe it as something involving structural disparities in education, employment, representation, or politics. One of the few mothers who defines racism in a way that acknowledges structural inequality is Andrea, who defines herself as white or brown, but not an African-descendant. She connects racial inequality to slavery by mentioning the overrepresentation of black women as maids. Moreover, she cites the government's failure to fund public education as a driving force for racial and class inequality.

A key question for families is how they view the quota system in Brazil, considering the links between one's definition of racism, one's racial identity, and one's political views.[30] One's racial consciousness or identity is significant because it functions as a "lens through which individuals interpret and make sense of the world around them" and as "a starting point for social action."[31] The quota system is intended to facilitate the entrance of black and indigenous students, and students of lower socioeconomic status in all racial categories, into college.[32] In Brazil, public universities are free, and they are considered the best universities in the country. In order to gain entrance, students must pass a rigorous college entrance exam (*vestibular*), which many students can only do after taking an expensive year-long *cursinho* (pre-exam course).

Students who attend the free public secondary schools in Brazil are predominately poor and black. They often have underpaid teachers, substandard school facilities, and few educational resources; furthermore, their families cannot afford to pay the expensive fees associated with the *cursinho*. Though public universities were developed so all students could have access to college, it has ultimately provided free education to students who come from the wealthiest and whitest families in the country. A large number of Brazilians, disproportionately Afro-Brazilians with dreams of attending college, must attend private universities, where they take on significant debt and end up graduating with degrees that are often less valued on the job market. After long struggles led by appeals from the black movement, the quota system, made national in 2013, was passed in order to make public universities more accessible to a larger number of underprivileged students.[33]

The core families overwhelmingly view education as the secret to success and social mobility, but this ideological commitment does not translate into support for affirmative action or the quota system in Brazil. Only seven people in all of the core families stated that they supported the quota system—less than 10 percent of respondents. After additional probing, I find the rationales of the majority of informants suspiciously similar. The main argument against the quota system is the idea that it leaves a negative impression of black competency. Consider the following responses:

> I am against quotas. I think the same way that I can study others can study. When you are black you have. . . . If I am black and you are white, the spot is mine. This is saying that a black person doesn't have the capability to get in on his own. I agree with affirmative action for public school students, but not racial [quotas]. (Walter, 19, student)

> I don't think I agree with that quota system because it is saying that blacks do not have the capability to enter into the university. . . . But I might be wrong. (Gloria, 47)

Interviewees problematize the quota system because of their perception that it unfairly privileges blacks by indiscriminately allowing unqualified black students to enroll in college. But the quota system does not give unqualified black students a free pass without regard to academics, and it is also not a program solely targeting black students.[34] Proponents of affirmative action counter these arguments by emphasizing that if any group has received preference during the several-centuries-long existence of universities, it has been and continues to be white Brazilians. They further argue that the term *preference* is misleading because it draws attention away from how these programs function as redress for historical and contemporary inequality.[35]

Walter, a black student who will soon be entering a private college, offers a very common response to questions about quotas and race-based mobilization. Not only does he disagree with quotas, he resents black organizations in Salvador that try to highlight racial inequality:

> What I don't like is this thing that exists right inside of many black institutions because they themselves promote prejudice. Saying things like, "Ah, because the black is discriminated against, ah, because black people are oppressed," you know, things like that.

Later in our conversation Walter admits that he is speaking principally about the Instituto Steve Biko in Salvador, which has played a pivotal role in advancing legislation to end racial inequality. Its programmatic goals are to use education and prevestibular programs to prepare black students for the college exam and prepare them for the job market. His argument that the Instituto promotes prejudice illustrates the extent to which Walter has internalized the idea that Brazil is a "racial democracy" and a meritocracy. Walter expresses anger at the Instituto Steve Biko and frames its legitimate concerns about access to education and redress for historical discrimination as themselves racist or prejudiced. While he is proud of the way that he has combated racism on the interpersonal level, he does not believe in linking racism to systemic inequality or organizing to combat racism, at least as it relates to blacks.

Walter continues by stating that quotas for indigenous people are different. Both the timbre of his voice and his words reflect his "affective disposition" of deep sympathy to the historical narratives of indigenous people.[36]

> Sometimes I feel like I see the indigenous population is disappearing and I feel so bad for them. So there should be a plan to continue their culture. Of course they need to develop, but their history is almost gone.

Not only does Walter frame blacks as a group undeserving of what he considers special treatment, he juxtaposes them to indigenous people, whom he views as true victims of racism and colonization.[37] I ask many respondents to comment on the history of indigenous people in Brazil with the question: "What happened to the *índios* [native people]?" They describe them as culturally very different from blacks in that they were "born to be free" and were not used as slaves because "they did not want to be slaves." In respondents' narratives, *índios* are given much more agency, and informants tend to naturalize Indians' desire to be free in a way that suggests that blacks passively accepted enslavement. They often overlook—or do not know about—the consistent and quite significant resistance efforts organized by blacks in Brazil.[38]

Men and fathers are seldom part of my interviews in the core families; however, once the quota system is broached, everyone wants to contribute and has strong emotional reactions. The vast majority agree that quotas are a bad idea, and they bond over their belief that quotas suggest that blacks are incapable or incompetent. On the day the women are discussing the quota system, Sérgio, Sonia's husband, appears at the door and angrily states:

> Blacks can't blame racism for everything! They have to get up and work for what they want. I get so tired of hearing people saying because of racism I can't do this or I can't do that. I can't get a job because I'm black. If you are poor it's because you want to be poor! (Sérgio, 36, father of seven)

The irony of this statement is that Sérgio has been underemployed for at least five years. His eleven-year-old confides that she prays at night that he will find a stable job. For years, Sérgio has woken up very early in the morning to sell ice cream or take odd jobs around the city, but he has not been able to find consistent work. He is the perfect example of a man who is working hard, waking up every day to find work, but still having trouble supporting his family. When Sérgio's family's water gets turned off, they ask their neighbor, Luana, if they can use her shower until they can pay to have the water reconnected. When they are unable to fix their water problem, they use the neighbor's shower for months, and this leaves her with a high water bill. His own personal trajectory contradicts his statement, as he works hard yet can barely pay his bills. Moreover, I interviewed over one hundred people for this study, and I never met the proverbial black person who sits around only complaining about racism. In fact, those who are most likely to voice their opinions against racism tend to be college-educated Afro-Brazilians who are in a position to observe firsthand the complications of mobility in white spaces.[39]

MEDIA AND CULTURE

In her work *Negras in Brazil*, Kia Caldwell deploys the term *cultural citizenship* to analyze how in various domains, including popular culture, black women are racialized and gendered in ways that shape their experiences of citizenship.[40] Over a decade after production of the song "Veja os cabelos dela" (Look at Her Hair), written and recorded by Tiriríca, Sony was ordered to pay $1.2 million because the song was considered racist.[41] It was the largest settlement ever for an infraction involving racism. The lyrics, which have been heavily criticized because of the injury they have caused to black women, compare a black woman's hair to a scouring pad and say that her "stench" is worse than that of an animal.[42]

As a gauge of cultural citizenship, Afro-Brazilians and women find themselves virtually absent from mainstream television programming, which is a considerable cultural space. Families enjoy watching "Everybody Hates Chris," a popular show from the United States about a black working-class family, but they do not have a similar show about black families in Brazil. Daniel explains the contradiction:

> They [blacks] are not as valued (*valorizados*) as it seems. It's just an image. I think that nowadays he has to affirm himself. The world is starting to see that the black in Salvador is arriving, he is going to arrive. If you see tourism, there is space. If he wants to do art and dance there are spaces. The musicality of blacks is being valued and some of it is sincere. Tourists come. They think the women are beautiful. They fall in love and take them back to Italy, . . . but sometimes they prostitute them.

Daniel, like many *Baianos*, embraces cultural entrepreneurship as a way for blacks to use their artistic and musical abilities for social mobility. His comments also reveal the tenuousness of this strategy, because increased tourism has not translated into opportunities for Afro-Brazilians to move into the role of business owners. Instead they often only have access to limited roles as performers and to limited cultural spaces. This corresponds to Jocélio Teles dos Santos's concept of "symbolic integration," which emphasizes how the state suppresses and mobilizes blackness at strategic times and for certain purposes.[43] The new initiative to rebrand Salvador is seen as part of a strategic effort to make profits but may not reflect any true commitment to antiracism or to sustained opportunities for blacks to move into spaces from which they have been historically excluded.[44]

In the same way that black dolls are sold to tourists, not to blacks who live in the city, many of the major museums and cultural spaces that are featured in the African heritage tourism book are inexpensive for the public to enjoy, but many of the core families are so marginalized from the cultural center that they have never been to these locations.[45] Some interviewees have never been to the historic city center, Pelourinho. The cost of transportation is prohibitive, and awareness of activities and happenings there is limited. So while foreigners are enticed by the image of an exotic, black Bahia, the self-references for families in the study are overwhelmingly white. The city and state have invested in an initiative to bring Afro-Brazilian cultural heritage to foreigners when many of its own citizens do not have access to these same spaces. Activists had hoped that the re-Africanization of Bahia would affirm Afro-Brazilian culture, but the result has been to "paradoxically reify the myth of racial democracy" by subsuming African culture under a large umbrella of Brazilian culture.[46]

The symbolic presence of Candomblé and *capoeira* create the illusion that cultural space is democratic, but even this reflects conditional cultural inclusion. Carnaval represents a microcosm of spatialized dynamics that mirrors the city's racial and gender dynamics. At Carnaval, the juxtaposition of the largely black cord-pullers (*cordeiros*) who protect white partygoers riding atop floats or as they walk among the black masses (*pipoca*) reflect this. The middle-class and largely white elite who are not on floats watch the street party from above in expensive balcony-like seats (*camarotes*) that overlook the streets at a safe distance from the supposedly dangerous black masses.

Cultural sports and events are a significant element of implicit racial socialization, because they convey ideas about what and who is culturally valuable.[47] Cultural experiences such as soccer, Carnaval, and *telenovelas* occupy a substantial role in the lives of families. The centrality of these activities to family life in Brazil is not coincidental, but reflects an "intentional project by the state to create an inclusive national identity above ethno-racial identity."[48]

Telenovelas are a particularly powerful source of implicit racial socialization because it is customary for every home to have a television, sometimes even a flat-screen. Television serves as the primary source of family entertainment, so the investment is considered worthwhile. With popular layaway plans, families can divide payments over a year until the balance is paid off.

Telenovelas are a national phenomenon in Brazil, traversing gender, age, racial, and color barriers, and the majority of Brazilians watch and become emotionally invested in them. Watching *telenovelas* is an important diversion for families, and their cultural relevance rests in their ability to contribute to Brazilians' pride in and passion for patriotism and the national family.[49] With a poor public education system, few books or other reading materials at home, and ambiguous conversations about race, Brazilian history and race relations as told on the *telenovelas* can significantly influence the thinking of even the poorest family. The objective of the programs is not to be accurate. Instead, *telenovelas* entertain while simultaneously presenting misrepresentations of the world for their audience to enjoy and reproduce.[50]

Engagement with the dramatic story lines of *telenovelas* is a normalized part of what it means to be Brazilian. During my interviews with children, it is apparent that the programs are socializing agents on issues ranging from fashion, beauty, and romance to the history of race in Brazil. I asked children whether and how racism is discussed in their families, and these answers are representative:

> No, they don't talk about that. I learned about slavery from the *novela*. There was a program that showed how whites beat on blacks, and they punished them when they wanted them to work. You know there is a *novela* that comes on about slavery. What is it called? It's called *Sinha Moça*! They have lots of blacks on that *novela*. (Melissa, 9)

> My mom taught me some things, but a lot [I learn] from television. They have lots of shows talking about this. A lot of stuff I learned on TV and many other places. (Marilda, 11)

At least eight children in the study use *telenovelas* to understand the history of slavery in Brazil. I observe others watching *Sinha Moça*, a soap opera set during the slave era, with their families daily. This *telenovela*, like others, is fraught with inaccuracies and silences. Blacks tend to be seen disproportionately or only in inferior and "demeaning roles, as slaves, or in marginal positions such as villains, and in a situation of servitude."[51]

As with young Leo, when I ask children about what they know about slavery, they excitedly recount narratives of slaves being brutally whipped or punished. In some cases, they act out these brutal scenes happily and laugh as they pretend to be tied to a whipping post to be beaten. It is as though the dramatization of slavery has left them desensitized to slave imagery. Slavery is connected to a very distant past, and it is framed as existing completely outside of the realm of how they understand themselves.

The dominant hegemonic narratives of Brazil's history shape the portrayal of slavery in the *telenovelas*. In *Sinha Moça* blacks are shown as slaves in the fields, but they are filmed working in slow motion and always with pleasant, relaxing music playing in the background. This perpetuates historical portrayals of Brazil as having had a less brutal form of slavery, in which punishment was exceptional and reserved only for bad slaves.[52] This type of *telenovela* features the largest number of black characters, and the story lines are predictable. There is often a love triangle involving the usual suspects: a racially mixed woman (usually a *mulata*) and a white man. The white man feels torn between slavery and his love for the enslaved woman, and eventually ends up being the white savior. There is also the requisite evil black person who is jealous of the relationship between the *mulata* and her white boyfriend and tries to destroy the relationship. The *telenovelas* construct simple dichotomies between good and bad, underemphasizing explicit references to race and whiteness as much as possible.[53]

The socialization that Brazilians receive from *telenovelas* is not just about slavery, but also about race, color, and desire. In virtually all of the *telenovelas*, whites are the object of blacks' romantic affections, while whites mainly have relationships with other whites.[54] A *telenovela* that features a couple composed of two Afro-Brazilians is rarely produced.

In 2014, a new telenovela was launched titled *Sexo e As Negas* (Sex and the Negresses), which was created with the idea that it would be an extension of the U.S. series *Sex in the City*. Unfortunately, the show juxtaposes a white, female protagonist who seeks a stable romantic relationship to four black women who spend their time and energy aggressively seeking sex. The show has been fiercely critiqued by black Brazilian feminists for recycling racist and sexist stereotypes about black hypersexuality.

In a *telenovela* that airs during the research period, *Viver a Vida*, Tais Araújo, considered the most popular black Brazilian actress and one of the most beautiful, plays the starring role. In what is perhaps an unintended consequence, her presence in the *telenovela* has a transformative impact on the visual experience of walking down the streets. Magazine kiosks along the street often feature her picture, one of the only images of a black woman in a sea of magazines on the stand. In the *telenovela* she plays a model, Helena, who dates a much older white divorced man. In one significant episode, Helena has to beg forgiveness from her lover's ex-wife for a car accident for which she is blamed. In the apology scene, Helena is stripped of all makeup, wears tattered, rag-like clothing, is barefoot, and falls to her knees with her hands clasped high and head lowered to ask for forgiveness.[55] In what might be considered the hit heard around Brazil, Helena is slapped across the face by the angry white woman and says nothing as the woman turns and leaves.

Adding insult to injury, this episode aired during the week of Black Consciousness Day, November 20 in Brazil. Black activists were indignant with the portrayal of Helena and focused on how her body was staged in a way reminiscent of the deferential posture of slaves. The one *telenovela* character that young black girls commonly reference as a role model is reduced to a silenced slave. As with scenes of slavery, the children are often so immersed in the dramatization of the scene that they do not respond to it other than by letting out surprised gasps and covering their mouths in anticipation of the next episode.

DISCUSSION

Of blackness, Frantz Fanon writes, "The Negro is unaware of it as long as his existence is limited to his own environment; but the first encounter with a white man oppresses him with the whole weight of his blackness."[56] This sentiment is echoed by Felipe, who reports on some of his first experiences outside the circle of Afro-Brazilians with whom he had always interacted. His class mobility was associated with spatial mobility, a new consciousness about his blackness, and an awareness of how he was differentiated from privileged whites.

Some mothers, specifically middle-class mothers, insist on preparing their children for this. Both Raíssa and Taynara socialize their children and families into transgressive practices that use embodied capital to guide their negotiation of racialized discursive, cultural, and physical space. Their strategies are designed with the anticipation that their children will enter the middle class and that, voluntarily or not, they will represent all black people. Their efforts to teach their children how not to bring shame on the family is a reflection of the weight of their racial history. For other parents, universal ideas about respect and egalitarianism are important, and while race is not explicit, it is a subtext. The majority of mothers and other respondents recognize that racism exists but define it as an individual-level phenomenon. This perspective shapes their political commitments and explains why public policies, including affirmative action and quotas, are often viewed adversely.

Schools are a generally antagonistic spaces for black students. History textbooks carry racist overtones and, as Ana Célia Silva notes, schools need to address the "presence of blacks in books frequently as a slave, without reference to his past of being a free man before slavery and the struggles for freedom that he developed during the slavery period."[57] In addition to this racialized curriculum, Afro-Brazilian students experience racial insults that are tolerated by both teachers and students and are treated in ways that suggest they are incompetent, less desirable, less intelligent, and even less worthy of affection than white children.[58] Again, silence and the absence of critical commentary have a role in normalizing racist representations and legitimating differential treatment of children in schools.

Cultural participation provides an important form of implicit racial socialization. Watching *telenovelas* is a daily family activity, and their messages and images perpetuate racial hierarchies through negative portrayals of blacks and the absence of a counterdiscourse. Also, *telenovelas* that focus on slavery not only desensitize children to the horrors of slavery, but reinforce notions of white saviors and the virtues of *mestiçagem* through interracial relationships, implicitly framed as blacks seeking white partners. Participation in some of the most popular cultural activities, such as soccer and Carnaval, help to foster nationalistic ties, which provide a temporary affective reward but often leave Afro-Brazilians at the margins of full citizenship.

In terms of making diasporic connections, the socialization practices of the middle class mothers (Raíssa and Taynara) resonate with the socialization practices found in black families in the United States. Specifically, their emphasis on embodied racial capital, reflected by concern for cleanliness and appropriate behavior, parallel the politics of respectability that has been observed in earlier periods of history in Brazil and the United States.[59] Raíssa's assertion that her son's behavior will reflect on the entire racial group mirrors the earlier emphasis in the United States on middle-class blacks needing to be a "credit to their race." Though I critique Lúcio's focus on dress as a way to avoid problems with the police, in the United States there is a plethora of "instructional videos, brochures, and wallet cards by civil rights organizations, which are intended to aide those who encounter the police." Some of these advise monitoring one's emotions, dress, and body language in anticipation of police encounters.[60]

Barbara's grandmother's advice about respecting the ways that race shapes public spaces and social relations puts severe limitations on the movements of blacks. This can and should be problematized as reproducing inequality, but these strategies are also rooted in real fears about what might happen when racialized spaces are transgressed. Black families in Brazil find themselves in a complicated situation. On one hand, they are supportive and encouraging of education, and on the other, they remain vigilant and assert agency, using the practices learned through racial socialization. In other diasporic regions, black mothers use spatial and emotional limits particularly when raising their sons, urging them to "live lives of limited, restricted, and controlled affect and expression" in order to avoid dangerous situations and death.[61] Overall, in their negotiations of spatial mobility and embodied racial capital, Afro-Brazilians are both resilient and resourceful. They want family members to be successful, and many teach them to do so, while underscoring that in a racialized social system they must also mind their blackness.

CHAPTER 6

ANTIRACISM IN TRANSGRESSIVE FAMILIES

Discovering your blackness is to have had your identity massacred. . . .
But it is also and above all the experience of committing yourself to
rescuing your history and re-creating yourself by your own capabilities.
NEUSA SANTOS SOUZA, *TORNAR-SE NEGRO*

IN A SOCIAL SYSTEM ORGANIZED so thoroughly by race, explicit and implicit racial socialization assists family members as they negotiate their embodied and affective capital in the private and public spheres of their lives. In this chapter, I illustrate that "where there is power, there is also resistance" by focusing on how three consistently transgressive families engage in antiracism.[1] I highlight these three families because of their explicit and exceptionally creative strategies of antiracism, which illustrate the complex ways that families use socialization to negotiate and challenge racial hierarchies. I present evidence that recognizes these complexities, and by deploying the notion of resistance and accommodation, I explore the tension between families' ability to resist racial hierarchies and simultaneously engage in practices, discourses, and affective exchanges that undermine or contradict their resistance.[2] To be sure, resistance and accommodation occur in all families and for all groups, but I argue that racial socialization is not overdetermined by hegemonic whiteness. Each of these three families use affective and embodied capital to redefine racial and color hierarchies, transform national myths, transgress spatial and discursive boundaries, and refashion themselves in opposition to the structures that constrain them.

NASCIMENTO FAMILY VALUES

Come out from the slave quarters and wash the dishes!

This is what Irma and Fabiana playfully yell to their younger sister Joana as we finish our meal. Neide, their mother, has invited me to lunch, and she has cooked a special meal consisting of *mocotó*, rice, and *aipim*. Mo-cotó is a decidedly Brazilian dish consisting of cow's feet stewed over beans and vegetables and served with *aipim* (manioc) over white rice. A humorous argument ensues about who will wash the dishes, and the three determine that it is, in fact, Joana's turn. All three laugh as Joana playfully pushes them out of the kitchen. While other families have been shown to downplay their African heritage, Neide proudly explains to me the history of this special meal and its origins as "slave food" that she says everyone in Brazil loves to eat. The racial banter as well as their empha-sis on African culture is standard in the Nascimento home. This stands in contrast to the way that the topic of slavery emerges in other homes, where it is seldom mentioned except in relation to the *telenovelas* and where it is not mobilized as a social critique. Neide is insistent that her three daughters and two sons understand their racial history, prepare for the racial challenges they will face, and are aware enough not to "confun-dir a realidade" (confuse the reality) of their racial positionality.

All of the members of the Nascimento family are very dark skinned with features that mark them as *pretos*. The strategic semantic ambigu-ity that is used by other families to ambiguously racialize family mem-bers is much less relevant among the Nascimentos, where family members define themselves uniformly in color and racial terms as *preta* or *negra*, the most unambiguous racial and color terms. However, they do perceive slight differences in skin color and features; this is reflected in their de-scriptions of family members as just a little darker or lighter than one an-other. Though Neide's sons and their father are emotionally distant, they are physically present during my visits. Neide's husband is a relatively re-served man who contributes to the conversation with periodic nods and the occasional comment, but he is rarely engaged in the interviews or ob-servations. In one casual conversation, Neide's son Roberto begins to tell me his color. He is on the verge of saying *moreno* when he glances over in the direction of his mother and corrects himself, classifying himself by color and race as *negro*. His mother cannot hear our conversation but her instruction looms closely.

Neide is a custodian at a large company in Salvador, but a work-related injury means that she is available for hours to speak with me about her life, her family, and Brazil. She openly addresses a wide range of issues and always finds a way to weave race and class politics into the interviews. Her interest in discussing inequality is a deviation from the way socialization in Brazil is usually described, as using messages to "promote discrimination while simultaneously denying its existence."[3] She has socialized her daughters and sons into a more critical understanding of Brazilian society, as evidenced by their comments, jokes, and day-to-day interactions. If most families are characterized by socialization practices that maximize racial ambiguity, Neide's family demonstrates an approach that is based on brutal honesty, sharp wit, and direct racial statements. Their interactions border on theatrical as they use jokes and interactions to challenge dominant discourses and narratives about race in Salvador.

Racial nicknames or names that refer to racial appearance are quite common in Brazil and Latin America, and they can be used as terms of endearment.[4] In the Nascimento family, Neide has a nickname that she uses for all of her children and grandchildren. They are her *torradinhos* (literally translated as little burnt ones), but her use of the term is nuanced. When asked about the meaning of *torradinho*, she and her daughter Fabiana laugh and reply together that it means, "He's black, black, black, black, black!"[5] Fabiana now uses the term to endearingly refer to her baby boy, Roquinaldo, incorporating the same language in the socialization of her son. Within the span of two hours, Neide uses the term more than twenty times as a descriptor of her children, grandchildren, and poor blacks in Salvador. She uses it as a conscious critique and a way of mocking how color terms have been deployed as part of the strategic semantic ambiguity that allows Brazilians to avoid labeling themselves as black. So, while there is a tendency for Brazilians to categorize or even whiten themselves by using intermediary color terms, her use of *torradinho* functions in the exact opposite way, embracing her family's location at the polar end of the racialized color continuum. They are unapologetically black—past black: they are burnt.

Consider the following conversation, in which Neide discusses Fabiana's pregnancy with Roquinaldo:

> NEIDE: Fabiana did not want a boy, she wanted a girl. When she went to do the ultrasound, she found out it was a boy. That's why you should have two, one for mom and one for dad. Your husband is American. Right? So, the baby is going to come out just a little brown with his dad's eyes. They are blue, right?
>
> ELIZABETH: (chuckle) My husband is black.
>
> NEIDE: He's black too?!

ELIZABETH: Yes, he's black.

NEIDE: So, then, the baby will be born *torradinho* like this (*points to her five-year-old grandson*), with this beautiful skin. Right, my black African, my good black boy, my honey, my African. I call him my beautiful black boy. Isn't that right, beautiful black boy? I love African music, if we had the money I would buy a lot of African music.[6]

Neide has an entire arsenal of racialized terms that she uses to refer to her grandson, each of them qualified by a complimentary adjective in order to emphasize the positive associations between blackness and beauty. Instead of deracializing the term *torradinho*, she makes the racial connotation even stronger by explicitly linking his beauty to Africanness and affirming her passion for African culture. In other families not only do respondents fail to connect blackness with Africa, they distance themselves from all things explicitly African, especially Afro-Brazilian religion and physical features.[7] Neide embraces her grandson's racial phenotype, links his appearance to Africa, and creates a term to convey his location on the extreme end of the color spectrum rather than toward the middle. For Neide, it is a term of endearment, consciously constructed to embody unambiguous blackness, and it is used as a strategy to help her family learn how not to "confuse the reality" about their color and race.

Neide's initial assumption that my husband is white with blue eyes is consistent with the assumption of virtually everyone when they discover that my husband is American. For the vast majority of Brazilians, to be American means to be white with blue eyes. Her assumptions about Americanness and whiteness are incorrect, but she corrects herself and then affirms that my future child will be "beautiful" and "good" like her grandson, whom she praises with compliments that emphasize his dark skin and Africanness. This interaction contrasts with requests that I consistently receive from women asking if I can introduce them to one of my American (presumably white male) friends, with the reasoning, "I want to have a baby with blue eyes."

Neide's inventive strategies do not merely encompass the discursive terrain, but they include other creative constructions that reflect how she fosters antiracism in her family. When I first meet Neide and her family, she shows me an end table in the living room with picture frames on top and informs me that it is *só pra gente branca*, or only for white people. Neide states this matter-of-factly, laughs, and then again repeats that the end table is used only for pictures of white people. She jests that she might consider adding a picture of me to the side table, considering I have white teeth.

Unsure how to interpret this interaction, I document it and plan to ask her about it at a later date. However, the meaning comes to life organically when a white friend and patron of the family comes to visit. As Neide sits on the sofa with him, they laugh and discuss a range of issues. Eventually she tells him to look at the pictures on the end table, a space that is reserved "For whites only; only for pretty people," and she laughs loudly. She brilliantly uses the table to mock exclusionary racialized spaces and to critique the conflation of whiteness with beauty. She forces her white visitor to confront the reality of his privilege and reminds him that although they are friends, there are significant structural barriers that separate them. It would normally be considered inappropriate to speak about race as Neide does. She is in violation of tacit rules of racial etiquette and cordiality. So Neide lightens the tone of the conversation with an exaggerated laugh in order to creatively accomplish her goal. Laughter has been used to trivialize racist comments in other families, but Neide appropriates it to challenge white privilege.

Neide's use of creative antiracist strategies extends to her interpretation of the relevance of race and class in Brazil and her criticisms of U.S. consumption. She states:

> You Americans are fat because you eat food that has lots of fat, like McDonald's. You all like McDonald's there, don't you? Here, you will only see rich people, you do not see *torradinhos* in McDonald's. We eat a dessert that we get on the street for seventy-five cents and fruit juice. When we want a snack, we do the same thing.

Her statement acknowledges class and racial inequality, framing blacks and wealthy people as mutually exclusive categories. But in addition, she compliments resourceful, poor blacks, who, she claims, develop smart and healthy strategies to deal with the reality of their situation. Instead of consuming expensive and unhealthy food, they find an affordable meal and snack for just a fraction of the price. Few respondents in this study complimented poor Brazilian blacks for how they navigate a stratified society in which they are in the most disadvantaged position. Her critique of the United States on the basis of its overconsumption and overspending also contrasts with other Afro-Brazilian families' tendency to idealize everything about the United States, except with regard to issues of race, in which case the United States is constructed as blatantly and "truly" racist.[8]

Inevitably, in a family with four women the question of hair arises. The symbolic and racialized meanings attached to hair and beauty have been studied extensively, highlighting how black families and cultural movements transform racist evaluations of hair to foster antiracism and racial pride.[9] In a family where antiracism is central to racialization and racial learning, I anticipate that hair might also be a site of racial contestation. In fact, while women in other families maximize their embodied capital by accommodating dominant beauty norms, I observe that the Nascimento women have chosen an alternative approach. Neide and two of her daughters wear their hair in synthetic braids, a style whose popularity has grown as part of the afro-aesthetics movement. One of her daughters, Joana, makes a living braiding hair in Salvador and offers to braid my hair if I am interested.[10] This stands in contrast to Sonia's offer to chemically straighten my hair.

Conversations about hair have a distinctly gendered element. Young boys often wear their hair cut very low, and there is little conversation about this. However, on one occasion, Neide's oldest daughter, Fabiana, arrives for lunch and begins talking about how she wishes that she had a baby girl rather than a boy:

> FABIANA: If Roquinaldo were a girl, I would put Mega Hair[11] in his head.
> ELIZABETH: You would really put Mega Hair in a baby's head, a two-year-old's head? (*all of us laugh*)
> FABIANA: Yes (*chuckles*).
> NEIDE: The right thing to do would be to go ahead and straighten it.

All indications so far have been that Neide's household is one in which blackness and Africa, including afro-textured hair, are embraced and celebrated, but her daughter's statement suggests that this is not necessarily the case. The assertion that she would put fake hair in her daughter's head and Neide's further affirmation that the "right thing to do" would be to straighten it seems inconsistent with the earlier messages of African pride. With all the talk about hair, Neide is reminded of her two-year-old great-niece (her sister's granddaughter), whom she wants me to meet:

> Oh, you have to see this little girl! She's just this size, just two years old (*uses her hands to show that the girl comes up to her knee*). You have to hear her sing, "Beautiful girl with nappy hair, put a straightener in your hair so that it'll look nice, a straightener will fix it up. Brush it, brush it, brush it." (*Neide pretends to have a brush in her hand as she smiles broadly and laughs, imitating the way her niece sings the lyrics.*)

What is jarring about the song is that it seems explicitly derogatory toward black hair and frames it as something to be fixed. This is yet another instance where family interactions contradict the mother's earlier commitment to antiracism. In a separate visit with the family, I am introduced to the little girl, and she is told to perform the song, which she does with the help of her grandmother, who sings the same lyrics with her and acts out the brushing gestures.

The entire interaction strikes me as perplexing in light of the family's strong antiracist discourse, which affirms blackness and challenges racial norms and etiquette. However, once I research the lyrics, I discover that the particular lines that Neide loves to hear her niece sing are part of a popular song by the group Rapaziada da Baixa Fria titled "Cabelo da desgraça" (Shameful Hair). This song, contrary to the words that the little girl sings, was developed with the intention of validating a black aesthetic. The song critiques the internalization of racial stereotypes and norms and attempts to foster positive self-esteem among blacks in Brazil. Though not apparent from the line the little girl sings, the song is about self-love and antiracism. It uses lyrics about brushing one's hair to critique those who try to eliminate or straighten their natural hair. Having researched the song, I develop a new appreciation of its message and of its significance as a critical intervention into popular music that often degrades, animalizes, and insults black women and their bodies.

But I still wonder why they focus on the lyrics about brushing hair rather than those that more clearly articulate these positive ideas. It is possible that consistent with the ways that Neide flips racial concepts and ideas, this one line is also being used subversively. However, Neide's niece, the mother of the young girl, goes on to tell the two year old:

> That's right, brush it, brush it, brush it! Oh, if only I had married a white guy with good hair and a thin nose, then you wouldn't have that hair! (*she laughs loudly*)

Researchers have offered a sharp analysis of the use of laughter and humorous talk in Brazil, arguing that humor opens "a discursive space within which it becomes possible to speak about matters that are otherwise naturalized, unquestioned, or silenced."[12] In this family, the unexpected laughs, chuckles, and giggles that permeate conversations illustrate a unique use of this emotional aesthetic. But because it becomes difficult to distinguish between humor and truth, now I am starting to understand how easy it is to "confuse the reality" about color and race.

Neide is intentional about her discussions of race, weaving the topic into conversations whenever possible in order to help her children develop critical racial fluency. She initiates a seemingly nonracial conversation about traveling to the United States and inquires about the regulations that stipulate that Brazilian tourists can only stay in the United States for a maximum of three months:

> NEIDE: How do they know if I have been there for three months?
> ELIZABETH: Your passport gets a stamp.
> NEIDE: A stamp? You know in the past, they used iron to brand blacks and I see things are not that different now (*laughs*).

Neide makes this conversation into a teaching moment. The passport stamp has some very tangential similarities to the iron brands that were used to mark slaves to control and monitor their movement. The comparison is an imperfect and problematic one, but Neide's use of it is one example of how she incorporates her radical applications of racial history into day-to-day conversations.

Fabiana is not amused:

> FABIANA: Mom, it's not just for blacks, it's for whites, blacks, yellow, everybody.
> NEIDE: My daughter, let's have lunch. (*She has asked her daughter to come eat several times now, but Fabiana continues sitting on the couch talking to me and I have already eaten. She continues in a loud voice.*) The first people to eat are the masters and then the maid. Now it's time to call the slave, the little slave from the slave quarters, but nobody wants to come. Come here right now my "torradinho," my little black one![13]

Neide's references to slavery are another strategy of educating her children about racial hierarchy and slavery while also locating her daughter in this history. Both she and her daughters laugh but understand that the hierarchy she describes is based on real social relations. In the same way that Neide emphasizes white privilege with the end table, she makes black disadvantage clear through these slave references. The family can make these references and laugh, knowing that the days of slavery have ended, but they also serve as reminders of both the history and the contemporary status of blacks in Brazil.

I do not observe this type of racial subversion in other families. The closest example to another use of an image or reference to slavery to describe current-day conditions occurs in the Ribeira family. Vânia states:

I feel like I am a slave [at work]. I can't go to the bathroom when I want. When I leave my desk, they are watching me wherever I go. Ten minutes to go to a break; they have a paper that says when I can go. If I start feeling badly I can't go to the bathroom until they tell me I can take a break. If you have to pee, you have to hold it until you can take a break. As it relates to color, I think that blacks make less than whites. Mainly, women. (Vânia, 31)

In this example, not only does Vânia link labor exploitation and restrictive rules of behavior to slavery and gender inequality, she directly identifies how whites are privileged vis-à-vis black women. Vânia is exceptional in the Ribeira family because she is college educated, but she is not actually a biological member of the family because she is Paulo's girlfriend. She is more radical in terms of how she views blackness and public policy, and in her understanding of how race shapes contemporary Brazilian society. Vânia is also among the few respondents to support the quota system, but given her education and class, these differences are not surprising.

One of the reasons Neide speaks so openly and often about race is that she wants her children to be prepared to confront situations in which they have to stand up for themselves. This is a concern all mothers have, but it is normally framed as "a gente não deve abaixar a cabeça" (we shouldn't lower our heads). Contrary to the generalized messages that other families convey to their children, Neide speaks in direct racial terms and in ways that address race, phenotype, and class. When explaining racism she states:

Oh, because you are white and have straight hair, and you dress in name-brand clothes I am not going to sit down because I am black? I have the same rights as you. I am going sit here because I am a person, and I have my rights. I am going to sit.

She explicitly tells her children that it is important to protect their self-esteem from racial assaults and not to feel inferior on the basis of race, appearance, or class. Rather than encouraging them to avoid situations where whites are present, she encourages them to resist and stake a claim to their citizenship and their right to challenge racialized public spaces. She acknowledges that this is not necessarily an easy process:

NEIDE: You have some people that have racism within themselves. What I mean is, they call themselves black but they don't value themselves. We have to value ourselves. They think that they are inferior. They don't have much education, they don't have nice clothes, they don't think they are pretty, they don't value themselves.

ELIZABETH: Where do these ideas come from?

NEIDE: It comes from themselves.

Neide's comment acknowledges the existence of internalized racism and acknowledges that education and appearance affect the self-esteem of black people. However, Neide stops short of linking internalized racism to broader racial hierarchies and systems of oppression, instead framing it as an individual problem that comes from within. In this sense, her response is consistent with the astructural way that other families explain internalized racism: as coming from individuals rather than as a product of the racial ideologies promoted by the broader society.

Neide's family is unique in many ways, but it is also replete with racial contradictions. I join her daughter, Joana, as she cruises the internet on the family computer, which is located in her parents' room. She is using social media and looking at pictures of dark-skinned black models who are considered very attractive, including Tyson Beckford, arguably the most famous black male supermodel in the United States. She clicks through his pictures and comments:

> He is very good-looking, but I would never date a big, dark-skinned black man (*negão*). I prefer lighter men. I've always preferred lighter men. My white friends date black men because they say they know how to work it, but I'm not interested.

In the context of racial socialization in this family, which I describe as transgressive because of the frequency of pro-African and pro-black messages, Joana's comments are startlingly inconsistent. I glance over to her mother, anticipating a clever, subversive response. Instead of problematizing Joana's comments in a way that would be consistent with her earlier assertions about black beauty, Neide looks at me sincerely and says:

> What? (*shrugs*) They [dark-skinned black men] seem kind of aggressive and vulgar. Don't you ever dream of marrying a white man? You know, to have children with blue eyes?

With this comment, Neide confirms that even while she creatively resists racism in her day-to-day life, racial hierarchies based on white supremacy affect her consciousness and views in fundamental ways. Resistance, much like domination, is not total. Neide's contradictions are illustrative of both the possibilities and the limits of resistance.

THE SANTOS FAMILY: BLACK INFLATION

Dona Elena is the matriarch of the Santos family. A widow partnered three times, she has nine children. She is very dark skinned with features that mark her as *preta*, but she wears her hair in long, black, straight Mega Hair extensions and wears gold rings on each of her fingers. She defines herself and all of her children as *negros legítimos* (legitimate blacks), though they vary considerably in phenotype. Dona Elena asserts her racial identity proudly, and the strength of her claims to blackness are evidenced by her questioning of my blackness:

> DONA ELENA: You, you are a black woman, but you do not have black features (*aspetos do negro*).
>
> ELIZABETH: What do you mean?
>
> DONA ELENA: You do not. You have a nose, . . . you do not have a wide nose. You do not have thick lips. You do not have a black appearance. You probably have someone in your family who is not black. Because blacks have what? Thick lips, flat nose. So black beauty has to be that. To be black beauty it has to be that you have to have thick lips and a flat nose. This is what black beauty looks like. You know? Everybody in my family is *negro*, there is not even one person who is not.
>
> ELIZABETH: Are you sure? (*I lean in toward her and smile.*)
>
> DONA ELENA: Black, black, black.
>
> ELIZABETH: There is not one person in your family that is not black? (*I lean in again and smile.*)
>
> DONA ELENA: Black, black, black (*pauses*). . . . Well, listen, wait a minute. My great-grandmother was an Indian woman, and my grandmother never knew her mother. My great-grandmother was a slave who escaped. But that is going way, way back. But, but! On my father's side everybody is black, coming straight from Africa. So much so that my name is not our name, it is the name of the master. They took the name that came with us from Africa and gave us Santos. So this name was a given name.

Confident in her blackness and African authenticity, she does not rely on the ideology of *mestiçagem* (racial mixture) to describe her family, but affirms that "not one person" in her family is nonblack, which is a point of pride rather than shame. As we delve into her family history, she only reluctantly admits that there is an Indian woman somewhere in her family. However, her hurried transition from talking about her mother's side to talking about her unmixed black father's side reinforces her claims to true African heritage.

This is markedly different from the eagerness of other families to deconstruct their lineage with particular emphasis on white or nonblack family members, what researchers have referred to as "white inflation."[14] Dona Elena's is one of the few families that engages in what could alternatively be called *black inflation*, offering a reading of racial authenticity that privileges the importance of black culture, black beauty, and black family history. For Dona Elena, embodied racial capital is attained by one's possession of black features. In contrast to the disgust that her partner displays when her daughter, Neguinha, is born, Dona Elena describes her daughter as being born "really, really black, but pretty" (*preta, preta, mas linda*). Although the phrase suggests that very dark skin and beauty are conflicting descriptors, Dona Elena embraces her daughter's blackness and enters her in beauty competitions.

Her notions of beauty are based on essentialist ideas about Africanness and blackness and are used in a way that challenges antiblack racism in Brazil. Yet researchers note that the problem with essentialism is that it restricts blackness to a limited set of symbols and to criteria that many who identify as black do not meet.[15] At the same time, it is a powerful gesture challenging white aesthetic norms and ideologies of black inferiority.

Dona Elena's linkage of her blackness to Africa and her explanation of how slavery played a role in her family's name illustrate a level of familiarity with Brazil's racial history that few outside of these three families demonstrate. Moreover, her willingness to place herself and family in that history is unique among the sample. Perhaps even more telling is Dona Elena's version of how Brazil began and her understanding of how blacks arrived. She departs drastically from the scripted narrative I heard in other families. Instead, she explains:

> There were three princesses that came from Africa and founded three houses of Candomblé. There were three that came from Africa and from there they started Candomblé here. This was a long time ago. What else do I think? In Pernambuco there were huge slave ships and when they arrived to the shores white men would say, "The chickens have arrived!" Nowadays they call it Porto das Galinhas,[16] but it was not originally a port. It was where they raped the women when they arrived. You understand? In Pernambuco, it was not Porto das Galinhas it was the port

where the women arrived and were raped. Today we, we are still suffering from discrimination, but it will never be like it was before, like having to sleep with those white men.

Dona Elena's historical account challenges the dominant narrative of European discovery in Brazil. First, she begins by recognizing that blacks came from Africa. Not only does she place slavery at the beginning of Brazil's history, but she also highlights the importance of regal African princesses bringing the religion Candomblé to Brazil. The royal lineage of these princesses is important because it is indicative of an African civilization that existed before the Africa-Europe encounter, which is seldom mentioned in history books or interviews.

The power of national mythologies and narratives is less about their accuracy and more about how they function to perpetuate broader ideologies.[17] Dona Elena's interpretation of Brazil's beginning highlights how the contributions and violations of black women, exploitation of Africa, and transfer of Candomblé religion make up the core elements of the country's development. This revisionist approach to Brazilian history contrasts sharply with other, popularly retold versions focusing on a benevolent Princesa Isabel. A testament to Dona Elena's ability to transmit this consciousness and alternative readings of Brazil to her children are her thirty-four-year-old son Felipe's answers to my questions about Brazil's history:

> You want to know about the beginning of Brazil? Well, look, there are two versions of this. The real one and the fake, which one do you want? (*laughs*)

Her son mocks the fake version, which involves "the good little Princess who brings freedom to the slaves." Not only does Dona Elena speak about the importance of talking to her children about racism and slavery, but her aunts passed on to her important cultural practices, including highly decorated embroidery that she reveals has roots in Africa. Dona Elena's connections to Africa also include her membership in Candomblé. Throughout our conversations, she gives thanks to the Orixás (Candomblé deities) for helping her to survive the difficult times in her life.

Dona Elena's adoption of an essentialist view of black beauty and an alternative reading of Brazilian history does not mean that she completely rejects the racial rituals discussed in previous chapters. Her approach to socialization reflects both resistance and accommodation to racial hierarchies. When asked about racial rituals, she reveals that not only is she knowledgeable about the practice of modifying a baby's nose, she has participated in it:

> Pinch it! Get a match, light some incense, when the smoke comes up pass a finger through it and pinch the nose. Everyday I did that to thin (*afinar*) the nose. But that stuff doesn't even work. It's a lie! (*sucks her teeth*) I did it to all of them and they still all came out with wide noses like mine. It did not help. It does not work. No, it does not work! Nowadays people do not do this. Everything has changed.

Despite Dona Elena's insistence on an alternative reading of Brazil's racial history and her pride in what she presents as her authentically black ancestry, she is not exempt from attempting to modify her children's noses. Her participation in the racial ritual suggests how embedded the racial stigma of a wide nose is and the level of consensus about the importance of controlling racialized features. While some may suggest that nose modification is connected to beauty rather than race, Dona Elena's earlier reference to a wide nose as being a trait of blackness and black beauty suggests that the connection for her is a clear one.

Dona Elena is 68 years old, and she wears a long, expensive hair weave that is neatly done and cascades down her shoulders. With hopes of discussing her hair, I ask her about the meaning of good hair and bad hair in Brazil. She replies:

> Our hair, black people's hair is bad (*pointing at both of us*). My hair is nappy (*duro*). Look at my hair, it is nappy. Look at it. (*She parts her hair with her fingers, showing me her roots where the hair extensions are attached.*) I do not wear my hair out because it takes work to comb it. This is not my hair here (*pointing to the extensions*). Even though I wear these extensions my hair grows a lot. It is the type of hair that grows, I have good hair growth but I don't like it nappy. Nappy hair? I do not like it. I do not like it. I accept it, but for me no (*shakes her head and sucks her teeth three times*).

Though in the beginning of our conversations she emphasized the beauty of black features and black cultural forms, her view of afro-textured hair is not very different from other respondents'. In fact, she explicitly describes afro-textured hair as bad hair and does not hesitate to lump my hair into that category as well.

Dona Elena's normalization of afro-textured hair as bad hair is not done maliciously; rather, she speaks of it as an objective fact. The contradictions are best illustrated in the remaining portion of the conversation:

> DONA ELENA: Nappy hair takes so much work. Who does your hair for you like that when you are in the United States? (*She is referencing the twisted natural hairstyle that I am wearing.*)
> ELIZABETH: I do it myself. I did this; it does not take long.
> DONA ELENA: Wait, you did that yourself? You, yourself did it?
> ELIZABETH: Yes.
> DONA ELENA: Wow, how beautiful! But not for me. Honestly, I love my color. I like my color, you know. But my hair, no. I want to be the dark-skinned black woman (*negona*) that I am now, except with straight hair. I would love to have straight hair. I do not like nappy hair.

Here Dona Elena's statements aptly represent the complexities and contradictions of race, gender, and hair politics. She wants to remain the dark-skinned woman that she is except that her hair, one of the most defining racial characteristics, is what she would like to have changed. I find her compliments of my hair interesting because though she often tells me that my hair looks nice, she would not wear her natural hair. Despite his mother's comments, Dona Elena's son Felipe has a more critical view of what he calls the "business about hair" and beauty:

> We, the truth is, we learned to admire European beauty. If you were to stop and think about Jesus, you will see that the images of Jesus are of a European man. Blue eyes, straight hair, light skin, but it has nothing to do with the religion. It's the image that is being sold.

It is an image being sold, an image being purchased, but also an image being reimagined. That Dona Elena asserts her strong racial identity, embraces Afro-Brazilian culture, and affirms black beauty while lamenting her *cabelo ruim* (bad hair) should not be reduced to an illustration of the reproduction of racial hierarchies.

As Chela Sandoval suggests, these contradictions are representative of how women "weave 'between and among' oppositional ideologies" of femininity and antiracism to find self-valorization and liberation from hegemonic power structures.[18] In a society that devalues what it means to be a *negona*, the fact that Dona Elena wants to keep her very dark skin and only change her hair represents a crack in the hegemony of the racial commonsense that would have her alter all of her features. Her comments also reflect the ideological impasse that black women face as they negotiate hegemonic notions of femininity and antiracism and work to create spaces where the two do not have to be mutually exclusive. For these reasons, Dona Elena can be described as having a "differential oppositional consciousness," which is a signal of the permeability of hegemonic structures.[19]

THE DE JESUS FAMILY: THE BRAZILIAN BLACK PANTHERS

The de Jesus family is the only family in the study that consistently socializes family members into positive racial messages, illustrates complex understandings of race and color, and links racial consciousness to political action. To refer to this family as the Brazilian Black Panthers may seem specious but not only is it appropriate, it was requested. In this family, Andrés de Jesus is married to Claudia, and they have three children together, one girl and two boys. Andrés is a very tall, medium- to dark-skinned man with short hair, a friendly face with African features, and a gentle demeanor. His wife is darker than he is, with African facial features and straightened hair. Two of their children are the same deep brown color as Andrés, and the middle child has a dark butterscotch color and wears an afro.

Early on in my interview with Andrés and his family, he kindly requests that I call him by his nickname Pantera Negra (Black Panther). When I forget to do so and call him Andrés, he corrects me, and I do not make that mistake again. I am fascinated by his nickname, especially when he hands me a black business card with an image of a black panther and his contact information listed on the front. During our initial meeting, I assume that Andrés simply has an overzealous interest in the 1960s in the United States. In other families in the study, the nicknames that are given to family members are generic, based on skin color or shortened versions of their original names. However, in this family, Andrés has renamed himself Pantera Negra, and he goes by Pantera for short. His children are called Panterinhos (little panthers) and his wife, Panterona (big female panther). After perusing several tattered albums and boxes filled with thousands of pages of old newspaper clippings, legal documents, and pictures of him wearing a large afro while organizing community events, I understand that he has fashioned himself in the tradition of the radical Black Panthers in the United States. Not only has he adopted their nomenclature and style, but it is clear that he has also adopted their racial pol-

itics, with an emphasis on his community action and over a decade as a
leader in his workers' union.

Pantera Negra is fifty-five years old, and when he is asked about his
color and race he states *"negro"* for both without hesitation and with a
proud nod of his head. He was born one of twenty-two children in Salvador to a poor black domestic servant from the interior part of the state.
His mother, much like many black women during her time, was very poor
and worked in the homes of white Brazilians. He describes his mother and
his birth in the following way:

> My mom had her first child and gave it away to a white family. She had
> the second child and gave it away. Right after I was born, a white family
> adopted me. But in my heart I am black, I never stopped being black. I am
> always with my people, which is why I have done social work in the com-
> munity geared toward improving the living conditions of our people.

In his statement, his use of the pronoun *our*, reflects his strong racial identity and sense of racial solidarity. He wants to be certain that I understand
that his connections to the black community are strong despite his upbringing in a white family. In fact, he attributes his racial consciousness
both to his exploitation in the white family and to the technical training
that this same family provided him.

I am curious about how his twenty-one siblings identify themselves.
When I ask him, "Are your siblings *negros?*" he responds:

> I don't know, I never asked them. The blackest of the group is me and Ge-
> rardo. My dad is without a doubt black. Roseane is white. You already
> saw my mom's picture. I'm going to grab it. Roseane, Samuel, Cleiber, and
> Patricia are a little lighter. But I'm the only one who assumes my black-
> ness, but just saying I am black isn't enough. This *(pointing at himself)* is
> someone who is black and assumes his blackness. I assume it because I am
> black, I truly identify as an African-descendant. You understand? Even if
> I were a little lighter I am black because that is how I define myself. A per-
> son can be white or black but I am black.[20] There is either white or black,
> I don't see *pardo*. I see white or black.

In just the first few minutes of our conversation, Pantera Negra clearly
outlines what might be considered a radical position on race and color,
and educates me on the importance of knowing the difference between
racial classification and racial consciousness. He explains that his sib-

lings are of a variety of colors and phenotypes (the lightest he refers to as white), but while they are all of African descent, they do not have the same consciousness and sense of solidarity and shared fate that Pantera feels toward black people. He actively assumes his racial identity as a personal choice, connects it explicitly to Africa, and considers intermediate categories such as *pardo* meaningless since, to him, *pardos* are also African-descendants.

His wife is present during our interviews and during my observations because she does not work outside of the home. She is a relatively soft-spoken person but has insight to offer when the conversation shifts to racial socialization of children and babies. She explains:

> When a baby is a newborn, and if it is born with a nose, . . . um, with a, a, "a nose that the ox smashed" (*she and Pantera say this at the same time, and she laughs*), you take it like this and you massage it. And they say when the baby is born kind of red looking (*vermelinho*), they say it'll be born *preto*. They say, "This is going to be a *negão*." I never did this. I would never do this type of thing to my child. I never did it. They say, "This baby was born with good hair, but then it is going to fall out, and the normal hair will come in, and you'll have to straighten it right away" (laughs).

Both Pantera and Claudia laugh at the absurdity of these beliefs, but Claudia becomes very serious when she mentions that she would never engage in this behavior. She also rejects the comparisons people make between the varying skin tones of her two sons, João and Fábio (discussed in chapter 3).

Eager to share evidence of his leadership in various social movements in his neighborhood, Pantera Negra spends several hours bringing out photos and newspaper clippings—some are organized in boxes but most are in piles of loose papers—that document the numerous impressive community projects he has organized. He speaks very quickly and passionately as he flips through the pages and explains both what he organized and why it was important to the community. The crinkled, yellowish brown paper is a clear indication that his community work spans decades. He links his community efforts to the importance of giving blacks access to resources and basic infrastructure. He has a sharp understanding about how one's racialization in a racial socialized system is connected to access to resources. With this understanding, he is less concerned about affirmation through culture and more invested in addressing concrete examples of racial disparities and lack of access to important resources.

One of his major achievements is having restructured the water sanitation system and community roads so clean water would be available to community members. His photos show huge tractors and machinery that he convinced the city to provide in order to address the water sanitation problem. Pleased with his accomplishments, he shows me pictures of himself posing with several council members in front of the new water pipes, with his small daughter and his sons working alongside other community members. He mentions that this water project is critical to him because many black women support their families using the money they earn from washing clothes. He explains that when the water is not working properly, black women cannot do their jobs, and it affects families. It was their concerns, he suggests, that were the impetus for the water project. But, he explains:

> You can't say this. You can't tell them what you're doing. If you say it is something about black woman and jobs, they won't support it. If you say it as being about having water they will do it. You have to be smart about it. We're smart people. You have to be smart.

Using his own racial fluency and knowledge about how ideologies of racial democracy function, Pantera recognizes the importance of cordial race relations and that he must negotiate his community project delicately because an initiative that targets black women is unlikely to be funded. He has a firm sense of intersectionality and of how race, class, and gender are all important considerations when he presents the community project to local politicians. He strategically subverts the system by framing the project in universal terms without losing sight of his explicitly racial and gender-oriented goal. This is an example of how he engages in *critical accommodation* in the short term in order to make significant gains for the community in the long run.

Pantera tells his children the racial motivation behind the seemingly nonracial initiative, and he teaches them how to navigate social institutions in Brazil in a "smart" way. Instead of socializing his children with the general idea that everyone is equal, his approach is to teach his children that in Brazilian society everyone is not treated equally, but that with strategic appeals to universal ideas of equality and water, racial equality can be achieved. I ask Pantera Negra about what he teaches his children explicitly about race and discrimination. He states:

> It's like this. The behavior of the family is already teaching them this. In my interview I showed you all the things related to the person who I call

Pantera. Pantera raises his children and his children look up to him. There is no secret. Everything about my life is open and my children participated in every movement. It's natural teaching.

He speaks of himself in the third person, which I find important, as he wants to show that he has taken on this identity for a particular political reason. Because Pantera's children have been so active in the community movements he has organized and have heard him speak about racial equality, he is less concerned about formal socialization. In this way, the implicit socialization or natural teaching that some families use to reproduce racial hierarchy is used in this family to promote racial activism and resistance to racism and sexism.

Two of Pantera's children are in college, and in their rooms are several books with familiar titles, including classic works by Frantz Fanon, Malcolm X, and W. E. B. Du Bois. His older son and I have an enlightening conversation about the United States and Brazil, as he has many questions about comparative race relations. Pantera feels he does not have to worry about his children, so he places more emphasis on his notion of the neighborhood family:

> You can't just be a father to your child, but you need to be a father to your
> neighbor's son as well. Your child is also your neighbor's child. When
> your child goes out, the outside world is there. You are the father of your
> son, fine, ok. What are you going to do? You are going to work, pay for
> his college, give him clothes, food, protect him. And now he goes out
> in the outside world, and there is your neighbor's son. Your neighbor's
> son isn't well behaved. If you can do something for your neighbor, do it!
> When you help your neighbor's son, you protect your kids too.

Pantera is both practically and philosophically invested in the well-being of the children and young adults in the neighborhood. He organizes practical job training for young men who live in the community and allows them to shadow him and other men as they work. He uses his nonbiological kinship ties to empower the community and maximize its human resources, employing an alternative notion of family that is similar to the "trope of kinship" to convey his feeling that he is connected to community members on the basis of their common racial struggle.[21] Pantera views the future of his children and that of the neighborhood children as linked, a logical extension of his commitment to ideas about linked racial fate. He says that as motivation to the community, he asks, "How is it possible for us to build their world but not build our own? Let's build our world." Pantera's political participation confirms what other researchers have written about the relationship between strong racial identity, racial solidarity, and political activity.[22]

In another race-based project, he challenged his employer's use of uniforms, which he felt were being used to oppress the overwhelmingly black workforce. He explains that his desire to organize the workers to achieve this goal was based on something deeper than simply uniforms:

> If you were to see this company where we worked—the monuments, the architecture—you sense this thing, it's like, like it is from slavery times, like the slave quarters (*senzala*). In the clothing and even in the architecture itself, you feel the past in the present. So it was important to break with that for our own freedom. In the uniform of the workers, I felt that they were trying hit (*bater*) the workers in a subtle way. Because in those uniforms I felt a type of oppression. It wasn't even the uniform itself; it was what was behind those uniforms. There was a manager there, and he would say, "You have to wear this uniform." But I felt like behind that uniform there was something more there.

In collaboration with fifteen black seamstresses in his neighborhood, the workers designed and organized the production of new uniforms that they felt did not have the baggage of slavery that the other uniforms had. Cognizant of the ways that clothing can affect the way racial inequality is embodied, Pantera successfully undermined the normalization of oppression through embodied practices.

Throughout the interview, Pantera discusses in elaborate detail how structural racism affects the distribution of state resources in communities, contributes to economic and educational disparities, and fosters racial stereotypes in Brazilian society. Moreover, in our formal interviews, lasting over six hours, he analyzes racism in a detailed and insightful way that spans the entire history of Brazil.

Our interviews are both exhausting and exhilarating, as it is rare to hear regular folks (or academics, for that matter) speak with such passion, paired with a sociological and diasporic historical analysis. In the course of our interviews, I even learn a few things about Brazil's history. In addition to structural racism, Pantera addresses internalized racism:

> Black-against-black discrimination is worse than white. And this makes me uncomfortable; that is why I am fighting against this. It exists but for

blacks it's unconscious. He discriminates because of how he was raised and because of the culture of this country. This happens because his own family upbringing discriminates. It has put it in his mind that white is prettier than black. And that when a black has a lighter son it is an achievement. For me, it's not. It doesn't matter your color, what is important is the education of that citizen and human being.

Pantera, unlike any of the other respondents in this study, links internalized racism to individual, family-level, and structural factors, which he refers to as the "culture of the country." His sophisticated, multilevel analysis is engaging and thoughtful. The practices of racial socialization in the de Jesus family are singular because they are radical and systematic, and because they have material outcomes for Pantera's family and his community. His legacy of community organizing bears the mark of the Black Panther Party in the United States; however, with his emphasis on the needs and agency of women, he forges an even more inclusive model for racial and gender liberation than the Black Panther Party managed to achieve.

TRANSGRESSIVE FAMILIES AND INSTITUTIONAL COLLABORATORS

In Salvador, families are not alone in their struggles to exert radical agency in the face of racism. Cultural groups such as Ilê Aiyê developed in the 1970s as a way to encourage the visibility of Afro-Brazilian cultural forms and to combat cultural exclusion.[23] It hosts "A Noite de Beleza Negra" (Black Beauty Night), and each year a young black woman is crowned Deusa de Ébano (Ebony Goddess) and Queen of Ilê Aiyê, and rides atop a Carnaval float to represent black beauty.[24] Ilê Carnaval–goers have a reputation for being the "the most beautiful of the most beautiful blacks." Their African-inspired costumes and Axé music is visually appealing and culturally important. Young Afro-Brazilian girls who live in Liberdade, where Ilê Aiyê is based, grow up dreaming of becoming an Ebony Goddess, rather than Xuxa, a blonde, blue-eyed Brazilian of German descent who has served as the famous host of several children's shows on Globo television.[25] The Ebony Goddess title recognizes beauty that is redefined on the basis of a black aesthetic that values dark skin, black features, natural hair, and the ability to embody Afro-Brazilian culture through dance. Many of the recent winners are college-bound, dark-skinned Afro-Brazilian women whose success and popularity in the neighborhood are symbolically significant.

Cultural and beauty politics are significant, but they can also derail a political movement and be co-opted in ways that reinforce hierarchies or overemphasize superficial beauty.[26] This is why organizations like Instituto Steve Biko (called Biko for short) emerged. With a history of serving the black community for over twenty years in Salvador, it has as its prime objective redressing the exclusion of young black Brazilians from college and racial affirmation. Having pioneered prevestibular classes that prepare students for the college entrance exam, it has been a critical element in the pipeline connecting Afro-Brazilian students with colleges and universities. It also supports the development of political consciousness and addresses questions of self-esteem and racial consciousness through its black consciousness and citizenship course. In 2012, Silvio Humberto, founder of the Institute, was elected city council member in Salvador. He models the connections between substance and style by wearing his hair in dreadlocks and serving as a political leader with an aggressive agenda and a political stance that some consider radical. Supported by a team of Biko colleagues, he has developed a platform that is attuned to the conditions of Afro-Brazilians and their families.

Not all families have access to the organizations and transnational discourses that articulate linkages between slavery, racism, and white supremacy. Indeed, if researchers from around the world struggle to understand the complicated nature of race relations in Brazil, this is even more difficult for members of vulnerable groups whose "perception of themselves as oppressed is impaired by their submersion in the reality of oppression."[27] However, as is evident from the interviews with respondents in this study, the knowledge gained through participation in Candomblé, *capoeira*, and various seminars and community classes has served as the basis on which some Afro-Brazilians have learned to connect seemingly personal barriers to broader systemic issues.

I focus on Instituto Steve Biko because six of the respondents in this study reported that they had ties to this community organization. However, there are several organizations whose prime goal is to address both racial and gender disparities. Specifically, an organized black feminist movement has developed because while black women's "concerns about race largely went unheeded by the feminist movement, their concerns about gender were often marginalized by the black movement."[28] Organizations such as Geledés, Fala Preta!, and the Domestic Workers Union are critical spaces for political mobilization and consciousness building for black women in Brazil.

As for the respondents in this study, Raíssa and Taynara attribute their more politically engaged racial consciousness to their previous participation as students and leaders in the Instituto Steve Biko. Similarly, Ismara and Barbara have both been actively involved in Biko and credit their enrollment in the prevestibular program and its black consciousness and citizenship courses as their first introduction to questions of racial inequality in Brazil. This more political identity has also corresponded with embodied changes, as Ismara reports that after attending classes at Biko, she decided to wear her hair in its naturally curly state. She boasts that she was the first in her family to make this bold step. The decision to cut her hair represents the externalization of her racial consciousness and an affront to dominant beauty hierarchies that tend to devalue black hair and chain women's sense of self to the length of their hair. In our interviews, she is giddy as she takes credit for resocializing her initially stubborn sister and her mother, Inês, who previously did not identify as *negra* but is contemplating wearing her hair naturally, as well. Barbara and Ismara hope this will be her first step toward assuming her blackness.

In a different family, Maurício describes his membership in Biko as personally transformative, and he introduces me to his mother, whom he introduced to the organization. She started taking courses at Biko because she was hoping to return to school, and because of her son she knew they offered free preparatory classes. But as she attended classes there, her exposure to ideas about racial consciousness and activism helped foster the development of a more political racial consciousness. She laughs as she explains that she did not understand race before and used to refer to herself as *morena*, but now she is "proud to be black."

The Instituto Steve Biko promotes community partnerships that build on a model in which families and communities work together. This is the same philosophy that drives the efforts of Pantera Negra of the de Jesus family, and the community organizing approach is similar to that of black women activists in Gamboa de Baixo in Salvador.[29]

But for all the success stories of Biko students who have been able to recruit their parents and family members, there are also narratives of those who feel empowered by Biko but disheartened by the racism they face in their families and the broader society. At an afro-aesthetics conference in Salvador in 2013, a panel of young Bikudos (members of Instituto Steve Biko) were asked, "Where do you get the will to go on, the strength to wear your hair in afros in spite of it all?" Some of the conference participants held back tears as they listened to the resilience of the young panelists. For some panelists, the honest response was "I don't know," but for others the answer was clear: the students are able to do what they do because Biko functions as a second family for them, in which their goals can be nurtured, their consciousness developed, and their blackness supported. In this way, the mission of the Instituto Steve Biko addresses educational capital by offering coursework and pre-college training, embodied capital by emphasizing the value of a black racial aesthetic, and affective capital by providing the affirmation and emotional resources that Afro-Brazilians sometimes lack in their own homes. Most important, affection and support are there not despite students' blackness but because of it.

DISCUSSION

In a poignant articulation of racial identity in Brazil, Neusa Santos Souza argues, "Discovering your blackness is to live the experience of having your identity massacred, being confused by your perspectives, subjected to demands, compelled by alienated expectations. But it is also and above all the experience of committing yourself to rescuing your history and recreating yourself by your own capabilities."[30] By highlighting the strategies of some of the most transgressive families in this study, I argue for the importance of recognizing both isolated and sustained "moments of rupture" as significant contestations to hegemonic structures.[31] These three families are "ideological dissidents" who redefine racial meanings, reconstruct a new sense of self, and forge resistance strategies that have material consequences.[32] Neide's redefinition is mainly discursive, evident in how she valorizes blackness by employing specific words such as *torradinho* and subversively using racial jokes. Dona Elena redefines hegemonic ideologies through her African-centered narratives of Brazil's discovery and her celebration of her African ancestry. Lastly, Pantera redefines himself by embodying a consciously racialized black persona to successfully mobilize the community to work toward their social goals. Pantera's family model is most distinctive because he moves from the ideological level to concrete community projects, reflecting the importance of "developing resistant forms of racial consciousness" involving both "the recognition of how race and racism operate and the development of strategies to resist their influence."[33]

Throughout this chapter, I focus on how racial socialization, particularly in the first two families, is simultaneously characterized by both systematic ruptures and accommodation to racial ideologies. These families illustrate that even in homes with some of the most radical discourses and practices, people do not escape the influence of white supremacy. But while hegemony is often defined as totalitarian and multidimensional, it is not static, and there are ways to shift the balance of power. In the same way that families can be sites of the reproduction of racism, they can also be sites of racial resistance. Pantera's mission, for example, extends beyond his front door to the rest of his community:

> Our family is an example for the entire street. They themselves have said this to me. . . . Look at it this way, when you become a reference you are careful not to make mistakes.

The limitations of their resistance are as much a testament to the hegemonic dominance of racial hierarchies as they are evidence of vulnerability. In the end, these families' resistance is a glimmer of hope that oppressive structures are not impenetrable but can be contested and dismantled.

Though these three families are exceptional within the context of the core families in this study, resistance by Afro-Brazilians in Salvador, and in Brazil more broadly, has a distinct history beginning as early as slavery. Quilombos, or maroon communities populated by fugitive slaves, were among the first manifestations of resistance, serving as spaces where *negros* pursued self-determination through the "creation of parallel and alternative communities coexisting within national cultures."[34] The longest surviving runaway slave community in the Americas was located in Brazil and led by Zumbi dos Palmares. Later the establishment of the political party Frente Negra Brasileira, in 1931, was among the first efforts to politically mobilize blacks around a race-based identity.[35] Though unsuccessful in garnering widespread support from the majority of Afro-Brazilians, the party paved the way for the development of the contemporary black movement. Black Brazilian feminists including Lélia Gonzalez, Vilma Reis, and Luiza Bairros (Minister of the Secretariat for Policies to Promote Racial Equality) have been at the forefront of political resistance by challenging the notion of racial democracy, promoting critical analysis of racial inequalities, and mobilizing both domestic and international resources to leverage significant changes that can improve living conditions and opportunities for blacks in Brazil.

Taken together, the long history of black resistance in Brazil, "moments of rupture" exhibited in families, and the concrete legislative gains of the black movement and black feminist organizations confirm that, indeed, "where there is power, there is resistance."[36]

THE TIES THAT BIND

Herein lies buried many things that if read with patience may show the strange meaning of being black here at the dawn of the twentieth century. This meaning is not without interest to you . . . for the problem of the twentieth century is the problem of the colorline . . . the relation of the darker to the lighter races of men in Asia and Africa and the islands of the sea.

W. E. B. DU BOIS, *THE SOULS OF BLACK FOLK*

SOCIOLOGIST W. E. B. DU BOIS'S prescient conclusion about the "strange meaning of being black" in the twentieth century continues to have relevance in the twenty-first century.[1] One of the most important elements of his intellectual contribution is how he connects the color line to his interest in the "souls" of black folk. Du Bois eloquently navigates the territory between psychology and sociology, structure and agency, emotions and behavior, addressing themes that parallel concepts articulated by black diasporic scholars, such as Brazilian Neusa Santos Souza and Martiniquen Frantz Fanon.

Among the common threads that link these researchers is how life under racial domination leads to internal turmoil, an ongoing quest to prove one's humanity, and an irreconcilable struggle for survival. Moreover, the affective experience of terror that those in the diaspora have shared since the time of slavery informs their affective experience of intense alienation caused by existing in societies structured by white supremacy. One is left to ponder whether Souza's brilliant observation that racism causes "the massacre of one's identity" was a contributing factor in her own untimely death by suicide in 2008.[2] This is the angst to which Du Bois was referring when he asked, "How does it feel to be a problem?" This question is at the heart of this study, and it is addressed most directly in the sociological analysis of embodied racial capital and affective capital. Specifically, the theoretical concept of affective capital highlights how the emotional and personal resources that one accumulates over one's life shape one's outcomes and life chances.

Building on an approach that is grounded in similar concerns expressed by earlier scholars, my foray into the realm of family reveals how "strange meanings" lead to relationships of intimacy and cruelty, of love and shame—and to reproduction of and resistance to racism. None of these dynamics exists as a mutually exclusive dichotomy; rather, these elements exist simultaneously. Brazilians who fall closest to the black pole of the phenotypic continuum can answer Du Bois's question because they are considered a problem for the national family, and often a problem for their own biological families. From infancy, every part of the black body is scrutinized: skin color, hair texture and color, eye color, ear color, nail color, penis size, and the shape and color of buttocks are all measured against white normativity and treated accordingly. The intense surveillance of the racialized body of a black baby implores even the most skeptical researcher to consider the relationship between stigma, embodied capital, and racialization. Through racial rituals, concrete practices are used to control and modify racial features as though blackness were a disease rather than a social product. And it is here that we observe the destructive ideology of whiteness shaping embodied practices and structuring close family relationships.

RELEVANCE FOR FAMILY RESEARCHERS

This research brings into dialogue two groups of researchers: those examining racial socialization in Brazil and those studying racial socialization in the United States. It responds to Tânia Gebara and Nilma Gomes's critique of current Brazilian research, which they argue is characterized by the invisibility of black families or narrow portrayals of them as passive victims.[3] Likewise, I address the limitations of extant U.S.-based research, including the critique that "racial socialization could be strengthened by fully incorporating the theoretical insights of race and stratification scholars working in the critical race theory and colorism traditions."[4] To address these shortcomings, I bridge critical race and feminist theoretical perspectives, and intentionally engage an intersectional approach to explore the diverse ways that gender, class, racialization (rather than simply race), and colorism (expanded to include phenotype, rather than simply skin color) shape the strategies that Afro-Brazilian families use in the context of racial socialization.[5]

Theoretically I rely heavily on notions of capital, specifically embodied racial capital, but I also introduce *gendered racial bargains* to address the within-group complexity of gender and race that characterizes Afro-Brazilians' strategies. Recognizing the variability in the meanings that people attach to social identities, I deploy the term *racial fluency* to capture these negotiations, which are also informed by race, class, and gender. For many Afro-Brazilians in this study, their task is not only to learn racial meanings, but to use their knowledge as the basis for creating ideological and embodied practices that simultaneously resist and accommodate racial hierarchies. Afro-Brazilians can resist and accommodate discourses about race and beauty in the same conversation and sometimes in the same sentence, as do Zica and Natalia (chapter 3), Sonia (chapter 4), and Neide and Dona Elena (chapter 6). Racialization processes and the meanings attached to race are dynamic and can shift within generations, or within the course of one's own life as the racial identity processes of *negras assumidas*, including Barbara and Ismara (chapter 6), illustrate. These shifts do not happen spontaneously but occur within a particular historical and political context, including Brazil's burgeoning black movement, the successes of black Brazilian women's organizations, and an afro-aesthetics cultural movement.

One of the additional contributions of an intersectional approach is that it can address "how people 'do' or perform close relationships and roles within multiple systems . . . across the life course, generations, and time."[6] In this research specifically, affective capital captures how one's racialization influences affective exchanges in families, as well as family formation (as for Tânia and Rebeca; see chapter 3). Beyond this, I link these differences in affective capital to their concrete implications for racial and gender inequality. Within the context of family, race and gender are inextricably linked as Afro-Brazilian women are saddled with the responsibility of being the source of love and affection for their family, while also managing racial features through embodied strategies and racial rituals, as Dona Ceci outlines (chapter 2). Afro-Brazilian men are also affected by this process, but their male privilege means that they have alternative avenues of gaining social mobility and capital that are unavailable to *negras*. *Capoeira* serves this purpose for Arivaldo and Thiago (chapters 3 and 5).

Some mixed-race Afro-Brazilians describe themselves as "walking between two worlds," but everyone is stumbling through the unpredictable elements of racial life, encountering multiple situations and contexts that speak to the importance of "an analysis of race more nuanced and polyvalent."[7] Even the idea of walking between two worlds is a point of privilege for mixed-race Brazilians in comparison to *pretos* such as Dilson (chapter 3), who move through a more unforgiving world that devalues everything about their existence. Class adds an additional layer, as family members who are viewed as *preto e pobre* (poor and black) might be monetarily supported but socially rejected by black family members with more economic resources, as happens to Dona Lara (chapter 5). These relationships function as they do because people use internalized racial rules to guide their decisions and interactions.

I hope that this study influences future research agendas to bridge several sociological and interdisciplinary themes related to racialization, socialization, and capital. In Brazil, this calls for researchers to acknowledge the existence of black families (beyond those that involve white-black interracial relationships) and make a commitment to exploring their agency and complexity in the face of racialization.[8] In the United States, research on how families produce unequal childhoods should be extended to incorporate differential outcomes for individuals within the same family.[9] Moreover, in the United States the pursuit of more intersectional studies that include critical race theory and colorism is not only prudent, but absolutely necessary because of the shifting demographic reality.

MOTHERING

Some of the most sustained analysis in this book is related to mothers. I discuss how Afro-Brazilian women are bound by notions of motherhood and womanhood (as are Damiana and Corina, in chapter 1), and risk being labeled bad mothers if they do not conform to racial and gender norms.[10] The strategies they use are not random; rather, parents and caregivers are "likely to follow to some extent the role requirements for parents in their culture, which they have learned as a result of their own experiences of socialization."[11] In the absence of biological family, policing comes from nonbiological kin, who may also serve as surrogate overseers and proxies for the male gaze and often a patriarchal gaze.

Some mothers consider their negative responses to black features and their participation in rituals to modify them to be nearly as important as formal education to ensure the success of their children. For other mothers and families their concern is less about their children's futures and more about their immediate personal status and search for whiteness (as for Damiana, chapter 1). Still other families and young adults engage in *critical accommodation*, in which they temporarily abide by racial rules in the short term in order to subvert and even challenge racism in the long term, as do Barbara and Fernando (chapter 2) and Pantera Negra (chapter 6).

To be clear, a mother's experiences with racial socialization do not revolve entirely around visibility management and cannot be understood simply as the reproduction of racism. As I have illustrated, embodied racial capital is a matter of phenotype, but it also entails behavioral and cultural traits. Some of the more unexpected findings are related to how Afro-Brazilian families prepare members to encounter a racialized world in terms of behavior, dress, etiquette, and spatial mobility. In chapter 5 the mothering practices of Raíssa and Taynara focus on socializing their children to reject racial hierarchies, but also teaching them to display embodied racial capital in their encounters with whites. Imposing physical and social limitations on their children's behavior and encouraging intentional self-surveillance is laborious and may be perceived as extreme, but for some it is the best way to exercise agency when confronting racialization. These parenting strategies challenge previous research that portrays black Brazilian families as being shrouded in silence and submission; instead, they show how some black families actively and explicitly engage in racial socialization.[12] There are also clear class differences that would make for fertile ground for future research.

Mother-daughter relationships can be fraught with complications, painful emotions, and strained interactions. Most Afro-Brazilian mothers are sincerely concerned with protecting their daughters from a world in which *negras* are disadvantaged, preparing family members for a marriage market that racializes and frequently rejects the blackest-looking prospects, and confronting a job market unwilling to negotiate its racist standards of appearance. Overall, Afro-Brazilian mothers struggle to do what they feel is right and what they know to be legitimate. In a tearful plea for others to understand some of the difficult decisions she has made regarding her children that have resulted in strained relationships, sixty-three-year-old Magda states:

> People just don't know how hard it is to be a black woman. People don't understand the decisions that we have to make. We do what we have to do. We do the best we can, but nobody understands.

The complexities of mothers' decisions and actions should be situated in the context of the racist and sexist society in which they live. Mothers seeking to protect their children rely on racial rituals, embodied capital, and self-imposed limitations, often with the goal of helping rather than hurting family members. They find themselves torn by the gendered racial bargains they must strike as they battle to prepare their children for an outside world that treats them as subhuman, while also attempting to preserve and even cherish their children's humanity.[13] At the core of this work is evidence that the affective exchanges, language, and concrete practices of racial socialization must be contextualized as responses to an absurd and perverse society where simply existing while black is considered an offense.

WHERE IS THE LOVE?

I theorize about emotions not as emotional labor, but regarding their role in reproducing racial stigma and determining one's access to affective capital, which I argue shapes life chances. By shifting the analysis away from emotional labor, I explicitly connect affect and emotion to racialization and the structure of inequality. I refer to the *socialization of racial affect* to describe how racial stigma is both produced and reproduced in family interactions. The learned and seemingly visceral elements of racial affect are transmitted by the expression of companionate love in nonromantic relationships.[14] Affect is essential because intimacy and family bonds require closeness, closeness requires emotion, and positive emotion fosters solidarity. These bonds of closeness and solidarity are what make otherwise unacceptable systems of inequality, like racism, bearable. But intimacy and family closeness do not imply equality. Instead, the tender, positive experiences in these relationships compel family members to discount numerous tense racial slights, and these dismissed slights can be reproduced in interactions with others.

Racial affect is punctuated during life transitions, but even after critical moments have passed, the residual emotions and racial hierarchies that shape these affective exchanges influence peoples' lives. In the same way that one's racial location affects access to material and social goods, it also shapes one's access to affective resources. Stated differently, love and affection are experienced very differently within families depending on one's racial position. Affective capital, the intangible resources that a person gains from being positively evaluated and supported, and from frequently receiving meaningful displays of affection, can change the course of a person's life. Positive emotions and experiences lead to people displaying more creativity, becoming more resilient, and making healthier choices.[15] Low affective capital reflects one's racial position in a racialized social system, but it also helps to perpetuate one's position by compromising the motivation, self-esteem, and confidence needed to be successful.[16] (As for Dilson, Yasmin, and Elisa, see chapter 3.)

Though I agree that love, especially self-love, can be revolutionary, in no way should my emphasis on affective capital be interpreted as a suggestion that personal emotional resources are to blame for racism.[17] To the contrary, I suggest that there is a cyclic interaction between racialization and racial socialization, which creates a feedback loop that shapes affective and material capital. This loop can only be broken when the social structure and system of disadvantage that sustains it are dismantled. Historically these types of shifts are the products of social movements involving organizations and people who, as Pantera Negra argues, are not afraid of fighting (*não têm medo da luta*).

A CULTURAL CHIMERA: SALVADOR, BAHIA AS A RESEARCH SITE

Salvador, Bahia, Brazil, is not frozen in time; instead, it is constantly shifting as a result of its position at the interstices of local and global currents.[18] Afro-Brazilian families are poised to benefit from significant legislation, including a national affirmative action policy and sweeping domestic labor laws. These developments indicate that change is possible, but they do not guarantee that change will necessarily be transformative. How long will affirmative action policies be enforced, and are these policies sufficient to address several centuries of cumulative disadvantage and contemporary inequality? Moreover, though the domestic labor laws are promising, black women continue to be exploited in the homes of middle-class families, albeit in different ways.[19]

Despite the significant progress these laws signify, symbolic racial violence and structural inequality remain high. In Bahia, the state tourism machine can be likened to a *cultural chimera*, strategically constructing the region's identity on the basis of a grotesque amalgamation of stereotypes about race, gender, sexuality, and Africanness that fosters feelings of cultural belonging while compounding racial disparities. The products of this cultural chimera are symbols and events that create the illusion that Afro-Brazilian culture is valuable, when the truth is simply that it has monetary value. This value is contingent on the promotion of notions of nonthreatening cultural blackness, or "domesticated blackness," where elements are extracted, modified, sanitized, and deblackened for commercial consumption. This phenomenon is as much about selling people as it is about commercializing cultural artifacts. These local dynamics are inextricably linked to questions of embodied capital, as the nonwhite body can be affirmed as long as it is portrayed as sensual rather than beautiful and only after it has been made more racially palatable.[20]

No less complicated for Bahia is that the international gaze, which is often presumed to be a white gaze, has long been a black, North American gaze.[21] So, the investment in constructing Salvador as an authentically black space with close connections to Africa responds to ideas about an imagined homeland, which it will produce at any cost, "milking Mama Africa."[22] In the aftermath of these cultural productions, Afro-Brazilian families are left to pick up the pieces of foreigners' seasonal participation in Carnaval and the affective reward—national pride and a sense of belonging—that comes from sporadic engagement with Brazil during international events, including the World Cup and the Olympics. All that is asked is that they mind their blackness and be reduced to background props, serving as hair braiders, ostentatious *capoeiristas*, and coconut vendors for a clientele that reserves the real money for white foreign business owners. Even well-meaning and inquisitive black North American researchers have to be careful about how they interact in order not to reproduce these same dynamics of voyeurism and exploitation.[23]

There are likely lingering questions about my selection of Salvador and about whether this selection affects the generalizability of the study. This research was designed as a theory-building project, so the practices that I highlight are part of a diverse array of racial socialization practices deployed by Afro-Brazilian families. I believe that additional studies should be developed to broaden our understanding of the diverse forms and consequences of racial socialization, with an emphasis on the concepts that appear here, including embodied racial capital, affective capital, and racial fluency.

Salvador does have a history that in some ways sets it apart from other regions in Brazil. But these differences only add validity to my argument, which emphasizes the pernicious ways that white supremacy orchestrates relationships and socialization in phenotypically diverse families. Given its distinction as the blackest city in Brazil and its strategic emphasis on Afro-Brazilian culture, Salvador is a location where one might expect Afro-Brazilians to be somewhat shielded from white supremacy, though I find the opposite happening. I view Salvador as a vantage point from which the local, regional, national, and international dynamics that shape it offer insight into racialization processes and socialization practices.

The practices observed in these families are not unique to Bahia, but reflect how Afro-Brazilian families and, in some cases, other diasporic families respond to white supremacy. Might these same processes be apparent in other regions of Brazil? In the southern region of Brazil, where the criteria of whiteness are more strict, visibility management for Afro-Brazilians may not go far in moving one's position in the racial hierarchy. In that case there might be much more formal organizing, rather than racial accommodation through visibility management. In Rio de Janeiro, where the image of the *mulata* figures prominently, efforts to maximize embodied capital might look very different. The Amazon may share all of the practices observed here or none at all. These are empirical questions that I implore future researchers to pursue.

AN AFRICAN DIASPORIC LENS

Throughout this book, in order to highlight transnational linkages, I have incorporated examples that allow me to triangulate my findings with data from diasporic contexts.[24] This orientation is consistent with the goals of researchers of the "Black Atlantic," whose work seeks "to transcend both the structures of the nation state and the constraints of ethnicity and national particularity, in order to develop theoretical and conceptual frames that make unique contributions."[25] This diasporic lens is not an assumption of sameness, but there are similarities, as well as differences, that I implore researchers to seriously engage in order to achieve new theoretical and conceptual insights.

One of the reasons making diasporic connections is feasible is the shared history of the trans-Atlantic slave trade and racial oppression in Latin America and the Caribbean. I began the book by discussing how white elites in Brazil developed a racial project using a discourse of racial mixture, or *mestiçagem*, as the solution to its race problem. In Spanish-speaking Latin America notions of Iberian exceptionalism also led to the development of ideological constructs that promoted the development of a national identity that downplayed race and supported efforts at racial hygiene.[26] In the Dominican Republic both quantitative and qualitative research provide evidence of "strong and nearly universal agreement that it is better to be European than African in appearance, the more European, the better."[27] Using a rhetoric connecting race with modernity, Dominican president Joaquín Balaguer asserted that whiteness is "a necessary condition for the existence of the nation" and associated moral decay and delayed national progress to the nation's "anthropological traits" and "contact with blacks."[28] Making the connections between race and eugenics explicit, Dominican writers as late as 1913 argued that African influences, like "corrosive germs," needed to destroyed.[29] The Dominican Republic and Haiti share the island of Hispaniola and histories of slavery, yet the Dominican identity has been predicated on "Negrophobia, white supremacy, and Anti-Haitianism."[30] Though Haiti has been the target of antiblack sentiment, it also reproduces similar antiblack dynamics that emerge in tensions between mulattoes and unmixed blacks.[31]

Racial anxieties in Puerto Rico led some to claim that Puerto Rico was the whitest island in the Antilles with the hope that this affirmation would facilitate the island's development.[32] In Cuba—which in 1886 was the second-to-last country or territory in the Americas to abolish slavery, two years before Brazil became the last—the government also relied on immigration to whiten the population, in addition to promoting cultural whitening through a segregated school system.[33] In the 1980s Fidel Castro referred to Cuba as an "African Latin Nation," and while communist policies significantly advantaged Afro-Cubans, limited discursive space to discuss racial inequality has exacerbated inequality.[34] Hence, Afro-Cubans are still discriminated against and among the most vulnerable people in the country.[35] In the United States racial purity was promoted and viciously protected via the imposition of racial segregation, which is most succinctly captured by Jim Crow laws, explicit racial codes that led many to characterize the United States as the home of true racism.[36]

Recognizing divergent approaches to racialization (with the "one-drop rule" in the United States being the exceptional case), differences in strategies of rule, and variations in racial rhetoric, there are still a number of fundamental ideas that remain central to these societies. Indeed, researchers question whether these societies were all that different to begin with in terms of racialization, and are examining the extent to which they have diverged and converged in terms of their racial structure.[37] Colorism emerges as a useful frame for understanding differential treatment based on skin color *and* physical features, as the pervasiveness of whiteness means that strategies of domination circulate throughout the Americas.[38] As it relates to romantic partnerships, colorism is evident in the ideological commitment to *limpar a raça* (clean the race) in Brazil and is reflected in desires to *mejorar la raza* (improve the race) in Spanish-speaking Latin America.[39] Efforts at whitening in Portuguese and Spanish Latin America (*branqueamento* and *blanqueamiento*, respectively), find some points of convergence with the history of racial passing in the United States.[40] Scholars of Puerto Rico and Mexico have also explored within-family racial and phenotypic dynamics.[41] Though most of the contemporary work on colorism emerges from studies of blacks in the United States, research on how Latinos are affected by this phenomenon sheds light on its broader significance.[42]

With regard to evaluations and stigmatization of blackness, I discuss how whiteness and status are goods that can be exchanged in interracial relationships. These findings resonate with researchers who find that race functions as "symbolic capital" in a marriage market that advantages women whose racial appearance most closely approximates whiteness.[43] In his analyses of the small, French-speaking island of Martinique, Frantz Fanon shows the naturalization of a pervasive whitening ideology. He writes:

> The race must be whitened; every woman in Martinique knows this, says it, repeats it. Whiten the race, save the race, but not in the sense that one might think; not "preserve the uniqueness of that part of the world in which we grew up" but make sure it will be white.[44]

But these relationships are complicated negotiations. Historical data on interracial relationships in Brazil, in the United States, elsewhere in Latin America, and in the African diaspora in Europe have been instructive in exploring how whiteness shapes such pairings. This research has revealed how white families respond to the entrance of black members into the family and how white parents learn to negotiate with black spouses and mixed-race children.[45]

Less commonly discussed are what I refer to as the racial rituals used to modify or police the features of children and babies, which represent the embodied negotiations of race. Paralleling the examples given in this book are the ways that concerns with "bad hair" manifest as efforts to construct racialized "identity displays" and beauty rituals that discipline afro-textured hair in the Dominican Republic.[46] Beyond hair, reminders to clamp one's nose, close one's lips, and *vete por la sombrita!* (go into the shade!) to avoid becoming darker can be heard throughout the Spanish-speaking Americas.[47] Similar racial constructions are spoken in multiple languages across the diaspora and across generations.

Moving beyond academic research to multimedia, the recent production of *Dark Girls* in the United States and the forthcoming project *Memoirs of Melanin* from the Bahamas reflect how palpable questions of colorism are in contemporary diasporic societies.[48] The overall conclusion from this research is clear: the presence of multiracial or phenotypically diverse people does not signify the existence of a racial democracy or entrance into a postracial era. Instead, significant racial barriers, "racework" required to sustain interracial relationships, phenotypic hierarchies, and the gendered racial bargains required to survive suggests that the end of racism remains elusive.[49]

In particular, discourses about hair predominate in conversations about race, body, and beauty; specifically, hair functions as a major signifier of race and criterion of beauty in the Americas.[50] This is an issue not merely in Brazil but throughout the African diaspora. It is perhaps unsurprising that in both the United States and Brazil, the first self-made black female millionaires were women whose careers were based on cosmetic products and hair treatments for black women. It is important to clarify, however, that hair styling and even hair straightening does not always reflect the reproduction of hegemonic whiteness or internalized racism.[51] The notion of good appearance (*boa aparência*) in Brazil shares similarities with *buena presencia* in Spanish-speaking Latin America and with ideas of "professionalism" in parts of the English-speaking diaspora. All of these terms function as racialized code words that employers often use to exclude African-descendants on the basis of racialized physical and cultural standards. It is in this context that research concludes that sometimes black women's decisions are based on internalized racism, at other times they are calculated decisions that consider marriageability and social mobility, and at still other times they are about styling freedom, creativity, and versatility.[52]

It is difficult to recognize where one consideration ends and another begins. Some black women might view straightened hair as more versatile because their hair has always been straightened and they have never learned how to style their natural hair. At the same time, even in discussions of natural hair it is sometimes overlooked that all hair is worked on, but that African-descendant women are significantly constrained by hegemonic whiteness in their negotiations of beauty.[53] Nonetheless, their efforts to envision alternative avenues to beauty, even while sometimes reproducing white gender and beauty norms, represent a rupture in hegemony and signal the possibility of resistance.

Less studied is the way that whitening ideologies not only exist in diasporic regions of the Americas, but have a way of folding back on themselves to shape how Africans, not just African-descendants, view themselves. Neither a paradox nor a contradiction, the rise in skin bleaching across Africa should come as no surprise to those familiar with "global white supremacy."[54] Despite warnings that associate skin bleaching with kidney damage, with dangers related to the use of mercury in the skin-whitening creams, and with purported risks to pregnant women and their unborn children, beauty stores are "flooded with toxic skin bleaching products that [are] sold to African women to specifically lighten their skin color."[55] Many women consider skin bleaching a strategy for acquiring "feminine social capital" in Ghana and Tanzania, where it is perceived as a "necessary procedure to undergo for ensuring economic and social success."[56]

TOWARD A CONCEPTUALIZATION
OF A GLOBAL TRAITOCRACY

Researchers are invested in thinking about race beyond its corporeal or embodied dimensions. This is critically important, but it should not occur at the expense of fully appreciating people's lived and embodied experiences with racialization. Hybridity, racial mixture, and racial fluidity are important trends in social science research, and this book promotes these forward advancements without underestimating phenotypic and cultural distinctions. Historically, the notion of whitening has been limited primarily to conversations related to African-descendants and skin color. The terms *pigmentocracy* and *colorism* have often been used to describe systems that assign advantages on the basis of racial phenotype, but both of these constructions implicitly privilege pigment and skin color over other phenotypic markers. The embodiment of race means that skin color is important but it is only one of many phenotypic markers that shape racialization processes. In many cases, hair texture is more decisive than skin color in racial classification, especially in the Americas.

Frantz Fanon's classic work *Black Skin, White Masks* represents one of the earliest and most sophisticated efforts at deconstructing how both racial physical features and cultural features matter. At this juncture, expanding our lexicon beyond *pigmentocracy* and *colorism* might allow researchers to engage how hierarchies of culture and phenotype (not merely of skin color) can disrupt racial and color hierarchies. As opposed to *pigmentocracy*, researchers might consider a term such as a *traitocracy*, which captures how the ranking of both physical and cultural traits affects racialization processes. It does so without privileging one racial feature over another, or even physical traits over cultural traits. The term *traitocracy* provides flexibility to explore how certain physical and cultural traits can be selectively and situationally valued even if they are not considered white or European, which is critical for examining the global circulation of whiteness and cultural appropriation.

This is also crucial because the traitocracy does not affect only people of African descent. In India commercials for the global brand "Fair and Lovely," targeting both men and women, sell skin-lightening products with the promise of marriage, career promotions, and improved well-being. Internet communities allow easy access to these products and yield a plethora of data on family socialization practices of parents who promote these embodied practices, particularly on skin-whitening sites such as IndiaParenting.com.[57]

For people of East Asian descent, particularly in Korea, a procedure known as the Asian double-eyelid surgery promises to improve appearance by making the eyes look more Western and less Asian. For many families this expensive surgery is the capstone for students completing high school or college. Those who cannot afford the procedure can access online instructional videos dedicated to demonstrating alternative methods of "correcting" the eye by using makeup and invisible tape to create the illusion of an eye fold. More research is needed on how families discuss these practices and promote or discourage them as part of racial socialization. Such practices are situated alongside efforts to "contour" facial features—to achieve a thinner nose, for example—so they reflect Western notions of beauty. At the same time, researchers must examine these procedures carefully and cautiously to understand people's agency in these aesthetic negotiations. As Kathleen Zane points out, "surgically transforming the eyelid is a far more complex cultural production than a simply imitative media-instructed practice that reasserts Western, white patriarchy."[58]

Several decades ago, colored contact lenses emerged on the market, providing the opportunity to lighten the iris. More recently, a surgically inserted iris implant called Brightocular was developed to permanently change the color of a person's eyes. Over 75 percent of the world's people have black, brown, or chestnut-colored eyes, so the globalizing ideology of whiteness that favors lightened eyes means that the company has a large potential clientele. Client testimonials on the company's website refer to ways that families were initially skeptical and concerned about the dangers but ultimately accepted the procedure and supported family members who opted to undergo it.[59] Whiteness also affects whites who are considered less white than others. In fact, ethnic white women were among the original targets for whitening creams in the United States.[60]

In October 2013, the international community was in an uproar when the discovery of a blonde girl in a dark-skinned Roma family precipitated accusations that she had been abducted.[61] Globally people rallied in their concern for the "blonde angel," whose picture was displayed on media outlets around the world. Her presence in the midst of the dark-skinned but white Roma community was assumed to be a blatant example of human trafficking and exploitation. Reports suggested that she was "being used to beg on the streets" and appeared "frightened and neglected."[62]

Despite the pleas of her parents, officials wasted no time taking the parents into custody and removing the girl from the home. After DNA tests were conducted, the conclusion was clear: the young blonde girl was not abducted but was the biological child of her dark-skinned white parents. Most disturbing about this situation is the speed with which officials swooped in to remove the "mystery blonde girl" and take her parents into custody with no evidence except that there was "lack of resemblance between the blonde-haired, green-eyed, pale-skinned little girl and her parents."[63] Proponents of the official actions suggest that the response was reasonable given concerns with illegal adoptions and trafficking of children in the Roma community.[64] Despite the young girl's frowning and tousled appearance in photos, appeals in the media to her beauty and, above all, innocence resonated with emotions that are familiar in our racial repertoire. Sympathies soared and donations poured in from every corner of the world, reinforcing her value.

Across waters and around the globe, particularly in Latin America, this is a familiar story. Almost exactly a year before the situation involving the Roma family, a photographer in Mexico captured a picture of a blonde Mexican child beggar and posted it on social media, urging his friends to "spread this photo around."[65] His gut instinct told him that something was awry; something must be awry if a blonde child was begging on the streets. Officials sprang into action to save the young blonde girl from a life of begging that was apparently acceptable for darker-skinned family members and children but not for her. She was subsequently removed from the streets and placed in an orphanage. Given what we know about race, phenotype, and adoptions, chances are she will not languish for long. Families will clamor to welcome her as a fixture in their home; her lightness will serve as embodied capital in the competition for what all orphans desire and deserve: love.

These incidents reveal the contemporary significance of embodied capital and racialization. On a global level racial socialization, racialization, and cultivated self-consciousness about racialized features is based on the reality that whiteness functions as capital translating into economic, cultural, and affective resources. Though this study focuses on a particular region at a particular historical moment, "whiteness must be analyzed both as an interconnected global system and by focusing on its local specificities."[66] These points of intersection are not surprising for postcolonial researchers who have for decades worked to elucidate the transnational connections of black people throughout the diaspora. What the elements of a global white traitocracy suggest is that these connections need to go beyond the diaspora in order to capture the negotiations of people of color as well as those who are categorized as white or are aspiring to be white.

If race has "polyvalent mobility" and white supremacy is multidimensional, then agency can be exerted at the individual and institutional levels by all groups.[67] The gendered racial bargains that are deconstructed in this research are not Brazilian idiosyncrasies but are very much part of global strategies of power negotiation, contestation, and accommodation. Illustrating these diasporic and global connections allows researchers to understand the pernicious ways that white supremacy shapes intimate family relationships around the globe, but researchers are also challenged to "tell the truth about racism without causing disabling despair."[68] This is best accomplished by reiterating how families exhibit "moments of rupture" that contest hegemonic structures.[69] This is true because if "the family functions as a privileged exemplar of intersectionality in structuring hierarchy, it potentially can serve a similar function in challenging that hierarchy."[70]

While some families grapple with controlling racial features of family members, others, like Dona Elena, strive to highlight how blackness makes their family members distinct, more authentic, and more beautiful. Some families and mothers reappropriate the use of racial humor to subvert ideologies of whiteness, like Neide and the Nascimento family. Other families, like Pantera Negra's, manipulate the rules of cordial race relations in order to convince city officials to make significant improvements to the black community in which they live. Still others use their involvement with race-based organizing to fight for the visibility of Afro-Brazilians not merely in the cultural realm, but in ways that offer inclusion at the economic, political, and social levels. Their participation in these groups also serves as a recruitment tool for their own family members, who later join and begin to develop a particular type of racial consciousness that is associated with self-acceptance, political mobilization, and material gain. For those, especially women, for whom formal organizing is not possible, there is day-to-day resistance related to beauty. The women in this study may not be shouting "Black is beautiful!" but their qualified cry that "Black is beautiful *when*" is an example of their negotiations and potentially a step toward their own liberation. In addition to all the ways that countries in the diaspora confront white supremacy, they benefit from developing successful transnational forms of contestation and racial resistance, as well.[71]

FINAL THOUGHTS

Afro-Brazilian families find themselves in a moment of incredible globalization and increased transnational circulation of cultural products, ideas, and bodies. For the city of Salvador, transnational interaction is not new, but the speed at which information is being transferred and is affecting families is phenomenal. Speaking of dualities is no longer sufficient, and attempting to organize families into discrete categories of socialization strategies is futile. For researchers the challenge is to identify how all families manage racial hierarchies in ways that simultaneously reproduce and resist racial structures.

At the same time, it is critical to shift the gaze away from black families in order to focus on white families and whiteness. Du Bois's contribution in *The Souls of Black Folk* has often been referenced by researchers around the world, but we rarely discuss his work "The Souls of White Folk."[72] Engaging with black Brazilians only as research subjects reinforces the hierarchies that are responsible for racial inequality. Taking this critique seriously, a number of scholars have shifted their academic gaze to provide the missing data that would expose the inner workings of racial domination and whiteness from the perspective of the oppressor.[73] In the same way that I write about affective capital as it relates to blacks in Brazil, future studies should seek to unveil the affective investment of whites in domination, as well as how they develop racial fluency, actively construct and preserve racial boundaries, and promote their access to material, embodied, and affective capital.

Highlighting Afro-Brazilian families' simultaneous reproduction of and resistance to racism offers a dynamic and innovative conceptual approach that enriches our understanding of how individuals "do race," reproducing and managing intersectional identities in the context of families. These processes are shaped by structural factors, including dominant racial hierarchies and structural inequality that disadvantage blacks vis-à-vis whites and uniquely stigmatize the most black-looking family members vis-à-vis those who more closely approximate whiteness.

For all of the black Brazilian families in this study it takes courage simply to exist in a world that has historically tried to eliminate evidence of their existence. But existing is not enough for them. The intensity of their

socialization practices suggests that each day these families rise equipped
with the tools that they have available, determined to manage and negotiate their racial position with the hope of forging a better future for
themselves and their families. This is best conveyed by Pantera Negra in
his reflections about fostering a politically oriented racial consciousness in
black families:

> A house that is constructed with a foundation, every house that is con-
> structed with a strong foundation will be too solid to collapse. It will
> never collapse. Our family and our future generations will be even stron-
> ger because they have a foundation, a strong seed, and it's going to de-
> velop this black family and it's going to reflect in all black families around
> the country. Because now there are already many *negros* striving like this.
> Because even if you come from a family with nothing—I was the child of
> a laundry woman, and look, my son is in college now. Whether they want
> it or not, our children who are in college have within their hearts a seed
> planted inside of them. And their children, following their example, will
> have one, too. What were difficulties for me, were sacrifices for them, and
> what awaits the children of my children is freedom.

Racial socialization in the family is one of the most effective tools—indeed the linchpin—of racial domination. Home is where the hurt is, precisely because of our strong belief that home is where the heart should be.
Our human desire for belonging, for safety, and for refuge is promised by
the notion of family, but it is betrayed when these relationships are used
to reproduce inequality. Racial hegemony and gender oppression depend
heavily on families to guide the hand of domination. At the same time,
this research illustrates that the destruction of racial domination might be
linked to that same institution: family.

Because of the global traitocracy's adaptive capability and manifestation in multiple arenas, challenging it requires a multilevel approach and
a social movement that spans continents. As the transgressive families in
this study demonstrate, white supremacy is not impenetrable. Resistance
is possible, though it is inherently rife with contradictions and complexities, especially when it takes us from the four corners of the world back to
our own front door.

On the van ride from Rio de Janeiro's airport during my first trip to Brazil in 2008, I took notes furiously, noting how the dilapidated favelas were juxtaposed with the beauty of Rio's beaches and the upscale community in which I would reside. These observations were consistent with how researchers have discussed the spatial topography of racial inequality in Brazil.[1] On a narrow street in Copacabana, the airport van came to a halt, and directly outside the van window I noticed a very dark-skinned woman identifiable as black (*preta*) sitting on the edge of a sidewalk near the corner. She sat on a dusty, dull blue blanket with sundry knickknacks, including dishes, plastic bottles, newspapers, and a tattered pillow. Next to her sat a little girl who could not have been over four years old. The tiny brown-skinned girl wore her hair parted down the middle and gathered in two matted puffs, with stray afro-textured hair peeking out across her hairline. In the girl's hand was a worn baby doll with dirt spots on her face and patches that hinted at the doll's original blond hair.

This image of an apparently homeless black mother and daughter living on a blanket on a sidewalk was provocative and deeply disturbing. It represented Brazil's stark social inequality and the face of racial inequality and poverty in Brazil. I fumbled through my bag to find my camera, hoping to beat the change of the traffic light, and did not take my eyes off the girl. As I brought the camera up to my face, suddenly and unexpectedly the little girl pulled the tattered blanket over her head to cover her face. I was mortified. Frozen with embarrassment, I lowered the camera, feeling as though I had betrayed her with my imposing gaze. I would later describe this encounter to interested colleagues, explaining that the girl and I were locked in a gaze. But after reviewing my field notes later on, I realized that though my eyes were fixed on her, her eyes darted around uncomfortably, only coming back to meet mine to see if I was still looking. This fleeting moment in Rio left an indelible impression on me and raised questions about my privilege and positionality.

In this first encounter in Rio, I had naively presumed that privilege and exploitation were mainly issues for white researchers to work out. I had not anticipated the degree to which I would also feel ambivalent about the researcher gaze and the activist posture. As a black North American, I felt solidarity with Afro-Brazilians, but "sharing certain identities is not enough to presume an insider status. Idiosyncrasies are embedded in our identities that inevitably create moments of intimacy and distance between the informant and researcher."[2] My sincere investment in documenting racial disparity by taking a photo did not inevitably translate to solidarity, and at worst could be considered exploitive and dehumanizing.

Aiming to push the criticality of my research even further, I heeded the advice of others who suggested that "good qualitative feminist research must not only be able to assist the researcher in gathering accurate and useful data, but, more importantly, the researcher must ensure that the informant is central in the research process."[3] Despite the fact that a significant portion of my own academic experience had been spent embracing the importance of "decolonizing methodologies," denormalizing epistemological approaches, and resisting expectations to produce a particular narrative of race and inequality, I still found myself in a position where, in practice, I was poised to do quite the opposite.[4]

In retrospect, my propensity to so easily slip into the problematic researcher gaze reflected my inculcation into the norms of sociology and a particular social-science tradition that includes the casual dismissal and manipulation of marginalized communities.[5] This made me potentially complicit in the reproduction of inequality; as researchers have argued, "White rule, or the theoretical, methodological, epistemological, and practical domination of Whites . . . can happen without Whites at the helm."[6] Not only had this moment uncomfortably revealed my privilege, but the experience clarified the extent to which I would need to closely monitor my gaze and more consciously reevaluate how my socialization in the academy influenced how I interacted with marginalized communities.[7] When the van drove away to deliver me to my nice apartment in Copacabana, I was feeling ambivalent. What I knew about who I was, about my research, and about what I was doing in Brazil were now fragmented ideas that needed to be reconfigured and reassessed.

During the time I was conducting research in Brazil, I was constantly challenged to manage my positionalities in ways that I did not expect, and admittedly I did not always manage them well. Black diasporic scholars find themselves in a unique position to provide insight into these negotiations.[8] Angela Gilliam and Onik'a Gilliam write of their experience in Brazil, "We were white to the degree that we spoke English and refused to speak Portuguese properly, since it reinforced our status as foreigners. We were black to the degree that we seemed Brazilian. This bifurcation of the subject position was to become more complex in Bahia."[9] While this statement is persuasive, I argue that positionality is characterized by multilevel fragmentation rather than a dual or bifurcated negotiation. Along these same lines, black researchers in Brazil are perhaps best framed as being positioned "out of bounds." Rather than moving back and forth over boundaries strategically or unpredictably, they are never completely in or out. They hover in the uncertainty of constantly shifting positions, but they also exert agency in guiding these transitions.

The ways in which the implications of my racialization and positionality shifted, sometimes rapidly and unexpectedly, were both fascinating and disconcerting. Some of the most valuable experiences with this process were those that occurred with white Brazilians, rather than black Brazilians. For half of my time, I lived in an apartment in the Upper City, in one of the most exclusive neighborhoods in Salvador. Walking into an expensive restaurant in Salvador with a white, male colleague felt like a scene in a movie: everyone's head turned as they tried to understand why I was in "their" white space. My white colleague explained that the restaurant-goers likely thought I was his mistress or a casual fling. He and I received those same imposing and presumptuous gazes whenever we traveled the city together. Not realizing we have a professional relationship, one of his neighbors actually stopped speaking to him because he had seen us out in the city together and assumed I was his mistress.

White Brazilians welcomed the opportunity to take me to chic places and used me as a status symbol. At the same time, they spoke to me about "dirty *negros* who smell and do not bathe," as though I were not also black. To them I was not *negra*, at least not in the same way as black Brazilians. To them I was an honorary white, so they viewed it as a compliment to say to me: "Blacks are ugly! But not you. Your blacks are better looking than our blacks." In conversations with a couple of white

Brazilian friends, I rejected their efforts to call me *morena* and emphatically requested that if they insisted on using racial terms to describe me they should call me *negra*. As a humorous way to deal with my stubborn rejection of the more ambiguous label, they referred to me as "Rainha Negra" (Black Queen) and "Deusa de Ébano" (Ebony Goddess) whenever I approached. I was more than happy to respond to those monikers.

At a party I attended, a white Brazilian who previously had visited the United States called to me from across a room full of people by yelling, "Hey nigger, come here!" (in English). I assumed he had heard this word on the radio and did not really understand that it is offensive. I politely explained that the term is highly offensive and racist. I suggested that he never use it again to refer to a black person. He explained that it was I who did not understand, and he proceeded to call me a "discriminatory racist," arguing that only a racist would object to being called a nigger.

Because of these experiences and many others, I was privy to many "intimate secrets of white society" in Brazil.[10] Exposure to antiblack racism and prejudice from both whites and blacks angered me, but I learned to "suppress a sense of outrage while in the field . . . and take advantage of [my] rage" in order to make key inferences about racial discourse and white habitus in Brazil.[11] The social interactions I had with white Brazilians suggest that studies of whiteness in Brazil will make an important contribution to the field of social science.

I chose not to live in Lua Cheia both because I thought it would be overwhelming and because it would be inconvenient to live so far from the center of the city. In retrospect, this was a good decision with a number of positive unintended consequences. Families felt the need to fill me in on occurrences that I missed, the time away from the neighborhood provided me with opportunities to process the data, and the distance allowed me to have a life outside of the families. I am certain that if I had lived in the community, it would have been much more difficult to attend cultural events around the city and develop a sense of the cultural politics that guide the local landscape. In many ways, constantly moving between these two spaces was extraordinarily useful for understanding the racialized spatial dimensions of the city.

My research approach was deliberately both feminist and activist, which I found to be flexible and dynamic, and a way to deliberately reject "white methods."[12] This approach anticipates empathy and action with research participants, rather than just distant observation. I draw heavily on black feminist theory to argue that it is beneficial and necessary for scholars to reject the false dichotomy of insider and outsider status, in exchange for discussing complex negotiations of identity, power, and positionality. But my closeness with participants was not without complications. Participants with whom I had spent a significant amount of time would ask me for money, and I had to find ways to work around those situations. I did not want to reproduce problematic relations of patronage that some of them had had with wealthier Brazilians, in which case our relationship would be viewed as part of an exchange involving economic support and protection. At the same time, I needed to recognize the rules of reciprocity in Brazil that require embracing elements of patronage, but to do so without violating ethical boundaries. When people asked to borrow money, I had to say no. But I did buy goods and services from informants, like lunches they were selling from their homes; I invited them to lunch; and I bought birthday gifts out of respect for the social and moral code of reciprocity.

In chapter 1 of this book, I write about observing violence. I did witness children getting spanked by their parents, and there was one woman who refused to go home out of fear that her husband would beat her. However, it was the symbolic and emotional violence that was most disturbing. This emotional abuse is best exemplified in the case of Regane, the nine-year-old girl who was relentlessly humiliated by family and neighbors. One of the roles I took on in the neighborhood was that of braiding or twisting the hair of young Afro-Brazilian girls who wanted a new hairstyle. In this role, I provided a desired service to the community and created a place for young girls to be exposed to counterdiscourses about blackness and beauty. Realizing how much racialization processes and notions of beauty are framed in terms of hair, I began to manipulate my own hair in response to racialized comments about "cabelo bom" and "cabelo ruim" (good and bad hair). Every several days, I changed my natural afro-textured hair, using hairstyles ranging from intricate braid and twist patterns to a natural afro style. Both young girls and women became curious about my hair designs and started to request them for themselves or ask me to teach them how to do them. Contrary to the argument that social scientists are not necessarily conscious of subjectivity, I was manipulating my subjectivity and destabilizing the status quo in ways that had implications for my theoretical insights.[13] Offering this service was also the best way to address or attempt to counteract some of the emotional abuse Regane experienced.

In terms of physical violence, several women confessed that they were or had been suicidal. Per my Institutional Review Board protocol, I was required to have information about mental health services available given the type of work I was conducting. Though I had information about where they could get help, respondents promptly and uniformly declined this information, claiming that speaking with me about their "traumas" was enough to help them cope with their pain.

During my research visits it was evident that respondents felt completely comfortable including me in their responses even if their statements were insults. These insults were constant and can be summed up by the sting of hearing one of the respondents declare that I was considered to be valueless and having nothing to offer because I am *preta*. These comments and other experiences in Brazil allowed me to personally experience the degradation about which others spoke or hinted. There were moments when I felt ungrounded simply trying to hold on to myself in the midst of social interactions that misread and mistreated me. Managing relationships with Afro-Brazilian families, decompressing with black U.S. researchers and black Brazilian activists, carving out personal time for myself, and maintaining a long-distance marriage are all elements of research that are seldom mentioned but that are necessary with this type of work. I hope that this book contributes insights about the embodied dilemmas of transnational research alongside its main goal of analyzing racial socialization in Afro-Brazilian families.

METHODOLOGY AND POSITIONALITY

This is a multimethod qualitative research study based on ethnographic observations in ten core families and five extended families. In addition, I conducted semistructured interviews with a total of 116 Brazilians (60 percent from the core community and families). Due to space constraints, I am limited in terms of the quantity of observations that can be included in this book. Nonetheless, the ethnographic observations were fundamental in helping me understand the complexities of families' daily lives, with both a temporal and a limited longitudinal perspective. The interview extracts I have included are representative of the types of responses I received during the research. When appropriate I incorporate outliers or exceptions for contrast.

SELECTION OF FAMILIES

Before I arrived in Salvador, I had arranged to work with a faculty member at a local university to help me meet families in a very large area of Salvador called the Lower City. Given the number of large black and brown families who lived in the area, as well as previous research conducted there by researchers from the university, we determined that the setting was ideal. When for personal reasons the faculty member was no longer available to assist me, I was on my own to find an entry point into a community.

For the first several months I was in Brazil, I struggled to figure out how I would locate and gain entrance into a predominately black neighborhood in the Lower City. In retrospect this was advantageous because it gave me ample time to learn the lay of the land and become more comfortable with the city. Over those months, my casual daily conversations with Luana, a domestic worker who worked in my apartment building, led to what seemed like a miracle when she told me she was moving to a neighborhood in the Lower City (*Cidade Baixa*) and wanted me to see her home. Luana invited me to the neighborhood, Lua Cheia, which was the ideal setting for the study because it was located within the area I had originally planned to study; Luana was connected to a number of families in the neighborhood, and she could vouch for me. We had known each other for two months and had developed a friendly relationship, so she invited me to come to the neighborhood and to stay at her home whenever I needed to in order to conduct interviews and observations. Excited about the invitation, I eagerly accepted her offer.

During my first visit to Lua Cheia I was overwhelmed by the number of families and individuals who wanted to be interviewed. My criteria for inclusion included having a phenotypically diverse household, more than three children living in the home, and poor or working-class status. That described the majority of the families I met. In order to select the ten core families, I began by meeting more than ten families and inquiring about their openness to my visits and the feasibility of my conducting multiple visits over several months. Proximity to Luana's house was also a significant factor. Those who had a closer relationship with Luana and were her neighbors were much more likely to be open to me visiting them with such frequency. In addition, two families who lived around the corner but interacted with the families in Luana's neighborhood were selected for inclusion as well. In addition to members of the core families, I interviewed members of other families who lived near and interacted with the core families.

PRE-INTERVIEWS AND INTERVIEWS

Moving to a new country and learning to speak a different language can be an adjustment. I learned Portuguese before arriving in Brazil and had spent a summer in Rio de Janeiro previously. Nonetheless, during the first three months I was in Salvador, I tried out some of my research questions on unsuspecting Brazilians to determine whether people could understand me and to see how they would respond to my questions. These pre-interviews are not included in the study. Three months later, when I began my formal interviews, I was much better prepared in terms of my comfort level with Brazil, my self-presentation, my fluency in Portuguese, and confidence in the appropriateness of my questions.

I was interested in studying four major questions: How do people racially identify? How do race and phenotype affect family relationships? What do Afro-Brazilians learn about race in their families? And how does gender shape the first three questions? In addition to these core questions, I addressed several subthemes in the interviews as well. (See Appendix B for details.) I continuously updated this thematic interview schedule to reflect the emergence of new concepts and themes. By the time I was conducting the last third of the interviews, I had learned how to maximize my interview time not simply because I was becoming more fluent, but because I had developed a better understanding of timing and appropriateness. I spent much less time resolving confusions in terms of the questions and hence could discuss key themes more deeply. Toward the end of the research period, I had virtually memorized the order in which I addressed themes. I had also developed a strategy for seamlessly transitioning from one theme to another and had learned when and how to ask questions. When I was able to accurately predict my informants' responses because I was receiving the same answers, I knew I was arriving at the point of theoretical saturation.

I would schedule interviews, and people would cancel very often. Frequently they did not cancel and we would meet, but they would inform me that they did not feel like being interviewed. When this happened, I would hang out at Luana's home, which was my base, and in the neighborhood common area observing and taking notes. This was awkward at first, but as people got to know me they would strike up conversations, which led to the collection of some of the most interesting data. Family members preferred that our conversations happen more organically, not in a scheduled fashion. They would answer questions in an informal conversation but were hesitant to schedule formal interviews.

Likewise, families preferred that I visit spontaneously or whenever I wanted to stop by (*venha quando você quiser*) rather than make prearrangements. Early on when I would stop by during *telenovelas*, the sound of the television would often drown out the family in the background, and informants would conspicuously split their attention between my questions and the dramatic story lines of the *telenovela*. Initially I naively dismissed *telenovelas* as obstacles to my research, but soon I realized that they are fundamental to how Brazilians learn to situate themselves in broader society. I did not travel when there was a soccer game because buses stopped functioning, as did the entire city. And I was left with no resort but to participate in Carnaval because trips to the Lower City became impossible.[14]

The uncertainty of the timing of interviews and observations was initially stressful and led to anxiety. Some interviewees knew that I would be in Brazil for a year and continued to postpone our formal interviews and would cancel observations in their homes with the belief that we had plenty of time. Ultimately I determined that this was a blessing rather a curse. All of the families were willing for me to hang around and observe them and would informally answer the questions that I would normally have asked in a formal setting. In addition to approaching the semistructured interviews thematically and in a much more informal manner, I was more flexible about where I conducted interviews. At times interviews occurred in interviewees' homes; at other times they occurred as we walked around the neighborhood or sat listening to the rolling beach waves. Most often they happened with a beer (*cerveja*) in hand, which required adjustment on my part because I don't drink, but this was a social requirement in Brazil.

Ensuring privacy was particularly important because the questions I asked were often sensitive and could potentially be the cause of conflict if the topics were discussed openly. During the formal interviews, interviewees were interviewed separately. In some cases, they insisted on being interviewed while watching children, watching television, or being in the presence of others whom they did not mind listening to the interview. Sometimes after I interviewed several family members in one day, the family wanted to debrief together. Without my revealing what anyone had said, the family would discuss their responses and were often surprised by experiences of family members that they had never known about. This debriefing did not happen with all families, but when it did, it was almost always a positive experience. Negative memories were not often shared during these debriefings.

Having planned to interview broadly, I encountered significant barriers to interviewing men because of their violations or perceived violations of professional interview standards. In a patriarchal society where machismo has a strong influence, men feel the need to flirt or make otherwise sexually inappropriate comments to women, even to researchers. The perception that this behavior did or could occur in private interviews with men threatened my most valued relationships with women and mothers. Although I did not eliminate men from the study altogether, early on I stopped pursuing private interviews with them unless I had known them for several months and was confident that the interview would not negatively affect the relationships I had with families and mothers.

ETHNOGRAPHY: THE VISITS

This project is a qualitative and inductive study that uses a symbolic interactionist approach to study process and meaning in families.[15] While there are several ways that researchers can become involved in a community, I adopted a highly active membership approach, in which I participated in the community and neighborhood as a researcher and adopted other roles as they became available, including homework helper, hair braider, and English instructor.[16] My ethnographic fieldwork and observations of daily life in the ten families were complemented by the semistructured interviews in families and in the community. Admittedly, I entered the field with some theoretical leanings and general ideas, but I was insistent on creating the space for concepts to emerge organically from my ethnographic fieldwork.[17]

I visited the ten core families at least once a week, and most often two to three times a week, for over nine months. The frequency decreased during holidays and large events such as Carnaval. This number of visits was only possible because I selected families who lived very close to one another so I could engage in ethnographic observations focusing on one family in particular, but still be observing others at the same time. Because the families were economically disadvantaged, they did not move around the city much at all. I would accompany them to the grocery store, to church (rarely), to the beach, to the local bar, to the bus stop, and to take their children to school and pick them up. We had to walk everywhere, as no one owned a car. When families were invited to parties, they would sometimes take me along and would always invite me to parties being hosted in their own home.

Almost all my ethnographic observations come from the interactions that occurred directly outside the front door of families' homes, in the neighborhood common area. To provide an idea of how limited space is, sitting in what I am calling the common area of the neighborhood, I could see and hear inside the homes of three families. This common area is where everyone tended to congregate every day unless it was raining. In the book I try to balance interview data with ethnographic observations, but most of the book is based on interview data.

Given the number of families included, during the first stage of my research my observations and field notes were prolific. I would visit every day and spend the whole day in the neighborhood so I could meet everyone and become more familiar with the area. During these initial days, I returned home completely exhausted from having collected and recorded impressions and general observations about Salvador, about the families, and about interactions in the community.[18] As I conducted interviews and collected field notes with families, I scheduled days off to process the data and perform the initial coding of the interviews and field notes. My observation schedule varied widely. I would sometimes conduct formal interviews in the morning, then remain in the neighborhood for the rest of the day conducting observations. Alternatively, I would spend the earlier part of the day observing families and then conduct formal interviews in the evening, before or after the *telenovelas*. After a few weeks of observations, I had learned about all the family routines and had interviewed many of the family members. Following this point, I would sit in the neighborhood common area where people from the community would walk through or sit and talk. As I got to know people, I would ask them for interviews, and they often accepted.

Once I determined who my ten core families would be, my family visits became more spaced out. I did not visit every day because I needed time in between to process considerable amounts of data. Once I had collected general observations about main actors, the settings of socialization, and the families, my field notes focused less on general impressions and more on observations of practices, events, and relationships that were thematically relevant or "incidents of interest."[19] With the ethnographic visits I had the goal of emphasizing one family, but would be open to recording any observations that were relevant about other families who agreed to be in the study. After several months of observations, because families interacted outside of their homes so often, I no longer focused on one family per visit, but was able to make observations about several families with ease.

I never spent the night inside the homes of the core families, but I did have overnight visits with five extended families. Admittedly something gets lost during these missing hours, but none of the homes of the core families could accommodate an additional person. I did spend numerous nights in Luana's home only because she lived by herself, and even then we shared a queen-sized bed. There is a selection effect in terms of the extended families that invited me for an overnight visit. These were one-time weekend visits, and only families with larger homes and extra space were able to comfortably accommodate me. These class differences were valuable to the research.

During my ethnographic observations, informal conversations would be sparked or participants would bring something to my attention that they believed I would find interesting on the basis of our previous interview. These informal conversations were much more productive than the formal interviews and the observations. The respondents were obviously nervous during formal interviews, when I sat in front of them one-on-one with a recorder and notepad. They were much more open and comfortable when they could talk around others or in a less formal situation. In addition, some of the most interesting data emerged when there were unexpected interruptions or interventions in both casual and formal conversations. Often the respondents would struggle to answer my questions and would call in someone to help them understand or respond. I looked forward to these moments to see how they uniquely approached and resolved race and color discrepancies. Still, conducting the initial private interview first was important because it gave me the context in which to understand the family. It also helped to clue me in to some of the family dynamics that might be important to observe.

In chapter 5, I discuss a party for a dog in another region of Salvador. This party was located in a section of the city that is considered dangerous. It is a large neighborhood with smaller areas that are protected by gang members who walk the streets, sometimes armed with large semi-automatic weapons. Violence is a normalized element in the lives of some of the residents. For example, both of the young girls (Natalia and Zica) and their families had had young school friends who died as a result of *balas perdidas* (stray bullets) in the neighborhood, and Zica's uncle had died not long before in a shoot-out with the police. The longer I remained there, revelations about violence made me rethink the significance of racial socialization given the challenges of residents' day-to-day lives. The doubts were not enough to convince me to abandon my research, but they did make me more conscious about portraying and analyzing the lives of these families as complex, full, and multilayered.

DATA ANALYSIS

As a researcher rooted in a symbolic interactionism and interested in investigating how structural inequalities and ideologies affect microsocial interactions, I rely on constructivist grounded theory to examine how informants make meaning of racial socialization, racial stigma, and phenotype and translate these meanings into practices.[20] This project emphasizes interviews and ethnographic observations of the day-to-day lived experience of informants, which is why constructivism is useful.[21]

Coding was an essential method used to organize key concepts and themes. I used a three-phase coding process involving open, axial, and selective coding.[22] Key concepts consisted of single words or labels, and themes were phrases that were suggestive of process—for example, hair is a concept, and modifying hair is an analytical theme. The first stage of analysis involved open coding, with an emphasis on "sensitizing concepts," based on line-by-line readings of my field notes and interview content in order to identify broad concepts.[23] For example, I employed open coding to identify concepts and themes related to how mothers used explicit messages to engage in phenotypic differentiation. Comments such as "Why didn't I marry someone with 'good hair?,'" "We need to pinch her nose down," and "Straighten it well enough to hide my roots" were coded as indicators of phenotypic differentiation.

Using axial coding I emphasized how situational factors affected whether and when mothers engaged in these practices.[24] I assessed what criteria were used to determine whether hair was good or bad, as well as how age and gender affected how phenotypic features were managed. Selective coding was used to relate maternal practices involving phenotypic differentiation to racial socialization. This category included the behaviors and verbal messages involving phenotypic differentiation that more broadly constitute racial socialization. With this data, I created a codebook that included an extensive list of constructed categories, codes, and subcodes.[25] With each iteration of data collection and data analysis, I combined codes, added new codes, removed codes, and developed or refined my themes.[26] This strategy of constant comparison and constant revision and refinement of categories is the hallmark of grounded theory. While in the field, I wrote several formal memos for my dissertation committee and numerous private memos and short statements that allowed me to develop my theoretical inclinations. These memos were important for capturing a diverse array of experiences, including isolated events, specific practices, and "incidents of interest," which included conflicts, family arguments, and the birth of a child.[27]

After data collection I reorganized major concepts and codes and organized my observations and informant quotes thematically. Inevitably some quotes and observations appeared multiple times if they were relevant to more than one thematic area. In the book I include comments that are most representative of how participants responded to questions and themes, but I also juxtapose them to contrasting statements to illustrate the complexity of families and individuals. I translated all of the interviews myself and had them reviewed by a native speaker when there were doubts about double meanings. In some cases, translations into English lose some of their original meaning, so when the original Portuguese quote or word offers a nuanced meaning, I include the Portuguese translation.

I began this study with an interview instrument that included over fifty different questions. In the field this instrument was too detailed and was not useful for interviews that tended to be much more informal. So instead of using formal questions, I engaged informants by addressing broader themes. Below are the major themes that I discussed with informants during formal and informal interviews:

Settings and actors in racial socialization
Family and individual racial classification
Family and individual color classification
Defining important family actors and socialization sources
Families' daily routines
Participation in racial rituals
Socialization messages in the home (explicit or implicit)
Role of schools in socialization
Socialization about Brazilian history and slavery
Phenotypic hierarchies: What is good hair and bad hair?
Participation in Afro-Brazilian cultural activities
Who is beautiful? What does it mean to be beautiful?
Importance of cultural participation
Informal use of color and racial terms and what they mean
Definition of racism and experiences or examples of racism
Perceptions of differential treatment in families (not asked directly)
Relationships with siblings and extended family
Romantic relationships and ideal partners
Beauty and self-presentation
Family heritage and history

A significant portion of the section titled "Second Sight or Double Vision?" was previously published in Elizabeth Hordge-Freeman, "Out of Bounds: Negotiating Researcher Positionality in Brazil," in *Bridging Scholarship and Activism: Reflections from the Frontlines of Collaborative Research*, ed. Bernd Reiter and Ulrich Oslender (East Lansing: Michigan State University Press, 2015).

1. Sylvia van Kirk introduces this phrase to describe the contradictory nature but nonetheless "human dimension" of relationships that developed during the colonial encounter. See van Kirk, *Many Tender Ties*.

2. See Stoler, "Carnal Knowledge and Imperial Power," 18.

3. Historian Scott Ickes has produced a thorough historiography about Salvador, Bahia, Brazil, in which he traces the development of the term *Black Rome*, as well as important shifts that are ushering in the re-Africanization of Bahia. See Ickes, *African-Brazilian Culture and Regional Identity in Bahia, Brazil*.

4. See Steinbugler, *Beyond Loving*, xiii.

5. Instituto Brasileiro de Geografia e Estatística, http://www.ibge.gov.br/english/.

6. Edward E. Telles provides an exhaustive contemporary analysis of racial inequality in Brazil, addressing how color shapes opportunities in various areas including education, marriage, and housing. See Telles, *Race in Another America*. In their analysis of economic inequality, Carlos Hasenbalg and Nelson do Valle Silva note that "non-whites are subject to a 'process of cumulative disadvantages' in their social trajectories." See Hasenbalg and Silva, "Educação e diferenças raciais na mobilidade ocupacional no Brasil," 218.

7. See Hellwig, *African-American Reflections on Brazil's Racial Paradise*.

8. See Telles, "Who Are the Morenas?"; Baran, "'Girl, You Are Not Morena. We Are Negras!'"

9. See Twine, *Racism in a Racial Democracy*; Sheriff, *Dreaming Equality*; Patricia Pinho, "White But Not Quite," 49.

10. See Dominguez, "A Taste for 'the Other,'" 333.

11. In his pioneering theoretical piece, Eduardo Bonilla-Silva offers an alternative framework for conceptualizing how race functions as an organizing principle in societies. Instead of focusing on racism, a term that he argues has been overused and misused, Bonilla-Silva suggests that researchers use a framework that defines "societies in which economic, political, social, and ideological levels are partially structured by the placement of actors in racial categories or races" as racialized social systems. Racism is merely one part of the inner workings of a racialized social system. See Bonilla-Silva, "Rethinking Racism," 469.

12. Racial socialization is defined as "verbal and behavioral messages transmitted to younger generations for the development of values, attitudes, behaviors, and beliefs regarding the meaning and significance of race and racial stratification. See Scottham and Smalls, "Unpacking Racial Socialization," 807.

13. There are relatively few examples of contemporary research on racial socialization in black families in Brazil. See Souza, *Tornar-se negro*; Cavalleiro, "Processo de socialização na educação infantil"; Brito and Mantoani, "Processo de socialização em famílias negras"; Pacheco, "Raça, gênero e relações sexual-afetivas na produção bibliográfica das ciências sociais brasileiras"; Moutinho, "Razão, 'Cor' e Desejo"; Barbosa, "Socialização e relações raciais." For critiques outlining the limitations of research produced on socialization in black families in Brazil, see Gebara and Gomes, "Gênero, família e relações étnicorraciais."

14. Annette Lareau offers an innovative analysis of families in the United States that suggests that class is more decisive than race in shaping child-rearing practices. However, I argue that she overlooks evidence that race shapes seemingly class-based child-rearing decisions, and her work does not address racialization. Despite this limitation, her study was instructive in developing this book, which also studies unequal childhoods in the context of the same families. See Lareau, *Unequal Childhoods*.

15. See Steinbugler, *Beyond Loving*, xv.

16. See Rebhun, *The Heart Is Unknown Country*, 166. Nancy Scheper-Hughes describes the way poverty undermines the affective relationship between mothers and their children; see Scheper-Hughes, *Death Without Weeping*.

17. See Barsade and O'Neill, "What's Love Got to Do with It?," 2.

18. The "broaden-and-build" theory of positive emotions is a contribution from the field of psychology. By linking one's access to experiences of positive emotions to one's racialization or position in a racialized society, this innovative theory becomes useful to social scientists. With it, sociologists can begin to conceptualize emotions not simply as emotion work or psychological distress but as both the product and reproducer of inequality. See Fredrickson, "The Role of Positive Emotions in Positive Psychology," 220–223.

19. Ibid.

20. See Kane, *The Gender Trap*, 199.

21. Sociologists have studied differential treatment in families by parents, but very few address the ways that race may shape differential treatment. See Jensen et al., "'Life Still Isn't Fair.'"

22. The term *patriarchal bargain* has been used to describe how women may decide to accommodate certain elements of patriarchal norms for individual gain, even at the expense of reproducing gender inequality. Critiques of the use of the term *bargain* argue that the concept is an overly simplistic portrayal of women's decision making because it understates the fact that women make decisions within the context of limited structural options. I address this by defining bargains as inherently ambivalent negotiations reflecting one's vulnerable social position. See Kandiyoti, "Bargaining with Patriarchy."

23. See West and Zimmerman, "Doing Gender," 125.

24. See Collins, *Black Feminist Thought*.

25. See Bourdieu, "Cultural Reproduction and Social Reproduction."

26. See Bourdieu, *Distinction*.

27. In her research on interracial couples, Amy Steinbugler provides an analysis of how "racework" is used to navigate relationships. Her model has been useful in developing the schema of embodied racial capital and visibility management that I discuss in this book. See Steinbugler, *Beyond Loving*.

28. An abundance of research discusses how people of African descent negotiate day-to-day racism. See Essed, *Understanding Everyday Racism*, and Twine, *White Side of Black Britain*. Rose Weitz discusses the ways that women engage in "resistance and accommodation" to combat oppressive gender and beauty norms. I draw on this idea as well in order to explore the relationship between race, beauty, and gender. See Weitz, "Women and Their Hair."

29. See Twine, *White Side of Black Britain*, 8.

30. Twine describes racial literacy as the "discursive, material, and cultural practices in which parents train themselves and their children to recognize, name, challenge, and manage various forms of everyday racism." This concept does not focus on affective interactions, and it is also geared towards antiracism. See Twine, *White Side*, 8.

31. Ibid. Twine's book contributes to an understanding of white motherhood of nonwhite children, but it focuses mainly on childhood rather than on how racialization processes are learned and refined throughout one's life.

32. Ibid. Twine provides a model for how multivocality can capture the perspectives of black family members who serve as resources to white mothers as they negotiate their roles as mothers and partners of African-descended Britons.

33. See Burton et al., "Critical Race Theories, Colorism, and the Decade's Research on Families of Color," 144.

34. See Harris, "From Color Line to Color Chart."

35. See Russell, Wilson, and Hall, *The Color Complex*; Harris, "From Color Line," 54.

36. See Daniel, *Race and Multiraciality in Brazil and the United States*; Bonilla-Silva, "From Bi-Racial to Tri-Racial"; Skidmore, "Bi-Racial USA vs. Multi-Racial Brazil."

37. See Bonilla-Silva and Dietrich, "The Latin Americanization of Racial Stratification in the U.S.," 155.

38. See Conrad, *Children of God's Fire*; de Queirós Mattoso, *To Be a Slave in Brazil, 1550–1888*.

39. The Brazilian population was described as a "fearfully mongrel population." Borges, "'Puffy, Ugly, Slothful, and Inert,'" 244.

40. Dain Borges offers concise, yet thorough, historical overviews of the development of eugenics, identifying which features were racialized and deemed degenerate. See Borges, "'Puffy,'" 235.

41. See Costa, *As cores de Ercília*; Hofbauer, *Uma história de branqueamento ou o negro em questão*.

42. See Borges, "'Puffy,'" 238.

43. See Nuttall, "Rethinking Beauty," 9.

44. Nancy Leys Stepan outlines the emergence of the eugenics movement in Europe, then its spread to the Americas. She describes how craniology, phrenology, and physiognomy refer to the analysis of facial features and head size and shape to determine a person's personality, intelligence, and level of humanity. This pseudoscience was also used to promote a hierarchy among Europeans, with some Europeans being considered inferior to others. These methods were also used to promote patriarchy by arguing that women were intellectually inferior to men. See Stepan, *"The Hour of Eugenics."*

45. Ibid., 45.

46. See Sales Augusto dos Santos and Laurence Hallewell, "Historical Roots of the 'Whitening' of Brazil," 64–65.

47. See Stepan, *Hour of Eugenics*," 44–49.

48. See Seyferth, "A antropologia e teoria do branqueamento de raça no Brasil," 96, as cited in Sales Augusto dos Santos and Laurence Hallewell, "Historical Roots."

49. See Hasenbalg and Silva, *Relações raciais no Brasil contemporâneo*, 2; Guimarães, *Classes, Raças e Democracias*.

50. See Sales Augusto dos Santos and Laurence Hallewell, "Historical Roots."

51. The assumption was that in order for the nation to be whitened, black and brown women would mix with the European immigrants and improve the racial stock of the nation. This strategy only makes sense in the context of the belief that interracial relationships would successively lead to the whitening of the population, rather than population darkening.

52. See Nascimento, *Mixture or Massacre?*; d'Adesky, *Pluralismo étnico e multiculturalismo*, 173–174.

53. See Freyre, *The Masters and the Slaves*.

54. Ibid.; Skidmore, *Black into White*; Viotti da Costa, *The Brazilian Empire*.

55. See Freyre, *Masters and Slaves*, 85, 200.

56. See Reichmann, *Race in Contemporary Brazil*, 8.

57. See Schwartz, "The Manumission of Slaves in Colonial Brazil," 635.

58. See Nishida, "Manumission and Ethnicity in Urban Slavery," 386.

59. See Schwartz, "Manumission of Slaves," 635–636. In a debate that has come to shape the field of race studies in Brazil, Carl Degler suggested that the offspring of black and white Brazilians had access to privileges through a "mulatto escape hatch." A decade later, Carlos Hasenbalg and Nelson do Valle Silva suggested that outcomes over the lifetime for browns and blacks are relatively similar. See Degler, *Neither Black nor White*; Hasenbalg and Silva, "Educação e diferenças raciais na mobilidade ocupacional no Brasil."

60. Ibid.

61. Ibid., 635.

62. See Collins, "It's All in the Family," 66.

63. Race and colorism in families has been explored with most detail in the realm of literature and fiction. See Toni Morrison's *The Bluest Eye* and *Tar Baby* for brilliant portrayals of the importance of phenotype in black families in the United States.

64. There are significant debates that address concerns about superimposing ideas from the United States onto Brazil. Several scholars outline the benefits and the possibilities of developing research that makes these connections without ignoring regional and national specificities. See French, "The Missteps of Anti-Imperialist reason"; French, "Translation, Diasporic Dialogue, and the Errors of Pierre Bourdieu and Loïc Wacquant"; Segato, "The Color-Blind Subject of Myth"; da Silva, *Violência e racismo no Rio de Janeiro*; Costa Vargas, "The Inner City and the Favela."

65. As a sociologist, Frazier drew heavily on a social disorganization approach and a cultural deficiency model characteristic of the Chicago School of Sociology, and argued that there were no significant African cultural survivals in Brazil. In contrast, Herskovits is recognized in the field of anthropology for offering a paradigm-shifting conceptualization of black families that describes the numerous ways that cultural

forms were transported to the New World and transformed by enslaved Africans. See Frazier, "The Negro Family in Bahia, Brazil"; Herskovits, *The Myth of the Negro Past.* For an excellent analysis of this debate, see Yelvington, "The Anthropology of Afro-Latin America and the Caribbean," 228.

66. See Stack, *All Our Kin*; McLoyd, et al., "Marital Processes and Parental Socialization in Families of Color"; Lesane-Brown, "A Review of Race Socialization within Black Families"; and Maxine S. Thompson and Verna M. Keith, "The Blacker the Berry." The reason the contemporary framing of racial socialization in black families is positive is that this research was produced as a response to Daniel Patrick Moynihan's scathing and racist attack on black families and black mothers in 1965.

67. A number of books discuss the role of black women as mothers, leaders, and community organizers in Brazil. See Landes, *City of Women*; Caldwell, *Negras in Brazil*; Perry, *Black Women against the Land Grab.*

68. Burton and colleagues critique "a lack of attention to colorism and how it shapes within-race/ethnic socialization practices of families, specifically immigrants from countries of origin with racialized and color-conscious hierarchies." See Burton, et al., "Critical Race Theories," 453. Few-Demo outlines the contributions resulting from incorporation of intersectionality into family studies. See April Few-Demo, "Intersectionality as the 'New' Critical Approach in Feminist Family Studies."

69. In what he calls the "ultimate test," Telles studies multiracial families in Brazil and concludes that among siblings of a different race there are educational differences, including differences in the likelihood of being in age-appropriate schooling. See Telles, *Race in another America*, 149–150.

70. Beginning in the 1990s many African Americans have traveled to Salvador. Rather than seeing Africa as a homeland, many feel more connected to Brazil as home because it captures the diasporic slave experience while also having close ties to Africa that are not as visible in the U.S. The presence of African American tourists in Brazil became such a significant force that it sparked conversations about marketing Salvador as an African heritage site. See Jocélio Teles dos Santos, "A Mixed-Raced Nation"; Patricia de Santana Pinho, *Mama Africa.*

71. See Shirey, "Transforming the Orixás," 66.

72. African Heritage tourism, driven by black U.S. tourists, is at the core of the tourism boom in Bahia. This is ironic given that in the early 1900s black North Americans were denied entry to Brazil because their presence was considered to introduce a negative racial element and to stifle whitening processes. See Hellwig, *African-American Reflections*; Kraay, *Afro-Brazilian Culture and Politics*; Paschel, "Re-Africanization and the Cultural Politics of Bahianidade."

73. See Shirey, "Transforming the Orixás," 62.

74. See Jocélio Teles dos Santos, "A Mixed-Race Nation," 127.

75. Erica Williams discusses the way that Salvador's image is sexualized in order to appeal to an international audience. See Williams, *Sex Tourism in Bahia.*

76. See Patricia de Santana Pinho, *Mama Africa.*

77. See Patricia Pinho, "Afro-Aesthetics in Brazil" and *Mama Africa*; Osmundo de Araujo Pinho, "Espaço, poder e relações raciais"; Sansone, *Blackness without Ethnicity*; Paschel, "Re-Africanization."

78. See Armstrong, "The Aesthetic Escape Hatch," 69.

79. In her analysis of regional dynamics in Brazil, Barbara Weinstein mentions

work by Mario de Andrade suggesting that President Getúlio Vargas's populist approach was jokingly referred to as the *dictanegra* to highlight the fact that its base was composed of the darker elements of Brazilian society. See Weinstein, "Racializing Regional Difference," 246.

80. See Telles, *Race in Another America*; Lovell, "Race, Gender and Regional Labor Market Inequalities in Brazil."

81. In October 2012, Brazil passed the Law of Quotas (Lei de Cotas n. 12.711) requiring federal universities to enroll students from public schools (to address class inequality) and students who are representative of the racial composition of the local population.

82. See Telles, *Race in Another America*, 206.

83. Keisha-Khan Perry provides a detailed analysis of how the community Gamboa de Baixo, in Salvador's "Lower City," is constructed as a dangerous black space and is the target of urban renewal, against which community members, particularly women, are fighting. See Perry, *Black Women against the Land Grab*.

84. Jacqueline Nassy Brown writes about the role that Liverpool, England, plays in the black diaspora as one of the oldest cities with a diasporic community and with the emergence of new social relations that reflect its simultaneous local and global characteristics. Her analysis shuttles between the local and global and considers Liverpool a vantage point from which to understand race. See Brown, *Dropping Anchor, Setting Sail*.

85. The interviews that lasted six hours involved Afro-Brazilians whom I either met with over a period of several days or met with and interviewed over the course of one day with periodic breaks for snacks, lunch, and dinner. In the latter case, I often insisted on stopping the interviews so the respondents could take a break, but they often insisted on continuing, wanting to free themselves of a life history that they had not told anyone. The subjects of these long interviews were largely part of the special group called *filhas de criação* (raised daughters). Though I discuss the lives of three of these women in this book, their narratives will be analyzed more deeply in a forthcoming book project. See Hordge-Freeman and Harrington, "Ties that Bind," for a more in-depth analysis of this group.

86. See LaRossa, "Grounded Theory Methods and Qualitative Family Research"; Charmaz, *Constructing Grounded Theory*.

87. See Hochschild and Machung, *Second Shift*, as referred to in Lareau, *Unequal Childhoods*.

88. See Emerson, Fretz, and Shaw, *Writing Ethnographic Field Notes*, 2.

89. See Gordilha-Souza, *Limites do habitar*, 167.

90. See McCallum, "Racialized Bodies, Naturalized Classes."

91. See Perry, *Black Women against the Land Grab*.

92. See Da Matta, *A casa e a Rua*.

93. These findings were also made by Livio Sansone in his analysis of Salvador. See Sansone, *Blackness without Ethnicity*.

94. See Du Bois, *The Souls of Black Folk*.

95. See Kia Lilly Caldwell, *Negras in Brazil*, xv.

96. See Kia Lilly Caldwell, *Negras in Brazil*; Gilliam and Gilliam, "Odyssey"; Butler, *Freedoms Given, Freedoms Won*, 228; Hanchard, *Orpheus and Power*; Twine, *Racism in a Racial Democracy*; Twine and Warren, *Racing Research, Researching Race*.

97. See Kia Lilly Caldwell, "Look at Her Hair."

98. I remained conscious of avoiding interacting with Afro-Brazilians in ways that were consistent with "imperialism in blackface," as I had critiqued white research-ers for the way they interacted with poor Brazilians. I spent the entirety of my time grappling with how I would ensure that my approach, conclusions, and relationships would be critical and community-engaged. See Guridy, *Forging Diaspora*, 12; Hordge-Freeman, "Out of Bounds."

99. There are ethical and methodological issues involved when ethnographers are exposed to traumatic narratives of domestic violence during the course of their re-search. See Burton, Purvin, and Garrett-Peters, "Longitudinal Ethnography"; Ether-ington, "Working with Traumatic Stories"; and Dickson-Swift et al., "Blurring Bound-aries in Qualitative Health Research on Sensitive Topics."

100. There have been considerable debates surrounding the limitations of census data and the diverse and complex understandings Brazilians have of the color cate-gories that are used to describe phenotypic characteristics. See Telles, "Who Are the Morenas?"; Loveman, Muniz, and Bailey, "Brazil in Black and White?"; and Harris et al., "Who Are the Whites?"

101. See Telles, *Race in Another America*.

102. See hooks, *Black Looks*, 131.

CHAPTER 1

1. Bete is the nickname that Brazilians uniformly give me. It is a shortened version of my name.

2. See Stoler, "Tense and Tender Ties," 864, and Stoler, "Carnal Knowledge and Imperial Power," 57.

3. Goffman, *Stigma*; Link and Phelan, "Conceptualizing Stigma."

4. In her work on "tense and tender ties," Ann Laura Stoler draws on work pub-lished by Sylvia van Kirk. See Stoler, "Tense and Tender Ties," 830; van Kirk, *Many Tender Ties*.

5. See Kane, *The Gender Trap*, 199.

6. This is true for both exogamous and endogamous pairings because the relational quality of race and phenotype in Brazil privileges "degrees of whiteness" so that phe-notypic difference has meaning for all families. See Patricia de Santana Pinho, "White but Not Quite," 39.

7. See Gomes, *A mulher negra que vi de perto*.

8. See Burdick, *Blessed Anastácia*; Rebhun, *The Heart Is Unknown Country*, 166.

9. See Patricia Pinho, "Afro-Aesthetics in Brazil"; Adelman and Ruggi, "The Beau-tiful and the Abject."

10. In Robin Sheriff's work on race in a favela in Rio de Janeiro, she mentions that in families "one senses a kind of anticipation and concern over color before the birth of a child." She also suggests that it is not openly discussed, which stands in contrast to how babies are discussed in this study. See Sheriff, *Dreaming Equality*, 144.

11. The notion of *barriga suja* has been discussed in other research in Brazil. See Twine, *Racism in a Racial Democracy*; Baran, "Girl, You Are Not Morena"; Burdick, *Blessed Anastácia*.

12. See McClintock, *Imperial Leather*.

13. France Winddance Twine writes that hospitals have historically been a site of

surveillance for all women, and particularly for white women who might be suspected of having had an interracial relationship. See Twine, "Transgressive Women and Transracial Mothers," 133–137.

14. The Portuguese captures the nuance: "Bom, quando eu nasci ela [Jani] ficou morrendo de enveja porque a filha dela nasceu mulata. Ela é clara mas o marido dela é negro, . . . mas tem cabelo melhor, bonzinho, né, melhor. O cabelo dele é liso, o cabelo dela é mais crespo mas ela é branca e clara. Quem é branco aqui? Não tem ninguém? Né? Ai ela teve a filha dela nasceu mulata mesmo cabelo crespo com pele morena, negra. E a filha da minha mãe a pesar de minha mãe ser negra eu nasci branca com olhos claros. Aí ela olhou para minha mãe e falou assim: 'Queria que a minha filha tivesse nascido loira com olhos azuis.' É até hoje ela fica comparando a filha dela comigo. Entendeu? Até quando eu entrei na faculdade disse que não queria que sua filha entrasse porque tem maconhera. Que a faculdade era lugar de drogado. Porque na verdade ela se sentiu incomodada."

15. In an analysis of popular songs, Martha Abreu discusses the ways that women who fall into these categories are racialized and sexualized differently. See Abreu, "Mulatas, Crioulos, and Morenas"; Giacomini, "Mulatas Profissionais."

16. See Adelman and Ruggi, "Beautiful and the Abject."

17. Donald Pierson cites the work of João Varella, who writes in *Da Bahia do Senhor do Bonfim*, "When the child was black and ugly, he was usually carried in this fashion. If, however, he was a *coisa mais limpa* (literally, 'a cleaner one'), he was borne in front, in his mother's arms, so that all the world might the more readily see him." See Pierson, *Negros in Brazil*, 121.

18. Personal space, including the body, is public space in Salvador. I offer this example: A passerby, a complete stranger, approached me and asked me why I had so many pimples on my face. (I was having a reaction to the heat.) She said that I was too pretty to have pimples ruin my face, and she proceeded to try to pop one of them!

19. See Wilder and Cain, "Teaching and Learning Color Consciousness in Black Families."

20. Donna Goldstein discusses the "emotional aesthetic" families and women in Brazil use in their conversations about otherwise offensive or violent acts. Other scholars write about the history of voicing racist statements under the guise of humor. See Goldstein, *Laughter Out of Place*; Sue and Golash-Boza, "'It Was Only a Joke.'"

21. See Foucault, *Discipline and Punish*; Waskul and Vannini, "Introduction: The Body in Symbolic Interaction."

22. Scholars have written about how mothers are blamed when children are born with problems or "defects." See Blum, "Mother-Blame in the Prozac Nation"; Arendell, "Conceiving and Investigating Motherhood."

23. See Edmonds, "'The Poor Have the Right to Be Beautiful.'"

24. See Sansone, *Blackness without Ethnicity*.

25. See Nascimento, *Mixture or Massacre?*

26. See Larson and Almeida, "Emotional Transmission in the Daily Lives of Families"; Stocker et al., "Family Emotional Processes and Adolescents' Adjustment."

27. See Blum, "Mother-Blame," 202.

28. See Pitt-Rivers, "The Fate of Shechem, or the Politics of Sex."

29. See da Matta, *A casa e a rua*; Gregg, *Virtually Virgins*.

30. See Stepan, *The Hour of Eugenics*.

31. See Rebhun, *Heart Is Unknown Country.*

32. Ginetta Candelario explores the notion of being "black behind the ears," which suggests that a person has hints of black heritage in the Dominican Republic. See Candelario, *Black behind the Ears.*

33. See Volling, "The Family Correlates of Maternal and Paternal Perceptions of Differential Treatment in Early Childhood," 228; Stocker, "Differences in Mothers' and Fathers' Relationships with Siblings."

34. Angela Jorge contends that negative comments that mothers make about their daughters' hair can be a traumatic experience with lifelong implications. Writing of her experiences in Puerto Rico, she mentions that when combing coarse or afro-textured hair mothers can be heard saying, "Maldito sea este pelo!" (Damn this hair!), or "Dios mío, este pelo!" (Dear God, this hair!), which leads to negative feelings. See Jorge, "The Black Puerto Rican Woman in Contemporary American Society," 194.

35. See Lewis, "Hair Combing Interactions."

36. See Stoler, "Tense and Tender Ties," 864

37. Nuttall, "Rethinking Beauty," 29. Nuttall quotes Denis Donoghue; Donoghue, *Speaking of Beauty.*

38. Theories of social comparison suggest that people are more likely to compare themselves to similar others, though there is some agency in determining who these similar others are. Women view each other in complex ways as collaborators, competitors, and evaluators. See Rosenberg, *Conceiving the Self.*

39. See Ribeiro and Silva, "Cor, educação e casamento"; Petruccelli, "Seletividade por cor e escolhas conjugais no Brasil dos 90"; Goldstein, "'Interracial' sex and racial democracy in Brazil."

40. See Burdick, *Blessed Anastácia*; Telles, *Race in Another America.*

41. See Telles, *Race in Another America,* 231.

42. See Adelman and Ruggi, "Beautiful and the Abject," 560.

43. Erica Williams suggests that black women who are involved in sex tourism should not be viewed as one-dimensional victims. Focusing on their agency, Williams examines the variety of relationships and arrangements that shape sexual "entanglements" between mainly black Bahian women and white European tourists. Some black women may want marriage, while others express their preference for short-term monthly or even week-long relationships. Williams, *Sex Tourism in Bahia.*

44. See Sansone, *Blackness without Ethnicity.*

45. See Peterson and Leigh, "The Family and Social Competence in Adolescence"; Henry, "Family System Characteristics, Parental Behaviors, and Adolescent Family Life Satisfaction."

46. Wilder and Cain, "Teaching and Learning," 585.

47. In her ethnography of a favela in Rio, Goldstein uses the term *emotional aesthetic* to describe how poor women use dark humor to discuss harsh realities including rape, abuse, and child death. Goldstein, *Laughter Out of Place,* 45.

48. See Telles, *Race in Another America.*

49. See Burdick, *Blessed Anastácia*; Hunter, *Race, Gender, and the Politics of Skin Tone*; Hill, *Black Intimacies.*

50. See Gregg, *Virtually Virgins.*

51. See Osuji, "Divergence or Convergence in the U.S. and Brazil," 110.

52. The idea of dating and loving other black people has been promoted by the

black movement. However, I had numerous conversations with black women in the movement who were frustrated that many black men in the movement who promoted the idea consistently dated or married white or very light women.

53. See Twine, *A White Side of Black Britain*.

54. See Gilroy, *The Black Atlantic*, 218.

55. See Relethford et al., "Social Class, Admixture, and Skin Color Variation in Mexican-Americans and Anglo-Americans Living in San Antonio, Texas"; Candelario, *Black behind the Ears*; Comas-Díaz, "LatiNegra."

56. See Comas-Díaz, "LatiNegra," 40.

57. See Comas-Díaz, "LatiNegra."

58. As Comas-Díaz describes, the term *requintar* comes from the word *fifth* and represents the number of generations that black traits can "stain" a family. Ibid., 41.

59. See Jorge, "Black Puerto Rican Woman," 194.

60. See Fanon, *Black Skin, White Masks*, 42.

61. See Torres-Saillant, "The Tribulations of Blackness."

62. See "Dear Mother," SNCC Newsletter, September–October 1967, 7, Cleveland Sellers Collection at the Avery Research Center for African-American History at the College of Charleston, Box 18, Folder 4.

63. See Comas-Díaz, "LatiNegra," 54.

64. See Boyd-Franklin, *Black Families in Therapy*; Russell, Wilson, and Hall, *The Color Complex*; Graham, *Our Kind of People*; Frazier, *Black Bourgeoisie*.

65. See Boyd-Franklin, *Black Families*; Wilder and Cain, "Teaching and Learning."

66. See Goldstein, *Laughter Out of Place*.

67. See Relethford et al. "Social Class"; Twine, *Racism in a Racial Democracy*.

68. See Sue and Golash-Boza, "'It Was Only a Joke,'" 1596. In this analysis of Mexico and Peru, Christina Sue and Tonya Golash-Boza make a compelling case that a "systematic comparison between black-related and indigenous-related humour in Latin America could provide a much-needed bridge between studies of these two populations."

69. See Patricia de Santana Pinho, "White but Not Quite," 40.

70. See Hunter, *Race, Gender*; Maxine S. Thompson and Verna M. Keith, "The Blacker the Berry."

71. See Petrucelli, "Seletividade"; Baran, "Girl, You Are Not Morena," 388.

72. JeffriAnne Wilder and Colleen Cain offer a compelling analysis of how in "color socialization" maternal figures often believe that they are helping, not hurting their family members. See Wilder and Cain, "Teaching and Learning," 591.

CHAPTER 2

1. See Guerreiro Ramos, "O negro desde dentro," 240.

2. See Tracey Owens Patton, "Hey Girl, Am I More than My Hair?," 131.

3. See Morrison, *The Bluest Eye*, 95.

4. See Nuttall, "Rethinking Beauty," 9. In this quote, Sarah Nuttall is citing philosopher Immanuel Kant.

5. See Adelman and Ruggi, "The Beautiful and the Abject," 559.

6. See Gossett, *Race: The History of an Idea in America*.

7. See Mays, *Women in Early America*.

8. See Nuttall,"Rethinking Beauty."

9. In 2014, the *Revista da Associação Brasileira de Pesquisadores Negros* published its first issue, which was dedicated solely to the understudied area of whiteness (*branquitude*) in Brazil. For exemplary works, see Oliveira, "Representações sociais de branquitude em Salvador"; Sovik, "Preto no branco"; Malomalo, "Branquitude como dominação do corpo negro."

10. The term literally means "thanks to be taken out." See Twinam, *Public Lives, Private Secrets*; Dávila, *Diploma of Whiteness*. This document also represents concerns over "cleanliness of blood" that originated in Spain when there were anti-Semitic concerns about Jews infiltrating the Spanish aristocracy.

11. Reiter, "Whiteness as Capital," 25.

12. See Foucault, *Discipline and Punish*, 155.

13. See McClintock, *Imperial Leather*; Souza, *Tornar-se Negro*, 29.

14. See Sheriff, *Dreaming Equality*, 57.

15. See Adelman and Ruggi, "Beautiful and the Abject."

16. See Dworkin, *Women Hating*, 113–114.

17. In their cross-anthropological study of "infant head molding," Ellen Fitz-Simmons, Jack H. Prost, and Sharon Peniston found that families may apply pressure or even use bindings on an infant's head in order to shape the cranial bones. This cultural practice is used throughout the world—by Caribbeans, Europeans, Asians, and Native American groups—with no apparent racial connection. Mothers and other women, who are often responsible for managing these features, describe the importance of infant head molding in terms of its effect on beauty, health, and even intelligence. See FitzSimmons, Prost, and Peniston, "Infant Head Molding"; Anthony Synnott discusses early sociological theorizations of the body, including the relationship between face and body, but with an emphasis on gender, not race. See Synnott, *The Body Social*.

18. The medical terms *therapy* and *massage* connote an almost scientific aspect of nose modification. A broad nose is like any other "problem," like a sore muscle or joint that needs to be massaged.

19. See Baran, "Girl, You Are Not Morena," 388.

20. See Patricia Pinho, "Afro-Aesthetics in Brazil." See Collins, *Black Feminist Thought*, for the implications of this for sexuality.

21. See Candelario, *Black behind the Ears*; Frazier, "The Negro Family in Bahia, Brazil."

22. My translation. Cavalleiro, "Processo de socialização na educação infantil," 42.

23. See Patricia Pinho, "Afro-Aesthetics in Brazil," 271–272.

24. This observation was made in only one family, though they claimed that the idea was accepted throughout their family. Although I expected to observe additional examples of racial phenotype informing personality or character attributions in families, I did not observe other examples of this directly.

25. See Comas-Díaz, "LatiNegra," 44.

26. See Wilder and Cain, "Teaching and Learning Color Consciousness"; Boyd-Franklin, *Black Families in Therapy*.

27. See Abreu, "Mulatas, Crioulos, and Morenas"; Giacomini, "Mulatas profissionais."

28. Across the diaspora, women's buttocks are one of many traits that have been

racialized as an indicator of black blood. See Alleyne, *The Construction and Representation of Race and Ethnicity in the Caribbean and the World*, 6.

29. See Gregg, *Virtually Virgins*.

30. See Cheryl Thompson, "Black Women, Beauty, and Hair as a Matter of Being," 836.

31. See Craig, *Ain't I a Beauty Queen?*, 29.

32. See Omi and Winant, *Racial Formation in the United States*, 106.

33. See Patricia Pinho, "Afro-Aesthetics in Brazil."

34. See Craig, *Ain't I a Beauty Queen?*; Candelario, *Black behind the Ears*; Alleyne, *Construction and Representation*.

35. See Gordon, "A Beleza abre Portas."

36. See de Casanova, "'No Ugly Women,'" 292.

37. See Twine, *Racism in a Racial Democracy*; Figueiredo, "Beleza Pura."

38. Erynn Masi de Casanova describes the importance of being *bien arreglada* (well put together) in Ecuador, which is influenced by racialized notions of beauty, along with what de Casanova argues are personality traits. She notes, "Peers and family members encourage these young women to pay attention to their appearance, and from the participants' responses, it appears that the opinions of their school peers matter more than those of their parents or siblings." See de Casanova, "'No Ugly Women,'" 292.

39. See Gordon, "A Beleza abre Portas."

40. See Kia Lilly Caldwell, "'Look at Her Hair,'" 27.

41. In the United States some black women refer to chemical relaxers as "creamy crack" to convey how chemically straightening one's hair creates a dependency, because women must have their hair restraightened every few weeks in order for any new hair growth to match the texture of their straightened hair.

42. See Figueiredo, "Beleza pura"; Jocélio Teles dos Santos, "O negro no espelho"; Gomes, *Sem Perder a raiz*; Lody, *Cabelos do axé*.

43. See Patricia de Santana Pinho, *Mama Africa*, 287.

44. Ibid.

45. See Butler, *Freedoms Given, Freedoms Won*.

46. See Patricia de Santana Pinho, *Mama Africa*.

47. See Craig, *Ain't I a Beauty Queen?*; Banks, *Hair Matters*.

48. See Jocélio Teles dos Santos, "O negro no espelho"; Figueiredo, *Beleza pura*.

49. See Jocélio Teles dos Santos, "A Mixed-Raced Nation"; Patricia de Santana Pinho, *Mama Africa*.

50. See Craig, *Ain't I a Beauty Queen?*

51. See Patricia de Santana Pinho, *Mama Africa*.

52. See Douglas, "Nappy."

53. http://belezanatural.com.br/en#.

54. See Cruz, "Os cabelos mágicos."

55. Ibid.

56. The regional manager who was called in from Rio de Janeiro to give a presentation to the group of black faculty from the United States and Brazil studying afro-aesthetics was a white woman with European features and straightened black hair. White upper managers are not required to undergo this treatment.

57. Cruz offers a detailed description of how the physical organization of the Institute corresponds with a Ford or McDonald's production line, an organizational strategy used to lower costs. See Cruz, "Os cabelos mágicos."

58. See Candelario, *Black behind the Ears*, 129.

59. See Cruz, "Os cabelos mágicos."

60. See Owens, "Hey Girl, Am I More than My Hair?"

61. See Cruz, "Os cabelos mágicos."

62. Currently the vast majority of black men wear their hair cut less than a quarter-inch from their scalp. Seldom do researchers discuss why that decision has been uniformly made, even though there is a history of black men also using their hair as a symbol of racial resistance and racial accommodation. See Alexander, *Performing Black Masculinity*.

63. Angela Figueiredo discusses the challenges that middle-class blacks face because there are very few blacks in the Brazilian middle class. Figueiredo, *Classe média negra*.

64. See Candelario, *Black behind the Ears*, 254.

65. Ibid.

66. See Paulette M. Caldwell, "A Hair Piece."

67. See Comas-Díaz, "LatiNegra," 54; Jorge, "The Black Puerto Rican Woman."

68. Laurence Prescott notes that in 1883 in Colombia, "there appeared in the 'Folletines' supplement of the Bogotá newspaper *La Luz*, a notice titled 'No más negros' 'No more Blacks,' which reported on a doctor in South Carolina who was experimenting with 'una agua milagrosa que da a la piel de los negros la blancura de la nieve' 'a miraculous water which gives to Negroes' skin the whiteness of snow.'" See Prescott, "Liberating Blackness," 477.

69. See Glenn, "Yearning for Lightness," 282.

70. See Brown-Glaude, "The Fact of Blackness?," 34.

71. See Wolf, *The Beauty Myth*.

72. See Edmonds, *Pretty Modern*; Bradford, "Brazil's Poor Receiving Plastic Surgery Free of Charge."

73. See Edmonds, *Pretty Modern*.

74. This is another representation of what Jocélio Teles dos Santos refers to as "strategic integration" of Afro-Brazilian culture. See Jocélio Teles dos Santos, "Mixed-Race Nation."

CHAPTER 3

1. See Gonçalves Filho, "Humilhação social"; Podkameni et al., "Afro-descendência, família e prevenção."

2. See Sampaoi, "Ecos da hipertensão."

3. See Goffman, *Stigma*, 3.

4. See Link and Phelan, "Conceptualizing Stigma."

5. See Wickrama et al., "Family Antecedents and Consequences of Trajectories of Depressive Symptoms from Adolescence to Young Adulthood," 471.

6. See McHale et al., "Congruence between Mothers' and Fathers' Differential Treatment of Siblings."

7. See Essed, *Understanding Everyday Racism*; Burdick, *Blessed Anastácia*.

8. See Kia Lilly Caldwell, *Negras in Brazil*, 113; Moura, "Dialética radical do Brasil negro."

9. France Winddance Twine uses the term *criada* for young girls who are informally adopted in Rio de Janeiro. In Bahia, they are more commonly referred to as *filhas de criação*. See Twine, *Racism in a Racial Democracy*; Fonseca, "Inequality Near and Far."

10. See Twine, *Racism in a Racial Democracy*.

11. Original Portuguese, provided here for nuance: "A gente sente a distancia na maneira de tratar, na maneira de ofender, de humilhar, tudo isso fica. De humilhar em frente de outros, de me xingar, de me bater... e deixar você assim com a cara no chão mesmo. Marcante eram as coisas ditas, as palavras, as humilhações; procura sua baixa posição vagabunda, frases, sabe em frente de outras . . . você não tem nada, não vai ter nada. Percebe que você é uma propriedade mesma. Na minha propriedade posso bater, posso pedir, posso fazer qualquer coisa."

12. See Twine, *Racism in a Racial Democracy*, 35–38.

13. Original Portuguese for nuance: "E muito fácil abrir a boca e dizer assim: 'É minha filha adotiva.' Mas você não é tratada como uma filha. Acho que para você sentir você tem que sentir carinho. Você tem que receber carinho... receber atenção. Como a filha! . . . Eu não sinto. . . . Você não pode mudar sua maneira de pensar, de ver as coisas que você passou que você ouviu e você botar um pano encima disso e dizer 'Não, é minha filha . . .'

14. Camila eventually rejected her mother's advice to distance herself from other blacks. Instead, she became an active practitioner of Candomblé.

15. See Sheriff, *Dreaming Equality*.

16. Lillian Comas-Díaz illustrates the way in which sibling relationships can be strained by internalized racism. See Comas-Díaz, "LatiNegra," 45.

17. Ibid.

18. See Burdick, *Blessed Anastácia*, 43.

19. Ibid.

20. See Ronilda Iyakẹmi Ribeiro, *Alma Africana no Brasil*, 171.

21. See Perry, *Black Women against the Land Grab*, 153.

22. See Jones and Shorter-Gooden, *Shifting*, 177.

23. See Ronilda Iyakẹmi Ribeiro, *Alma africana no Brasil*, 171.

24. She later begins to date a black man whose family is from another area and is supposedly wealthy. Months later, she is heartbroken to find out that he has been cheating on her during their entire relationship and even has a child from another woman.

25. See Fanon, *Black Skin, White Masks*, 116.

26. See Assunção, *Capoeira*.

27. Osmundo Pinho provides an excellent overview of the research on the ways black Brazilian men use corporeality and their bodies to embody an aesthetic that is nonwhite and is inspired by discourses and performances of black soul and hip-hop in the United States. See Osmundo Pinho, "Ethnographies of the *Brau*."

28. See Sansone, "Funk baiano," 225 (my translation).

29. See Osmundo Pinho, "Ethnographies," 6.

30. Although studies of differential treatment do not always focus on treatment based on race or phenotype, they do provide a model for understanding and studying

the consequences of parental differential treatment on sibling relationships. See Brody, Stoneman, and Burke, "Child Temperaments, Maternal Differential Behavior, and Sibling Relationships"; Brody, Stoneman, and McCoy, "Associations of Maternal and Paternal Direct and Differential Behavior with Sibling Relationships"; Volling, "The Family Correlates of Maternal and Paternal Perceptions of Differential Treatment in Early Childhood."

31. See Essed, *Understanding Everyday Racism*; Burdick, *Blessed Anastácia*.

32. See Burdick, *Blessed Anastácia*, 25.

33. See Fredrickson, "The Role of Positive Emotions in Positive Psychology," 220, 223.

34. See Henry, "Family System Characteristics, Parental Behaviors, and Adolescent Family Life Satisfaction"; Stocker, "Family Emotional Processes and Adolescents' Adjustment."

35. See Wickrama, "Family antecedents"; Thoits, "Identity-Relevant Events and Psychological Symptoms."

36. See hooks, *Black Looks*, 2.

37. See Sheriff, *Dreaming Equality*, 129.

CHAPTER 4

1. See Freire, *Pedagogy of the Oppressed*, 34.

2. The literature on racial socialization has been most prolific in the United States, where racial classification is viewed as more rigid than in Brazil. I argue that racial socialization is characterized by efforts to manipulate race, through an emphasis on color consciousness and efforts to manage racial appearance.

3. See Degler, *Neither Black or White*; Sheriff, *Dreaming Equality*; Sansone, *Blackness without Ethnicity*.

4. See Sansone, *Blackness without Ethnicity*.

5. Several researchers have studied the negotiation of racial and color terms in Brazil and in Latin America. Ginetta Candelario uses the phrase *strategic ambiguity* to describe the ways that Dominicans negotiate racial and color terms. Sheriff terms a similar process *semantic ambiguity*. A combination of both terms, strategic semantic ambiguity reflects how Afro-Brazilians exert agency in their manipulations of racial terms and recognizes that "meanings shift according to implicit and explicit points of reference." Sheriff, *Dreaming Equality*, 34; see also Candelario, *Black behind the Ears*.

6. Researchers who have discussed this phenomenon include Sheriff, *Dreaming Equality*; Twine, *Racism in a Racial Democracy*; and Burdick, *Blessed Anastácia*.

7. These issues of jealousy often appear when I am dealing with children or with women whom some call *carente* because they crave attention and tend to forge close relationships quickly.

8. See Telles, *Race in Another America*, 99

9. Brazil recently passed Lei 10.639/03, which requires that students be taught about the culture and history of Afro-Brazilians. See Gomes, "Limites e possibilidades da implementação da Lei 10.639/03 no contexto das políticas públicas em educação."

10. A cousin *de consideração* is a type of fictive kin, or "play cousin." It is a person who is not biologically related but is considered family because of their close relationship.

11. See Twine, *Racism in a Racial Democracy*, and Kia Lilly Caldwell, *Negras in Brazil*, for examples of this.

12. See Golash-Boza, *Yo Soy Negro*.

13. See Sansone, *Blackness without Ethnicity*.

14. See Telles, *Race in Another America*, 99.

15. I include the Portuguese translation to highlight that Dona Lara refers to her sons as "*negões.*" This distinction is important because it shows the extent to which she wants to convey that her sons are black. The term *negão* accentuates rather than minimizes blackness; colloquially it is used to describe dark-skinned black men who are large or strong. It is also often invoked to sexualize black men. Dona Lara's intention is to argue that intermediate terms are inaccurate descriptions for her black sons.

16. Roseane's mother is one of two people who question my authentic racial identity as *negra*. She argues that I am not as black as she is, even though she is several shades lighter than me. She explains that this is because she is from Brazil and I am from the United States.

17. See Twine, *Racism in a Racial Democracy*.

18. Not only does the purchase of whiteness certificates provide evidence for the construction of race, but the emotional investment in the strategy of changing race through legal forms transmits a strong message about racial hierarchies. See Dávila, *Diploma of Whiteness*.

19. See Skidmore, "Bi-Racial USA vs. Multi-Racial Brazil."

20. See Sansone, *Blackness without Ethnicity*.

21. See Twine, *A White Side of Black Britain*.

22. In her research on a large favela in Rio, Robin Sheriff found that residents used a variety of color categories though they understood themselves as either black or white. Sheriff, *Dreaming Equality*.

23. See Pierson, *Negroes in Brazil*; Butler, *Freedoms Given, Freedoms Won*.

24. Original Portuguese: "Nós temos uma piada que as pessoas no Brasil sempre se perguntam 'quem é branco?,' sobretudo na Bahia. Mas é uma falsa discussão porque a ideia que todos somos misturados . . . biologicamente até somos mesmos. Mas socialmente o que é que conta é que nós não somos. É isso que nos acostumamos a falar que na Bahia os que são considerados brancos baianos nao conseguem resistir ao teste do aeroporto de Guarulhos de São Paulo. Porque em São Paulo dizem, 'Aqui nós sabemos quem é branco.' Mas isso nao diminui as hierarquias sociais e raciais da Bahia. Porque também tem um modelo que é uma pigmentocracia. Quanto mais claro você for, maior é sua possibilidade de ascensão."

25. See Bonilla-Silva, Lewis, and Embrick, "'I Did Not Get That Job Because of a Black Man . . . ,'" 556.

26. See Freyre, *Masters and Slaves*, originally published in 1933.

27. See Bonilla-Silva, Lewis, and Embrick, "'I Did Not Get That Job,'" 556.

28. See Somers, "The Narrative Constitution of Identity"; Joyce, "Race Matters."

29. See Daniel, *Race and Multiraciality in Brazil and the United States*.

30. After our initial meetings, Leo, having turned nine years old, decides that he is interested in conducting his own research. During my visits to his home, he entertains my presence and often asks me to help him do research on the types of jewels given to the royal family. Eventually his research expands to me helping him find images about the Afro-Brazilian religion Candomblé on my iPad. Growing up in an avowedly Catholic family, he is curious about the religion.

31. See Scottham and Smalls, "Unpacking Racial Socialization"; Lesane-Brown, "A Review of Race Socialization within Black Families."

32. See Hanchard, *Orpheus and Power*.

33. See Nobles, *Shades of Citizenship*.

34. Kia Lilly Caldwell notes that the phrase "foot in the kitchen" is typically used by white Brazilians to acknowledge distant African ancestry. The use of the term *kitchen* is suggestive of domestic labor and the history of slavery. That only a foot is in the kitchen suggests that only a small part of the person's history can be traced back to slavery. See Caldwell, *Negras in Brazil*, 38.

CHAPTER 5

1. See Perry, *Black Women against the Land Grab*, 54.

2. Ibid., 43.

3. In a groundbreaking piece on how spatialized racial dimensions can shape multi-racial communities in the United States, Sarah Mayorga-Gallo speaks to the importance of considering the quality of interracial relationships in ostensibly multiracial environments. See Mayorga-Gallo, *Behind the White Picket Fence*.

4. See Telles, *Race in Another America*, 206. Michael George Hanchard discusses the consequences of transgressing racialized spaces in the public sphere, offering a poignant example in which he begins by analyzing a case of "elevator apartheid" and connecting it to structural exclusion. See Hanchard, "Black Cinderella?"

5. See Perry, *Black Women against the Land Grab*, 27.

6. See Figueiredo, "Out of Place," 62; see also Figueiredo, *Classe média negra*.

7. See Twine, *Racism in a Racial Democracy*; Sue and Golash-Boza, "It Was Only a Joke."

8. See Souza, *Tornar-se Negro*; Figueiredo, *Novas elites de cor*. Both of these works represent the most contemporary and comprehensive analyses of middle-class blacks in Brazil. Souza's work is considered a classic in psychology and the social sciences.

9. Cecilia McCallum captures this dynamic well. See McCallum, "Racialized Bodies, Naturalized Classes."

10. See Costa Vargas, *The Inner City and the Favela*.

11. I have previously written about the situation, in which Matheus and his cousins were accused of robbery and assault during a visit to the island of Itaparíca. He explained to the officers that they had arrived to the island minutes before, and there was no way they could have been involved with the robbery or assault. The police continued to harass the group of young men, and Matheus stated that as a law student he believed that the police had no just cause to accuse them. Matheus's "arrogance" angered police officers, who not only brutally beat him and his friends, but also forced them into the police vehicle, planted drugs on them once they arrived at the police station, and threatened to charge Matheus with drug trafficking. His wife and I went to the Public Ministry to report the situation. Matheus was in jail for over a month before he was released after agreeing to pay a bribe to the officer in charge of his case. See Hordge-Freeman, "Out of Bounds."

12. See Jorge da Silva, *Violência e racismo no Rio de Janeiro*; Costa Vargas, "The Inner City and the Favela."

13. See de Oliveira Rocha, "Black mothers' Experiences of Violence in Rio de Janeiro."

14. Sonia is eager to introduce me to the white family because she wants to show off the fact that an American is attending her birthday party. The white family is also interested in speaking to me, so they invite me over to sit down in their special area, and I have drinks with them. They ask to take pictures with me, and the men begin to harmlessly flirt with me. I sit for a while with them, but I have to negotiate this carefully, as neighborhood residents might view this interaction as betrayal or may even become jealous of my special treatment.

15. See Harding, *A Refuge in Thunder.*

16. See Scottham and Smalls, "Unpacking Racial Socialization"; Hughes et al. "Parents' Ethnic-Racial Socialization Practices."

17. See Figueiredo, *Classe média negra*; Figueiredo, "Out of Place."

18. Raíssa recognizes that she may be too protective, but she figures it is better to be safe than sorry. She describes another rule she uses: if Murilo comes home with something that he did not leave the house with and says it was given to him, she always calls the home of the parent of the child to confirm that he can, in fact, have the item so there are no misunderstandings. Considering how blacks are viewed suspiciously and that her young black son is thus vulnerable to suspicion, she considers this important to enforce.

19. See Figueiredo, "Out of Place," 53.

20. See Chvaicer, "The Criminalization of Capoeira in Nineteenth-Century Brazil," 525.

21. Ibid.

22. See Shirey, "Transforming the Orixás," 77.

23. See Brislola, "Umbanda e candomblé nao são religiões, diz juiz federal."

24. See Candelario, *Black behind the Ears*, 253.

25. At the same time, my natural, afro-textured hair may have been appropriate if it were not coarse, but rather a variation of spirally, curly, or wavy. These distinctions of hair gradations sometimes get lost in conversation that polarize "good" and "bad" hair.

26. See Candelario, "Hair-raceing," 136.

27. See Cavalleiro, "Processo de socialização na educação infantil."

28. See Gonçalves Filho, "Humilhação social."

29. Nineteen-year-old Danilo, interviewed for this study, is hoping to become an initiate of Candomblé. He reveals: "Candomblé is not viewed very well in Salvador. They only talk about it to 'chamar turista' (to attract tourists) because it is totally different."

30. See Bailey, *Legacies of Race*; Mitchell-Walthour, "Afro-Brazilian Black Linked Fate in Salvador and São Paulo, Brazil."

31. See Daniel, *Race and the Multiraciality in Brazil and the United States*, 199.

32. See Guimarães, *Racismo e anti-racismo no Brasil.*

33. Arguments against affirmative action are in some ways similar to the arguments that have been heard in the U.S. It has been discounted as reverse racism or special preferences to black students. However, in Brazil opponents also argue that it is difficult to know who is actually black and who is not. To this objection, Vilma Reis, a militant black activist, argues that the police do not seem to have difficulty determining who is black.

34. See Astor, "Brazil Tries Quotas to Get Racial Equality."

35. See Bernardino-Costa, "Levando a raça serio"; Guimarães, "Ações afirmativas para a população negra nas universidades brasileiras."

36. See Bonilla-Silva, Lewis, and Embrick, "I Did Not Get That Job because of a Black Man . . . ," 559.

37. Jan Hoffman French recognizes the tendency of the state to acknowledge indigenous rights while ignoring the rights of African-descendants and points out the ways that this has affected identity processes. See French, *Legalizing Identities*.

38. While the state of Bahia took pride in erecting a statue of Zumbi, the leader of the longest-lasting runaway slave community in the Americas, in the Pelourinho area respondents are overwhelmingly unaware of his significance. They know his name but not why he is important. When asked, one young girl erroneously explains that Zumbi was the president of Brazil.

39. Racial consciousness has historically been lower for poorer Brazilians. In my research I was much more likely to hear an educated Afro-Brazilian who had a professional job complain about the relationship between race and inequality than to hear someone with less education voice such a complaint. This reflects how class differences affect racial experiences and racial consciousness. See Figueiredo, *Classe média negra*; Figueiredo, "Out of Place."

40. See Caldwell, *Negras in Brazil*, 4.

41. See Wilson, "Natural Hair Song by Tirírica Deemed Racist, Sony Music Ordered to Pay $1.2 Million."

42. See Caldwell, *Negras in Brazil*.

43. See Jocélio Teles dos Santos, "A Mixed-Raced Nation."

44. See Paschel, "Re-Africanization and the Cultural Politics of Bahianidade."

45. There are initiatives requiring schools to incorporate Afro-Brazilian culture and history into classes and to phase out racist books that portray blacks as offensive caricatures.

46. See Paschel, "Re-Africanization," 423.

47. See Hughes and Chen, "The Nature of Caregivers' Race-Related Communications to Children."

48. See Paschel, "Re-Africanization and the Cultural Politics of Bahianidade," 428.

49. See Sommer, "Love and Country in Latin America."

50. See Joyce, "Race Matters: Race, Telenovela Representation, and Discourse in Contemporary Brazil."

51. Ibid., 28. Regarding the original film, see Araújo, *A negação do Brasil*.

52. See Freyre, *The Masters and the Slaves*.

53. See Araújo, *A negação do Brasil*.

54. Ibid.

55. The entire scene is filled with racial symbolism: her clothing, the bareness of her face and feet, and the image of her pleading on her knees with perhaps the most understood gesture of racial inferiority—a bowed head.

56. See Fanon, *Black Skin, White Masks*, 143.

57. Author's translation. See Ana Célia da Silva, "A desconstrução da discriminação no livro didático," 25.

58. Cavalleiro provides evidence that teachers are less likely to hug and show affection to nonwhite students than to other students. See Cavalleiro, "Processo de socialização."

59. For examples of the politics of respectability in Brazil and the United States, see Patricia Pinho, "Afro-aesthetics in Brazil." Also Frazier, *Black Bourgeoisie.*

60. See Brunson and Weitzer, "Negotiating Unwelcome Police Encounters," 426.

61. See Smith, "Race, Emotions, and Socialization," 103.

CHAPTER 6

1. See Foucault, *The History of Sexuality,* 95–96.

2. See Weitz, "Women and Their Hair," 667.

3. See Hanchard, *Orpheus and Power,* 6.

4. See Sansone, *Blackness without Ethnicity.*

5. Original Portuguese for nuance: "É pretinho, pretinho, pretinho, pretinho, pretinho." The term *pretinho* is a diminutive construction for the word *preto*, which, when referring to skin color, means unambiguously black or African-looking.

6. Original Portuguese for nuance: "Então, ele vai nascer torradinho assim. Com esta pele bonita, não é meu negro africano? Meu negro bom. Não é meu nego, meu africano? Chamei ele de meu nego lindo. Não é meu nego lindo? Adoro música africana, se a gente tivesse condições, compraria muita música africana."

7. See Twine, *Racism in a Racial Democracy*; Patricia de Santana Pinho, "White but Not Quite."

8. Two separate interviewees reference the movie *Mississippi Burning* to illustrate how bad race relations are in the United States. They do not emphasize the resistance of the black community but focus on the overt displays of racism by whites.

9. The significance of hair in fostering antiracism and racial pride has been addressed by a number of scholars from Brazil, as well as diasporic researchers. See Figueiredo, "Beleza pura"; Kia Lilly Caldwell, *Negras in Brazil*; Banks, *Hair Matters*; Leeds, *Ain't I a Beauty Queen?*; hooks, "Straightening Our Hair."

10. Tempted by the offer as an opportunity to engage in more hair talk and understand whether, if at all, Joana links her profession to the afro-aesthetics movement, I schedule an appointment. She cancels at the last minute.

11. Mega Hair is synthetic hair weave that is braided into a person's hair to add length and thickness. Many black women use Mega Hair to achieve a desired hairstyle, usually worn loose.

12. See Goldstein, *Laughter Out of Place,* 10.

13. Original Portuguese: "Primeiro, quem come é [são] as patroas e depois a empregada. É a hora de chamar a escrava . . . a escravinha da senzala mas ninguém quer ir. Agora aqui meu torradinho, pretinho!"

14. Twine, *Racism in a Racial Democracy,* 111.

15. Patricia Pinho, "Afro-Aesthetics in Brazil."

16. Porto das Galinhas, translated "the port of chickens," earned its name because contraband slaves arrived there with shipments of chickens. When the ships arrived, the porters would yell, "The chickens have arrived!"—code for the arrival of the enslaved Africans.

17. See Van Dijk, *Ideology.*

18. See Sandoval, "U.S. Third World Feminism," 270–271.

19. Ibid.

20. Original Portuguese for nuance: "Mas negro assumindo só sou eu. Sou negro,

mas não é só dizer que sou negro, dizer que é negro e assumir a negritude. Eu assumo porque sou negro me identifico como um descendente africano mesmo. Esta certo? Eu posso ser um pouco mais claro mais sou negro porque é como eu vou me definir. Posso ser branco ou negro e eu sou negro."

21. See Gilroy, "It's a Family Affair," 87.

22. See Mitchell, "Racism and Brazilian Democracy."

23. See Patricia Pinho, "Afro-Aesthetics."

24. See Moraes-Liu, *Deusa do Ébano*.

25. Amelia Simpson analyzes how the confluence of race, gender, and sexuality plays a critical role in Xuxa's rise to fame. She ultimately became an important aesthetic point of reference for Brazilian girls and women, and for Brazil as a nation.

26. See Patricia de Santana Pinho, *Mama Africa*.

27. See Freire, *Pedagogy of the Oppressed*, 45.

28. See Caldwell, *Negras in Brazil*, 155.

29. See Perry, *Black Women against the Land Grab*.

30. My translation: "Saber-se negra é viver a experiência de ter sido massacrada em sua identidade, confundida em suas perspectivas, submetida a exigências, compelida a expectativas alienadas. Mas é também, e, sobretudo, a experiência de comprometer-se a resgatar sua história e recriar-se em suas potencialidades." Neusa Santos Souza, *Tornar-se negro*.

31. See hooks, *Black Looks*.

32. See van Dijk, "Ideology."

33. See Kia Lilly Caldwell, *Negras in Brazil*, 17.

34. See Butler, *Freedoms Given, Freedoms Won*, 62.

35. See Butler, *Freedoms Given*; Hanchard, *Orpheus and Power*.

36. See Foucault, "History of Sexuality," 95–96.

CONCLUSION

1. See Du Bois, *The Souls of Black Folk*, 21.

2. Neusa Santos Souza's book *Tornar-se negro* is one of the best known books on black psychology in Brazil. Souza's tragic suicide was a devastating loss to the research community in Brazil. Coincidentally, two respondents in this study named black activists who had committed suicide during the course of their careers and insinuated that their deaths were connected to the angst about which Souza wrote. See Souza, *Tornar-se negro*.

3. See Gebara and Gomes, "Gênero, família e relações étnicorraciais."

4. See Burton et al., "Critical Race Theories, Colorism, and the Decade's Research on Families of Color," 455.

5. April Few-Demo provides a detailed overview of how intersectionality has been incorporated into family studies, often by researchers whose work is identified as critical race theory or feminist. See Few-Demo, "Intersectionality as the 'New' Critical Approach in Feminist Family Studies," 175.

6. See Few-Demo, "Intersectionality," 180; see also De Reus, Few, and Blume, "Multicultural and Critical Race Feminisms."

7. See Lewis, "Transcending the Grosser Physical Differences of Race in Contemporary Society," 26.

8. See Gebara and Gomes, "Gênero, família e relações étnicorraciais."

9. Researchers who study the ways in which emotions influence family dynamics do not always analyze the implications of this relationship for racialization and racial socialization. See Stocker, "Family Emotional Processes and Adolescents' Adjustment"; Stocker, Dunn, and Ploman, "Sibling Relationships."

10. See Collins, "Shifting the Center."

11. See Arnett, "Broad and Narrow Socialization," 619.

12. See Cavalleiro, Do silêncio do lar ao silêncio escolar.

13. See Parks and Banks-Wallace, "'So that Our Souls Don't Get Damaged.'"

14. See Barsade and O'Neill, "What's Love Got to Do with It?," 12.

15. See Frederickson, "The Role of Positive Emotions."

16. See Brown, "Critical Race Theory Speaks to the Sociology of Mental Health."

17. See hooks, Salvation.

18. Anadelia Romo critiques static portrayals of Salvador as a "living museum," which she argues is part of the marketing strategy supported by its tourist industry. See Romo, Brazil's Living Museum.

19. Jaira Harrington and I discuss how Afro-Brazilian women who are called filhas de criação continue to be exploited in their families, despite the passage of these laws. See Hordge-Freeman and Harrington, "Ties that Bind."

20. The notion of "mulatas de exportação" (export-quality mulatas) is suggestive of the way in which the European and international gaze shapes cultural and racial politics. See Giacomini, "Mulatas profissionais."

21. See Hellwig, African-American Reflections on Brazil's Racial Paradise.

22. Patricia de Santana Pinho uses this phrase to describe the use of images of cultural iconography that connect to Africa to promote the cultural project of Bahia. See Pinho, Mama Africa.

23. This theme is taken up in more detail in Appendix A, "Doing Diaspora."

24. Bonilla-Silva's Latin Americanization thesis of race relations in the U.S. illustrates how these global connections are sociologically important. Bonilla-Silva, "From Bi-Racial to Tri-Racial."

25. See Gilroy, Black Atlantic, 19.

26. See Wade, Race and Ethnicity in Latin America.

27. See Sidanius, et al., Inclusionary Discrimination; Torres-Saillant, "Creoleness or Blackness"; Candelario, Black behind the Ears.

28. See Torres-Saillant, "The Tribulations of Blackness," 1091.

29. Ibid., 1103; quote originally from García Godoy, "El derrumbe."

30. See Candelario, Black behind the Ears, 3; Trouillot, "Culture, Color, and Politics in Haiti."

31. See Trouillot, "Culture, Color, and Politics in Haiti."

32. See Santiago-Valles, "Puerto Rico."

33. See de la Fuente, A Nation for All.

34. See Sawyer, Peña, and Sidanius, "Cuban Exceptionalism."

35. Ibid.

36. See Daniel, Race and Multiraciality in Brazil and the United States.

37. See Bonilla-Silva, "From Bi-Racial to Tri-Racial"; Daniels, Race and Multiraciality; and Skidmore, "Bi-Racial USA vs. Multi-Racial Brazil."

38. See Russell, Wilson, and Hall, The Color Complex (Revised).

39. See Relethford et al., "Social Class, Admixture, and Skin Color Variation in

Mexican-Americans and Anglo-Americans living in San Antonio, Texas"; Candelario, *Black behind the Ears*; Jorge, "The Black Puerto Rican Woman in Contemporary American Society"; Blue Vein Societies are designed to foster relationships between blacks who were light enough for their veins to be seen through their skin. See Graham, *Our Kind of People*.

40. See Wade, *Race and Ethnicity in Latin America*; Graham, *Our Kind of People*.

41. See Castillo, "Massacre of the Dreamers"; Suárez-Findlay, *Imposing Decency*; Jorge, "Black Puerto Rican Woman."

42. See Wilder and Cain, "Teaching and Learning Color Consciousness in Black Families"; Hill, *Black Intimacies*; Hunter, "Colorstruck"; Thompson and Keith, "The Blacker the Berry"; Collins, *Black Sexual Politics*; Chavez-Dueñas, Adames, and Organista, "Skin-Color Prejudice and Within-Group Racial Discrimination: Historical and Current Impact on Latino/a Populations."

43. See Hill, *Black Intimacies*; Hunter, *Race, Gender, and the Politics of Skin Tone*; Herring, Keith, and Horton, *Skin Deep*; Telles, *Race in Another America*; Burdick, *Blessed Anastácia*; Goldstein, "'Interracial' Sex and Racial Democracy in Brazil."

44. See Fanon, *Black Skin, White Masks*, 47.

45. See Twine, *A White Side of Black Britain*; Steinbugler, *Beyond Loving*; Osuji, "Divergence or Convergence in the U.S. and Brazil"; Twine, *Racism in a Racial Democracy*.

46. See Candelario, *Black behind the Ears*; Banks, *Hair Matters*; Craig, *Ain't I a Beauty Queen?*

47. See Chavez-Dueñas, Adames, and Organista, "Skin-Color Prejudice," 17; Golden, *Don't Play in the Sun*; Jorge, "Black Puerto Rican Woman."

48. See Duke Media, *Dark Girls*, http://officialdarkgirlsmovie.com; Dale Wells-Marshall, director, *Memoirs of Melanin: Colorism in a Modern Bahamian Society*, forthcoming.

49. See Steinbugler, *Beyond Loving*; Twine, *A White Side of Black Britain*.

50. See Rahier, "Blackness, the Racial/Spatial Order, Migrations, and Miss Ecuador 1995–96"; Candelario, *Black behind the Ears*.

51. See hooks, *Black Looks*; Paulette M. Caldwell, "A Hair Piece"; hooks, "Straightening Our Hair"; Figueiredo, "Beleza pura"; Tate, "Black Beauty"; Banks, *Hair Matters*.

52. See Tate, *Black Beauty*; Paulette M. Caldwell, "A Hair Piece."

53. See Pinho, "Afro-Aesthetics in Brazil."

54. See Glenn, "Yearning for Lightness"; Lewis et. al, "The Tanzanian Response to Dangerous Skin Bleaching Products and the Gendered Politics Involved."

55. See Hall, "The Euro-Americanization of Race," 123.

56. See Fokuo, "The Lighter Side of Marriage," 133.

57. See Glenn, *Shades of Difference*.

58. See Zane, "Reflections on a Yellow Eye," 361.

59. See http://www.brightocular.com/aboutus.htm.

60. See Tracey Owens Patton, "Hey Girl, Am I More than My Hair?"

61. See Lowen, "Greek Roma Community Denies 'Blonde Angel' Abduction."

62. BBC News, "Greek Police Appeal over Mystery Blonde Girl."

63. Ibid.

64. A similar phenomenon in the United States, the missing white woman syndrome, functions in the same way. Young, white, attractive women and girls are the

most likely missing persons to be shown on television, and their overrepresentation creates the illusion that they suffer a unique vulnerability and are most worthy of saving because of their beauty and innocence.

65. See Adame, "The Blond 'Mexican Beggar Child' Story Holds a Mirror to US Perceptions of Race."

66. See Ware and Back, *Out of Whiteness*, 19.

67. See Stoler, "Carnal Knowledge and Imperial Power," 68–89.

68. See Bell, *Faces at the Bottom of the Well*, 10.

69. See hooks, *Black Looks*, 117.

70. See Collins, "The Meaning of Motherhood in Black Culture and Black Mother/Daughter Relationships," 77.

71. See Mullings, ed. *New Social Movements in the African Diaspora*.

72. See Du Bois, "The Souls of White Folk."

73. See Malomalo, "Branquitude como dominação do corpo"; Oliveira, "Representações sociais de branquitude em Salvador."

APPENDIX A

Much of what appears in this appendix has been previously published in Elizabeth Hordge-Freeman, "Out of Bounds: Negotiating Researcher Positionality in Brazil," in *Bridging Scholarship and Activism: Reflections from the Frontlines of Collaborative Research*, ed. Bernd Reiter and Ulrich Oslender (East Lansing: Michigan State University Press, 2015).

1. See McCallum, "Racialized Bodies, Naturalized Classes."

2. See Few, Stephens, and Rouse-Arnett, "Sister-to-Sister Talk," 207.

3. Ibid.

4. See Linda Tuhiwai Smith, *Decolonizing Methodologies*, 3; Hordge-Freeman, Mayorga, and Bonilla-Silva, "Exposing Whiteness because We Are Free."

5. See Ladner, *The Death of White Sociology*; Smith, *Decolonizing Methodologies*; Zuberi and Bonilla-Silva, *White Logic, White Methods*.

6. See Hordge-Freeman, Mayorga, and Bonilla-Silva, "Exposing Whiteness," 96; Zuberi and Bonilla-Silva, *White Logic*.

7. See Collins, "Learning from the Outsider Within"; Zuberi and Bonilla-Silva, *White Logic*.

8. See Twine and Warren, *Racing Research, Researching Race*.

9. See Gilliam and Gilliam, "Odyssey," 72.

10. See Collins, "Learning from the Outsider," 35.

11. See Erickson, "Rhetoric, Anecdote, and Rhapsody," 61.

12. See Zuberi and Bonilla-Silva, *White Logic, White Methods*.

13. See Peshkin, "In Search of Subjectivity—One's Own," 17.

14. Carnaval was both a wonderful diversion and also an incredibly important social space in which to watch racial dynamics unfold.

15. See Blumer, *Symbolic Interactionism*; Denzin and Lincoln, "Introduction: Entering the Field of Qualitative Research."

16. See Adler, Adler, and Rochford. "The Politics of Participation in Field Research."

17. See Glaser, *Emergence vs. Forcing*; Charmaz and Belgrave, "Qualitative Interviewing and Grounded Theory Analysis."

18. See Adler, Adler, and Rochford, "Politics of Participation."

19. See Emerson, et al., *Writing Ethnographic Fieldnotes*, 40.

20. See Charmaz, *The Grounded Theory Method*; Miller and Salkind, *Handbook of Research Design and Social Measurement*.

21. See Essed, *Understanding Everyday Racism*.

22. See Burton et al., "The Role of Trust in Low-Income Mothers' Intimate Unions"; LaRossa, "Grounded Theory Methods and Qualitative Family Research."

23. See Blumer, *Symbolic Interactionism*.

24. See Burton et al., "Role of Trust"; LaRossa, "Grounded Theory Methods."

25. See Emerson, *Writing Ethnographic Fieldnotes*.

26. See LaRossa, "Grounded Theory Methods."

27. See Emerson, *Writing Ethnographic Fieldnotes*.

Abreu, Martha. "Mulatas, Crioulos, and Morenas: Racial Hierarchy, Gender Relations, and National Identity in Postabolition Popular Song: Southeastern Brazil, 1890–1920," trans. Amy Chazkel and Junia Claudia Zaidan. In *Gender and Slave Emancipation in the Atlantic World*, ed. Pamela Scully and Diana Paton, 267–288. Durham, N.C.: Duke University Press, 2005.

Adame, Susana. "The Blond 'Mexican Beggar Child' Story Holds a Mirror to US Perceptions of Race." *The Guardian*, October 30, 2012. http://www.theguardian.com /commentisfree/2012/oct/30/blond-mexican-beggar-child-story-us-race.

Adelman, Miriam, and Lennita Ruggi. "The Beautiful and the Abject: Gender, Identity, and Constructions of the Body in Contemporary Brazilian Culture." *Current Sociology* 56, no. 4 (2008): 555–586.

Adler, Patricia A., Peter Adler, and E. Burke Rochford. "The Politics of Participation in Field Research." *Journal of Contemporary Ethnography* 14, no. 4 (1986): 363–376.

Alexander, Bryant Keith. *Performing Black Masculinity: Race, Culture, and Queer Identity*. New York: AltaMira, 2006.

Alleyne, Mervyn C. *The Construction and Representation of Race and Ethnicity in the Caribbean and the World*. Kingston, Jamaica: University of the West Indies Press, 2005.

Araújo, Joel Zito. *A negação do Brasil: O negro na telenovela brasileira*. São Paulo: Senac, 2000.

Arendell, Terry. "Conceiving and Investigating Motherhood: The Decade's Scholarship." *Journal of Marriage and Family* 62, no. 4 (2000): 1192–1207.

Armstrong, Piers. "The Aesthetic Escape Hatch: Carnaval, Blocos Afro and the Mutations of Baianidade under the Signs of Globalisation and Re-Africanisation." *Journal of Iberian and Latin American Research* 5, no. 2 (1999): 65–98.

Arnett, Jeffrey Jensen. "Broad and Narrow Socialization: The Family in the Context of a Cultural Theory." *Journal of Marriage and the Family* (1995): 617–628.

Assunção, Matthias Röhrig. *Capoeira: The History of an Afro-Brazilian Martial Art*. New York: Routledge, 2004.

Astor, Michael. "Brazil Tries Quotas to Get Racial Equality." *Los Angeles Times*, February 29, 2004, A3.

Bailey, Stanley R. *Legacies of Race: Identities, Attitudes, and Politics in Brazil*. Redwood City, Calif.: Stanford University Press, 2009.

Banks, Ingrid. *Hair Matters: Beauty, Power, and Black Women's Consciousness*. New York: NYU Press. 2000

Baran, Michael D. "'Girl, You Are Not Morena. We Are Negras!': Questioning the Concept of 'Race' in Southern Bahia, Brazil." *Ethos* 35, no. 3 (2007): 383–409.

Barbosa, Irene María F. *Socialização e relações raciais: Um estudo de família negra em Campinas*, Vol. 5. São Paulo: FFLCH Fac. de Filosofia, Letras e Ciências Humanas, 1983.

Barsade, Sigal, and Olivia A. O'Neill. "What's Love Got to Do with It?: The Influence of a Culture of Companionate Love in the Long-term Care Setting." *Administrative Science Quarterly* (May 29, 2014).

BBC News. "Greek Police Appeal over Mystery Blonde Girl." October 19, 2013. http://www.bbc.com/news/world-europe-24589614.

Bell, Derrick A. *Faces at the Bottom of the Well: The Permanence of Racism.* New York: Basic Books, 1992.

Bernardino-Costa, Joaze. "Levando a raça a sério: Ação afirmativa correto reconhecimento." In *Levando a raça a sério: Ação afirmativa e universidade,* ed. Joaze Bernardino-Costa and Daniela Galdino. Rio de Janeiro: DP&A editores, 2004.

Blum, Linda M. "Mother-Blame in the Prozac Nation: Raising Kids with Invisible Disabilities." *Gender and Society* 21, no. 2 (2007): 202–226.

Blumer, Herbert. *Symbolic Interactionism: Perspective and Method.* Berkeley: University of California Press, 1969.

Bonilla-Silva, Eduardo. "From Bi-Racial to Tri-Racial: Towards a New System of Racial Stratification in the USA." *Ethnic and Racial Studies* 27, no. 6 (2004): 931–950.

———. "Rethinking Racism: Toward a Structural Interpretation." *American Sociological Review* 62, no. 3 (1997): 465–480.

Bonilla-Silva, Eduardo, and David Dietrich. "The Latin Americanization of Racial Stratification in the U.S." In *Racism in the 21st Century,* ed. Ronald Hall, 151–170. New York: Springer, 2008.

Bonilla-Silva, Eduardo, Amanda Lewis, and David G. Embrick. "'I Did Not Get That Job because of a Black Man . . .'": The Story Lines and Testimonies of Color-Blind Racism." *Sociological Forum* 19, no. 4 (2004): 555–581.

Borges, Dain. "'Puffy, Ugly, Slothful, and Inert': Degeneration in Brazilian Social Thought, 1880–1940." *Journal of Latin American Studies* 25, no. 02 (1993): 235–256.

Bourdieu, Pierre. "Cultural Reproduction and Social Reproduction." In *Knowledge, Education, and Cultural Change,* ed. Richard Brown, 71–84. London: Tavistock, 1973.

———. *Distinction: A Social Critique of the Judgement of Taste.* Cambridge, Mass.: Harvard University Press, 1984.

Boyd-Franklin, Nancy. *Black Families in Therapy: Understanding the African American Experience.* New York: Guilford, 2013.

Bradford, Harry. "Brazil's Poor Receiving Plastic Surgery Free of Charge." *Huffington Post,* March 23, 2012. www.huffingtonpost.com/2012/03/23/plastic-surgery-brazil-poor_n_1375242.html.

Brisolla, Fabio. "Umbanda e candomblé nao são religiões, diz juiz federal," *Folha de São Paulo,* May 16, 2014. http://www1.folha.uol.com.br/poder/2014/05/1455758-umbanda-e-candomble-nao-sao-religioes-diz-juiz-federal.shtml.

Brito, Angela. "Lares negros olhares negros: Identidade e socialização em famílias negras e inter-raciais." *Revista Serviço Social, Londrina* 15, no. 2 (2013): 74–102.

Brody, Gene H., Zolinda Stoneman, and Michelle Burke. "Child Temperaments, Maternal Differential Behavior, and Sibling Relationships." *Developmental Psychology* 23, no. 3 (1987): 354–362.

Brody, Gene H., Zolinda Stoneman, and J. Kelly McCoy. "Associations of Maternal and Paternal Direct and Differential Behavior with Sibling Relationships: Contemporaneous and Longitudinal Analyses." *Child Development* 63, no. 1 (1992): 82–92.

Brown, Jacqueline Nassy. *Dropping Anchor, Setting Sail: Geographies of Race in Black Liverpool.* Princeton, N.J.: Princeton University Press, 2005.

Brown, Tony N. "Critical Race Theory Speaks to the Sociology of Mental Health: Mental Health Problems Produced by Racial Stratification." *Journal of Health and Social Behavior* 44, no. 3 (2003): 292–301.

Brown-Glaude, Winnifred. "The Fact of Blackness? The Bleached Body in Contemporary Jamaica." *Small Axe* 11, no. 3 (2007): 34–51.

Brunson, Rod K., and Ronald Weitzer. "Negotiating Unwelcome Police Encounters: The Intergenerational Transmission of Conduct Norms." *Journal of Contemporary Ethnography* 40, no. 4 (2011): 425–456.

Burdick, John. *Blessed Anastácia: Women, Race, and Popular Christianity in Brazil.* New York: Psychology Press, 1998.

Burton, Linda M., Eduardo Bonilla-Silva, Victor Ray, Rose Buckelew, and Elizabeth Hordge-Freeman. "Critical Race Theories, Colorism, and the Decade's Research on Families of Color." *Journal of Marriage and Family* 72, no. 3 (2010): 440–459.

Burton, Linda M., Andrew Cherlin, Donna-Marie Winn, Angela Estacion, and Clara Holder-Taylor. "The Role of Trust in Low-Income Mothers' Intimate Unions." *Journal of Marriage and Family* 71, no. 5 (2009): 1107–1124.

Burton, Linda M., Diane Purvin, and Raymond Garrett-Peters. "Longitudinal Ethnography: Uncovering Domestic Abuse in Low-Income Women's Lives." In *The Craft of Life Course Research*, ed. Glen H. Elder and Janet Z. Giele, 70–92. New York: Guildford, 2009.

Butler, Kim D. *Freedoms Given, Freedoms Won: Afro-Brazilians in Post-Abolition Sao Paulo and Salvador.* New Brunswick, N.J.: Rutgers University Press, 1998.

Caldwell, Kia Lilly. "'Look at Her Hair': The Body Politics of Black Womanhood in Brazil." *Transforming Anthropology* 11, no. 2 (2003): 18–29.

———. *Negras in Brazil: Re-Envisioning Black Women, Citizenship, and the Politics of Identity.* New Brunswick, N.J.: Rutgers University Press, 2007.

Caldwell, Paulette M. "A Hair Piece: Perspectives on the Intersection of Race and Gender." *Duke Law Journal* (1991): 365–396.

Candelario, Ginetta. *Black behind the Ears: Dominican Racial Identity from Museums to Beauty Shops.* Durham, N.C.: Duke University Press, 2007.

———. "Hair Race-ing: Dominican Beauty Culture and Identity Production." *Meridians* 1, no. 1 (2000): 128–156.

Castillo, Ana. "Massacre of Dreams: Essays on Xicanisma." In *Chicana Feminist Thought: The Basic Historical Writings*, ed. Alma M. Garcia and Mario T. Garcia, 310–312. New York: Routledge, 2014.

Cavalleiro, E. S. "Processo de socialização na educação infantil: Construção do silêncio e da submissão." *Revista Brasileira de Crescimento e Desenvolvimento Humano* 9, no. 2 (1999): 33–45.

Cavalleiro, Eliane dos Santos. *Do silêncio do lar ao silêncio escolar: Racismo, preconceito e discriminação na educação infantil.* São Paulo: Editora Contexto, 2000.

Charmaz, Kathy. *Constructing Grounded Theory: A Practical Guide through Qualitative Research.* Thousand Oaks, Calif.: SAGE, 2006.

———. "The Grounded Theory Method: An Explication and Interpretation." In *Contemporary Field Research*, ed. Robert M. Emerson, 109–126. Boston: Little, Brown, 1983.

Charmaz, Kathy, and Linda Liska Belgrave. "Qualitative Interviewing and Grounded Theory Analysis." In *The SAGE Handbook of Interview Research: The Complex-*

ity of the Craft, 2nd edition, ed. Jaber F. Gubrium et al. Thousand Oaks, Calif.: SAGE, 2002.

Chavez-Dueñas, Nayeli Y., Hector Y. Adames, and Kurt C. Organista. "Skin-Color Prejudice and Within-Group Racial Discrimination: Historical and Current Impact on Latino/a Populations." *Hispanic Journal of Behavioral Sciences* 36, no. 1 (2014): 3–26.

Chvaicer, Maya Talmon. "The Criminalization of Capoeira in Nineteenth-Century Brazil." *Hispanic American Historical Review* 82, no. 3 (2002): 525–547.

Collins, Patricia Hill. *Black Feminist Thought: Knowledge, Consciousness, and the Politics of Empowerment.* New York: Routledge, 1999.

———. *Black Sexual Politics: African Americans, Gender, and the New Racism.* New York: Routledge, 2005.

———. "It's All in the Family: Intersections of Gender, Race, and Nation." *Hypatia* 13, no. 3 (1998): 62–82.

———. "Learning from the Outsider Within: The Sociological Significance of Black Feminist Thought." In *Beyond Methodology: Feminist Research as Lived Research,* ed. M. Fonow and J. Cook, 35–39. Bloomington: Indiana University Press, 1991.

———. "The Meaning of Motherhood in Black Culture and Black Mother/Daughter Relationships." In *Toward a New Psychology of Gender: A Reader,* ed. Mary M. Gergen and Sara N. Davis, 325–340. New York: Routledge, 1997.

———. "Shifting the Center: Race, Class, and Feminist Theorizing about Motherhood." *Mothering: Ideology, Experience, and Agency,* ed. Evelyn Nakano Glenn, Grace Chang, and Linda Rennie Forcey, 45–65. New York: Psychology Press, 1994.

Comas-Díaz, Lillian. "LatiNegra: Mental Health Issues of African Latinas." *Journal of Feminist Family Therapy* 5, no. 3–4 (1994): 35–74.

Conrad, Robert. *Children of God's Fire: A Documentary History of Brazilian Slavery.* Princeton, N.J.: Princeton University Press, 1994.

Costa, Sérgio. *As cores de Ercília: esfera pública, democracia, configurações pós-nacionais.* Belo Horizonta, Brazil: Editora UFMG, 2002.

Costa Vargas, João. "The Inner City and the Favela: Transnational Black Politics." *Race and Class* 44, no. 4 (2003): 19–40.

Craig, Maxine Leeds. *Ain't I a Beauty Queen? Black Women, Beauty, and the Politics of Race.* Oxford: Oxford University Press, 2002.

Cruz, Cíntia Câmara Pinto da. "Os cabelos mágicos: Identidade e consumo de mulheres afrodescendentes no Instituto Beleza Natural." Dissertation, Universidade Federal do Recôncavo da Bahia, 2013.

d'Adesky, Jacques. *Pluralismo étnico e multiculturalismo: racismos e anti-racismos no Brasil.* Rio de Janeiro: Pallas, 2001.

da Matta, Roberto. *A casa e a rua: espaço, cidadania, mulher e morte no Brasil.* São Paulo: Brasiliense, 1985.

Daniel, G. Reginald. *Race and Multiraciality in Brazil and the United States: Converging Paths?* University Park, Pa.: Penn State University Press, 2010.

da Silva, Ana Célia. "A desconstrução da discriminação no livro didático." In *Superando o racismo na escola,* 2nd revised edition, organized by Kabengele Munanga, 21–37. Brasília: MEC, 2005.

da Silva, Jorge. *Violência e racismo no Rio de Janeiro.* Niterói, Brazil: Editora da Universidade Federal Fluminense, 2003.

Dávila, Jerry. *Diploma of Whiteness: Race and Social Policy in Brazil, 1917–1945.* Durham, N.C.: Duke University Press, 2003.

de Casanova, Erynn Masi. "'No Ugly Women': Concepts of Race and Beauty among Adolescent Women in Ecuador." *Gender and Society* 18, no. 3 (2004): 287–308.

Degler, Carl N. *Neither Black nor White: Slavery and Race Relations in Brazil and the United States.* Madison: University of Wisconsin Press, 1971.

de la Fuente, Alejandro. *A Nation for All: Race, Inequality, and Politics in Twentieth-Century Cuba.* Chapel Hill: North Carolina University Press, 2001.

Denzin, Norman K., and Yvonna S. Lincoln. "Introduction: Entering the Field of Qualitative Research." In *Handbook of Qualitative Research,* ed. Norman K. Denzin and Yvonna S. Lincoln, 1–19. Thousand Oaks, Calif.: SAGE.

de Oliveira Rocha, Luciane. "Black Mothers' Experiences of Violence in Rio de Janeiro." *Cultural Dynamics* 24, no. 1 (2012): 59–73.

de Queirós Mattoso, Kátia M. *To Be a Slave in Brazil, 1550–1888.* New Brunswick, N.J.: Rutgers University Press, 1986.

De Reus, Lee Ann, April L. Few, and Libby Balter Blume. "Multicultural and Critical Race Feminisms: Theorizing Families in the Third Wave." In *Sourcebook of Family Theory and Research,* ed. Vern L. Bengston, Alan C. Acock, Katherine R. Allen, Peggye Dilworth-Anderson, and David M. Klein, 447–468. Thousand Oaks, Calif.: SAGE, 2004.

Dickson-Swift, Virginia, Erica L. James, Sandra Kippen, and Pranee Liamputtong. "Blurring Boundaries in Qualitative Health Research on Sensitive Topics." *Qualitative Health Research* 16, no. 6 (2006): 853–871.

Dominguez, Virginia R. "A Taste for 'the Other': Intellectual Complicity in Racializing Practices." *Current Anthropology* 35, no. 4 (1994): 333–348.

Donoghue, Denis. *Speaking of Beauty.* New Haven: Yale University Press, 2003.

dos Santos, Jocélio Teles. "A Mixed-Race Nation: Afro-Brazilians and Cultural Policy in Bahia, 1970–1990." *Afro-Brazilian Culture and Politics: Bahia, 1790s to 1990s,* ed. Hendrik Kraay, 117–133. Armonk, N.Y.: M. E. Sharpe, 1998.

———. "O negro no espelho: imagens e discursos nos salões de beleza étnicos." *Estudos afro-asiáticos* 38 (2000): 49–65.

dos Santos, Sales Augusto, and Laurence Hallewell. "Historical Roots of the 'Whitening' of Brazil." *Latin American Perspectives* 20, no. 1 (2002): 61–82.

Douglas, Lydia Ann. "Nappy." Video recording. Howard University, Peazey Head Productions and Women Make Movies, 1997.

Du Bois, W. E. B. *The Souls of Black Folk.* Oxford: Oxford University Press, 1903.

———. "The Souls of White Folk." In *Darkwater: Voices from within the Veil.* New York: Harcourt, Brace and Company, 1920.

Dworkin, Andrea. *Woman Hating.* New York: Dutton, 1974.

Edmonds, Alexander. "'The Poor Have the Right to Be Beautiful': Cosmetic Surgery in Neoliberal Brazil." *Journal of the Royal Anthropological Institute* 13, no. 2 (2007): 363–381.

———. *Pretty Modern: Beauty, Sex, and Plastic Surgery in Brazil.* Durham, N.C.: Duke University Press, 2010.

Emerson, Robert M., Rachel I. Fretz, and Linda L. Shaw. *Writing Ethnographic Fieldnotes.* Chicago: University of Chicago Press, 2011.

Erickson, Frederick. "Rhetoric, Anecdote, and Rhapsody: Coherence Strategies in a Conversation among Black American Adolescents." In *Coherence in Spoken and*

Written Discourse, ed. Deborah Tannen, 81–154. Santa Barbara, Calif.: Praeger, 1984.

Essed, Philomena. *Understanding Everyday Racism: An Interdisciplinary Theory.* Thousand Oaks, Calif.: SAGE, 1991.

Etherington, Kim. "Working with Traumatic Stories: From Transcriber to Witness." *International Journal of Social Research Methodology* 10, no. 2 (2007): 85–97.

Fanon, Frantz. *Black Skin, White Masks*, ed. Charles Lam Markmann. New York: Grove, 1952/1967.

Few, April L., Dionne P. Stephens, and Marlo Rouse-Arnett. "Sister-to-Sister Talk: Transcending Boundaries and Challenges in Qualitative Research with Black Women." *Family Relations* 52, no. 3 (2003): 205–215.

Few-Demo, April L. "Intersectionality as the 'New' Critical Approach in Feminist Family Studies: Evolving Racial/Ethnic Feminisms and Critical Race Theories." *Journal of Family Theory and Review* 6, no. 2 (2014): 169–183.

Figueiredo, Angela. "Beleza pura: Símbolos e economia ao redor do cabelo negro." Monografia para conclusão do curso de Ciências Sociais. Universidade Federal da Bahia, 1984.

———. *Classe média negra: Trajetórias e perfis.* Salvador, Brazil: Editora da Universidade Federal da Bahia, 2012.

———. *Novas elites de cor: Estudo sobre os profissionais liberais negros de Salvador.* São Paulo: Annablume, 2002.

———. "Out of Place: The Experience of the Black Middle Class." In *Brazil's New Racial Politics*, ed. Bernd Reiter and Gladys L. Mitchell, 89–122. Boulder, Colo.: Lynne Rienner, 2010.

FitzSimmons, Ellen, Jack H. Prost, and Sharon Peniston. "Infant Head Molding: A Cultural Practice." *Archives of Family Medicine* 7, no. 1 (1998): 88.

Fokuo, Konadu J. "The Lighter Side of Marriage: Skin Bleaching in Post-Colonial Ghana." *African and Asian Studies* 8, no. 1 (2009): 125–146.

Fonseca, Claudia. "Inequality Near and Far: Adoption as Seen from the Brazilian Favelas." *Law and Society Review* (2002): 397–432.

Foucault, Michel. *Discipline and Punish: The Birth of the Prison.* New York: Random House, 1977.

———. *The History of Sexuality*, Vol. I: *An Introduction*, trans. R. Hurley. New York: Vintage, 1978.

Frazier, E. Franklin. *Black Bourgeoisie.* New York: Simon and Schuster, 1957.

———. "The Negro Family in Bahia, Brazil." *American Sociological Review* 7, no. 4 (1942): 465–478.

Fredrickson, Barbara L. "The Role of Positive Emotions in Positive Psychology: The Broaden-and-Build Theory of Positive Emotions." *American Psychologist* 56, no. 3 (2001): 218–226.

Freire, Paulo. *Pedagogy of the Oppressed.* New York: Bloomsbury, 2000.

French, Jan Hoffman. *Legalizing Identities: Becoming Black or Indian in Brazil's Northeast.* Chapel Hill: University of North Carolina Press, 2009.

French, John D. "The Missteps Of Anti-Imperialist Reason: Bourdieu, Wacquant and Hanchard's Orpheus and Power." *Theory, Culture and Society* 17, no. 1 (2000): 107–128.

———. "Translation, Diasporic Dialogue, and the Errors of Pierre Bourdieu and Loïc Wacquant." *Nepantla: Views from South* 4, no. 2 (2003): 375–389.

Freyre, Gilberto. *The Masters and the Slaves (Casa-grande e Senzala): A Study in the Development of Brazilian Civilization*, trans. Samuel Putnam, abridged from the 2nd English-language ed., rev. New York: Knopf, 1964.

García Godoy, Federico. "El derrumbe." Santo Domingo: Editora de la Universidad Autónoma de Santo Domingo (1975).

Gebara, Tânia, and Nilma Gomes. "Gênero, família e relações étnicorraciais: Um estudo sobre as estratégias elaboradas por mulheres negras e brancas provedoras nas relações estabelecem com a educação de seus filhos(as)." *Revista Fórum Identidades* 10, no. 10 (2011): 115–133.

Giacomini, Sônia. "Mulatas profissionais: Raça, gênero e ocupação." *Revista Estudos Feministas* 14, no. 1 (2006): 85–101.

Gilliam, Angela, and Onik'a Gilliam. "Odyssey: Negotiating the Subjectivity of *Mulata* Identity in Brazil." *Latin American Perspectives* 26, no. 3 (1999): 60–84.

Gilroy, Paul. *The Black Atlantic: Modernity and Double Consciousness.* Cambridge, Mass.: Harvard University Press, 1993.

———. "It's a Family Affair." In *That's the Joint: The Hip-Hop Studies Reader,* ed. Murray Forman and Mark Anthony Neal, 87–103. New York: Taylor and Francis, 2004.

Glaser, Barney G. *Emergence vs. Forcing: Basics of Grounded Theory Analysis.* Mill Valley, Calif.: Sociology Press, 1992.

Glenn, Evelyn Nakano, ed. *Shades of Difference: Why Skin Color Matters.* Redwood City, Calif.: Stanford University Press, 2009.

———. "Yearning for Lightness: Transnational Circuits in the Marketing and Consumption of Skin Lighteners." *Gender and Society* 22, no. 3 (2008): 281–302.

Goffman, Erving. *Stigma: Notes on the Management of Spoiled Identity.* New York: Simon and Schuster, 2009.

Golash-Boza, Tanya Maria. *Yo Soy Negro: Blackness in Peru.* Gainesville: University Press of Florida, 2011.

Golden, Marita. *Don't Play in the Sun: One Woman's Journey through the Color Complex.* New York: Random House, 2007.

Goldstein, Donna. "'Interracial' Sex and Racial Democracy in Brazil: Twin Concepts?" *American Anthropologist* 101, no. 3 (1999): 563–578.

———. *Laughter Out of Place: Race, Class, Violence, and Sexuality in a Rio Shantytown.* Oakland: University of California Press, 2013.

Gomes, Nilma Lino. *A mulher negra que vi de perto: O processo de construção da identidade racial de professoras negras.* Belo Horizonte, Brazil: Mazza Edições, 1995.

———. "Limites e possibilidades da implementação da Lei 10.639/03 no contexto das políticas públicas em educação." In *Caminhos convergentes: Estado e sociedade na superação das desigualdades raciais no Brasil,* 39–74. Rio de Janeiro: Fundação Heinrich Boll, ActionAid, 2009.

———. *Sem perder a raiz: Corpo e cabelo como símbolos da identidade negra.* Belo Horizonte, Brazil: Autêntica, 2006.

Gonçalves Filho, José Moura. "Humilhação social: Um problema político em psicologia." *Psicologia USP* 9, no. 2 (1998): 11–67.

Gordilho-Souza, Angela. *Limites do habitar: Segregação e exclusão na configuração urbana contemporânea de Salvador e perspectivas no final do século XX.* Salvador, Brazil: EDUFBA, 2000.

Gordon, Doreen. "A Beleza abre Portas: Beauty and the Racialised Body among Black Middle-Class Women in Salvador, Brazil." *Feminist Theory* 14, no. 2 (2013): 203–218.

Gossett, Thomas F. *Race: The History of an Idea in America*. Oxford: Oxford University Press, 1997.

Graham, Lawrence Otis. *Our Kind of People*. New York: HarperCollins, 2009.

Gregg, Jessica L. *Virtually Virgins: Sexual Strategies and Cervical Cancer in Recife, Brazil*. Redwood City, Calif.: Stanford University Press, 2003.

Guerreiro Ramos, Alberto. "O negro desde dentro." *Revista Forma* 3 (1954).

Guimarães, Antônio Sergio Alfredo. "Ações afirmativas para a população negra nas universidades brasileiras." In *Ações afirmativas políticas públicas contra as desigualdades raciais*, ed. Renato Emerson dos Santos and Fátima Lobato. Rio de Janeiro: Lamparina Editora, 2003.

———. *Classes, Raças e Democracias*. São Paulo: Editora 34, 2002.

———. *Racismo e anti-racismo no Brasil*. São Paulo: Editora 34, 1999.

Guridy, Frank Andre. *Forging Diaspora: Afro-Cubans and African Americans in a World of Empire and Jim Crow*. Chapel Hill: University of North Carolina Press, 2010.

Hall, Ronald E. "The Euro-Americanization of Race: Alien Perspective of African Americans vis-à-vis Trivialization of Skin Color." *Journal of Black Studies* 36, no. 1 (2005): 116–128.

Hanchard, Michael. "Black Cinderella?: Race and the Public Sphere in Brazil." *Public Culture* 7, no. 1 (1994): 165–185.

Hanchard, Michael George. *Orpheus and Power: The Movimento Negro of Rio de Janeiro and São Paulo, Brazil 1945–1988*. Princeton, N.J.: Princeton University Press, 1998.

Harding, Rachel E. *A Refuge in Thunder: Candomblé and Alternative Spaces of Blackness*. Bloomington: Indiana University Press, 2003.

Harris, Angela P. "From Color Line to Color Chart: Racism and Colorism in the New Century." *Berkeley Journal of African-American Law and Policy* 10 (2008): 52.

Harris, Marvin, Josildeth Gomes Consorte, Joseph Lang, and Bryan Byrne. "Who Are the Whites?: Imposed Census Categories and the Racial Demography of Brazil." *Social Forces* 72, no. 2 (1993): 451–462.

Hasenbalg, Carlos, and Nelson do Valle Silva. "Educação e diferenças raciais na mobilidade ocupacional no Brasil." In *Cor e estratificação social*, ed. C. Hasenbalg, N. V. Silva, and M. Lima, 217–230. Rio de Janeiro: Contracapa, 1999.

———. *Relações raciais no Brasil contemporâneo*. Rio de Janeiro: Rio Fundo Editora, 1992.

Hellwig, David J., ed. *African-American Reflections on Brazil's Racial Paradise*. Philadelphia: Temple University Press, 1992.

Henry, Carolyn S. "Family System Characteristics, Parental Behaviors, and Adolescent Family Life Satisfaction." *Family Relations* 43, no. 4 (1994): 447–455.

Herring, Cedric, Verna Keith, and Hayward Derrick Horton, eds. *Skin Deep: How Race and Complexion Matter in the "Color-Blind" Era*. Champaign: University of Illinois Press, 2004.

Herskovits, Melville Jean. *The Myth of the Negro Past*. Boston: Beacon, 1990.

Hill, Shirley A. *Black Intimacies: A Gender Perspective on Families and Relationships*. New York: AltaMira, 2004.

Hochschild, Arlie, and Anne Machung. *The Second Shift: Working Families and the Revolution at Home*. New York: Penguin, 2012.

Hofbauer, Andreas. *Uma história de branqueamento ou o negro em questão*. São Paulo: Editora UNESP, 2006.

hooks, bell. *Black Looks: Race and Representation*. Boston: South End Press, 1992.

———. *Salvation: Black People and Love*. New York: William Morrow, 2001.

———. "Straightening Our Hair." *Z Magazine*, September 1988.

Hordge-Freeman, Elizabeth. "Out of Bounds: Negotiating Researcher Positionality in Brazil." In *Bridging Scholarship and Activism: Reflections from the Frontlines of Collaborative Research*, ed. Bernd Reiter and Ulrich Oslender. East Lansing: Michigan State University Press, 2015.

———. "What's Love Got to Do with It?: Racial Features, Stigma, and Socialization in Afro-Brazilian Families." *Ethnic and Racial Studies* 36, no. 10 (2013): 1507–1523.

Hordge-Freeman, Elizabeth, and Jaira Harrington. "Ties that Bind: Localizing the Occupational Motivations that Drive Non-Affiliated Domestic Workers in Salvador, Brazil." In *Perspectives on Domestic and Caregiving Work: A Global Approach*, ed. Marcel van der Lindon. Leiden: Brill, forthcoming in 2015.

Hordge-Freeman, Elizabeth, Sarah Mayorga, and Eduardo Bonilla-Silva. "Exposing Whiteness because We Are Free: Emancipation Methodological Practice in Identifying and Challenging Racial Practices in Sociology Departments." In *Rethinking Race and Ethnicity in Research Methods*, ed. John Stanfield, 95–122. Walnut Creek, Calif: Left Coast Press, 2011.

Hughes, D., and Chen, L. "The Nature of Caregivers' Race-Related Communications to Children: A Developmental Perspective." In *Child Psychology: A Handbook of Contemporary Issues*, ed. Lawrence Balter and Catherine S. Tamis-LeMonda, 467–490. New York: Psychology Press, 1999.

Hughes, Diane, James Rodriguez, Emilie P. Smith, Deborah J. Johnson, Howard C. Stevenson, and Paul Spicer. "Parents' Ethnic-Racial Socialization Practices: A Review of Research and Directions for Future Study." *Developmental Psychology* 42, no. 5 (2006): 747.

Hunter, Margaret L. "Colorstruck: Skin Color Stratification in the Lives of African American Women." *Sociological Inquiry* 68, no. 4 (1998): 517–535.

———. *Race, Gender, and the Politics of Skin Tone*. New York, Routledge, 2013.

Ickes, Scott. *African-Brazilian Culture and Regional Identity in Bahia, Brazil*. Gainesville: University Press of Florida, 2013.

Jenson, Alexander C., Shawn D. Whiteman, Karen L. Fingerman, and Kira S. Birditt. "'Life Still Isn't Fair': Parental Differential Treatment of Young Adult Siblings." *Journal of Marriage and Family* 75, no. 2 (2013): 438–452.

Jones, Charisse, and Kumea Shorter-Gooden. *Shifting: The Double Lives of Black Women in America*. New York: Harper Perennial, 2004.

Jorge, Angela. "The Black Puerto Rican Woman in Contemporary American Society." In *The Puerto Rican Woman: Perspectives on Culture, History, and Society*, ed. Edna Acosta-Belén, 180–187. New York: Praeger, 1979.

Joyce, Samantha Nogueira. "Race Matters: Race, Telenovela Representation, and Discourse in Contemporary Brazil." Ph.D. diss., University of Iowa, 2010.

Kandiyoti, Deniz. "Bargaining with Patriarchy." *Gender and Society* 2, no. 3 (1988): 274–290.

Kane, Emily W. *The Gender Trap: Parents and the Pitfalls of Raising Boys and Girls.* New York: NYU Press, 2012.

Kraay, Hendrik, ed. *Afro-Brazilian Culture and Politics: Bahia, 1790s to 1990s.* Armonk, N.Y.: M. E. Sharpe, 1998.

Ladner, Joyce A. *The Death of White Sociology: Essays on Race and Culture.* New York: Vintage, 1973.

Landes, Ruth. *City of Women.* New York: Macmillan, 1947.

Lareau, Annette. *Unequal Childhoods: Race, Class, and Family Life.* Berkeley: University of California Press, 2003.

LaRossa, Ralph. "Grounded Theory Methods and Qualitative Family Research." *Journal of Marriage and Family* 67, no. 4 (2005): 837–857.

Larson, Reed W., and David M. Almeida. "Emotional Transmission in the Daily Lives of Families: A New Paradigm for Studying Family Process." *Journal of Marriage and the Family* (1999): 5–20.

Lesane-Brown, Chase L. "A Review of Race Socialization within Black Families." *Developmental Review* 26, no. 4 (2006): 400–426.

Lewis, K. M., N. Robkin, K. Gaska, L. C. Njoki, E. Andrews, and K. Jetha. "The Tanzanian Response to Dangerous Skin Bleaching Products and the Gendered Politics Involved: A Critical Analysis." *JENdA: Journal of Culture and African Women Studies* 10 (2009): 18–35.

Lewis, Linden. "Transcending the Grosser Physical Differences of Race in Contemporary Society: Introduction." In *Color, Hair, and Bone: Race in the Twenty-First Century,* ed. Linden Lewis, Glyne A. Griffith, and Elizabeth Crespo Kebler, 11–29. Plainsboro, N.J.: Associated University Press, 2008.

Lewis, Marva L. "Hair Combing Interactions: A New Paradigm for Research with African-American Mothers." *American Journal of Orthopsychiatry* 69, no. 4 (1999): 504–514.

Link, Bruce G., and Jo C. Phelan. "Conceptualizing Stigma." *Annual Review of Sociology* (2001): 363–385.

Lody, Raul. *Cabelos de axé: Identidade e resistência.* São Paulo: Editora Senac, 2004.

Lovell, Peggy A. "Race, Gender and Regional Labor Market Inequalities in Brazil." *Review of Social Economy* 58, no. 3 (2000): 277–293.

Loveman, Mara, Jeronimo O. Muniz, and Stanley R. Bailey. "Brazil in Black and White? Race Categories, the Census, and the Study of Inequality." *Ethnic and Racial Studies* 35, no. 8 (2012): 1466–1483.

Lowen, Mark. "Greek Roma Community Denies 'Blonde Angel' Abduction," October 20, 2013, http://www.bbc.co.uk/news/world-europe-24601917.

Malomalo, Basa Basilele. "Branquitude como dominação do corpo: Diálogo com a sociologia de Bourdieu." *Revista da Associação Brasileira de Pesquisadores Negros* 6, no. 13 (2014): 175–200.

Mayorga-Gallo, Sarah. *Behind the White Picket Fence: Power and Privilege in a Multiethnic Neighborhood.* Chapel Hill: University of North Carolina Press, 2014.

Mays, Dorothy A. *Women in Early America: Struggle, Survival, and Freedom in a New World.* Santa Barbara, Calif.: ABC-CLIO, 2004.

McCallum, Cecilia. "Racialized Bodies, Naturalized Classes: Moving through the City of Salvador da Bahia." *American Ethnologist* 32, no. 1 (2005): 100–117.

McClintock, Anne. *Imperial Leather: Race, Gender, and Sexuality in the Colonial Contest.* New York: Routledge, 2013.

McHale, Susan M., Ann C. Crouter, Shirley A. McGuire, and Kimberly A. Updegraff. "Congruence between Mothers' and Fathers' Differential Treatment of Siblings: Links with Family Relations and Children's Well-Being." *Child Development* 66, no. 1 (1995): 116–128.

McLoyd, Vonnie C., Ana Mari Cauce, David Takeuchi, and Leon Wilson. "Marital Processes and Parental Socialization in Families of Color: A Decade Review of Research." *Journal of Marriage and Family* 62, no. 4 (2000): 1070–1093.

Miller, Delbert C., and Neil J. Salkind, eds. *Handbook of Research Design and Social Measurement*. Thousand Oaks, Calif.: SAGE, 2002.

Mitchell, Gladys Lanier. "Racism and Brazilian Democracy: Two Sides of the Same Coin?" *Ethnic and Racial studies* 33, no. 10 (2010): 1776–1796.

Mitchell-Walthour, Gladys. "Afro-Brazilian Black Linked Fate in Salvador and São Paulo, Brazil." In *Black Politics in a Time of Transition*, ed. Michael Mitchell and David Covin, 41–62. Edison, N.J.: Transaction, 2011.

Moraes-Liu, Carolina, director. *Deusa do Ébano: Rainha do Ilê Aiyê*. DVD. New York: Third World Newsreel, 2010.

Morrison, Toni. *The Bluest Eye*. New York: Random House, 2007.

———. *Tar Baby*. New York: Knopf, 1981.

Moura, Clóvis. *Dialética radical do Brasil negro*. Editora Anita, 1994.

Moutinho, Laura. "Razão, 'Cor' e Desejo." *Population* 3 (2006): 377–380.

Mullings, Leith, ed. *New Social Movements in the African Diaspora: Challenging Global Apartheid*. London: Palgrave Macmillan, 2009.

Nascimento, Abdias do. *Mixture or Massacre? Essays in the Genocide of a Black People*, trans. Elisa Larkin Nascimento. Buffalo, N.Y.: Puerto Rican Studies and Research Center, State University of New York, 1979.

Nishida, Mieko. "Manumission and Ethnicity in Urban Slavery: Salvador, Brazil, 1808–1888." *Hispanic American Historical Review* (1993): 361–391.

Nobles, Melissa. *Shades of Citizenship: Race and the Census in Modern Politics*. Redwood City, Calif: Stanford University Press, 2000.

Nuttall, Sarah. "Rethinking Beauty." In *Beautiful/Ugly: African and Diaspora Aesthetics*, ed. Sarah Nuttall, 6–29. Cape Town: Kwela, 2006.

Oliveira, Lúcio. "Representações sociais de branquitude em Salvador." *Revista da Associação Brasileira de Pesquisadores Negros* 6, no. 13 (2014): 175–200.

Omi, Michael, and Howard Winant. *Racial Formation in the United States: From the 1960s to the 1990s*. New York: Psychology Press, 1994.

Osuji, Chinyere. "Divergence or Convergence in the U.S. and Brazil: Understanding Race Relations Through White Family Reactions to Black-White Interracial Couples." *Qualitative Sociology* 37, no. 1 (2014): 93–115.

Pacheco, Ana Cláudia Lemos. "Raça, gênero e relações sexual-afetivas na produção bibliográfica das ciências sociais brasileiras." *Afro-Ásia* 34 (2006): 153–188.

Parks, JoAnne, and Lenette Banks-Wallace. "'So that Our Souls Don't Get Damaged': The Impact of Racism on Maternal Thinking and Practice Related to the Protection of Daughters." *Issues in Mental Health Nursing* 22, no. 1 (2001): 77–98.

Paschel, Tianna. "Re-Africanization and the Cultural Politics of Bahianidade." *Souls: A Critical Journal of Black Politics, Society and Culture* 11, no. 4 (2008), 423–440.

Patton, Tracey Owens. "Hey Girl, Am I More than My Hair?: African-American Women and Their Struggles with Beauty, Body Image, and Hair." In *Contested*

Images: Women of Color in Popular Culture, ed. Alma M. Garcia, 111–136. New York: AltaMira,2012.

Perry, Keisha-Khan Y. *Black Women against the Land Grab: The Fight for Racial Justice in Brazil*. Minneapolis: University of Minnesota Press, 2013.

Peshkin, Alan. "In Search of Subjectivity—One's Own." *Educational Researcher* 17, no. 7 (1988): 17–21.

Peterson, Gary W., and Geoffry K. Leigh. "The Family and Social Competence in Adolescence." In *Developing Social Competency in Adolescence: Advances in Adolescent Development*, Vol. 3, ed. T. P. Gullotta, G. R. Adams, and R. Montemayor, 97–138. Newbury Park, Calif.: SAGE, 1990.

Petruccelli, José Luis. "Seletividade por cor e escolhas conjugais no Brasil dos 90." *Estudos afro-asiáticos* 23, no. 1 (2001): 29–51.

Pierre, Jemima. *The Predicament of Blackness: Postcolonial Ghana and the Politics of Race*. Chicago: University of Chicago Press, 2012.

Pierson, Donald. *Negroes in Brazil: A Study of Race Conflict in Bahia*. Carbondale: Southern Illinois University Press, 1967.

Pinho, Osmundo. "Ethnographies of the *Brau*: Body, Masculinity, and Race in the Reafricanization in Salvador." *Estudos Feministas* 13, no. 1 (2006): 127–145.

Pinho, Osmundo de Araújo. "Espaço, poder e relações raciais: O caso do centro histórico de Salvador." *Afro-Ásia*, nos. 21–22 (1998–1999): 257–274.

Pinho, Patricia. "Afro-Aesthetics in Brazil." In *Beautiful/Ugly: African and Diaspora Aesthetics*, ed. Sarah Nuttall, 266–289. Durham, N.C.: Duke University Press, 2006.

Pinho, Patricia de Santana. *Mama Africa: Reinventing Blackness in Bahia*. Durham, N.C.: Duke University Press, 2010.

———. "White but Not Quite: Tones and Overtones of Whiteness in Brazil." *Small Axe* 13, no. 2 (2009): 39–56.

Pitt-Rivers, Julian. *The Fate of Shechem, or the Politics of Sex: Essays in the Anthropology of the Mediterranean*. Cambridge, U.K.: Cambridge University Press, 1977.

Podkameni, A. B., M. A. C. Guimarães, J. Mello Filho, and M. Burd. "Afrodescendência, família e prevenção." In *Doença e família*, ed. J. Mello Filho and M. Burd, 123–139. São Paulo: Casa do Psicólogo, 2004.

Prescott, Laurence E. "Liberating Blackness: The Theme of Whitening in Two Colombian Short Stories." *Callaloo* 35, no. 2 (2012): 475–493.

Rahier, Jean Muteba. "Blackness, the Racial/Spatial Order, Migrations, and Miss Ecuador 1995–96." *American Anthropologist* 100, no. 2 (1998): 421–430.

Rebhun, Linda-Anne. *The Heart Is Unknown Country: Love in the Changing Economy of Northeast Brazil*. Redwood City, Calif.: Stanford University Press, 2002.

Reichmann, Rebecca L., ed. *Race in Contemporary Brazil: From Indifference to Inequality*. University Park, Pa.: Penn State University Press, 2010.

Reiter, Bernd. "Whiteness as Capital: Constructing Inclusion and Defending Privilege." In *Brazil's New Racial Politics*, ed. Bernd Reiter and Gladys L. Mitchell, 19–33. Boulder, Colo.: Lynne Rienner, 2010.

Relethford, John H., Michael P. Stern, Sharon P. Gaskill, and Helen P. Hazuda. "Social Class, Admixture, and Skin Color Variation in Mexican-Americans and Anglo-Americans Living in San Antonio, Texas." *American Journal of Physical Anthropology* 61, no. 1 (1983): 97–102.

Ribeiro, Carlos Antonio Costa, and Nelson do Valle Silva. "Cor, educação e casamento: Tendências da seletividade marital no Brasil, 1960 a 2000." *Dados* 52, no. 1 (2009): 7–51.

Ribeiro, Ronilda Iyakęmi. *Alma africana no Brasil: Os iorubas.* São Paulo: Editora Oduduwa, 1996.

Romo, Anadelia A. *Brazil's Living Museum: Race, Reform, and Tradition in Bahia.* Chapel Hill: University of North Carolina Press, 2010.

Rosenberg, Morris. *Conceiving the Self.* Malabar, Fla.: Krieger, 1986.

Russell, Kathy, Midge Wilson, and Ronald E. Hall. *The Color Complex: The Politics of Skin Color among African Americans.* New York: Random House, 1992.

———. *The Color Complex (Revised): The Politics of Skin Color in a New Millennium.* Rockland, Mass.: Anchor, 2013.

Sampaio, Adriana Soares. "Ecos da hipertensão: A vivência de mulheres negras no Rio de Janeiro." Mestrado em Psicologia Clínica–Psicossomática e Psicologia Hospitalar, Pontifícia Universidade Católica de São Paulo, 2009.

Sandoval, Chela. "U.S. Third World Feminism: The Theory and Method of Oppositional Consciousness in the Postmodern World." *Genders* 10 (1991): 1–24.

Sansone, Livio. *Blackness without Ethnicity: Constructing Race in Brazil.* Basingstoke, U.K.: Palgrave Macmillan, 2003.

———. "Funk baiano: Uma versão local de um fenômeno global." In *Ritmos em trânsito: Sócio-antropologia da música baiana,* ed. Livio Sansone and Jocélio Teles dos Santos. São Paulo: Dynamis Editorial, 1998.

Santiago-Valles, Kelvin A. "Puerto Rico." In *No Longer Invisible: Afro-Latin Americans Today,* ed. Minority Rights Group, 139–161. London: Minority Rights Publications, 1995.

Sawyer, Mark Q., Yesilernis Peña, and Jim Sidanius. "Cuban Exceptionalism: Group-Based Hierarchy and the Dynamics of Patriotism in Puerto Rico, the Dominican Republic, and Cuba." *Du Bois Review* 1, no. 1 (2004): 93–113.

Scheper-Hughes, Nancy. *Death without Weeping: The Violence of Everyday Life in Brazil.* Berkeley: University of California Press, 1993.

Schwartz, Stuart B. "The Manumission of Slaves in Colonial Brazil: Bahia, 1684–1745." *Hispanic American Historical Review* (1974): 603–635.

Scottham, Krista Maywalt, and Ciara P. Smalls. "Unpacking Racial Socialization: Considering Female African American Primary Caregivers' Racial Identity." *Journal of Marriage and Family* 71, no. 4 (2009): 807–818.

Segato, Rita Laura. "The Color-Blind Subject of Myth; or, Where to Find Africa in the Nation." *Annual Review of Anthropology* (1998): 129–151.

Seyferth, Giralda. "A antropologia e teoria do branqueamento de raça no Brasil: A tese de João Batista de Lacerda." *Revista do Museu Paulista,* n.s., 30 (1985): 81–98.

Sheriff, Robin E. *Dreaming Equality: Color, Race, and Racism in Urban Brazil.* New Brunswick, N.J.: Rutgers University Press, 2001.

Shirey, Heather. "Transforming the Orixás: Candomblé in Sacred and Secular Spaces in Salvador da Bahia, Brazil." *African Arts* 42, no. 4 (2009): 62–79.

Sidanius, Jim, Yesilernis Pena, and Mark Sawyer. "Inclusionary Discrimination: Pigmentocracy and Patriotism in the Dominican Republic." *Political Psychology* 22, no. 4 (2001): 827–851.

Simpson, Amelia. *Xuxa: The Mega-Marketing of Gender, Race, and Modernity.* Philadelphia: Temple University Press, 1993.

Skidmore, Thomas E. "Bi-Racial USA vs. Multi-Racial Brazil: Is the Contrast Still Valid?" *Journal of Latin American Studies* 25, no. 2 (1993): 373–386.

———. *Black into White: Race and Nationality in Brazilian Thought.* Durham, N.C.: Duke University Press, 1993.

Smith, James E. "Race, Emotions, and Socialization." *Race, Gender, and Class* (2002): 94–110.

Smith, Linda Tuhiwai. *Decolonizing Methodologies: Research and Indigenous Peoples.* London: Zed, 1999.

Somers, Margaret R. "The Narrative Constitution of Identity: A Relational and Network Approach." *Theory and Society* 23, no. 5 (1994): 605–649.

Sommer, Doris. "Love and Country in Latin America: An Allegorical Speculation." *Cultural Critique* (1990): 109–128.

Souza, Neusa Santos. *Tornar-se negro ou as vicissitudes da identidade do negro brasileiro em ascensão social.* Rio de Janeiro: Graal, 1983.

Sovik, Liv. "Preto no branco: Stuart Hall e a branquitude." *Revista da Associação Brasileira de Pesquisadores Negros* 6, no. 13 (2014): 162–174.

Stack, Carol B. *All Our Kin: Strategies for Survival in a Black Community.* New York: Basic Books, 1975.

Steinbugler, Amy C. *Beyond Loving: Intimate Racework in Lesbian, Gay, and Straight Interracial Relationships.* Oxford: Oxford University Press, 2012.

Stepan, Nancy Leys. *"The Hour of Eugenics": Race, Gender, and Nation in Latin America, 1890–1916.* Ithaca, N.Y.: Cornell University Press, 1991.

Stocker, Clare M. "Differences in Mothers' and Fathers' Relationships with Siblings: Links with Children's Behavior Problems." *Development and Psychopathology* 7, no. 3 (1995): 499–513.

Stocker, Clare, Judy Dunn, and Robert Plomin. "Sibling Relationships: Links with Child Temperament, Maternal Behavior, and Family Structure." *Child Development* (1989): 715–727.

Stocker, Clare M., Melissa K. Richmond, Galena K. Rhoades, and Lisa Kiang. "Family Emotional Processes and Adolescents' Adjustment." *Social Development* 16, no. 2 (2007): 310–325.

Stoler, Ann Laura. "Carnal Knowledge and Imperial Power: Gender, Race and Morality in Colonial Asia." In *Gender at the Crossroads of Knowledge: Feminist Anthropology in the Postmodern Era,* ed. Micaela di Leonardo, 51–101. Berkeley: University of California Press, 1991.

———. "Tense and Tender Ties: The Politics of Comparison in North American History and (Post) Colonial Studies." *The Journal of American History* 88, no. 3 (2001): 829–865.

Suárez-Findlay, Eileen. *Imposing Decency: The Politics of Sexuality and Race in Puerto Rico, 1870–1920.* Durham, N.C.: Duke University Press, 2000.

Sue, Christina A., and Tanya Golash-Boza. "'It Was Only a Joke': How Racial Humour Fuels Colour-Blind Ideologies in Mexico and Peru." *Ethnic and Racial Studies* 36, no. 10 (2013): 1582–1598.

Synnott, Anthony. *The Body Social: Symbolism, Self, and Society.* New York: Routledge, 1993.

Tate, Shirley Anne. *Black Beauty: Aesthetics, Stylization, Politics.* Farnham, Surrey, U.K.: Ashgate, 2009.

————. "Black Beauty: Shade, Hair, and Anti-Racist Aesthetics." *Ethnic and Racial Studies* 30, no. 2 (2007): 300–319.

Telles, Edward E. *Race in Another America: The Significance of Skin Color in Brazil.* Princeton, N.J.: Princeton University Press, 2004.

————. "Who Are the Morenas?" *Social Forces* 73, no. 4 (1995): 1609–1611.

Thoits, Peggy A. "Identity-Relevant Events and Psychological Symptoms: A Cautionary Tale." *Journal of Health and Social Behavior* 36, no. 1 (1995): 72–82.

Thompson, Cheryl. "Black Women, Beauty, and Hair as a Matter of Being." *Women's Studies* 38, no. 8 (2009): 831–856.

Thompson, Maxine S., and Verna M. Keith. "The Blacker the Berry: Gender, Skin Tone, Self-Esteem, and Self-Efficacy." *Gender and Society* 15, no. 3 (2001): 336–357.

Torres-Saillant, Silvio. "Creoleness or Blackness: A Dominican Dilemma." *Plantation Society in the Americas* 5, no. 1 (1998), 29–40.

————. "The Tribulations of Blackness: Stages in Dominican Racial Identity." *Calloo* 23, no. 3 (2000): 1086–1111.

Trouillot, Michel-Rolph. "Culture, Color, and Politics in Haiti." In *Race*, ed. Steven Gregory and Roger Sanjek, 146–174. New Brunswick, N.J.: Rutgers University Press.

Twinam, Ann. *Public Lives, Private Secrets: Gender, Honor, Sexuality, and Illegitimacy in Colonial Spanish America.* Redwood City, Calif.: Stanford University Press, 1999.

Twine, France Winddance. *Racism in a Racial Democracy: The Maintenance of White Supremacy in Brazil.* New Brunswick, N.J.: Rutgers University Press, 1998.

————. "Transgressive Women and Transracial Mothers: White Women and Critical Race Theory." *Meridians* 1, no. 2 (2001): 130–153.

————. *A White Side of Black Britain: Interracial Intimacy and Racial Literacy.* Durham, N.C.: Duke University Press, 2010.

Twine, France Winddance, and Jonathan W. Warren. *Racing Research, Researching Race: Methodological Dilemmas in Critical Race Studies.* New York: NYU Press, 2000.

van Dijk, Teun A. *Ideology: A Multidisciplinary Approach.* Thousand Oaks, Calif.: SAGE, 1998.

van Kirk, Sylvia. *Many Tender Ties: Women in Fur-Trade Society, 1670–1870.* Norman: University of Oklahoma Press, 1983.

Varella, João. *Da Bahia do Senhor do Bonfim: Factos, vultos e typos populares de tempos idos.* Salvador: Editora, 1936.

Viotti da Costa, Emilia. *The Brazilian Empire: Myths and Histories.* Belmont, Calif.: Wadsworth, 1985.

Volling, Brenda L. "The Family Correlates of Maternal and Paternal Perceptions of Differential Treatment in Early Childhood." *Family Relations* (1997): 227–236.

Wade, Peter. *Race and Ethnicity in Latin America.* London: Pluto, 1997.

Wade, T. Joel, and Sara Bielitz. "The Differential Effect of Skin Color on Attractiveness, Personality Evaluations, and Perceived Life Success of African Americans." *Journal of Black Psychology* 31, no. 3 (2005): 215–236.

Ware, Vron, and Les Back. *Out of Whiteness: Color, Politics, and Culture.* Chicago: University of Chicago Press, 2002.

Waskul, Dennis, and Phillip Vannini. "Introduction: The Body in Symbolic Interaction." *Body/Embodiment: Symbolic Interaction and the Sociology of the Body*, ed. Dennis Waskul and Phillip Vannini, 1–18. Aldershot, Hampshire, U.K.: Ashgate, 2006.

Weinstein, Barbara. "Racializing Regional Difference: São Paulo versus Brazil, 1932." In *Race and Nation in Modern Latin America*, ed. N. Appelbaum, A. Macpherson, and K. Rosemblatt, 237–262. Chapel Hill: University of North Carolina Press, 2003.

Weitz, Rose. "Women and Their Hair: Seeking Power through Resistance and Accommodation." *Gender and Society* 15, no. 5 (2001): 667–686.

West, Candace, and Don H. Zimmerman. "Doing Gender." *Gender and Society* 1, no. 2 (1987): 125–151.

Wickrama, K. A. S., Rand D. Conger, Frederick O. Lorenz, and Tony Jung. "Family Antecedents and Consequences of Trajectories of Depressive Symptoms from Adolescence to Young Adulthood: A Life Course Investigation." *Journal of Health and Social Behavior* 49, no. 4 (2008): 468–483.

Wilder, JeffriAnne, and Colleen Cain. "Teaching and Learning Color Consciousness in Black Families: Exploring Family Processes and Women's Experiences with Colorism." *Journal of Family Issues* 32, no. 5 (2010): 577–604.

Williams, Erica Lorraine. *Sex Tourism in Bahia: Ambiguous Entanglements*. Champaign: University of Illinois Press, 2013.

Wilson, Julee. "Natural Hair Song by Tiririca Deemed Racist, Sony Music Ordered to Pay $1.2 Million," *Huffington Post*, January 6, 2012. http://www.huffingtonpost.com/2012/01/06/natural-hair-racist-_n_1189068.html.

Wolf, Naomi. *The Beauty Myth: How Images of Beauty Are Used against Women*. New York: Perennial, 2002.

Wong, Carol A., Jacquelynne S. Eccles, and Arnold Sameroff. "The Influence of Ethnic Discrimination and Ethnic Identification on African American Adolescents' School and Socioemotional Adjustment." *Journal of Personality* 71, no. 6 (2003): 1197–1232.

Yelvington, Kevin A. "The Anthropology of Afro-Latin America and the Caribbean: Diasporic Dimensions." *Annual Review of Anthropology* (2001): 227–260.

Zane, Kathleen. "Reflections on a Yellow Eye: Asian i(\eye/)cons and Cosmetic Surgery." In *The Feminism and Visual Culture Reader*, ed. Amelia Jones, 354–364. New York: Routledge, 2003.

Zuberi, Tukufu, and Eduardo Bonilla-Silva, eds. *White Logic, White Methods: Racism and Methodology*. Lanham, Md.: Rowman and Littlefield, 2008.

Page numbers followed by the letter t indicate tables.